Pathways to Transformation

Learning in Relationship

A volume in
Innovative Perspectives of Higher Education—Research, Theory, and Practice
Kathleen P. King, *Series Editor*

Pathways to Transformation

Learning in Relationship

edited by

Carrie J. Boden McGill
Texas State University

Sola M. Kippers
Capella University

IAP
INFORMATION AGE PUBLISHING, INC.
Charlotte, NC • www.infoagepub.com

Library of Congress Cataloging-in-Publication Data

Pathways to transformation : learning in relationship / edited by Carrie J. Boden, Sola M. Kippers.
   p. cm. – (Innovative perspectives of higher education: research, theory, and practice)
 Includes bibliographical references.
  ISBN 978-1-61735-837-1 (pbk.) – ISBN 978-1-61735-838-8 (hardcover) – ISBN 978-1-61735-839-5 (ebook) 1. Adult learning. 2. Transformative learning. I. Boden, Carrie J. II. Kippers, Sola M.
 LC5225.L42P35 2012
 374–dc23
                                                    2012011518

Copyright © 2012 Information Age Publishing Inc.

All rights reserved. No part of this publication may be reproduced, stored in a retrieval system, or transmitted, in any form or by any means, electronic, mechanical, photocopying, microfilming, recording or otherwise, without written permission from the publisher.

Printed in the United States of America

CONTENTS

Foreword ix

Acknowledgements xiii

Introduction xv
    Carrie J. Boden McGill and Sola M. Kippers

RELATIONSHIP WITH SELF AND OTHERS

PART I

THE ROLE OF COMMUNICATION AND DIALOGUE IN TRANSFORMATIVE LEARNING

1. Meaningful Conversations: Coaching to Transform the Heart, Head, and Hands of Teaching and Learning 5
    Angela Webster-Smith, Shelly Albritton, and Patty Kohler-Evans

2. Learning About Learning in Relationships: Novice Teacher Educators Give Transformative Dialogue a Try 17
    Elizabeth Bondy, Lauren Tripp, and D. Alvarez Caron

3. Communication is the Relationship 31
    Julien C. Mirivel

4. Narrative Tools for Facilitating Research and Learning for Transformation 49
    Leann M. R. Kaiser and Elizabeth A. Erichsen

PART II
LEARNING IN RELATIONSHIP WITH SELF AND OTHERS

5 Narrative, Somatic, and Social/Constructivist Approaches to Transformative Learning in Training Programs for the Helping Professions 65
Daniel Stroud, Julie Prindle, and Stacy England

6 In Hope of Transformation: Teaching and Learning Through Relational Practice in the Adult Learning Classroom 83
Teresa J. Carter

7 Spiritual Autobiography: A Transformative Journey for a Counselor in Training 97
Michelle Kelley Shuler and Katrina Cook

8 Developing Scholarship Through Mentoring and Reflection: A Transformative Process for Doctoral Students 111
Brandé Flamez, Javier Cavazos Jr., Varunee Faii Sangganjanavanich, and Joshua C. Watson

9 The Transformative Relationship Within Teaching Counseling Skills and Methods: Implications for Training and Practice 131
Laura J. Fazio-Griffith

10 The Role of Faculty in Dispositional Development of Teacher Candidates: A Neglected Voice in Teacher Preparation 147
Janet Filer, Candice Dowd Barnes, and Mark Cooper

RELATIONSHIP WITH CULTURE, CONTEXT, AND TECHNOLOGY

PART I
TRANSFORMATIVE LEARNING IN MULTICULTURAL, CROSS-CULTURAL, AND INTERCULTURAL CONTEXTS

11 Easing Teacher Candidates Toward Cultural Competence Through the Multicultural Step Out 169
Freddie A. Bowles and Nancy P. Gallavan

12 The Transformative Path of Local, Cross-Cultural Relationships ... 191
Ellen L. Marmon

13 In Black and White: Transformation Through Examined
    Selves 207
    Gabriele Strohschen

14 Developing Intercultural Effectiveness Competencies: The
    Journey of Transformative Learning and Cross-Cultural
    Learning for Foreign-Born Faculty in American
    Higher Education 223
    Pi-Chi Han

15 Transformational Learning Experience of Haitian Americans
    in Response to the Earthquake in Haiti 241
    Emmanuel Jean Francois and William H. Young III

PART II

LEARNING IN RELATIONSHIP WITH CULTURE, CONTEXT, AND TECHNOLOGY

16 Rhythm, Rhyme, Reel, Resistance: Transformative Learning
    Using African American Popular Culture 261
    I. Malik Saafir

17 Transformative Learning Experiences of Black African
    International Students 275
    Alex Kumi Yeboah and William H. Young III

18 Facilitating Transformative Learning Opportunities in Higher
    Education Contexts for Adult Learners in Online and Virtual
    Spaces 291
    Kathleen P. King and Shelley Stewart

19 Video Technology: Transforming Reflective Practice 309
    Sejal Parikh and Christopher Janson

RELATIONSHIP WITH ADULT EDUCATION AND THE HUMAN SERVICES FIELDS

20 Advancing Transformative Theory: Multifold and Cyclical
    Transformation 325
    Fujuan Tan and Lee Nabb

21 The Self in Transformation: What Gets Transformed
   in Transformative Learning?..343
   Ted Fleming

22 Exploring Positive Life Changes in Response to Cancer:
   Perspective Transformation and Posttraumatic Growth.................355
   Allen C. Sherman, Avinash Thombre, and Stephanie Simonton

About the Editors **373**

About the Contributors **375**

FOREWORD

It has been more than 30 years since Jack Mezirow first described the conceptual framework known as transformative learning as a way to help understand and promote the development and maturation of adult learners. A wave of adult education scholars and scholar-practitioners have matured during this time—myself included. I have thought during the last few years that an interesting research question to pursue is "What did we call it before we called it transformative learning?" Was it an "aha" moment? Gaining an important insight? Getting closure on an issue? An epiphany? Experiential learning? Discovery learning? The authors of the chapters in the volume present research that is pertinent to my question. They also provide stimulating perspectives on moving forward with ways to activate transformative learning theory in practice.

This book explores very interesting and sometimes challenging pathways for transformative learning theory, research, and practice drawing on the disciplines of both adult and counselor education. It is particularly stimulating to me because over the years I have found my graduate training in counseling and adult education do interconnect with my philosophical perspectives and practice for facilitating the learning processes of adults. The adult and counselor educators writing these chapters have undertaken multiple tasks, chief among them an investigation of transformative learning from two different perspectives, counseling and adult education, with a focus on understanding the important relational questions and creating environments and activities to promote transformative learning.

The structure created by the editors, Carrie J. Boden McGill and Sola M. Kippers, is a very useful schema. The first main heading of the book is "Relationship with Self and Others." This first half is divided into two parts: "Part 1: The Role of Communication and Dialogue in Transformative Learning" and "Part 2: Learning in Relationship with Self and Others." These chapters present us with perspectives on communication theory focused on building relationships as fundamental to both a "helping" relationship and a "facilitating learning" context. The concepts and issues under consideration include the impact of Carl Rogers and a person-centered approach to helping relationships and development, coaching and mentoring relationships between faculty and graduate students, and holistic approaches to using narrative and other strategies in the helping professions.

If you identify primarily as an adult educator, you have probably participated in spirited discussions about whether or not your role as a teacher/facilitator of learning includes being in a "helping relationship" with learners. The roles and practices of therapist/counselor/teacher/facilitator of learning become much more difficult to define and separate under the transformative learning banner. You may find yourself engaging in these discussions with colleagues with renewed purpose.

The second half of the book is headed "Relationship with Culture, Context, and Technology." It is also divided into two parts: "Part 1: Transformative Learning in Multicultural, Cross-Cultural, and Intercultural Contexts" and "Part 2: Learning in Relationship with Culture, Context, and Technology." The chapters in Part 1 provide stimulating perspectives on navigating cultural competence, the importance of developing and understanding cross-cultural and intercultural relationships, and personal narratives of foreign-born colleagues describing their transformative learning from navigating multiple cultural engagements.

The development of many kinds of technologies was a major disruptive shift in our world during the 20th century. A particularly powerful one is in the area described as information communication technology (ICT). The development of motion pictures, radio, and television in the first half of the century were followed by the digital revolution. The Apple II computer appeared in 1977, followed by the IBM personal computer in 1981, and then the Apple Macintosh by the mid-1980s. Some of us reading this book remember the advent of the personal computer and mastering operating systems, navigating the early Internet, and struggling to find our voice to communicate via e-mail in the early or middle parts of our careers. However, others reading this book have grown up with these technologies as digital natives with a different frame of experiential learning using technology.

We are all experiencing the rapid change and new opportunities stimulated by mobile ICT devices and constantly evolving social learning/networking software. The chapters in this final section investigate the technologies and online virtual spaces they create. Additional theoretical perspectives investigating personal health challenges, the family bonds, and the levels and cycles of transformative learning in our lives round out this ambitious exploration of the concepts and issues of transformative learning.

I commend this book to colleagues engaged in dialogue with each other and the evolving theory, research, and practice of transformative learning. It provides a valuable set of perspectives from adult and counselor educators and descriptions of practices they have found effective. *Pathways to Transformation: Learning in Relationship* and *Adult Education Special Topics: Theory, Research, & Practice in Lifelong Learning* is an example of a group of books published recently that move forward our understanding of and work with transformative learning.

—**Henry S. Merrill**, EdD
Emeritus Associate Professor
School of Continuing Studies, Indiana University

ACKNOWLEDGEMENTS

I am grateful to my family, friends, colleagues, and students, whose interest in this project propelled it to completion. You have supported me with space and sustenance, been understanding when I've struggled under the weight of conflicting obligations, and encouraged me in many, many ways. I appreciate you taking this journey with me.

—Carrie J. Boden McGill

The words of the writings from the *Tao of Leadership* resonate in my reflection of the transformative power of the conversations and relationships that have influenced my process throughout the evolution of this body of work. "When I let go of what I am, I become what I might be. When I let go of what I have, I receive what I need" (Heider, 1985, *The Paradox of Letting Go*, p. 43).

—Sola M. Kippers

INTRODUCTION

Carrie J. Boden McGill and Sola M. Kippers

The book you hold in your hands or read on the screen in front of you began with conversations. The initial gleanings can be traced to conversations at conference dinners and in lobbies of hotels, to e-mail messages and quips scrawled on napkins, to telephone conversations and moments at coffee shops or walking along the river trail, to work completed at the office or at home, and to ideas expressed or understood in locales far away. These many conversations about various aspects of transformative learning and the forms through which it may occur came at fortuitous times and with a cavalcade of individuals, who spoke and listened with passion, intelligence, and care.

These early beginnings and initial conversations buzzed with excitement and promise, which prompted us to explore in more depth how our two fields—adult education and counseling—approach transformative learning. The connections very quickly became clear, and as we explored the commonalities, it was time for another conversation—one with the literature. A review of the past decade of literature related to transformative learning in the fields of adult education and counseling helped us contextualize "where the research has been" and also gave us a glimpse into "where the research could be going." We also followed the conversation into other fields; we were especially delighted to see how many other disciplines throughout education and the helping professions have adopted transformative learning theory and made it their own. As we examined the

Pathways to Transformation, pages xv–xx
Copyright © 2012 by Information Age Publishing
All rights of reproduction in any form reserved.

intersections of the disparate fields that transformative learning touches and the depth and breadth of conversations on the subject, we realized that while there were intersections of praxis, there were also diverging lines of research. To describe this phenomenon, we gravitated toward the metaphor of "pathways," and hence, selected the title, *Pathways to Transformation,* for this collection. The title solidified our mission to collect writings from voices from a multitude of contexts in order to highlight the distinct pathways through which transformative learning occurs and to broaden the conversation to include as many voices as possible.

It was during the review of literature that we also found what would become both the subtitle and the organizational structure for the book. Walters (2008) pointed out that transformation often occurs through "the mutuality of '*learning in relationship*'" (emphasis ours) and "holds every potential for making learning 'come alive'" (p. 114). We relished this notion of interconnectedness and were eager to explore the avenues of transformative learning made possible through connection. In the literature, we found resources that analyzed, synthesized, and categorized the empirical research on transformative learning to date. Studies of transformative learning were grouped into categories such as the cognitive rational approach (Fisher-Yoshida, Geller, & Schapiro, 2009), the neurobiological approach and the psychodevelopmental approach (Taylor, 2008), the structural developmental approach (Fisher-Yoshida et al., 2009), the psychoanalytic approach, the social emancipatory approach, the cultural-spiritual approach, the race-centric approach, and the planetary approach (Fisher-Yoshida et al., 2009; Taylor, 2008). These categories served as a starting place for this collection.

We also took note of areas that several researchers suggested were ripe for further investigation. These areas included how to foster and improve critical reflection (Gillingham, 2008; Mezirow & Taylor, 2009), the role of relationships in transformative learning (Clark & Dirkx, 2008; Jacobs, 2006; Taylor, 2007; Vescio, Bondy, & Pockert, 2009; Walters, 2008), the importance of context (Dirkx, 2006; Rush, 2008; Taylor, 2007), the nature of perspective transformation (Kasworm, Rose, & Ross-Gordon, 2010; Taylor, 2007), the role of emotion in learning (Clark & Dirkx, 2008; Dirkx, 2006; Meekums, 2008; Rush, 2008), the relationship between narrative learning and transformative learning (Avdi & Georgaca, 2007; Clark & Rossiter, 2008; Jacobs, 2006; Jarvis, 2006; Meekums, 2008; Refhus, 2009; Rossiter & Clark, 2007; Taylor, 2008), and the role of technology and other methods to foster transformative learning (Gillingham, 2008; Goodwin-Esola, Deely, & Powell, 2009; King, 2009; Meyers, 2008; Rush, 2008; Sill, Harward, & Cooper, 2009; Strom & Strom, 2011; Vescio et al., 2009).

We solicited chapters from authors writing in these and other areas. The proposals that came to us ranged greatly in scope. Sometimes we were enamored with possibilities we had not considered. Other times we had to take a step back and seriously evaluate if a chapter proposal fit within the framework we had established. We constantly considered our audiences and which chapters would be most appropriate for them. This was difficult and invigorating work, and each step included delightful moments of discovery woven into the process. As the proposals and then the completed chapters unfurled, we were part of many provocative, thoughtful, and challenging conversations. We began to feel that we knew some part of the authors, even those who we knew only via e-mail, because they wrote with such conviction as teachers, scholars, colleagues, and, sometimes, friends. We were part of such rich personal and academic conversations, and though they ranged in content, their similarities and the ways they fit together have given structure to this volume. As a whole, the collection reads like a manifesto, assuring the reader that moments for transformative learning are always available. Indeed, transformation is possible, contextual, individualized, and situated in real and virtual worlds. Most importantly, transformation occurs in relationship. In the words of Titus, "it is the relationship that teaches" (as cited in Henschke, 2009, p. 135).

The chapters in this volume are arranged by the sites where transformative learning occur in relationship. These include relationship with self and others; relationship with culture, context, and technology; and relationship with the adult education and the human services fields. The section on relationship to self and others describes transformative learning as it serves as a vehicle to "being," individuation, and one's relationship with oneself. The first part of this section includes chapters that focus on the importance of communication and dialogue. In "Meaningful Conversations: Coaching to Transform the Heart, Head, and Hands of Teaching and Learning," Webster-Smith, Albritton, and Kohler-Evans focus on utilizing conversational techniques to teach holistically through relationship in order to assist students to make decisions and discoveries in their learning. In the next chapter, Bondy, Tripp, and Caron report the results experienced by eight female doctoral students who engaged in critical reflection after utilizing transformative dialogue in personal and professional contexts. In "Communication is the Relationship," Mirivel proposes a model of communication behaviors that professors can use to create a climate conducive to transformative learning in the university classroom. Last, Kaiser and Erichsen discuss using narrative tools to promote whole-person learning, identity development, and transformative learning.

In the second part of the section, "Learning in Relationship with Self and Others," the chapters focus on specific practices to promote transformative learning. Stroud, Prindle, and England focus on using narrative, somatic, and social/constructivist approaches to facilitate transformative learning in programs preparing students to work in the helping professions. In the chapter "In Hope of Transformation: Teaching and Learning Through Relational Practice in the Adult Learning Classroom," Carter explores how relational practice in the adult education classroom supports growth-fostering change for those students and professors willing to engage in transformative learning experiences. Shuler and Cook reflect on the role of spirituality in transformative education and discuss how a spiritual autobiography assignment may be used for counseling students. Flamez, Cavazos, Sangganjanavanich, and Watson share two cases that demonstrate transformative learning experiences and propose a model of mentoring doctoral students as emerging scholars. In the next chapter in this section, "The Transformative Relationship with Teaching Counseling Skills and Methods: Implications for Training and Practice," Fazio-Griffith explores how reflection, feedback, and meaning-making can be used to promote transformative learning for students enrolled in a graduate counseling course. Finally, Filer, Barnes, and Cooper propose a model for disposition development in teacher preparation and espouse the importance of faculty in disposition development for students.

The next section of the book explores ways in which transformative learning occurs in relationship to culture, context, and technology. The first part of this section focuses on transformative learning in multi-, cross-, and intercultural contexts. Bowles and Gallavan propose a method to ease teacher candidates toward cultural competence through an assignment called the Multicultural Step Out, which often produces transformative experiences for students. Likewise, Marmon discusses the transformations of students enrolled in a local cross-cultural ministry course. Strohschen's chapter, "In Black and White: Transformation Through Examined Selves," presents vignettes, reflections, and analyses that give a framework for an adult education praxis that promotes personal and community transformation. In the next chapter, Han discusses the transformative learning experiences of foreign-born faculty developing intercultural competencies. Finally, Francois and Young analyze the transformative learning experiences of Haitian-Americans in response to the January 12, 2010, earthquake in Haiti.

In "Part 2: Learning in Relationship with Culture, Context, and Technology," in "Rhythm, Rhyme, Reel, Resistance: Transformative Learning Using African American Popular Culture," Saafir proffers how critical race theory, spirituality, and transformative learning are utilized in various courses that use pop culture to teach biblical concepts at the School for Practical Theology. Yeboah and Young discuss the transformative learning experiences of Black African international students before and upon their arrival in the United States. The next chapters focus on learning opportunities in online and virtual spaces. King and Stewart offer examples of transformative learning experiences for online learners while Parikh and Janson discuss the transformative possibilities of using video technology to encourage reflective practice through video journaling.

In the final section, "Relationship with the Adult Education and the Human Services Fields," the chapters include discussions of emerging theories and future directions for research in and between disciplines. Tan and Nabb offer a model of transformative learning that proposes that personal transformations may occur in multiple layers within the self and in more than one iteration or event. Tan and Nabb describe this phenomenon as multifold and cyclical transformation. Fleming argues that Bowlby's attachment theory offers insight into understanding and facilitating transformative learning. Fleming posits that it is one's internal working models and attachment styles that are changed as a result of transformative learning. Finally, Sherman, Thombre, and Simonton explore the parallels in the literature between posttraumatic growth and perspective transformation for cancer patients and suggest future lines of research and opportunities for interdisciplinary collaboration.

This volume, indeed, highlights the numerous pathways through which transformative learning may occur in relationship. After months of relishing these conversations for ourselves, we are very pleased to bring these conversations to you and to have you engage in them. At a recent retreat for women professors of adult education, a sage advised, "Even though there are those who have come before us and cleared a path, we still may make our own path by walking." Like the spirit of Horton and Freire (1990), which this quote evokes, our hope is that this collection intersects with your path in meaningful and important ways and that you take these concepts further into directions not yet imagined for your own yet-to-be trodden path.

REFERENCES

Avdi, E., & Georgaca, E. (2007). Narrative research in psychotherapy: A critical review. *Psychology and Psychotherapy: Theory, Research and Practice, 80,* 407–419.

Clark, M. C., & Dirkx, J. M. (2008). The emotional self in adult learning. *New Directions for Adult and Continuing Education, 120,* 89–95.

Clark, M. C., & Rossiter, M. (2008). Narrative learning in adulthood. *New Directions for Adult and Continuing Education, 119,* 61–70.

Dirkx, J. M. (2006). Engaging emotions in adult learning: A Jungian perspective on emotion and transformative learning. *New Directions for Adult and Continuing Education, 109,* 15–22.

Fisher-Yoshida, B., Geller, K., & Schapiro, S. (2009). *Innovations in transformative learning: Space, culture, and the arts.* New York, NY: Peter Lang.

Gillingham, P. (2008). Designing, implementing and evaluating a social work practice skills course: A case example. *Social Work Education, 27*(5), 474–488.

Goodwin-Esola, M., Deely, M., & Powell, N. (2009). Progress meetings: Facilitating role transition of the new graduate. *The Journal of Continuing Education in Nursing, 40*(9), 411–415.
Henschke, J. (2009). Engagement in active learning with Brazilian adult educators. In G. Strohschen (Ed.), *Handbook of blended shore education: Adult program development and delivery* (pp. 121–136). New York, NY: Springer.
Horton, M., & Freire, P. (1990). *We make the road by walking: Conversations on education and social change.* Philadelphia, PA: Temple University Press.
Jacobs, C. (2006). Transformation and kaleidoscope memories. *Smith College Studies in Social Work, 76*(4), 113–123.
Jarvis, C. (2006). Using fiction for transformation. *New Directions for Adult and Continuing Education, 109,* 69–77.
Kasworm, C., Rose, A., & Ross-Gordon, J. (Eds.). (2010). *Handbook of adult and continuing education.* Thousand Oaks, CA: Sage.
King, K. P. (2009). *The handbook of the evolving research of transformative learning.* Charlotte, NC: Information Age.
Meekums, B. (2008). Embodied narratives in becoming a counseling trainer: An autoethnographic study. *British Journal of Guidance & Counselling, 36*(3), 287–301.
Meyers, S. A. (2008). Using transformative pedagogy when teaching online. *College Teaching, 56*(4), 219–224.
Mezirow, J., & Taylor, E. (Eds.). (2009). *Transformative learning in practice: Insights from community, workplace, and higher education.* San Francisco, CA: Jossey-Bass.
Rehfus, M. C. (2009). The future career autobiography: A narrative measure of career intervention effectiveness. *The Career Development Quarterly, 58,* 82–90.
Rossiter, M., & Clark, M. C. (2007). *Narrative and the practice of adult education.* Malabar, FL: Krieger.
Rush, B. (2008). Mental health service user involvement in nurse education: A catalyst for transformative learning. *Journal of Mental Health, 17*(5), 531–542.
Sill, D., Harward, B. M., & Cooper, I. (2009). The disorienting dilemma: The senior capstone as a transformative experience. *Liberal Education, 95*(3), 50–55.
Strom, P., & Strom, R. (2011). *Adult learning and relationships.* Charlotte, NC: Information Age.
Taylor, E. M. (2007). An update of transformative learning theory: A critical review of the empirical research (1999–2005). *International Journal of Lifelong Education, 26*(2), 173–191.
Taylor, E. M. (2008). Transformative learning theory. *New Directions for Adult and Continuing Education, 119,* 5–15.
Vescio, V., Bondy, E., & Pockert, P. E. (2009, Spring). Preparing multicultural teacher educators: Toward a pedagogy of transformation, *Teacher Education Quarterly,* 5–25.
Walters, D. A. (2008). Existential being as transformative learning. *Pastoral Care in Education, 26*(2), 111–118.

RELATIONSHIP WITH SELF AND OTHERS

Part I

THE ROLE OF COMMUNICATION AND DIALOGUE
IN TRANSFORMATIVE LEARNING

CHAPTER 1

MEANINGFUL CONVERSATIONS

Coaching to Transform the Heart, Head, and Hands of Teaching and Learning

Angela Webster-Smith, Shelly Albritton, and Patty Kohler-Evans

Transformative learning transpires through meaningful conversations facilitated by instructors who adopt a coaching philosophy that influences the heart, the head, and the hands (Sergiovanni, 2007) of the instructor and the adult learner. The metaphor of the heart speaks to an excavation of the instructor's beliefs and philosophies pertaining to education. The unearthing of these beliefs liberates the instructor to move forward with a purity of heart that touches the heart of the students. The symbol of the head represents the thinking that leads to the highest levels of understanding content, whereas the figurative language of the hands represents ways in which the instructor helps the student apply, analyze, synthesize, and evaluate the content for optimal performance. This chapter offers insight on the powerful tenets of coaching that allow for meaningful conversations of discovery, dreaming, designing, and destiny (Orem, Binkert, & Clancy, 2007) to take place for holistic, transformative learning.

As university professors, the authors found themselves amidst a paradigm shift in higher education. Each earned her terminal degree during a time when the professor was historically the dominant character in the teacher-student relationship. The student had neither choice nor voice. While professors will always receive honor for their contributions to a learned society, the old teacher-centered professorial tone is not deemed the best method for fostering transformational learning in the adult student. Therefore, the authors recommend that professors learn the art of coaching, which puts forward meaningful conversations between them and their students. Coaching (Orem et al., 2007) takes professors away from the old professorial model of "telling" to a new leadership model of asking, listening, and directing, in that order (Scott, 2002). With a spirit of inquiry, professors may facilitate instruction and mentoring with conversations. By modeling meaningful conversations, those who teach sculpt a new paradigm for future teaching and learning relationships.

The authors of this chapter are more concerned with transforming students than conforming students. hooks (2003) expressed the sentiments of the authors when stating,

> My hope emerges from those places of struggle where I witness individuals positively transforming their lives and the world around them. Educating is always a vocation rooted in hopefulness. As teachers we believe that learning is possible, that nothing can keep an open mind from seeking after knowledge and finding a way to know. (p. xiv)

A closer examination of hooks's quote reveals that for those who are truly committed to fostering a sense of wonder and inquiry in the adult student, they must do everything possible to engage in the very behaviors that have traditionally not been a part of higher education. The teacher/professor must be one who listens and asks rather than one who simply imparts knowledge. In the following section, we closely examine the literature on these practices.

REVIEW OF RELATED LITERATURE

Influenced by their past, instructors of adult learners must continuously examine their beliefs and practices as they are often shaped by their school experiences as children (Taylor, 2003). This is especially critical considering that teachers in K–12 are unlikely to utilize the best practices for meeting the needs of the adult learner. To the contrary, teacher practices for children usually consist of unbalanced, authoritarian, dictatorial, and undemocratic methods. Hence, critical reflection of beliefs and practices is necessary for instructors of adult learners to acquire new practices that are active, collaborative, democratic, and engaging.

Weimer (2002) purported that oftentimes professors are unaware of their authoritarian approach. It is evident, however, in their syllabi, in their practices, and in their pedagogical styles. With a secret desire for students to revere them, professors become oblivious to how the imbalance of power can negatively impact student learning and motivation. Coaching, through meaningful conversations, helps to balance the power in the partnership by telling less and asking more. This is operationalized by allowing students to discover, dream, and design more through generating their own positive, probing yet challenging questions, exploring possibilities, and investigating hypotheses, for instance (Orem et al., 2007; Weimer, 2002).

At the heart of transformative learning is the notion of partnership. Partnership is accomplished through honoring the principles of equality and voice (Eisler, 1987). In order to foster transformative learning, voices traditionally silenced need to feel a sense of belonging (Johnson-Bailey & Alfred, 2006). Knight (2002) claims that "When you see the world through partnership glasses, you come to understand human relationships in new ways" (p. 7). Whether those relationships are parent-child, administrator-employee, or teacher-student, their critical elements are choice and voice. Conventional wisdom suggests that such relationships are inherently unequal and one-sided. However, the authors submit that regardless of the circumstances that birth a union, the relationship is cultivated when both partners choose to travel together as humans of equal value, with both having a say in the direction of their journey. The power of choice and voice is evident in the home of any rebellious teenager, in the organization of any disgruntled or resistant employee, or in the classroom of any educational institution where inattentive, unengaged, and unconnected students convene.

In the same way, Altman and Taylor's (1973) social penetration theory provides a window into partnership development by describing the progression of interpersonal communication using an "onion" analogy. In the professor-student relationship, the professor connects with the human essence of the student to develop trust to bring about transformational learning (Merizow, 1995). As the layers of the onion are slowly peeled away through meaningful conversations, the inner core of the onion lies bare so that the deeply held beliefs, attitudes, and even misconceptions of the student are conveyed. This relationship in learning is effective in that students become sophisticated learners who make more of their own discoveries in ways that resonate with their own experiences (Rock, 2006) and with structures that support students becoming agents of their own transformation.

Equally important is the type of education to which professors subscribe. Their personal philosophy will certainly play a role in whether they will endorse relational education. If professors are blissfully married to teaching but divorced, detached, or even dissociated from learning, they are less likely to understand the significance of associative schooling. Along this line of reasoning, Freire (2000) identified two kinds of education: banking/teacher-centered and learner-centered. Banking or teacher-centered education accepts students as passive and quiet, while learner-centered education poses dilemmas and quandaries that teachers and learners co-investigate. In learner-centered education, professors are likened to midwives (Ayers, 1986) and gardeners (Weimer, 2002). Midwives empower. They push and they pull. Then again, they know when to watch and wonder (Ayers, 1986). So it is with the gardener who tills, weeds, and waters. While the gardener is instrumental in the making of a beautiful garden, the glory belongs to the plants that grow, bloom, and bear the fruit (Weimer, 2002). Comparatively, the learner-centered instructor is a collaborator and a coach who helps learners share and revise their narratives as new meaning is made (Tisdell, 2003). Such collaboration promotes the ultimate goal of education, which is liberation for the purposes of transformation. In the same fashion, the goal of transformative learning is lifelong personal development (Freire, 2000). The professor then serves as mentor, guide, cheerleader, challenger, and supporter in the learning process (Daloz, 1986). Understanding that the process of transformation is constructed within the learner and begins with the learner's experiences, the authors recommend that coaching also becomes synonymous with the role of teacher, instructor, and professor. With a focus that is less on teaching and more on learning (Weimer, 2002), the professor may help learners critically examine their assumptions and beliefs, interpret their assumptions, and revise them as needed for transformation (Costa & Garmston, 1994). Fortunately, the notion of coaching through meaningful conversations is likely to be accepted by students since students aspire to engage in meaningful dialogue and accept a variety of opinions, even when those opinions challenge the status quo (Mezirow, 2000).

The Notion of Coaching

According to the work of Orem et al. (2007), the purpose of coaching is individual transformation. At the core of coaching is appreciation in all interactions and a focus on human potential and possibilities rather than problems. The foundation of coaching builds upon constructionist and positive principles. Constructionist principles are aligned with constructionist theory and how people view the world when considering their human potential, their limitless possibilities, and their relationships. Constructionists commend positive principles because positive attitudes, actions, and connections have a greater influence on change than negative ones. The notion of coaching assumes that each person has the potential to be motivated, and that under the right circumstances, all students can be motivated to make positive change. Coaching shares the core belief of teaching in that no one is uneducable; no one is unreachable.

Constructionist principles replace the significance of the "individual" with the significance of the "relationship" as the locus of knowledge (Orem et al., 2007). Those in a relationship create meaning, and through communication and language, so how one communicates and interacts with others creates their reality. Coaching generates and expresses positive emotions in order to foster an appreciative yet balanced view of self for the purposes of creating protracted and positive connections to others.

Positive principles, positive language, and positive questions are important because being positive and having feelings such as tranquility, joy, happiness, curiosity, and wonder can be transformational in expanding a person's ways of thinking and acting (Fredrickson, 1998). In fact, positive emotions create the urge to play. In the state of play, mental abilities are sharper, individuals are more intrinsically motivated, they take more intellectual risks, and they increase their involvement in exploration, invention, and skills acquisition. The more positive one's emotions remain, the longer lasting the change will be. Along these lines, coaches help individuals recognize, acknowledge, and believe in their own inner strength. They help individuals focus on and manage their positive history, strengths, and greatest accomplishments. Self-awareness is intertwined with destiny, so knowing what is best about oneself is at the base of positive change. Discovering what is best about self helps people to determine what they know and how it can be applied to a desirable future.

Language is also critical in the process in that negative words set in motion negative change or even resistance (Orem et al., 2007). Negativity focuses on problems and weaknesses that generate depressive and defensive responses. Even when individuals arrive with very negative circumstances and stories, coaches help them to reinterpret, reframe, reimagine, and refocus their life story to enable more hopeful and joyful action toward desired change. This is a valid process in that just as there are many interpretations of a poem, there can be numerous perspectives of an individual's life (Orem et al., 2007). Coaches use an individual's core skills, strong points, and proudest achievements to guide them into creating, exploring, and experimenting until their dream comes into clear view and they are able to design a plan for the dream. This plan of discovery, dreaming, designing, and destiny is more likely to occur when coaches possess the disposition of committed listening (Burley-Allen, 1995) and the norms of mimicry, feedback, positive language, care, confidentiality, and appreciative inquiry (Orem et al., 2007). In short, coaches help individuals generate and express positive emotions about themselves in ways that help them to create and sustain a bright future through the positive pursuit of a dream. While their hope is the blueprint of the dream, their positive attitude and actions are the constructions that take them to the destination.

The purpose, core, foundation, and principles of coaching would certainly be a boon in the classroom and in the instructor-student relationship. For instance, instructors would serve students well by helping them to discover the positives they bring to the learning opportunity. Instructors would take students to higher intellectual levels by affording them the deliberate process of dreaming. This includes helping students to create clear images of possibilities, to voice their preferred future, and to shift their focus from their current perceptions to the future they envision (Orem et al., 2007). Instructors would do well to affirm the dreams of their students by helping them to make mindful choices and actions and by directing their attention with patience, fortitude, and faith (Orem et al., 2007). Further, instructors demonstrate care for students when helping them expand their capacity (Orem et al., 2007) and competence through the course content as well as through extended learning opportunities. Discovery, dreaming, designing, and destiny, for some students, could be as narrow as using course content to earn a favorable grade, and for other students, as broad as using course content to fulfill greater, more long-term aspirations. In either case, students would benefit, in large measure, if instructors adopted the norms and dispositions of the coaching methodology as they would, no doubt, generate collaborative and meaningful conversations with students that afford transformational change.

The "Heart" of Transformative Learning

Operating with intelligence alone limits vision and wisdom. One is unable to see the complete picture absent the expanded intelligence of the heart in that it affords a broader perspective and understanding of the whole (McArthur & McArthur, 2004). Moreover, the heart is the place from which intentions and motivations emanate (Webster-Smith, 2010a, 2010b). This aspect is important considering the view that the heart houses the belief system. Beliefs can be pure or not, and they can also embrace truth or not (Walker, 2006). Therefore, an examination of one's heart is advisable.

An excavation of the heart was championed by Argyris and Schon (1974), because individuals can be unaware that their theories-in-use are inconsistent with their espoused theories. For instance, espoused theories are easily expressed but theories-in-use (or practices) confirm the beliefs, values, and worldviews that drive behavior and serve as the maps used to take action. To wit, worldview is a psychological construct and an essential element of human nature; hence, it is instructive for those who teach adult learners to examine their philosophy of education. It is quite possible that their classroom practices are deeply rooted in their philosophy about teaching and learning. Where there is misalignment between what instructors espouse and what they do in the classroom (practices), instructors must examine their philosophy and practices, uncover discrepancies, and through reflection, align the two (Tisdell & Taylor, 1999/2000).

Fortunately, life continuously presents opportunities to rebuild what has been created by the heart (McArthur & McArthur, 2004). For example, instructors can undertake an analysis of their teaching, including a complete instructional assessment (Weimer, 2002) to determine ways in which their philosophy and practices are not learner-centered. They can consider whether they have meaningful conversations with students and if their courses allow students to discover, dream, design, and shape their desired destiny (Orem et al., 2007). By and large, instructors must take the necessary steps to offer quality teaching that has learning as the explicit outcome (Weimer, 2002) while it reaches out to the essence, value, uniqueness, and complexity of each learner.

The "Head" of Transformative Learning

In order for students to gain the highest levels of understanding, instructors should help students uncover content rather than cover content (Weimer, 2002); and that content must accomplish at least two purposes. It must establish the foundation of knowledge on which subsequent learning is constructed as well as help learners develop the confidence they need to face future learning challenges on their own (Weimer, 2002). Brookfield (1996, 2000, 2005) supported higher-ordered thinking through content by encouraging scrutiny, analysis, critical thinking, and critical reflection, which lead to transformation through stages such as sense of inner discomfort, self-examination of the situation, examining new ways of explaining the situation, developing alternative perspectives, and integrating new ways of thinking.

As it is impossible to present all the possible information students need for a future that is yet to be imagined, instructors must become concerned with facilitating knowledge in ways that stimulate a thirst and quest for lifelong learning. The coaching method lends itself quite readily to the development of learning skills such as accessing information through various resources and evaluating their import (Weimer, 2002). The coaching model allows professors to go beyond teaching content to helping students develop their intellectual maturity, learning skills, and awareness so they can function as independent and interdependent learners (Weimer,

2002). The coaching model further assists instructors with motivating students to experience extended encounters with the course content. Similarly, when professors engage in meaningful conversations with students, it whets their appetite so that they might acquire a hunger and thirst for the content and its power to advance their professional development. They begin to see how content can explain or answer important questions and/or solve significant solutions in their field. Such cravings also overflow to reveal the ability of content to invigorate their personal development as well as help resolve larger societal ills (Weimer, 2002). As a result, students rise up to become solution-focused learners (Brookfield, 1996, 2000, 2005; Orem et al., 2007; Rock, 2006; Weimer, 2002), transforming their own education. Employing positive, constructionist, and constructivist principles helps students engage in courses in a reflective manner, which is critical for transformation.

The "Hands" of Transformative Learning

Given that the entire transformative experience is about change that is growth-enhancing and developmental (Tennant, 1993, 2000), taking action is the final part of transformative learning. The student may take "immediate action, delayed action, or reasoned affirmation of an existing pattern of action" (Mezirow, 2000, p. 24). The coaching model advances taking action and taking active ownership of learning in addition to making meaning of it for one's own life (Mezirow, 2000). Hence, professors must resist the temptation to be the center of attention to ensure that students become engaged in the authentic work of the discipline (Weimer, 2002). What is more, professors must give students opportunities to deal with the controversial and messy issues of the discipline so that they not only learn content but are able to argue, refute, collect evidence, and defend their positions. Meaningful conversations would cultivate the principles of reflection and praxis (Knight, 2002). Students would become able and proficient in order to understand, apply, analyze, synthesize, and evaluate the content for optimal performance. Through reflective thinking, adult learners would weigh the wisdom of accepting or rejecting course content, again for the benefit of their personal and professional advancement. The goal is to help students build the capacity to become interdependent learners as well as independent learners so that they are empowered to sustain their new understandings and achievements with new behaviors that become habitual through practice (Orem et al., 2007) and routine outside of the classroom environment.

RECOMMENDATIONS FOR PRACTICE

Consonant with the tenets of coaching, instructors should become vigilant in helping students see themselves in a holistic fashion, focusing on their talents and gifts rather than on their failings and shortcomings (Orem, et al., 2007). Instructors should also remember that optimal teaching and learning partnerships afford choice and voice, and an important feature of the dialog is having an "equal opportunity to participate in the various roles of discourse" (Mezirow, 2000, p. 13). All the same, instructors should listen to the language of students to help them rephrase when their language is negative and anchored in the present rather than in a brighter future (Orem et al., 2007) equipped with the arsenal of course content that has been critically considered, reflected upon, and evaluated. Strategies that challenge, support, and help students envision their future also help learners along their personal journeys (Daloz, 1986, 1999) toward discovery, dreaming, designing, and destiny.

CONCLUSION

Although the contextual framework offered here emerges from the collective experiences of faculty in higher education, the principles of coaching and meaningful conversations can apply to relationships in any setting in which there are at least two committed individuals who work together as equals and guide the direction of what they mutually share. When instructors do not impose, dominate, or control the dialogue but prompt meaningful conversations and balance, students can make key decisions about learning, make positive connections, discoveries, dream, and design a great destiny. By engaging in meaningful conversations, those who teach forge a new paradigm for future teaching and learning relationships.

REFERENCES

Altman, I., & Taylor, D. (1973). *Social penetration: The development of interpersonal relationships.* NewYork, NY: Holt, Rinehart and Winston.

Argyris, M., & Schön, D. (1974) *Theory in practice. Increasing professional effectiveness.* San Francisco, CA: Jossey-Bass.

Ayers, W. (1986). Thinking about teachers and the curriculum. *Harvard Educational Review, 56*(1), 49–51.

Brookfield, S. (1996). Breaking the code: Engaging practitioners in critical analysis of adult educational literature. In R. Edwards, A. Hanson, & P. Raggatt (Eds.), *Boundaries of adult learning* (pp. 57–81). New York, NY: Routledge.

Brookfield, S. (2000). Transformative learning as ideology critique. In J. Merizow & Associates (Eds.), *Learning as transformation: Critical perspectives on a theory of progress* (pp. 125–148). San Francisco, CA: Jossey-Bass.

Brookfield, S. (2005). Overcoming impostership, cultural suicide and lost innocence: Implications for teaching critical thinking in the community college. In C. M. McMahon (Ed.), Special issue: Critical thinking: Unfinished business (pp. 49–57). *New Directions for Community Colleges, 130.* San Francisco, CA: Jossey-Bass.

Burley-Allen, M. (1995). *Listening: The forgotten skill.* New York, NY: John Wiley & Sons.

Costa, A., & Garmston, R. (1994). *Cognitive coaching: A foundation for the renaissance school.* Norwood, MA: Christopher Gordon.

Daloz, L. A. (1986). *Effective teaching and mentoring: Realizing the transformational power of adult learning experiences.* San Francisco, CA: Jossey-Bass.

Daloz, L. A. (1999). *Mentor: Guiding the journey of adult learners* (2nd ed.). San Francisco, CA: Jossey-Bass.

Eisler, R. (1987). *The chalice and the blade: Our history, our future.* San Francisco, CA: Harper Collins.

Fredrickson, B. (1998). What good are positive emotions? *Review of General Psychology, 2,* 300–219.

Freire, P. (2000). *Pedagogy of the oppressed* (20th anniv. ed.). New York, NY: Continuum.

hooks, b. (2003). *Teaching community. A pedagogy of hope.* New York, NY: Routledge.

Johnson-Bailey, J., & Alfred, M. (2006). Transformational teaching and the practice of Black women educators. In E. W. Taylor (Ed.), Fostering transformative learning in the classroom: Challenges and innovations. *New Directions in Adult and Continuing Education, 102.* San Francisco, CA: Jossey-Bass.

Knight, J. (2002). *Partnership learning fieldbook.* Lawrence: Kansas University Center for Research on Learning.

McArthur, D., & McArthur, B. (2004). *The intelligent heart: Transform your life with the laws of love.* Virginia Beach, VA: A.R.E. Press.

Merizow, J. (1995). Transformation theory of adult learning. In M. R. Welton (Ed.), *In defense of the lifeworld* (pp. 39–70). Albany: State University of New York Press.

Merizow, J. (2000). Learning to think like an adult: Core concepts of transformation theory. In J. Merizow & Associates (Eds.), *Learning as transformation: Critical perspectives on a theory in progress* (pp. 3–33). San Francisco, CA: Jossey-Bass.

Orem, S., Binkert, J., & Clancy, A. (2007). *Appreciative coaching: A positive process for change.* San Francisco, CA: Jossey Bass.

Rock, D. (2006). *Quiet leadership: Six steps to transforming performance at work.* New York, NY: Harper Collins.

Scott, S. (2002). *Fierce conversations: Achieving success in work and in life, one conversation at a time.* New York, NY: Berkley.

Sergiovanni, T. (2007). *Rethinking leadership: A collection of articles* (2nd ed.). Thousand Oaks, CA: Corwin.

Taylor, E. (2003). The relationship between the prior school lives of adult educators and their beliefs about teaching adults. *International Journal of Lifelong Education, 22*(1), 59–77.

Tennant, M. C. (1993). Perspective transformation and adult development. *Adult Education Quarterly, 44*(1), 34–42.

Tennant, M. C. (2000). Adult learning for self-development and change. In A. L. Wilson & E. R. Hayes (Eds.), *Handbook of adult and continuing education* (pp. 87–100). San Francisco, CA: Jossey-Bass.

Tisdell, E. J. (2003). *Exploring spirituality and culture in adult and higher education.* San Francisco, CA: Jossey-Bass.

Tisdell, E. J., & Taylor, E. (1999/2000). Adult education philosophy informs practice. *Adult Learning, 11*(2), 6–10.

Walker, J. (2006). *The problem with beliefs.* Retrieved from http://www.nobeliefs.com/beliefs.htm

Webster-Smith, A. (2010a, August). *Reflective leadership that dispels demographic destiny.* Paper presented at the Annual Conference of the National Council of Professors of Educational Administration, Washington, DC.

Webster-Smith, A. (2010b, September). *Give yourself the gift of reflection.* Retrieved from http://reflectivelivingwithdrangela.com

Weimer, M. (2002). *Learner-centered teaching: Five key changes to practice.* San Francisco, CA: Jossey-Bass.

CHAPTER 2

LEARNING ABOUT LEARNING IN RELATIONSHIPS

Novice Teacher Educators Give Transformative Dialogue a Try

Elizabeth Bondy, Lauren Tripp, and D. Alvarez Caron

For more than two decades, educational scholars have called for changes in teacher education programs to prepare predominantly White, middle class prospective teachers to work effectively with the increasingly diverse student population in U.S. schools. Melnick and Zeichner (1998) point out that changes in teacher education programs have been difficult because teacher educators are very much like the population of students with whom they work, that is, overwhelmingly Caucasian, middle class, monolingual, and limited in cross-cultural experiences and understandings. They characterize the majority of teacher education programs as providing a monocultural approach that perpetuates the "kinds of teaching practices that have historically benefited middle class, White students but have largely failed to provide quality education for poor and ethnic and linguistic minority students" (p. 89). Melnick and Zeichner conclude, "The work of teacher educators and the institutional environment in which teacher education is embedded are critical in determining the success of efforts to prepare teachers to work with diverse students" (p. 89). Thus, an urgent and heretofore unaddressed challenge is how to prepare teacher educators with the strategies and habits of mind necessary for preparing culturally competent and responsive teachers. This kind of preparation requires transformative learning, which Mezirow (2000) defines as "the process by which we transform our taken-for-granted frames of reference" (p. 6) so that we are not held captive by the "sociocultural beliefs, values, and perspectives acquired (usually in childhood) through our family of origin, cultural assimilation, and stereotypical representations within our society" (Geller, 2009, p. 183).

The context for this chapter is the preparation of teacher educators who have the dispositions, knowledge, and skills needed for critical multicultural teacher education (Kincheloe, 2008), or what Keating (2007) has called "transformational multiculturalism." Specifically, the chapter reports an analysis of the experiences of teacher education doctoral students in a Critical Pedagogy Seminar, which attempted to encourage the development of multicultural knowledge and dispositions by providing future teacher educators with opportunities to examine their sociocultural identities. In particular, the basis of the chapter is an analysis of eight doctoral students' experience with one course assignment, called "Give it a Try." Challenged to enact one or more of the concepts and/or strategies studied in the seminar and to reflect (in an essay format) on what they learned from giving it a try, the students attempted to facilitate transformative learning in a wide range of contexts. The authors report on what the students learned about the features and challenges of dialogue for transformative learning in relationship with others.

THEORETICAL FRAMEWORK

The project is situated within the framework of Mezirow's (2000) theory of adult transformative learning as it has been enhanced by the work of other scholars and practitioners of transformative learning (e.g., Fisher-Yoshida, Geller, & Schapiro, 2009), and by Bakhtin's (1981) discussion of "ideological becoming," that is, the process by which people develop a worldview or ideological self. Mezirow asserts that transformative learning takes place through a process of critical reflection facilitated by open dialogue in a safe setting. This process is not necessarily rational; in fact, the whole person (not solely one's "logic") is often engaged in the learning process, and as such, "extrarational body, spirit, and emotion/feeling" can play as prominent a role as the rational and cognitive (Fisher-Yoshida et al., 2009, p. 290).

According to Bakhtin (1981), however, the social interactions that are most effective in promoting learning are those that embody conflict. As Geller (2009) summarizes, authors who work from a transformative learning perspective agree, and use various terms to refer to this conflict (e.g., disorienting dilemma, trigger event, disconfirmation, confusion, and withdrawal). Bakhtin explains, "The importance of struggling with another's discourse, its influence in the history of an individual's coming to ideological consciousness, is enormous" (1981, p. 348). This struggle, while integral to learning, is still more likely to be successful within a space characterized as open and emotionally safe, as Mezirow suggests. In short, as Ball and Freeman (2004) have written, "In a Bakhtinian sense, with whom, in what ways, and in what contexts we interact will determine what we stand to learn" (p. 9).

Schapiro's summary of the characteristics of transformative learning spaces also informed the authors:

> Learning happens in *relationships*, (2) in which there is *shared ownership* and control of the learning space, (3) room for the *whole person*—feelings as well as thoughts, body and soul, as well as mind, (4) and *sufficient time* for collaboration, action, reflection, and integration, (5) to pursue a process of *inquiry driven by* the questions, needs, and purposes of the *learners*. (Schapiro, 2009, pp. 111–112, emphasis in original)

Although the professional literature does include discussion of the features that are essential for dialogue to have the potential to be transformative, recent research indicates that novices can find enactment of these features to be challenging (Bondy, Tricarico, Dodman, & LaFramenta, 2010). In fact, there is likely to be, perhaps not surprisingly, a gap between a person's conceptual grasp of transformative practice and the individual's ability to enact that practice. Hence, this chapter reports on the experience of novice teacher educators who attempted to enact transformative dialogue within and outside of the university classroom.

INSIGHTS INTO TRANSFORMATIVE DIALOGUE

The eight female teacher education doctoral students reported on the following experiences:

- An attempt to problematize a male friend's beliefs about "chivalrous" behavior by having him read and discuss with the doctoral student a paper about chivalry as a form of oppression,

- A conversation with one's husband, a Southern Baptist divinity school student, about the potentially oppressive use of power from the pulpit,
- A Facebook discussion initiated by a Pakistani woman with her former students about the implications of traditional Pakistani beliefs for the Pakistani people,
- A challenge to students in a History of Education class to expand their definition of multiculturalism,
- Receiving and giving radical love, as defined by Paulo Freire and others, in the university context,
- The initiation of an online forum for students in a Social Foundations of Education class to encourage them to respond thoughtfully to each other's ideas,
- A confrontation with a local business owner and a fiancé about the use of a pornographic image to promote a popular local business, and
- An attempt to disrupt future teachers' assumptions about the purposes and practices of "classroom management."

The participants' essays yielded clues to the role of the teacher educator who wishes to facilitate transformative dialogue. That role includes enacting strategies we call "gentle" and strategies we call "brave." Together, these strategies create the conditions in which participants are willing to be disturbed (Wheatley, 2002). That is, the strategies create a psychologically supportive environment (Patrick, Turner, Meyer, & Midgley, 2003) that invites and enables honest participation and reconsideration of long-held, and typically unrecognized, tacit beliefs. The opportunity to consider and transform habits of thinking is particularly important for teachers who will work with children and families with whom they are likely to have little experience and perhaps little in common.

BEING GENTLE

While the concept of being "gentle" often assumes passivity, building a psychologically supportive environment requires a particular kind of gentleness and action. This gentleness establishes a foundation in which one may question previously unquestioned norms. In other words, the authors found that the gentle establishes the conditions in which the brave can be effective. The gentle strategies that create a safe space for transformation include the following:

Listening deeply entails a sense of responsiveness and an unconditional acceptance despite differences. Keating's (2007) description of deep listening captures well the experience of the novice teacher educators. Keating describes the strategy as including respect for the speaker and the individual's "intricate history" that is unknown to others; acknowledgement of the facilitator's uncertainty and willingness to change; requests for clarification of the speaker's meaning; remaining silent and withholding recommendations, solutions, and our own stories; and challenging ideas but not the speaker. The authors noticed these strategies at play in most of the essays and draw on two examples here: a feminist educator's withholding judgment of a proudly chivalrous male friend, and another educator allowing students to read and respond to their peers' reactions to course readings without her interference.

Elyse described sharing an article on oppression caused by traditional gender roles with a male friend whom Elyse knew strongly valued the concept of male "chivalry." Instead of informing him of all the ways the male friend's behavior oppressed women, Elyse simply asked him to read the article and then purposefully structured their conversation with statements like "Tell me more about how you feel about _____" or "Give me an example of what you mean by _____." Elyse's respectful and responsive listening maintained the friendly and open atmosphere between them, minimized any threat the male friend might feel, and helped the friend to share responses to the article that clearly challenged the male friend's beliefs.

Elyse hoped to enable the male friend to realize that those chivalrous gestures, such as always holding the door, paying for meals, and driving when with women, "send the message that women are incapable and conspire to the immobilization, reduction, and molding of them." Elyse's friend shared, however, that those cultural beliefs were the basis of these gestures, and that, in fact, he saw them as a result of Hispanic males' "admiration and reverence for women which begins, for most, as a deep-seated respect for their own mothers." This discussion revealed the divide between the male friend's intention and the reception of those gestures and allowed a broadening of concepts of what it means to respect women.

Lauren's example illustrates that listening can mean attending closely to what is not said in an effort to enable participants to engage openly with one another. An online discussion forum was set up in hopes to facilitate debate among students after they had hesitated to engage with one another during in-class large group discussion. Still, Lauren found little if any real wrestling with the ideas or with each other. Careful consideration of the students' very cautious online comments led Lauren to recognize what had gone awry. By asking students to debate, Lauren violated the ground rules for classroom engagement that Lauren had discussed with students on the first day of class: (a) I search for basic agreement; (b) I reflect on my position and, temporarily, suspend my beliefs; (c) I assume that many people have a piece of the answer and I want to find common ground. Lauren recognized the misstep and reconsidered the control of trying to enforce the format of the students' discussion. Lauren revised the approach and asked the students to respond freely to the text based on their own opinions. Immediately, the tenor of the discussion shifted toward greater engagement with one another's ideas and comments that were more thoughtful. By listening to what students were not saying (or writing, as the case may be), Lauren recognized that the initial directions to students had actually thwarted the very dialogue that she hoped to enable. By removing the instructor from the equation, the students enjoyed a much more enriching conversation.

Sharing authority is the facilitator's gentle stance of learning with others rather than delivering information to them. This orientation to teaching and learning requires that the facilitator allow multiple people to fill the role of expert. This was highlighted through one educator's request for students to share their stories of using "nonstandard" forms of English in the classroom rather than accepting a guest speaker's claim that only "standard" English should be used at all times.

Part of a critical teacher education program must involve questioning the traditional structure of the classroom: teacher as knowledge provider and students as knowledge recipients. Chris attempted to overturn this model and share authority with students in a classroom management course. First, Chris gave students permission to disagree with the text, thereby enabling them to exercise power. Students were also encouraged to question concrete, established school norms, such as the forms of English used in the classroom. When confronted with a guest speaker who encouraged the teacher education students to criticize and correct any "nonstandard" English dialects used in the classroom, Chris shared a story about a personal experience as a classroom teacher in which she collaborated with students to create a dictionary of slang terms. The goal was to value students' spoken language while acknowledging its similarities and differences with more academic forms of English required for school assignments. By providing a counterpoint to the message of the school district-approved authority figure, Chris empowered the student teachers to share their own experiences of feeling "dumb" for using nonstandard English and how it had silenced them in the classroom. Gently validating their experiences, Chris created the space for transformative dialogue.

Acknowledging the difficulty refers to the willingness of educators to admit the unstable ground onto which they hope to venture. Two educators provided insight into this strategy by attempting transformative dialogue with their partners: one publically questioning (through a letter to the editor of a local newspaper) an advertisement that she personally considered pornographic but her fiancé did not, and another discussing the ways in which her husband, a Southern Baptist seminary student, could use his power to empower his congregation instead of condemn them. While these conversations were risky, the gentle strategy involved laying the groundwork for transformation by acknowledging the inherent risk.

The first, Desi, was horrified to find that a bar that she and her fiancé frequented was using a pornographic image of a woman on a t-shirt to advertise the business. However, Desi's fiancé supported the bar owner's decision and told her she was overreacting. The risk Desi took publically by writing a letter to the editor protesting the t-shirt was clear, but the more subtle gentle act she undertook first was the discussion with her fiancé. Desi gently validated their relationship, acknowledged their differences of opinion, and noted the difficulty of disagreeing with him about an issue of enormous importance to her.

The second, Katrina, hoped to encourage her husband to acknowledge the power he could wield as a pastor and consider how to use it as a way to empower his congregants. By discussing the negative impact on her of their current pastor's condemnation of the Harry Potter series as "trash," read by "morons and idiots" who wanted their children to be Satan worshippers, Katrina was able to share with her husband how his own words from the pulpit could marginalize those in congregation, instead of uplift them. Katrina wrote,

> Of course I would want my husband to preach what he feels God has revealed to him about an issue, but in an empathetic way that does not marginalize others, instead helping them to seek out God's will on their own with his help as their pastor. I don't believe that God gives his revelation to one person, the pastor, only. I believe that He gives them to all his people.

The conversation Katrina had with her husband was successful in part because she admitted to him that she was struggling with these issues herself and that she wanted to work through the issues with him, not in opposition to him. This gentle act of saying, in effect, "This is difficult, and we're in it together" laid the foundation for a fresh vision of what a spiritual leader could be.

Using a variety of participation formats invites engagement in ways that are familiar and comfortable for participants. These educators did that by providing asynchronous formats, such as online forums, to collapse the walls of the classroom, and by allowing time for repeated reflection and conversations privately, in small groups, and in large groups. By encouraging many different formats for participation, previously silenced voices were empowered to share their ideas, creating a fertile ground for transformation.

Lauren, who had created the online forum to encourage student dialogue, found that the online structure provided yet another benefit: time out of class to expand on ideas shared in class. She structured one of the discussion forums with questions to consider during reading, such as "How does James Conant believe the SAT will overcome class bias?" and questions to answer after class discussion, such as "Is 'merit' a defining factor in the quality of education each student receives?" On the topic of merit, one student wrote the following in the online forum:

> We didn't get to discuss the NY Times article, *Shadowy Lines That Still Divide*, in class today, but I had written down a quote from it that related to the debate about meritocracy in education. At the end of the first page, the article wrote: "But merit, it turns out, is at least partly class-based. Parents with money, education and connections cultivate in their children the habits that the meritocracy rewards. When their children then succeed, their success is seen as earned." Basically, achievements cannot be based on merit alone, because not every student is coming from the same starting point. Even SAT scores cannot be judged the same for everyone, because one's class determines their experiences which may help their test scores. (So does being able to afford tutors!)

This insight was obviously a result of both a personal reaction to the course readings and also a further reflection on what other students had posted. Time to think about and return to class readings and classmates' reactions to those readings appeared to facilitate insights such as the one above.

Chris and Elyse's experiences highlight other examples of allowing time and different forms of participation as well. In questioning the guest speaker's "Standard English Only" message, Chris first asked the students to reflect on the message they heard about language, specifically what it meant, who it affected, and how it made them feel. By giving them this time for reflection, the instructor enabled the students to deepen their understanding of the dialogue and their own reactions to it. Elyse allowed for deeper participation in the conversation by sharing the article on chivalry as oppression, allowing the male friend time to think and write about it, and then having multiple conversations on the issue. Providing this time and space for reflection was a gentle strategy that paved the way for transformation of long-held beliefs.

BEING BRAVE

The authors refer to some strategies as "brave" because in using them, the teacher educator recognizes that by intentionally destabilizing participants' taken-for-granted beliefs, the teacher educator risks placing oneself and the students in the uncertain and uncomfortable (and even "harrowing," as one of the doctoral students wrote) arena of student resistance. Therefore, the work requires courage on the part of the teacher educator. Brave strategies include the following:

Examining beliefs from multiple perspectives refers to the ways in which teacher educators prompt participants to consider beliefs from a variety of vantage points. The authors noticed the educators attempting to do this in several ways. For instance, two drew on evidence (from American history in one case and the Indian subcontinent in the second) as a means of helping their students reconsider certain well-established beliefs in their countries.

Jess, the instructor of an undergraduate course on the history of U.S. education, expressed concern about the students in her course and their limited understanding of "multiculturalism." With a goal of enriching their understanding, Jess proceeded to "deliberately bring up more discussions about gender, including LGBTQ issues." For example, historical data was used and the writing of historical figures to raise the thorny and insistent issue of fair pay for women, how issues of social class played into the narratives of which women were valued, and how the meaning of morality was largely class dependent. Responding to the fact that women have "gained only 17 cents on the dollar in terms of pay equality since the antebellum era," a student let out a call for a "revolution" with an animated, affirmative response. The use of evidence to stimulate students' reflection on the status of women in the United States helped them to reconsider their belief that sexism was merely an ancient relic. Furthermore, by introducing gender as an aspect of multiculturalism, Jess helped the students to see how race, class, and gender are related and how multiculturalism is a relevant concept for all members of the community.

Interestingly, Jess notes that the primary factor that enabled the facilitation of risky conversations with the students in her class was the rapport that already existed among them. In Jess' estimation, the classroom community was intact and strong. In short, the gentle work allowed the class to wade into the potentially rough waters of destabilizing taken-for-granted beliefs.

Aliya, a Pakistani woman, wrote about interactions with former students from Pakistan on the networking site, Facebook. She initiated online dialogue by inviting the former students to read a published essay asserting the importance of faith in Allah. Aliya posted the following comment:

> In the Pakistani culture we are not raised with the belief that if we really want something we should keep trying to obtain it. Instead, most of us grow up with the faith that if something is your fate, you get it and vice versa.... It is this absence of that effort and relying solely on fate that I am contesting. I would appreciate diverse viewpoints.

In one of the posts, a student noted that "we cannot compare ourselves or the situation and mindset in Pakistan with the U.S. because the Pakistani people are concerned with achieving only basics like food, clothes, and shelter," implying that Americans would not share these concerns. Aliya responded by pointing out the problems related to poverty and education in the United States that are often unseen by others who are exposed to the carefully crafted vision of the land of opportunity. Another student related aspects of the history of the Indian subcontinent that was thought to explain why Pakistanis "believe in an external locus of control and think that our actions are not in our control." This student asserted that the very history of Pakistan explained why many people did not see that "destiny is a bridge you make for yourself." Aliya's essay illustrates how the facilitator (Aliya) and the participants can bring information to the dialogue that helps everyone consider beliefs, even fundamental religious beliefs, in a new light.

Aliya notes that the Facebook discussion is ongoing and has organically shifted to questions of how one can make education more equitable for, "ALL populations" in Pakistan. Aliya expressed great enthusiasm for the level of critique in which these former students engaged by encouraging consideration of diverse perspectives.

Using a variety of destabilizing texts facilitates wondering about and destabilizing tacit beliefs. The authors label the strategy as brave because of its intent to rock participants' very comfortable boats. Here the definition of texts is intentionally broad to include both print and nonprint sources, such as "mass media and popular culture practices (e.g., radio, TV, video, movies, CDs, the internet, gang graffiti, and cyberpunk culture)" (Alvermann & Hagood, 2000, p. 194). Texts, therefore, could include personal stories, e-mail messages, photographs, songs, newspaper articles, scholarly manuscripts, and any number of other visual and auditory messages. From Desi, who described experiences responding to an image on a t-shirt, the authors recognized the potential power of visual images in stimulating participants' willingness to be disturbed (Wheatley, 2002). In fact, Desi's essay revealed several kinds of texts, including a formal letter and e-mail messages.

In each essay, the authors noticed the use of texts to destabilize beliefs. For Katrina, the text was the pastor's sermon in which the Pastor condemned readers of the Harry Potter books. Elyse used the scholarly paper about men's oppression of women to challenge her male friend's beliefs about chivalry. Aliya relied on Facebook postings and material excerpted from course readings in her doctoral program. Chris treated the guest speaker's presentation as text and also legitimized as texts the students in her course's tales of their own experiences in schools. Jess drew on a variety of published textual material, including statistics, to facilitate students' reflection about the role of race, class, and gender in U.S. education. Lauren used course texts as well as students' online posts to disrupt what students took for granted about education. Alvarez used a peer's class presentation as a text to destabilize personal assumptions about the male student and his beliefs. In short, a variety of kinds of material can facilitate questioning of unexamined beliefs when introduced in a psychologically supportive environment.

Sharing thoughts and feelings honestly acknowledges that learning occurs through a variety of channels, and that although honesty can feel risky, it can be necessary to disrupt a person's comfort zone. When the facilitator presents and encourages both thoughts and feelings, this opens the door for cognitive and affective learning. This untraditional (in the academy) approach to teaching and learning encourages a mindful and whole-hearted struggle with new ideas.

The blend of the rational and extra-rational (Fisher-Yoshida et al., 2009) was particularly noteworthy in the experience of the educator, Alvarez, who had to cope with personal emotional distress upon recognizing that she had effectively "written off" a fellow male doctoral student based on assumptions made about the fellow student, only to learn that there was misjudgment as well as engagement in the same kind of oppressive practice that Alvarez condemned in others. In another emotionally charged incident, Alvarez was able to respond to a peer who stated that her presentation style in a class had seemed hostile. This honest (and brave!) moment facilitated dialogue about cultural differences and their impact on interaction patterns and perceptions of those patterns.

Of course, Desi's honest dialogue with her fiancé and Katrina's similar interaction with her husband highlight the power and bravery of the honest sharing of thoughts and feelings. Katrina's dialogue with her husband, the seminary student, illustrated the potentially disruptive power of frank communication in the context of a trusting relationship. The bravery needed to destabilize formerly comfortable relationships is also clear. Her own unique position as a devout Christian and wife allowed her to have frank conversations with her husband about the issues of power and marginalization in the church. In fact, Katrina acknowledged that it was the relationship with her husband that enabled an initiation of the examination of taken-for-granted beliefs.

It is important to note that although the gentle and brave strategies presented here are in the discrete and sequential format of traditional text, they are in reality neither discrete nor sequential. The strategies clearly overlap; for instance, using destabilizing texts can be a way to help participants view beliefs from multiple perspectives. In addition, one may enact the strategies in any number of possible sequences. In fact, although the authors think the gentle strategies generally establish the conditions in which the brave strategies can be effective, we do not claim that one must enact all strategies, that one must enact gentle strategies before a brave strategy is attempted, or that one does not need gentle strategies once one has used brave strategies. The goal was to report the insights of the doctoral students, all of whom are preparing to be teacher educators who can facilitate transformative learning, following their attempts to facilitate transformative practice in a variety of contexts. The authors were struck by the emergence of the qualitatively different kinds of strategies—the gentle and the brave—and the synergy among them. The authors recognized that an outcome of that synergy could well be a learning environment in which participants co-construct understanding as they engage in reflection that is both public and private, in the moment and extended over time, and collective and individual. Facilitating the development of this kind of environment requires practice, persistence, and deep respect for the differences among us.

CONCLUSIONS AND IMPLICATIONS

This chapter addresses a fundamental concern for those wishing to improve teacher education to acknowledge and cross the demographic divide: the preparation of critical teacher educators. Through the doctoral students' experiences with the "Give it a Try" essays, the authors gained insight into the kind of pedagogy critical teacher educators may wish to enact and what that enactment might look like. Specifically, the authors gained insight into the role of the teacher educator in creating the conditions in which transformative learning may occur. According to Ellsworth (1989), theorists often fail to provide concrete steps to help people enact critical (and transformative) pedagogy even as they focus on social justice goals within the curriculum. Although the authors do not wish to be prescriptive, it is necessary to acknowledge that a gap can exist between the conceptual and practical tools of critical teaching (Grossman et al., 2001). While the principles of transformative teaching certainly provide direction, one must study and practice the details of their enactment. The "Give it a Try" assignment provided this opportunity for future critical teacher educators.

There are challenges inherent in facilitating transformative dialogue. It may be obvious why the brave strategies are challenging. These strategies represent the facilitator's attempt to intentionally challenge participants' willingness to be disturbed (Wheatley, 2002), and the facilitator may be uncomfortable about pressing participants in this way and anxious about encountering resistance. Yet it is clear to us that those strategies we have labeled gentle may also be challenging for the facilitator. This is due to what may well be their strangeness. Listening more, talking less, sharing power, varying instructional formats, and thinking flexibly about the use of time may all require close attention and practice in order to implement effectively. In short, being gentle and brave may be challenging for the novice teacher educator because both are likely to require a transformed perspective about teaching and learning. Being gentle and brave may feel awkward and even intimidating. Even teacher educators, who can describe what to do, as we have done here, may stumble.

Grossman et al. (2001) describe the case of novice classroom teachers who did not sufficiently develop practical tools to enable them to enact that which they understood conceptually. Those authors argue that teacher education students need a balance of concepts that "help create a vision of teaching" (p. 96) and the "classroom practices, strategies, and resources that...have...local and immediate utility" (p. 81). Grossman et al.'s argument for careful balancing and integrating of conceptual and practical tools in the preparation of teachers appears to be relevant to the preparation of transformative teacher educators. If the goal is to transform teacher education and make possible the transformation of prospective teachers' frames of reference, one needs to consider how to scaffold the development of practical tools. Participation in a face-to-face or distant community of practice with colleagues who are striving to facilitate transformative dialogue could provide the context in which novices link the conceptual to the practical and refine their practical tools through individual and collaborative reflection. Although this blending of the conceptual and the practical may not be the norm in doctoral education, it may be necessary in order to prepare teacher educators to make critical multicultural teacher education a reality.

REFERENCES

Alvermann, D. E., & Hagood, M.C. (2000). Critical media literacy: Research, theory, and practice in "new times." *Journal of Educational Research, 93,* 193–205.

Bakhtin, M. M. (1981). *The dialogic imagination* (C. Emerson & M. Holquist, Trans.). Austin: University of Texas Press.

Ball, A. F., & Freedman, S. W. (2004). Ideological becoming: Bakhtinian concepts to guide the study of language, literacy, and learning. In A. F. Ball & S. W. Freedman (Eds.), *Bakhtinian perspectives on language, literacy, and learning* (pp. 3–33). Cambridge, England: Cambridge University Press.

Bondy, E., Tricarico, K., Dodman, S., & LaFramenta, J. (2010). *On the edges of critical teacher education: Promising practices and lingering dilemmas.* Paper presented at the annual meeting of the American Educational Research Association, Denver, CO.

Ellsworth, E. (1989). Why doesn't this feel empowering? Working through the repressive myths of critical pedagogy. *Harvard Educational Review, 59*(3), 297–324.

Fisher-Yoshida, B., Geller, K. D., & Schapiro, S. A. (Eds.). (2009). *Innovations in transformative learning.* New York, NY: Peter Lang.

Geller, K. D. (2009). Looking through the lens of culture, difference, and diversity. In B. Fisher-Yoshida, K. D. Geller, & S. A. Schapiro (Eds.), *Innovations in transformative learning* (pp. 201–204). New York, NY: Peter Lang.

Grossman, P. L., Valencia, S. W., Thompson, C., Martin, S. D., Place, N., & Evans, K. (2001). Transitions into teaching: Learning to teach writing in teacher education and beyond. In C. M. Roller (Ed.), *Learning to teach reading: Setting the research agenda* (pp. 80–99). Newark, DE: International Reading Association.

Keating, A. (2007). *Teaching transformation: Transcultural classroom dialogues*. New York, NY: Palgrave Macmillan.

Kincheloe, J. L. (2008). *Critical pedagogy* (2nd ed.). New York, NY: Peter Lang.

Melnick, S. L., & Zeichner, K. M. (1998). Teacher education's responsibility to address diversity issues: Enhancing institutional capacity. *Theory into Practice, 37*(2), 88–95.

Mezirow, J. (2000). Learning to think like an adult: Core concepts of transformation theory. In J. Mezirow & Associates (Eds.), *Learning as transformation* (pp. 3–34). San Francisco, CA: Jossey-Bass.

Patrick, H., Turner, J., Meyer, D. K., & Midgley, C. (2003). How teachers establish psychological environments during the first days of school: Associations with avoidance in mathematics. *Teachers College Record, 105*, 1521–1558.

Schapiro, S. (2009). Creating space for transformative learning. In B. Fisher-Yoshida, K. D. Geller, & S. A. Schapiro (Eds.), *Innovations in transformative learning* (pp. 111–116). New York, NY: Peter Lang.

Wheatley, M. (2002). *Turning to one another: Simple conversations to restore hope to the future*. San Francisco, CA: Berrett-Koehler.

CHAPTER 3

COMMUNICATION IS THE RELATIONSHIP

Julien C. Mirivel

> *While we teach knowledge, we are losing that teaching which is the most important one for human development: the teaching which can only be given by the simple presence of a mature, loving person.*
> —Fromm, 2006, p. 108

To enable students' transformation, teachers need to nurture positive relationships with them. As Buber (1965/2002) once argued, "The true teacher is not one who pours information into the student's head as through a funnel...it is the one who fosters genuine mutual contact and mutual trust" (p. xix). This point is well echoed by transformative learning theory (E. W. Taylor, 2007), which suggests that learning depends on genuine, authentic, relationships. As Taylor (2007) explained, "establishing relationships with others [is] one of the essential factors in a transformative experience" (p. 179; see also Mezirow, 2000; Taylor, 2008). Research in transformative learning or relational cultural theory (Carter, this volume), in fact, underscores the importance of relationship. As Teven (2001) explained, "in order to maximize learning, it is essential for teachers to develop a good relationship with their students, because the rapport established between teachers and students, in part, determines the interest and performance level of students" (p. 159). The process of relating with students in face-to-face encounters or in the classroom context inherently involves a communicative dimension. It is simply impossible to have a social or professional relationship without communication. With this perspective in mind, this chapter proposes several communication behaviors that teachers can choose to enact in interaction with students.

This chapter proceeds as follows. First, I introduce the constitutive model of communication to dilute a common misconception—that communication is simply an exchange of information. Instead, I argue that teachers should think about communication as a symbolic process of creation. The second part of the chapter describes three core communication behaviors that teachers can practice: (a) initiating greetings, (b) using open-ended questions, and (c) choosing to say something nice. For each, I draw on communication research and theory to support the claim. Next, I reflect on how embodying these behaviors can foster students' transformation. In the conclusion, I emphasize the importance of communicating well in the classroom and suggest avenues for future research.

WHY IS COMMUNICATION IMPORTANT?

Teaching is a communicative act. When teaching occurs in the classroom, it involves several individuals who communicate with one another in a localized spatio-temporal environment. To communicate, teachers and students perform a variety of actions that include conscious and unconscious behaviors. These behaviors can be audible as in utterances or speech acts (Austin, 1962) or visible, which includes microbehaviors (Streeck, 1983), small and often taken-for-granted actions such as gestures and gazes (for a review of research in this area, see Glenn, LeBaron, & Mandelbaum, 2003; Streeck, Goodwin, & LeBaron, in press; Streeck & Mehus, 2005). At any given moment of human interaction, thus, people perform a wide range of behaviors simultaneously, so that individuals might speak, move their body in space, initiate touch, maintain or lower their gaze, smile or frown (Koschmann & LeBaron, 2002). Through this interactional process, participants' behaviors *inherently* affect the nature of the relationship between individuals. For example, utterances can cue distance or closeness as well as the differing statuses between and among individuals (This explains why "What's up, honey bunny" is rarely a greeting professors use in the classroom). The point is that through interaction, teachers and students create a relational environment affected by moment-to-moment actions performed on a turn-by-turn basis. Through time, and much like a romantic relationship, members of a classroom create a relational history, experience significant turning points (Docan-Morgan, 2011; Docan-Morgan & Manusov, 2009) or conflicts, as well as nurture a positive or negative climate. Viewed from this perspective, teaching and learning is fundamentally a communicative process of relating. As Bateson (1972) claimed, "communication *is* the relationship" (as cited in Fairhurst, 2007, p. 13, emphasis in original).

There is a large body of literature that suggests that how teachers communicate affects students' learning in important ways. In the realm of nonverbal communication, for instance, research shows that nonverbal immediacy (Mehrabian, 1971), which includes smiling, nodding, and making eye contact, influences students' affective learning (Pogue & AhYun, 2006) as well as whole range of other variables such as the use of information-seeking behaviors, communication beyond the classroom, perceptions of effectiveness and credibility (respectively, e.g., Myers & Knox, 2001; Fusani, 1994; Chamberlin, 2000). Verbal communication, or what teachers say, also matters. Myers and Knox (2001), for example, showed a positive correlation between students' information-seeking behaviors and teachers' verbal immediacy and receptivity. These behaviors also affect students' affective and cognitive learning (Kramer & Pier, 1999). Other research suggests that humor affects learning (Banas, Dunbar, Rodriguez & Liu, 2011) and that instructional feedback that is well-designed is related to students' learning outcomes (Kerssen-Griep, Hess, & Trees, 2003; Kerssen-Griep, Trees, & Hess, 2008; Trees, Kerssen-Griep, & Hess, 2009). To put it shortly, what teachers say and do—how they communicate—matters extensively.

In sum, there is a substantial amount of communication research that documents the importance of communication processes in and outside of the classroom. Researchers know that faculty's communicative behaviors (e.g., caring attitude) affect students' perceptions as well as their affective and cognitive learning. However, to date, there is no practical model that suggests what teachers can do to communicate more effectively. In this chapter, I propose several behaviors that can facilitate the creation of positive, ethical relationships with students. Future research, of course, will need to further document how these behaviors occur in naturally occurring interaction and affect relationships.

WHAT WAYS OF THINKING AND BEHAVIORS FOSTER RELATIONSHIP?

This section introduces fundamental communication behaviors that teachers can *choose* to enact in interaction with students, whether it is in the classroom or in dyadic encounters. These behaviors are part of a larger practical theory of communication that I am developing. The larger system includes foundational principles, misconceptions, theoretical assumptions, and core skills. I have grounded the model in humanistic psychology (Frankl, 1984; Maslow, 1968; Rogers, 1961) and existential philosophy (Fromm, 1947; Sartre, 2007). The theory maps a system of thought and practice that individuals interested in communicating more effectively or wisely can adopt to grow as communicators. To proceed, I first address a common misconception. Then, I introduce three communication behaviors that teachers can choose to practice.

Moving From a Transmission to a Constitutive View of Communication

One dominant misconception about the nature of communication is the belief that the sole function of communication is to share information. This way of thinking stems from a model of communication developed in the 1800s called the transmission model (Peters, 1989). By definition, the transmission model suggests "communication is a process of sending and receiving messages or transferring information from one mind to another" (Craig, 1999, p. 125). From this perspective, communication is an information exchange.

Although the model is helpful is some ways, communication scholars have proposed another model called the constitutive model of communication (Deetz, 1994). This perspective highlights that "communication is a constitutive process that produces and reproduces shared meaning" (Craig, 1999, p. 125). More importantly, the constitutive model calls attention to the fact that when people talk to each other, they not only reflect reality but also actively construct it. What people say reflects the nature of the relationship between individuals and also actively produces, transforms, or affects the nature of their relationship. Utterances, as the language philosopher Austin (1962) showed, "do things." As an example, if I reveal to my students before class that I played tennis Sunday morning, the utterance does more that share information. By disclosing about my life, I foster closeness. If I tell a student, "I really like the work that you're doing," the talk functions as a compliment and can affect a student's sense of self. In sum, the constitutive view of communication suggests that "through communication participants perform and realize their relative roles, interactively negotiating the meanings of so-called messages, orienting toward some symbol systems as relevant and recognizable, in many ways constituting their communicative context" (LeBaron, Mandelbaum, & Glenn, 2003, p. 8). In a nutshell, the constitutive view foregrounds that relationships are always in the making and that communication is the process through which one manages relationships. It also highlights that small, taken-for-granted, behaviors can have large consequences on individuals and their relationship.

How a person thinks about communication naturally affects how they communicate with others. Communication researchers have shown that individuals develop logics of communication. O'Keefe and McCornack (1987) showed that communicators not only think differently about communication, but that their ways of thinking influences how they design messages. Changing how one thinks about communication can thus enable change in interaction.

In this section, I explained that communication is not simply a process of information exchange and message design. Instead, *communication is as an interactional, symbolic, process of co-creation.* Viewed in this way, teachers need to be attentive to the way they communicate, whether it is through their talk or with their body. The bottom line is that if one continuously manages relationships in and through communication, then one creates productive relationships through productive communication. In the next section, I introduce three communication behaviors that, if practiced consistently and regularly, can nurture positive relationships with students.

Initiating Greetings

First, teachers should choose to initiate greetings with students, both individually and collectively, as well as inside and outside of the classroom. Human interaction, across most cultures, begins with greetings. As Malinowski (1972) explained, "the breaking of silence, the communion of words is the first act to establish links of fellowship" (p. 150). In the United States, "what's up," "good morning," or "hello" are popular ways to begin interaction. In France, it is "bonjour." In Arabic culture, "assalamu-alaikum," or "peace be with you." In India, social interaction would start with "namaste," literally, "I bow to you." In many cultures, a greeting does not simply function to start conversation; it functions to recognize that another person exists. It also mitigates the possibility of being seen as a threat, reduces uncertainty, and immediately reproduces the degree of closeness and/or distance between individuals (Firth, 1972; Goffman, 1972). In some interactional contexts, how a greeting is conveyed can cue that an encounter will be difficult or that bad news is about to be delivered. A greeting can also create humor, but its absence, as we all know, will be noticeable, sometimes frustrating. Harvey Sacks, who pioneered research in conversation analysis, emphasized the importance of greetings. As he noted, "People can know each other for 35 years, talk to each other every day, and nonetheless greet each other when they begin a conversation" (Sacks, 1992, p. 97). Greetings, thus, make relationship possible.

There is a range of very interesting research on the topic of greetings and conversational openings (Firth, 1972; Goffman, 1972; Hopper, 1989; Hopper & Chen, 1996; Hopper & Drummond, 1992; Krivonos & Knapp, 1975; Schegloff, 1968; Schiffrin, 1977). For example, Youssouf, Grimshaw, and Bird (1976) showed how Tuareg men who travel the Sahara desert in solitude perform a sophisticated greeting sequence to assess the degree of threat that another traveling man carries. The greeting, in and of itself, is used to mark friendliness and is "critically important [as] lapses can have grave consequences for the offender or errant traveler" (p. 801). In and through the greeting sequence, participants also immediately cue the nature of the relationship. As Kendon (1990) explained, "how greeting exchanges performed are related to such matters as the relative status of the greeters or degree of acquaintance between them" (p. 206). Researchers also suggest that greeting sequences function as an interactive accomplishment through specific stages or phases of human behavior (Sacks, 1992; Schiffrin, 1977). In short, greetings serve important relational and social functions.

There are, of course, circumstances in which participants do not greet each other, or avoid mutual gaze altogether. The classroom might be a context prone for this kind of behavior. Students, for example, might not initiate a greeting with a faculty member because they are involved in side conversations, reading, writing, or sending a text. For teachers, the challenge might be to greet both individuals as well as the collective group. It can also feel redundant to greet multiple times. Sometimes, participants see and acknowledge each other but do not greet one another. Perhaps participants do not want to greet or think about it. There also are mental obstacles to overcome; in my own experience, I have noticed several forces that prevent me from *initiating* a greeting with others. One strong force is the desire to *be greeted*. This is an issue of power and status: "I will wait until you greet me first." Or it can illustrate our most powerful need: the need to be loved. As Maslow (1968) explained, "The need for love characterizes every being that is born" (p. 191). Another force is the fear of moving toward others, to engage in the process of relating and thus to become responsible for others. The writer Truss (2005) articulates this point well when she writes, "When present in person, people are interacting with each other as if they are in cars...People I believe are afraid of each other" (p. 64). Not greeting others, thus, can also simply be about fear.

If communication is relationship, then the greeting sequence is the foundational element of the process. Teachers have a responsibility to acknowledge each individual student. Practically, one can easily do this by initiating greetings with each student at the beginning of class. While taking attendance, for example, teachers can spend a few seconds to greet each individual member of the classroom, perhaps even asking a few questions about their lives (see below). If international students are present, greeting them in their native tongue can foster intercultural communication. As just one example, when a colleague and I taught a course in intercultural leadership with 15 Pakistani students who visited the United States for the first time, we intentionally greeted them with "assalamu-alaikum." Then they taught us to respond to the sequence, "walaikum-salam." Immediately, this greeting sequence affected our relationship with the students, who in fact quickly mentioned the struggle of intercultural contact: should they greet like an American or like a Pakistani? Should Pakistani women break their cultural norms and touch other (American) males or should they maintain their tradition? How to greet others became a fundamental challenge of intercultural communication. Over six months later, Derek Wingfield, one of my graduate students, interviewed these students for his master's project. In his analysis, Wingfield (2010) found that many students recalled our greetings and believed it enabled them to adapt to a new culture.

My point is simple: greeting others is one of the most essential acts of human communication. It can foster respectful communication and develop mutual trust. Its absence is noticeable and can work counterproductively.

Asking Open-Ended Questions

> A young man gets on a train and sits down next to an older man. The younger one asks, "Can you tell me the time?" and the older one says "No." "What do you mean no?" the younger one says. The older one says, "If I tell you the time we will have to get into a conversation. You'll ask me where I'm going. I'll ask you where you're going. It will turn out we're going to the same place. I'll have to invite you for dinner. I have a young marriageable daughter, and I don't want my daughter to marry someone who doesn't wear a watch. (Sacks, 1992, p. 50)

A second communication behavior that teachers can choose to enact is the use of open-ended questions. Much of human interaction involves asking and responding to questions. The question-answer sequence, in fact, lies at the heart of what relationships are all about. In his early analysis of question-answer sequences in conversations, Sacks (1992) noted, "there looks to be a rule that a person who asks a question has a right to talk again afterwards. And that rule can provide a simple way of generating enormous masses of sequences of talk: Question, talk, question, talk, etc., etc." (p. 49). In short, questions and answers are an intrinsic part of all relationships and serve important functions in the teacher-student relationship.

Communication researchers know that how a person asks a question carries important, sometimes immediate, consequences. Researchers in health communication, for instance, have worked since the 1970s to increase patient participation in medical encounters. Studies have shown that whether and how patients ask questions have implications for their health or their adherence to treatment (Roter, 1984). Researchers also know that physicians' use of questions can affect the diagnosis, patients' health outcomes, and their adherence to treatment (for a review, see Brown, Stewart, & Ryan, 2003; Roter & McNeilis, 2003). There is research that further documents that how one formulates a question can lead to positive or negative consequences. Tracy (2002), in her analysis of 911 phone calls, showed how the way call-takers frame their questions can be face-threatening to recipients and be interpreted by callers in emergency situations as "insulting their own definition of an emergency, or as impeding upon their quest to receive police help" (p. 130; also see Tracy & Tracy, 1998). Questions, thus, serve a number of functions that range from self-presentational and relational goals to instrumental goals. A question can cue doubt in the speaker, can challenge a person's comment, can mark the speaker's or the respondent's identity, or frame others as evading the question. In addition, "questions unavoidably encode attitudes and points of view" (Heritage, 2003, pp. 58–59). To put it simply, questions serve important, multiple, functions in naturally occurring interaction (Clayman & Heritage, 2002; Heritage, 2002).

In the classroom, and whether or not they have been trained to do it, teachers very regularly use questions to generate discussion, lead a lecture, and foster reflection. In his study of the best college professors, Bain (2004) noted that the use of questions is crucial: "In the learning literature and in the thinking of the best teachers, questions play an essential role in the process of learning and modifying mental models. Questions help us construct knowledge" (p. 31). Although questions can offer opportunities for learning, they do more than simply request an answer from students. Communication research, in fact, shows that "students see the value of effective questioning for both increasing quality participation and for discussion effectiveness" (Dallimore, Hertenstein, & Platt, 2004, p. 111). The content, style, and overall structure shape the quality of a question. Teachers' questions can foster learning, but they can also serve relational functions.

Questions that nurture relationships might lie outside of the disciplinary focus and be more attentive to the person(s) in the classroom. Rather than asking, "How does your brain work?" to jump-start a lecture, a teacher should first ask, "How was your weekend?" To develop questions that more naturally maintain relationship, teachers can choose to use open questions rather than closed questions. By design, open questions "encourage respondents to talk, determine the nature and amount of information to give, and volunteer information you might not think to ask for" (Stewart & Cash, 2011, p. 56). In contrast, closed questions "are narrow in focus and restrict the interviewee's freedom to determine the amount and kind of information to provide" (p. 57). In observations of my own behavior, I have noticed that my natural tendency is to ask closed questions, and that consistently developing open question is a challenging task. I have noted, however, that open questions tend to be more productive because they enable others to choose what to reveal and, if it is done authentically, communicate an interest in the person. As Stewart and Cash (2011) explained, "open questions communicate interest and trust in the respondent's judgment" (p. 56). Closed questions, however, tend to control others and privilege the interviewer's goals (e.g., "Do you like Diet Coke?"). In sum, how a question is formulated matters in that it affects the freedom the respondent has in responding to the question, but it also reveals a person's stance toward others.

In essence, asking questions is a way to show that another person is important. In the classroom, one may keep open questions relatively simple. Inquiries about students' lives such as "What did you do for fun this weekend?" or "Tell about your passions," or "What are some of your big dreams?" can foster genuine discussion with individual students as well as the collective group. Students can also greatly benefit from building and maintaining relationships with each other. Providing guided opportunities for short question-and-answer sessions can help cultivate a positive group climate. Open questions also foster learning that is more effective. In his work, Bain (2004), for instance, offered several examples of successful questions from the best teachers: "Why are human beings occasionally willing to leave home and hearth and march off into wilderness, desert, or jungle and kill each other in large numbers? Why are some people poor and other people rich? How does your brain work? What is the chemistry of life?" (p. 102). In each case, the question provides students with an opportunity to foreground their ways of thinking. Giving students voice and discovering more about them, including who they are as persons and what they think, is what good communication in and outside of the classroom is about.

Choosing to Say Something Nice

A third communication behavior is to choose to say something nice to students on a consistent basis. This suggestion stems from observing my behaviors in action. Specifically, I have noted a tendency to be critical of others' behaviors and to emphasize needed improvements rather than what is done well. I assume in this case that "that what is most personal is most general" (Rogers, 1961, p. 26). Scholars, writers, and thinkers, in fact, have noted this tendency. In his novel, for example, Dan Millman (2000) notes, "I started keeping a notebook in which I wrote down my thoughts during the day...I was astounded to see the bulk and general negativity of my thought processes" (p. 53). In his work, Rogers (1961) echoed this point for interpersonal communication. As he explained, "The major barrier to mutual interpersonal communication is our very natural tendency to judge, to evaluate, to approve or disapprove, the statement of the other person, or the other group" (p. 330). It is very difficult, indeed, to withhold judgment. This is particularly true for teachers who are in a position to evaluate students' work, their performance, or their progress.

To be frank, there is in academe a tendency to focus on the negative and to be critical of the self and others. In an autoethnographic essay that narrates a professor's life, Pelias (2000), for example, begins with these questions:

> You wonder: What does it mean to live with a critical eye, an eye that's always assessing, always deciding questions of worth, always saying what's good or bad? What does it mean to judge others? What does it mean to say someone else does not measure up? By what right do you set certain standards? (p. 111)

At the heart of the critical life, as Pelias calls it, is the evaluative process that professors engage in about student's performance. Pelias's point is also echoed by the inspiring Leo Buscaglia, who spoke internationally on the topic of love. In one of his talks, Buscaglia (1982) addresses the process of evaluation in education:

> How about giving up this nonsense about twenty-seven wrong. Wrong. Wrong. Wrong. Wrong. Wrong. Getting back papers with all of the things marked wrong. What about marking those things that are right? "You've got two right, Johnny. Good for you. Wow!" How about letting them know they can do something well and building from that instead of always counting what is wrong? (p. 37)

There is no doubt that interacting with students about their writing or their behavior can be challenging. Choosing to say something nice is a way of speaking that responds to internal and social pressures to evaluate work negatively and that thus emphasizes the positive in another's performance. Although it takes practice, it is a decision a communicator makes. As I see it, this communicative approach includes the frequent, consistent, use of speech acts (Austin, 1962; Searle, 1979) that will function positively in human interaction. These include complimenting, encouraging, and praising. By definition, a compliment is an "expression of esteem, respect, affection, and admiration." Praising is similar: it is to "express a favorable judgment." Encouraging is any act of talk that gives courage to others or inspires them to grow. These three speech acts can thus serve vital functions in mentoring students and can affect their cognitive and affective learning.

Choosing to say something nice can have short and long-term consequences. Communication researchers have shown, for instance that instructional feedback that communicates respects and mitigates the possible threat of an utterance is much better received by students and affects their learning (Trees et al., 2009). Other research suggests that "positive statements (praise) have been found to be more beneficial than verbal criticism"

(Burnett, 2002, p. 5; see also Brophy, 1991). Burnett (2002) also suggested that previous research showed that "praise was thought to occur when the teacher positively acknowledged students' work" and that "constructive encouragement was needed to enhance self-esteem" (p. 6). Praising or encouraging alone, of course, is not self-sufficient and can work counterproductively. As Witt and Kerssen-Griep (2011) point out, "the most effective feedback came from instructors who invoked high standards while believably assuring students that they could reach them, as opposed to instructors who offered praise alone or merely attempted to be friendly" (p. 77). The objective, thus, is not simply to be friendly, but to focus one's discursive energy on what students are doing well. Research on marital communication, for example, reveals that satisfied couples, "were those who maintained a five-to-one ratio of positive to negative moments" (Gottman, 2006, p. 231). Perhaps, this magic ratio can also help in the educational context.

In this section, I suggested that complimenting, praising, and encouraging are speech acts that function positively in relational communication. These behaviors, however, should not be used to control or manipulate students; they should reflect the teacher's genuine, authentic, assessment of an individual or a group's performance. Choosing to say something nice, in fact, is a communicative approach that the teacher works on for his or her own sake, in part because she or he knows that a single utterance can affect a person in the present and in the future.

HOW DOES RELATIONAL COMMUNICATION FOSTER TRANSFORMATIVE LEARNING?

By definition, transformative learning "is a process of examining, questioning, validating, and revising our perspectives" (Cranton, 2006, p. 23). Genuine and authentic communication fosters this form of learning. As Cranton (2006) explained, "Not only does authenticity in teaching help create honest and open relationships with students, but it also serves as a model for learners working to define who they are" (p. 116). How a teacher speaks and behaves in the classroom, in fact, often become sources of interpersonal influence. Students naturally learn from, and imitate, teacher's communicative behaviors. Said differently, and as is the case in most human interaction, students can directly or indirectly, consciously or unconsciously, learn to speak, walk, or move like their teacher. As one of my students explained it to me once, "In addition to the content, I learned so much from watching you in the classroom. I learned how to move in space and reach my audience as well as from the way you encourage us." When the same student wrote about her experience in a course on interpersonal communication that I teach, she wrote, "I have seen again the impact one human life can have upon another. I've witnessed first-hand how you have taught by example and given us a chance to grow, faltering and stumbling, in a safe environment." Students, thus, learn from our content but also from the way we interact and relate with them.

By embodying the behaviors described in this chapter, teachers can enable students to grow as communicators. They can nurture students' practical or communicative knowledge (Habermas, 1971) and thereby cultivate crucial social-communicative values. By modeling these behaviors, teachers will make possible their own and students' personal communicative transformation. From my perspective, this educational task is crucial. As Krishnamurti (1992), the Indian thinker, stressed in his lectures, "There must be a fundamental revolution in your relationship with people, with ideas. There must be a fundamental change, and that change must begin not outside of you, but in your relationship" (p. 33). For Krishnamurti, peace at the global level was only possible if produced in relationship. Other thinkers and philosophers, including those that inform transformative theory such as Martin Buber (1965/2002) and Paulo Freire (1970), echo this emphasis on relationship. This thinking also permeates contemporary research on learning (Bain, 2004; Bok, 2006; Brookfield, 1990; Weimer, 2002). Learners, in fact, describe their own transformative development as moving in the direction of others. Taylor (2000), for instance, labels this dimension of transformative learning "Toward connection with others" (p. 33). Said simply, communicating well can nudge students in the direction of ethical communicative conduct.

In her work, Cranton (2006) noted that "the better the relationship among the people, the more meaningful the communication will be" (p. 114). I would argue the opposite: communication is what creates relationship. To quote Virginia Satir (1976), "Communication is to relationship what breathing is to maintaining life" (p. 20). By consequence, positive and genuine communication is what will foster productive relationships. If teachers enact healthy communication, student transformation will occur through osmosis, and they will apply these behaviors at home with their spouses and children, or their friends and loved ones. By communicating well, teachers can enable students' own communicative transformation.

CONCLUSION

Teaching is a communicative-relational art. Teachers, thus, are intrinsically, albeit not solely, implicated in the nature of their relationship with students and the classroom context in which they operate. Communicating well is not easy. It is an art that requires patience, hard work, discipline, and practice. As Erich Fromm (2006) explained, "If one wants to become a master in any art, his whole life must be devoted to it, or at least, related to it" (p. 102). With this perspective in mind, I described three communication behaviors that teachers can practice to sustain productive relationships with students and to make transformative learning possible (Mezirow, 2000; Taylor, 2008). These behaviors are "white-belt moves" that teachers can work on as they grow as communicators. It is worth remembering, however, that communication is relationship, not technique.

REFERENCES

Austin, J. L. (1962). *How to do things with words.* Cambridge, MA: Harvard University Press.
Bain, K. (2004). *What the best college teachers do.* Cambridge, MA: Harvard University Press.
Banas, J. A., Dunbar, N., Rodriguez, D., & Liu, S. (2011). A review of humor in education settings: Four decades of research. *Communication Education, 60,* 115–144.
Bateson, G. (1972). *Steps toward an ecology of mind: Collected essays in anthropology, psychiatry, evolution, and epistemology.* Chicago, IL: University of Chicago Press.
Bok, D. (2006). *Our underachieving colleges: A candid look at how much students learn and why they should be learning more.* Princeton, NJ: Princeton University Press.
Brookfield, S. (1990). *The skillful teacher.* San Francisco, CA: Jossey-Bass.
Brophy, J. (1981). Teacher praise: A functional analysis. *Review of Educational Research, 51,* 5–32.
Brown, J. B., Stewart, M., & Ryan, B. L. (2003). Outcomes of patient-provider interaction. In T. L. Thompson, A. M. Dorsey, K. I. Miller, & R. Parrott (Eds.), *Handbook of health communication* (pp. 141–162). Mahwah, NJ: Lawrence Erlbaum.
Buber, M. (1965/2002). *Between man and man.* New York, NY: Routledge.
Burnett, P. C. (2002). Teacher praise and feedback and students' perceptions of the classroom environment. *Educational Psychology, 22,* 5–16.
Buscaglia, L. (1982). *Living, loving, and learning.* New York, NY: Holt, Rinehart & Winston.
Chamberlin, C. R. (2000). Nonverbal behaviors and initial impressions of trustworthiness in teacher-supervisor relationships. *Communication Education, 49*(4), 352–364.
Clayman, S. E., & Heritage, J. (2002). Questioning presidents: Journalistic deference and adversarialness in the press conferences of Eisenhower and Reagan. *Journal of Communication, 52,* 749–775.
Craig, C. T. (1999). Communication theory as a field. *Communication Theory, 9,* 119–161.
Cranton, P. (2006). *Understanding and promoting transformative learning: A guide for educators of adults* (2nd ed.). San Francisco, CA: Jossey-Bass.

Dallimore, E. J., Hertenstein, J. H., & Platt, M. B. (2004). Classroom participation and discussion effectiveness: Student-generated strategies. *Communication Education, 53,* 103–115. doi:10.1080/0363452032000135805

Deetz, S. A. (1994). Future of the discipline: The challenges, the research, and the social contribution. In S. A. Deetz (Ed.), *Communication yearbook 17* (pp. 565–600). Thousand Oaks, CA: Sage.

Docan-Morgan, T. (2011). "Everything changed": Relational turning point events in college teacher-student relationships from teacher's perspectives. *Communication Education, 60,* 20–50.

Docan-Morgan, T., & Manusov, V. (2009). Relational turning point events and their outcomes in college teacher-student relationships from students' perspectives. *Communication Education, 58,* 155–188.

Fairhurst, G. (2007). *Discursive leadership: In conversation with leadership psychology.* Thousand Oaks, CA: Sage.

Firth, R. (1972). Verbal and bodily rituals of greeting and parting. In J. S. LaFontaine (Ed.), *The interpretation of ritual: Essays in honour of A.I. Richards* (pp.1–38). London, England: Tavistock.

Frankl, V. (1984). *Man's search for meaning.* New York, NY: Washington Square.

Freire, P. (1970). *Pedagogy of the oppressed.* New York, NY: Continuum.

Fromm, E. (1947). *Man for himself: An inquiry into the psychology of ethics.* New York, NY: Henry Holt.

Fromm, E. (2006). *The art of loving.* New York, NY: Harper Collins.

Fusani, D. S. (1994). "Extra-class" communication: Frequency, immediacy, self-disclosure, and satisfaction in student-faculty interaction outside the classroom. *Communication Education, 49,* 207–219.

Glenn, P. J., LeBaron, C. D., & Mandelbaum, J. (Eds.). (2003). *Studies in language and social interaction.* Mahwah, NJ: Lawrence Erlbaum.

Goffman, E. (1972). *Relations in public: Microstudies of the public order.* Harmondsworth, England: Penguin.

Gottman, J. (2006). Why marriages fail. In K. M. Galvin & P. J. Cooper (Eds.), *Making connections: Readings in relational communication* (pp. 228–236). Los Angeles, CA: Roxbury.

Habermas, J. (1971). *Knowledge and human interests.* Boston, MA: Beacon.

Heritage, J. (2002). The limits of questioning: Negative interrogatives and hostile question content. *Journal of Pragmatics, 34,* 1427–1446. doi:10.1016/S0378-2166(02)00072-3

Heritage, J. (2003). Designing questions and setting agendas in the news interview. In P. Glenn, C. D. LeBaron, & J. Mandelbaum (Eds.), *Studies in language and social interaction: In honor of Robert Hopper* (pp. 57–90). Mahwah, NJ: Lawrence Erlbaum.

Hopper, R. (1989). Sequential ambiguity in telephone openings: "What are you doin." *Communication Monographs, 56,* 240–252.

Hopper, R., & Chen, C. (1996). Languages, cultures, relationships: Telephone openings in Taiwan. *Research on Language and Social Interaction, 29,* 291–313.

Hopper, R., & Drummond, K. (1992). Accomplishing interpersonal relationship: The telephone openings of strangers and intimates. *Western Journal of Communication, 56,* 185–199.

Kendon, A. (1990). *Conducting interaction: Patterns of behavior in focused encounters.* New York, NY: Cambridge University Press.

Kerssen-Griep, J., Hess, J. A., & Trees, A. R. (2003). Sustaining the desire to learn: Dimensions of perceived instructional facework related to student involvement and motivation to learn. *Western Journal of Communication, 67,* 357–381.

Kerssen-Griep, J., Trees, A. R., & Hess, J. A. (2008). Attentive facework during instructional feedback: Key to perceiving mentorship and an optimal learning environment. *Communication Education, 57,* 312–332.

Koschman, T., & Lebaron, C. D. (2002). Learner articulation as interactional achievement: Studying the conversation of gestures. *Cognition and Instruction, 20,* 249–282.

Kramer, M. W., & Pier, P. M. (1999). Students' perceptions of effective and ineffective communication by college teachers. *Southern Communication Journal, 65,* 16–33.

Krishnamurti, J. (1992). *On relationship.* Ojai, CA: Krishnamurti Foundation of America.

Krivonos, P. D., & Knapp, M. L. (1975). Initiating communication: What do you say when you say hello? *Central States Speech Journal, 26,* 115–125.

LeBaron, C. D., Mandelbaum, J., & Glenn, P. J. (2003). An overview of language and social interaction. In. P. J. Glenn, C. D. LeBaron, & J. Mandelbaum (Eds.), *Studies in language and social interaction: In honor of Robert Hopper* (pp. 1–40). Mahwah, NJ: Lawrence Erlbaum.

Malinowski, B. (1972). The problem of meaning in primitive languages. In C. K. Ogden & I. A. Richards (Eds.), *The meaning of meaning* (pp. 146–152). London, England: Routledge and Kegan Paul. (Original work published 1923)

Maslow, A. (1968). *Toward a psychology of being* (2nd ed.). New York, NY: Van Nostrand.

Mehrabian, A. (1971). *Silent messages.* Wadsworth, CA: Belmont.

Mezirow, J. (2000). Learning to think like an adult: Core concepts of transformation theory. In J. Mezirow & Associates (Eds.), *Learning as transformation: Critical perspectives on a theory in progress* (pp. 71–102). San Francisco, CA: Jossey-Bass.

Millman, D. (2000). *Way of the peaceful warrior: A book that changes lives.* Novato, CA: New World Library.

Myers, S. A., & Knox, R. L. (2001). The relationship between college student information-seeking behaviors and perceived instructor verbal behaviors. *Communication Education, 50,* 343–356.

O'Keefe, B. J., & McCornack, S. A. (1987). Message design logic and message goal structure effects on perceptions of message quality in regulative communication situations. *Human Communication Research, 14,* 68–92. doi:10.1111/j.1468-2958.1987.tb00122.x

Pelias, R. J. (2000). The critical life. *Communication Education, 49,* 220–229.

Peters, J. (1989). John Locke, the individual, and the origin of communication. *Quarterly Journal of Speech, 75,* 387–399.

Pogue, L., & Ahyun, K. (2006). The effect of teacher nonverbal immediacy and credibility on student motivation and affective learning. *Communication Education, 55,* 331–344. doi:10.1080/03634520600748623

Rogers, C. (1961). *On becoming a person.* Boston, MA: Houghton Mifflin.

Roter, D. L. (1984). Patient question asking in physician-patient interaction. *Health Psychology, 3*, 395–409.
Roter, D., & McNeilis, K. S. (2003). The nature of the therapeutic relationship and the assessment of its discourse in routine medical visits. In T. L. Thompson, A. M. Dorsey, K. I. Miller, & R. Parrott (Eds.), *Handbook of health communication* (pp. 121–140). Mahwah, NJ: Lawrence Erlbaum.
Sacks, H. (1992). *Lectures on conversation* (Vol 2; G. Jefferson, Ed.). Cambridge, MA: Blackwell.
Sartre, J. P. (2007). *Existentialism is a humanism.* New Haven, CT: Yale University Press.
Satir, V. (1976). *Making contact.* Millbrae, CA: Celestial Arts.
Schegloff, E. A. (1968). Sequencing in conversational openings. *American Anthropologist, 70*, 1075–1095.
Schiffrin, D. (1977). Opening encounters. *American Sociological Review, 42*, 679–691.
Searle, J. (1979). *Expression and meaning: Studies in the theory of speech acts.* New York, NY: Cambridge University Press.
Stewart, C. J., & Cash, W. B. (2011). *Interviewing: Principles and practices* (13th ed.). Dubuque, IA: McGraw-Hill.
Streeck, J. (1983). *Social order in child communication: A study in microethnography.* Philadelphia, PA: John Benjamins.
Streeck, J., Goodwin, C., & LeBaron, C. D. (Eds.). (in press). *Embodied interaction: Language and body in the material world.* Boston, MA: Cambridge University Press.
Streeck, J., & Mehus, S. (2005). Microethnography: The study of practices. In K. L. Fitch & R. E. Sanders (Eds.), *Handbook of language and social interaction* (pp. 381–404). Mahwah, NJ: Lawrence Erlbaum.
Taylor, E. W. (2007). An update of transformative learning theory: A critical review of the empirical research (1999–2005). *International Journal of Lifelong Education, 26*, 173–191. doi:10.1080/02601370701219475
Taylor, E. W. (2008). Transformative learning theory. *New Directions for Adult and Continuing Education, 119*, 5–15. doi:10.1002/ace.301
Taylor, K. (2000). Teaching with development intention. In J. Mezirow & Associates (Eds.), *Learning as transformation: Critical perspectives on a theory in progress.* San Francisco, CA: Jossey-Bass.
Teven, J. J. (2001). The relationship among teacher characteristics and perceived caring. *Communication Education, 50*, 159–170.
Tracy, S. J. (2002). When questioning turns to face threat: An interactional sensitivity in 911 call-taking. *Western Journal of Communication, 66*, 129–157.
Tracy, K., & Tracy, S. J. (1998). Rudeness at 911: Reconceptualizing face and face-attack. *Human Communication Research, 25*, 225–251.
Trees, A. R., Kerssen-Griep, J., & Hess, J. (2009). Earning influence by communicating respect: Facework's contributions to effective instructional feedback. *Communication Education, 58*, 397–416.
Truss, L. (2005). *Talk to the hand: The utter bloody rudeness of the world today, or six good reasons to stay home and bolt the door.* New York, NY: Gotham.
Weimer, M. (2002). *Learner-centered teaching: Five key changes to practice.* San Francisco, CA: Jossey-Bass.

Wingfield, D. (2010). *"We are more similar than different": An assessment of the impact of communication training on Pakistani students' cultural mindsets.* Unpublished master's paper, University of Arkansas at Little Rock.

Witt, P. L., & Kerssen-Griep, J. (2011). Instructional feedback I: The interaction of facework and immediacy on students' perceptions of instructor credibility. *Communication Education, 60,* 75–94. doi:10.1080/03634523.2010.507820

Youssouf, I. A., Grimshaw, A. D., & Bird, C. S. (1976). Greetings in the desert. *American Ethnologist, 3,* 797–824.

CHAPTER 4

NARRATIVE TOOLS FOR FACILITATING RESEARCH AND LEARNING FOR TRANSFORMATION

Leann M. R. Kaiser and Elizabeth A. Erichsen

Across cultures, narrative emerges early in communicative development and is a fundamental means of making sense of experience. Our personal narrative and conceptions of self are inseparable in that our narrative is simultaneously born out of our experiences and gives them shape. Ochs and Capps (1996) point out,

> Narrative activities provide tellers with an opportunity to impose order on otherwise disconnected events, and to create continuity between past, present, and imagined worlds. Narrative also interfaces self and society, constituting a crucial resource for socializing emotions, attitudes, and identities, developing interpersonal relationships, and constituting membership in a community. (p. 19)

Through sharing their personal experience, stories, and storytelling, adult learners become better able to make connections between past, present, and envisioned futures in meaningful ways that help them formulate new perspectives and possible selves (Rossiter, 2007).

The current research suggests that through the dynamics of exercising the narrative, cognitive, autoethnography, and personal storytelling, we bring to life multiple and partial selves (Bruner, 2004; Lee & Boud, 2003; Pfhal, 2003; Rossiter, 2007, Wiessner, 2001; Wortham, 2006). In reflecting on narrative cognitive functions as a means of developing our relationship to self (Pfahl & Wiessner, 2007), we propose that autoethnographic and personal narrative can be versatile tools that can be applied in the realms of research as well as facilitating transformative learning in education environments. This is significant in that facilitators can use this approach in a number of different settings for promoting whole-person learning and identity development, as well as a creative means for collecting qualitative data in researching learner development and transformative experience.

TRANSFORMATIVE LEARNING, NARRATIVE, AND THE SELF

In this chapter, the authors will define narratives of personal experience as verbalized, visualized, and/or embodied framings of a sequence of actual or possible life events. The authors are less concerned about the form or genre a personal narrative might take. Ochs and Capps (1996) point out, "While differing in complexity and circumstance, narratives transform life's journeys into sequences of events and evoke shifting and enduring perspectives on experience" (p. 20). Self, identity, and narrative are inseparable. Self is an unfolding reflective awareness of being-in-the world, including a sense of one's past and future. We come to know ourselves as we use narrative to attribute meaning to our experiences and navigate relationships with others and our varying contexts.

Transformative learning theory integrates with narration in various contexts in that it is "predicated on the idea that students are seriously challenged to assess their value system and worldview and are subsequently changed by the experience" (Quinnan, 1997, p. 42). As well, Brooks (2001) argues that narrative can be a central construct to understand transformational processes, and Clark (2010) discusses how shifts in a narrative perspective enrich transformative learning.

Transformative Learning and the Roles of Rational and Affective Thought

Mezirow (1978) describes transformational learning as "a structural reorganization in the way a person looks at himself [sic] and his relationships"

(p. 162). Distilled down to its most basic elements, transformative learning occurs when we have an experience that encourages us to critically reflect upon and transform a belief, attitude, or perspective (Mezirow, 2000). The meaning schemes or habits of mind that we formerly held no longer sufficiently describe or explain a phenomenon in our life, possibly leading to a changed perception, or transformation. Yet it is important to stress that simply having an experience is not sufficient for transformative learning to occur. Meaning schemes routinely change through learning and experience, but true perspective transformation occurs less frequently (Imel, 1998). The experience must be a "disorienting dilemma" (Mezirow, 1995, p. 50), and we must also "critically self-examine the assumptions and beliefs that have structured how the experience has been interpreted" (Merriam, Caffarella, & Baumgartner, 2007, p. 134). This, in turn, encourages us to change our frames of reference and revise our assumptions, leading to the outcome of personal development.

One of the major tenets of transformative learning lies in the importance of critical reflection on experience, which has also been one of the criticisms of the theory. Some have found that perspective transformation has been able to occur without critical reflection or rational discourse taking place as part of the process. Essentially, individuals in these situations were unaware of the change process that was occurring (Merriam, 2004; Taylor, 1994). The argument continues that Mezirow's (1978, 1997, 2000) view of transformative learning relies too heavily on rational thought and critical reflection as the catalyst to perspective transformation. Mezirow's framework does not give other ways of making meaning, such as a reliance on affective learning (intuition, emotions, and feeling), as much attention (Merriam et al., 2007).

Nevertheless, this potential weakness in Mezirow's (1978, 1997, 2000) view of transformative learning may actually still fit within the overall framework of the theory. While it is acknowledged that there are other ways of learning, a blending of these approaches along with critical reflection is possible and may lead to a "more holistic transformative paradigm" (Mulvihill, 2003, p. 325). Imel (1998) has argued that views of transformative learning that rely more heavily on intuition and emotion simply have a different emphasis. They still use rational processes but also rely on the extrarational.

The Narrative Cognitive

The utilization of narrative or autoethnography develops one alternative way of knowing (Rossiter, 2002). In order to construct the narrative, engaging in critical reflection on an experience is still necessary, but one reaches and solidifies new meaning schemes through storying, or narrating those experiences. A great deal of research explores the interconnection of transformative learning and narrative (Erichsen, Kaiser, Callahan, & Miller, 2009; Hale, Snow-Gerono, & Morales, 2008; Herrington & Curtis, 2000; Johnson, 2003; Karpiak, 2000; Kerka, 1996; King, 1987; Nelson, 1997; Rossiter & Clark, 2010). Bernhardt (2009) asserts, "Through this experience [autobiography] students... assimilate and accommodate new ideas and experiences, and engage in meaningful dialogue about values, beliefs and perspectives" (p. 61). Likewise, Merriam (2004) puts forward that transformative learning requires and promotes an advanced level of cognitive development, one that demonstrates a higher level of functioning in being able to integrate different kinds of learning experiences and compose them into a form of self-understanding, which one may communicate as personal narrative.

Essentially, the *narrative cognitive* and telling our own story is a relational thinking process. "Becoming more self-aware of implications of past experience for the present, and for a changed future, involves the whole person learning" (Pfahl & Wiessner, 2007, p. 10). The process of transforming experience requires learning at all levels. This kind of whole-person learning involves "awareness and use of all the functions we have available for knowing, including our cognitive, affective, somatic, intuitive, and spiritual dimensions" (thINQ, 1994, p. 171). Pfahl and Wiessner (2007) further elaborate:

> When we use our narrative cognitive function, we engage affective dimensions; envision action in relationship to context; draw upon intuition; and sometimes catalyze spiritual connection to others.... Thus, the essence of experiential narrative is re-invention of life story that holds potential to catalyze human development and change that transforms life experience. Intentionally bringing multiple dimensions together by using narrative processes empowers learners to reinterpret and reevaluate old ways of being and acting to explore new ways of life. (p. 10)

Stroobants (2005) describes life stories as a process of biographical learning in which the learning processes actually take place during the story-sharing process when participants reflect on their life. When telling their personal experience stories, learners actively give meaning to their life experiences and partly accomplish their learning process. Narrative can help learners gain insight into their different biographical strategies, and they have the chance to see their life in a different light, allowing them to analyze critically their own experience. While telling their story, learners can also reflect on their ongoing learning. The narrative cognitive offers the chance to view one's life experiences in terms of learning and to reflect on one's life as a learning process.

Relationship With Self Through the Narrative/Transformative Process

Spinning out their tellings through choice of words, degree of elaboration, attribution of causality and sequentiality, and the foregrounding and backgrounding of emotions, circumstances, and behavior, learners can build novel understandings of themselves-in-the-world. In this manner, selves evolve in the time frame of a single telling as well as in the course of the many tellings that eventually compose a life (Ochs & Capps, 1996). This self may construe new narrative readings, which in turn alter one's sense of being-in-the-world. "While narrative does not yield absolute truth, it can transport narrators and audiences to more authentic feelings, beliefs, and actions and ultimately to a more authentic sense of life" (Ochs & Capps, 1996, p. 23).

This evolution of self is a relationship with self. Inherent in the transformative learning process is the alteration of a personal meaning scheme, thus resulting in personal development. The relationship of the individual with the self is modified (Bandura, 1977, 1982, 1986). The individual transforms both *in* relationship with self and *because* of relationship with self (Josephs, Markus, & Tafarodi, 1992; Markus, 1977). Identities and conceptions of self must be both internalized and externalized. For one to confer an identity or an understanding of self, the person not only must become an active participant in the outside community, but they also must begin to accept and grapple with the meanings and expectations of those roles internally. Participation too must be both internalized and externalized. As understandings, roles, and dimensions of identity shift and vary in salience, a person begins to try on and either accept or deny new roles, norms, and behaviors (Baker & Lattuca, 2010). Ibarra's (1999) concept of "provisional selves" gives us a glimpse into this internal process of comparing potential selves against one's own values and standards and against external feedback.

This relationship with self in the narrative and transformative context manifests itself as a means of supporting this process and an individual's identity development. In particular, the development and understanding of multiple identities (Fairchild, 2003; Jones & McEwen, 2002) as well as possible identities or selves (Plimmer & Schmidt, 2007; Rossiter, 2007) occurs. Again, autoethnography can be a part of this development as narrative focuses on the self (Bloom, 2002). As Ochs and Capps (1996) state, "narrative brings multiple, partial selves to life . . . everyday narrative practices confront interlocutors with unanticipated emotions and ideas and ultimately with unanticipated selves" (p. 37).

Application: Using Transformative Learning and Narrative in Context

We are particularly interested in the process of narrative as a performative research methodology and as a way of knowing (Pelias, 1999). Kohut's (1991) theory on self-in-relationship-to-its-self-objects offers an articulation of the psychological need to make sense of our lives by creating coherence and continuity in our personal narrative, while Jarvis's (2006) categorizations and descriptions of learning express the human need to learn in order to reestablish harmony between one's lifeworld and context when they are no longer in alignment. Mezirow's (1978, 1997, 2000) transformative learning theory focuses on the need to reflect deeply on the discourses in which we are submerged and on how challenging these discourses changes our perspectives of the world and transforms our sense of self.

All of these elements contribute to the learner's need to reflect on their own personal story of where they are coming from, who they think they are, and where they think they might be going. The chronological dimension offers narrators a vehicle for imposing order on otherwise disconnected experiences. That is, chronology provides a reassuring coherence. By offering learners and participants in the co-authors' research such a vehicle, a means is provided for participants to construct new understandings of past experiences that they can then integrate into their present understandings and help them envision new possibilities for who they are becoming.

Narrative-Based Exercises as Research Tools

In one of the co-author's dissertation projects on female international graduate students' transformative learning experience (Erichsen, 2009), the findings suggest that a specific narrative exercise in combination with traditional in-depth interviews was particularly effective. This particular research project employed two tools. First, we collected traditional in-depth interviews, and participants shared their story of how they came to the United States and what they had experienced here. The other major component of the research was an exercise titled the "letter back home," in which participants wrote a letter to a family member or an old friend whom they had not seen since they had originally departed their home country. In this letter, they explained who they were as a person in the present as compared to the person they were when their friend knew them before. These two data collection tactics were remarkably complementary. On the one hand, the in-depth interviews offered an overview. Participants told detailed stories connecting the points of where they had been and what they had done. These interviews gave one side of their personal stories that I could analyze.

At first glimpse, the letters seemed a little superficial, but what they offered was a more precise articulation of how the participants felt they had personally changed, which provided a different picture than the stories they told during the interviews. The letters provided the participants with a vehicle for describing themselves in a very different way than the interviews had, and the data were rich and an invaluable addition to the data compiled during the interviewing process.

The participants in this study (Erichsen, 2009) were better able to interpret the meaning of their lived experiences as nontraditional, female, international graduate students through (re)narrating their lives. Their learning and transformation was reflected in the stories they told, and these revealed how they were "rewriting the self" (Freeman, 1993). As was demonstrated by the stories the participants shared, adult learners are continually in a process of restorying their life experiences and who they are in relation to their many contexts. The stories of the nontraditional female international graduate students illustrated this particularly well because of their need to function and bridge multiple worlds, which is a reminder of the multiple realities that can coexist in one's life. In a sense, multiple levels of learning occurred as the international student went through a process of social readjustment, composed of social dimensions of self and learning to relate and interact in a new context, before she moved on to the more reflective stages where the personal "I" is transformed and her narrative renegotiated.

Each one of these women's learning and experiences throughout their transformational process had affected their personal narrative and who they understood themselves to be and who they were becoming. Their learning and interactions within their many new contexts and social dimensions necessarily affected how they understood themselves. As they learned to make sense of their many contexts, they also had to rework their past and present narratives in order to make sense of who they were at that point in time. They began learning more consciously and reflectively where they were rebuilding a new understanding of their many worlds. They often felt as though they belonged to neither world, and narrative assisted them as they worked to resituate their many selves in relation to the multiplicity that defined their lifeworld and context. They were able to move to a more personal understanding of their socially split existence and begin to actively redefine their own lifeworld according to *their* unique experiences and multiplicities. It was a process of restorying lived experience and conceptions of identity, and the letter exercise provided a point of reference in reflecting on the complexity of their lives (Erichsen, 2009).

In another piece of research on the authors' own (Erichsen et al., 2009) transformative learning processes, the co-authors and others wrote about the transition from students to educators and found that personal dialogue and communication between group members in conjunction with writing and redrafting our own personal narratives provided rich data and contributed to personal insight into the role learning has played in our own personal stories. In this research, the co-authors wrote journal entries about experiences as students, educators, and mothers over a period of time. The co-authors met several times to discuss the developing written narratives and come to personal understandings of the deeper relationship and implications through the writing process. Through both the narrative process and the group communicative process (Canning & Callahan, 2010), the group was able to critically reflect both individually and collaboratively on the transformative events that had occurred and were occurring due to the intersecting facets of our lives. The journals captured the development and growth that occurred through various transformative experiences. However, we had not been able to reflect critically on those processes until we had the narrative tools at hand. The co-authors used the narrative as a method to encourage a process of transformative learning *already* begun. This was a more formalized manner to facilitate transformation and one that we could use in research, classroom, clinical, and personal contexts. Essentially, the journals provided a means to engage in the Habermasian concept of discourse wherein, "dialogue [is] devoted to searching for a common understanding and assessment of the justification of an interpretation or belief" (Mezirow, 2000, pp. 10–11). That "dialogue" or discourse was the use of the narrative as a tool in this research.

As a result of utilizing this research process, each of the authors was able to foster a stronger understanding of our own self-identities. We did not strive to create an overarching framework by which to understand our stories, but rather the process allowed each of us to better recognize and comprehend our "selves," both multiple and possible. Moreover, as this example shows, the use of the narrative as a data-collection tool can be multifunctional. It can be the catalyst to developing understanding of self and furthering transformative processes, as well as a method to use to collect and communicate research findings.

Narrative-Based Practices as Transformative Learning and Teaching Tools

Narrative and autobiographical exercises line up exceptionally well with transformative teaching and learning practice, because narratives naturally depict a temporal transition from one state of affairs to another. The task of storying one's own personal experience and change offers the opportunity to reflect on, articulate, and weave together a variety of a learner's life experiences in a way that is totally one's own. Narrative promotes self learning and a deeper understanding of one's own history, a path that can help facilitate the process of learning lifelong and lifewide (Pfahl & Wiessner, 2007; Stroobants, 2005). For example, Hale et al.'s (2008) research evidences the usefulness of narrative and autobiographical approaches in ELL/ESL/EFL learning environments, and Erichsen's (2009) research demonstrates the relevance in using these approaches with international learners to explore their learning processes. Rossiter (2007) and Plimmer and Schmidt's (2007) research also suggests that examining one's story at phases of transition in life can contribute to self-awareness and may promote transformative learning, especially in the midst of life and career changes.

Johnson's (2003) autobiographical account of employing autobiography as a teaching tool clearly makes the connection between our personal narrative and our capacity to learn:

> Autobiography can be done anytime. It does not need to become a component of formal learning. But if we give it a home next to learning, I believe we will find that we have created memories for our students beyond the scope of remembered facts. Autobiography allows the past to inform the future and bring the present into presence. Coupled with formal learning, autobiographical writing helps students engage in learning as life, rather than separate from it. The "whole" student comes to class because now there is room for the whole student to explore all that he or she can. (p. 242)

In the authors' teaching experience, a specific prompt that directs the learner to reflect critically on a particular kind of experience, or a particular kind of change over time, seems to be an effective way to open this narrative or autoethnographic process in a learning setting. Assignments with extremely broad aims without more direct goals can feel intimidating, and it is difficult to imagine where one should begin. Giving the person something manageable to begin with is important if engaging the learner in genuine self-reflection is to occur. Like the "letter back home" tool and the personal correspondence we have employed in our research, assigning similar tasks to learners can achieve similar effects.

For example, in beginning a class on the topic of learning styles, learners can tell a story about a time when they were particularly excited about and engaged in a learning situation. This does not have to be a long and drawn out story that class members tell, but the act of drawing on past experience and then reinterpreting it with new knowledge and then blending experience and knowledge in a social setting can be very powerful—it also makes for a much more engaging session in which learners build trust and relationships. In addition, it provides the facilitator with a number of handles with which to integrate personal experience and theoretical knowledge.

Another example we have used is having learners "bullet point" their professional narrative and how they have developed. After the class has created a brief personal outline, they can share them with the class. This also affords the opportunity for members to ask questions about the significance and selection of certain events or to ask whether they had ever imagined they would take the path they have taken and end up where they are. It is also a segue into material about possible selves, future training, and potential paths and personal change. One can talk about life transitions, stages of life, adult development, among many other conceivable topics.

In a final example, students entering a distance learning setting are often concerned about experiencing a disconnect between themselves, other students, and/or the instructor. Again, use of the narrative can serve to bridge this gap, encourage critical reflection, and enhance understanding of self-identity on the part of the learner. We have had learners create a timeline of their lives marking the "milestones" they have experienced. In addition, they have created a timeline of a course topic, such as the history of adult education or the history of their area of professional interest. Then they dovetail the two timelines, reflecting on who they were and who they are as well as what influenced changes and developments in their chosen topic. Posting these for other learners, or an instructor, to view in an online class serves several functions. First, it gives all learners their own stories and personalities beyond just a name and a brief introduction. The examination of their own lives, their intersection with history, and sharing these histories with others serves to connect them to other learners as well as the class content. In addition, it allows learners to involve themselves cognitively and personally in a course topic. It becomes something that has an effect on their ideas and development rather than a series of events outside of their own lives. They are encouraged to examine how and what may have affected their meaning schemes, or examine how they might be changed in the current time.

There are many other potential examples for the use of narrative tools to encourage transformative learning. The examples offered here serve to introduce this idea and to encourage others to think about potential applications within the classroom, clinical settings, and even in personal relationships.

CONCLUSION

The perspective developed in this chapter also allows for the exploration of many different dimensions in which a person can creatively apply autobiographical approaches and pursue learning for transformation, not limiting the individual to just formalized learning and rational thought, but also opening up the opportunity to recognize more emotive, spiritual, and personal dimensions of personal change. Many learning experiences of all kinds influence who we become and mold the many dimensions of who we are. Through autobiography we can engage in a process of personal discovery in which we learn about ourselves in order to change, and as we continue to learn and change, the more we feel compelled to restory ourselves and who we are becoming.

REFERENCES

Baker, V. L., & Lattuca, L. R. (2010). Developmental networks and learning: Toward an interdisciplinary perspective on identity development during doctoral study. *Studies in Higher Education, 35*(7), 807–827.
Bandura, A. (1977). *Social learning theory.* New York, NY: Prentice Hall.
Bandura, A. (1982). Self-efficacy mechanism in human agency. *American Psychologist, 37,* 122–147.
Bandura, A. (1986). *Social foundations of thought and action: A social cognitive theory.* New York, NY: Prentice Hall.
Bernhardt, P. (2009). Opening up classroom space: Student voice, autobiography, and the curriculum. *High School Journal, 92*(3), 61–67.
Bloom, L. (2002). From self to society: Reflections on the power of narrative inquiry. In S. Merriam & Associates (Eds.), *Qualitative research in practice: Examples for discussion and analysis* (pp. 310–313). San Francisco, CA: Jossey-Bass.
Brooks, A. (2001). *Narrative dimensions of transformative learning.* Paper presented at the Adult Education Research Conference. (ERIC Document Reproduction Service No. ED476042)
Bruner, J. (2004). *Making stories.* Cambridge, MA: Harvard University Press.
Canning, N., & Callahan, S. (2010). Heutagogy: Spirals of reflection to empower learners in higher education. *Reflective Practice, 11*(1), 71–82.
Clark, M. C. (2010). Narrative learning: Its contours and its possibilities. *New Directions for Adult and Continuing Education,* (126), 3–11. doi:10.1002/ace.367
Erichsen, E.A. (2009). *Reinventing selves: International students' conceptions of self and learning for transformation.* Unpublished doctoral dissertation. Retrieved from ProQuest Digital Dissertations.
Erichsen, E. A., Kaiser, L. M. R., Callahan, A., & Miller, K. (2009). Our quest: How we negotiate our multiple selves on a daily basis. *Journal of Adult Education, 38*(2), 1–18.
Fairchild, E. (2003). Multiple roles of adult learners. *New Directions for Student Services, 102,* 11–16.
Freeman, M. (1993). *Rewriting the self.* New York, NY: Routledge.
Hale, A., Snow-Gerono, J., & Morales, F. (2008). Transformative education for culturally diverse learners through narrative and ethnography. *Teaching and Teacher Education, 24*(6), 1413–1425. doi:10.1016/j.tate.2007.11.013
Herrington, A. J., & Curtis, M. (2000). *Persons in process: Four stories of writing and personal development in college.* Urbana, IL: National Council of Teachers of English.
Ibarra, H. (1999). Provisional selves: Experimenting with image and identity in professional adaptation. *Administrative Science Quarterly, 44*(4), 764–791.

Imel, S. (1998). *Transformative learning in adulthood.* Columbus, OH: ERIC Clearinghouse on Adult Career and Vocational Education. (ERIC Document Reproduction Service No. ED 423 426)

Jarvis, P. (2006). *Towards a comprehensive theory of human learning: Lifelong learning and the learning society, Volume 1.* London, England: Routledge.

Johnson, R. R. (2003). Autobiography and transformative learning: Narrative in search of self. *Journal of Transformative Education, 1,* 227–244.

Jones, S. R., & McEwen, M. (2002). A conceptual model of multiple dimensions of identity. In S. Merriam & Associates (Eds.), *Qualitative research in practice: Examples for discussion and analysis* (pp. 163–180). San Francisco, CA: Jossey-Bass.

Josephs, R., Markus, H., & Tafarodi, R. (1992). Gender and self-esteem. *Journal of Personality and Social Psychology, 63,* 391–402

Karpiak, I. E. (2000). Writing our life: Adult learning and teaching through autobiography. *Canadian Journal of University Continuing Education, 26*(1), 31–50.

Kerka, S. (1996). *Journal writing and adult learning.* (ERIC Document Reproduction Service No. ED 399 413)

King, K. M. (1987). Using retrospective autobiographies as a teaching tool. *Teaching Sociology, 15,* 410–413.

Kohut, H. (1991). *The search for the self: Selected writings of Heinz Kohut: 1978–1981.* Madison, CT: International Universities Press.

Lee, A., & Boud, D. (2003). Writing groups, change, and academic identity: Research development at local practice. *Studies in Higher Education, 28*(2), 187–200.

Markus, H. (1977). Self-schemas and processing information about the self. *Journal of Personality and Social Psychology, 35,* 63–78.

Merriam, S. B. (2004). The role of cognitive development in Mezirow's transformational learning theory. *Adult Education Quarterly, 55*(1), 60–68.

Merriam, S. B., Caffarella, R. S., & Baumgartner, L. M. (2007). *Learning in adulthood: A comprehensive guide.* San Francisco, CA: Jossey-Bass.

Mezirow, J. (1978). Perspective transformation. *Adult Education, 28,* 100–110.

Mezirow, J. (1995). Transformation theory of adult learning. In M. R. Welton (Ed.), *In defense of the lifeworld* (pp. 39–70). New York, NY: SUNY Press.

Mezirow, J. (1997). Transformative learning: Theory to practice. In P. Cranton (Ed.), *Transformative learning in action: Insights from practice* (p. 102). San Francisco, CA: Jossey-Bass.

Mezirow, J., & Associates. (2000). *Learning as transformation.* San Francisco, CA: Jossey-Bass.

Mulvihill, M. K. (2003). The Catholic church in crisis: Will transformative learning lead to social change through the uncovering of emotion? In C. A. Wiessner, S. R. Meyer, N. L. Pfahl, & P. G. Neaman (Eds.), *Proceedings of the Fifth International Conference on Transformative Learning* (pp. 320–325). New York, NY: Teachers College, Columbia University.

Nelson, A. (1997). Imagining and critical reflection in autobiography: An odd couple in adult transformative learning. In R. E. Nolan & H. Chelesvig. (Eds.), *Annual Adult Education Research Conference Proceedings* (pp. 191–196). Stillwater: Oklahoma State University.

Ochs, E., & Capps, L. (1996). Narrating the self. *Annual Review of Anthropology, 25,* 19–43.

Pelias, R. (1999). *Writing performance: Poeticizing the researcher's body.* Carbondale and Edwardsville: Southern Illinois University Press.

Pfahl, N. L. (2003). *Raising the bar for higher education: Using narrative processes to advance learning and change.* Unpublished doctoral dissertation. New York, NY: Teachers College, Columbia University.

Pfahl, N. L., & Wiessner, C. A. (2007). Creating new directions with story: Narrating life experience as story in community adult education contexts. *Adult Learning, 18*(3/4), 9–13.

Plimmer, G., & Schmidt, A. (2007). Possible selves and career transition: It's who you want to be not what you want to do. *New Directions for Adult and Continuing Education,* (114), 61–73.

Quinnan, T. W. (1997). *Adult students "at-risk": Culture bias in higher education.* Westport, CT: Bergin & Garvey.

Rossiter, M. (2002). *Narrative and stories in adult teaching and learning.* Columbus, OH: ERIC Clearinghouse on Adult Career and Vocational Education. (ERIC Document Reproduction Service No. EDO CE 02 214)

Rossiter, M. (2007). Possible selves in adult education. *New Directions for Adult and Continuing Education,* (114), 87–94.

Rossiter, M., & Clark, M. C. (2010). Narrative perspectives on adult education. *New Directions for Adult and Continuing Education,* (126), 89–91. doi:10.1002/ace.374

Stroobants, V. (2005). Stories about learning in narrative biographical research. *International Journal of Qualitative Studies in Education (QSE), 18*(1), 47–61. doi:10.1080/09518390412331318441.

Taylor, E. W. (1994). Intercultural competency: A transformative learning process. *Adult Education Quarterly, 44*(3), 154–174.

thINQ. (1994). *Collaborative inquiry in practice: Using collaborative inquiry as a strategy for learning and action.* Thousand Oaks, CA: Sage.

Wiessner, C. A. (2001). *Stories of change: Narrative in emancipatory adult education.* Unpublished doctoral dissertation. New York, NY: Teachers College, Columbia University.

Wortham, S. (2006). *Learning and identity: The joint emergence of social identification and academic learning.* Cambridge, England: Cambridge University Press.

Part II

LEARNING IN RELATIONSHIP WITH SELF AND OTHERS

CHAPTER 5

NARRATIVE, SOMATIC, AND SOCIAL/CONSTRUCTIVIST APPROACHES TO TRANSFORMATIVE LEARNING IN TRAINING PROGRAMS FOR THE HELPING PROFESSIONS

Daniel Stroud, Julie Prindle, and Stacy England

The focus of this chapter is transformation through somatic, narrative, and social/constructivist learning in relation to key concepts from transformative learning theory. From this, we highlight the importance of engaging the complete learner—mind, body, and spirit—and accentuating that focus in a classroom environment. We discuss implications and give examples to generate practice ideas for educators.

TRANSFORMATIVE LEARNING

Scholars often view transformative learning rather broadly, and traditionally the focus has been either on the individual or sociocultural context (Merriam, Caffarella, & Baumgartner, 2007). Of those who have taken a particular focus on the individual, Mezirow's psychocritical, Daloz's psychodevelopmental, and Boyd's psychoanalytic, Mezirow's approach has emerged as a thoroughly researched and developed theory that is augmented well by both the psychodevelopmental and psychoanalytic approaches of Daloz and Boyd (Merriam et al., 2007). Mezirow defines learning as "the process of using a prior interpretation of the meaning of one's experience in order to guide future action" (Wiessner & Mezirow, 2000, as cited in Merriam et al., 2007, p. 132). The process is what Mezirow coined *perspective transformation* and is arrived at by way of experience, critical reflection (to include questioning of one's previously held assumptions and beliefs), reflective discourse, and action (Dirkx, 1998). In contrast, Daloz views transformative learning in a less rational, more intuitive and developmental way. Although both Mezirow and Daloz view discourse as key to transformation, Daloz places emphasis on learners' stories. By bringing students' stories into the here and now of the learning environment, the teacher serves as a guide, challenger, and supporter. Students further their development via the mutual sharing of evolving personal narratives. "Through storytelling, Daloz and his students journey toward a more holistic and transformed worldview" (Merriam et al., 2007, p. 139). Combined, their work allows for a holistic view of learners.

So what is it about our stories and the way we experience them—mind and body—that is important to learning environments? In answering this question, we first explore narrative learning as means of understanding our personal narratives. We follow with a section on somatic learning that highlights the ways in which we may experience learning with more of a focus on affect than cognitions. We then transition to social/constructivist approaches to establish a foundation for the co-construction of knowledge in a learning environment. We conclude with three examples that illustrate narrative, somatic, and social/constructivist activities applied to the four components of *experience, critical reflection, reflective discourse,* and *action*.

NARRATIVE LEARNING

Transformative learning seeks to facilitate change. And the same is true of Narrative. Good stories take us to new places in our heads and hearts and narrative learning uses this power to create highly effective, compelling, and meaningful teaching.
—Rossiter & Clark (2010)

Stories inform our lives, touch people profoundly, guide us toward new directions, and provide roots from which we can grow. Narratives, as a deeply woven ancestry, are rich with meaning and unveil one's understanding of the world and how one comes to understand and digest new information. Adult learners enter the learning environment with their stories, and their stories' meanings, embedded in their experience. As adult learners begin to learn something new, the process of restorying this new knowledge, as a way of understanding the information, begins to unfold (Rossiter, 1999). The process of bringing learners' rich stories into the learning experience through narrative creates a transformative learning environment, which supports and honors the experiences of students, encourages connectedness in the learning environment, instills a value of reflective learning, and empowers adult learners to trust their stories and expand them through reflective and shared learning experience (Merriam et al., 2007). Employing narrative techniques enriches the teacher-student relationship and provides the educator with a profound teaching journey (Dirkx, 1998).

The use of narrative learning comes to life in the educational environment through the narratives adult learners bring with them and the process by which students begin to story the new information. According to Brooks (2001),

> We make meaning of our lives in terms of narrative. When asked to identify ourselves, we usually go on to elaborate with a story that brings feelings, context and value to our lives. Another way to say this is that we learn by constructing and reconstructing narratives to make meaning of information and events... The task of constructing what we are trying to learn into a meaningful narrative, whether represented in words or by other means, pushes us to integrate and reformulate new information, ideas, and ultimately, our own identity. That is a highly visible example of narrative learning. Thus, we make meaning for ourselves through a process of developing narratives. (p. 2)

Educators can tap into the cultural, familial, educational, personal, and socially constructed narratives of students to establish a foundation for connecting with students and presenting curriculum in a way that furthers their learning (Clark & Rossiter, 2008). Teachers can use their genuine interest to connect, incorporate, and at times challenge these narratives, and ultimately, co-author new narratives with students. Adult learners arrive loaded down with personal narratives built over years and generations, which are often socially constructed, some empowering and some constraining (Brooks, 2001). These rich narratives can have a powerful impact on the teacher, other students, and the person telling the story (Merriam et al., 2007). It is through telling and sharing that meaning deepens, stories evolve, and transformation occurs; these changes come about through the listening and shared experience as a witness to the story (Brooks, 2001). In short, narrative learning embraces the stories students possess and seeks innovative ways to incorporate the sharing of stories through curriculum, assignments, group experiences, role-plays, and reflective practices.

The students learn deeply as they take the course material presented and restory it into a new and more developed narrative. Some material may translate easily into students' current understanding according to their narrative. Other material may inspire, challenge, and encourage stories to evolve further. Adult learners may encounter new information that enhances and transforms the story they once held about a particular idea or subject matter. This, in turn, adds branches by way of critical reflection and engaging in reflective discourse, to the deeply rooted narratives they hold—in essence, new information restored in a way that illustrates transformed learners operating in a transformative environment (Merriam et al., 2007).

Creating a place for adult learners to share their stories and restory the new information through critical reflection and reflective discourse gives rise to a transformative learning environment in which learners can feel free to be themselves and participate fully. This new learning space encourages the building of a strong and supportive community and deepens the relationships among students. As intentional listeners and holders of special and transformative stories, educators and students honor the relationship that has evolved between them. Allowing students and educators to hear and welcome stories in the classroom is a process that demonstrates that the educator values what the students bring to the classroom and recognizes that each individual is an integral part of the learning environment, as illustrated by the new narratives that unfold. When learners allow themselves to be vulnerable to this experience and bring their stories to the surface to share, reflect, challenge, and grow, they evolve as students. When individual students bring their stories to the forefront of the learning environment, a logical next step is a focus on how students' cognitions, affect, and physiological responses influence them in the present moment. An embodied, somatic approach is a step in this direction.

SOMATIC LEARNING

To follow the structure generally attributed to Descartes and the Scientific Revolution (Beckett & Morris 2001; Clark, 2001; Goldenberg, Pyszczynski, Greenberg & Solomon, 2000), information would be delivered through a lecture, directly from the educator's mouth to the students' brains. In the Cartesian view, the mind and the body are very separate entities. Students internalize the given information, contemplate and question the ideas, and then arrive at an abstract understanding of *the* truth. Truth and knowledge in this process exist outside of the body and are available only to individuals through thought and reason (Dirkx, 1998). As explained earlier in this chapter, however, transformative learning is in contrast to this idea. Transformative learning "is about change—dramatic fundamental change in the way we see ourselves and the world in which we live" (Merriam et al., 2007, p. 130). Scholars who describe how educators may help facilitate this change often cite the use of techniques such as writing or journaling, portfolios, collaborative learning/group work, role-play, and case studies (King, 2005; Mezirow, 1997). As Mezirow (1997) states, "The key idea is to help the learners actively engage the concepts presented in the context of their own lives and collectively critically assess the justification of new knowledge" (p. 10).

The environment created to encourage transformative learning is congruent with the philosophy and strategies of somatic or embodied (used here interchangeably) learning. Somatic learning assumes a basic premise that the body is not separate from the mind; the two linked inextricably. Even in the dualism described by Descartes (as cited in Beckett & Morris, 2001), the body is the center. The learner's mind develops an understanding of the information relayed to her through a unique and essential biological process of firing neurons. Previous experiences, culture, economics, and politics, among other factors, also shape the integration of the material (Clark & Dirkx, 2008). If the room is too hot or too cold, the chair is stiff, or the learner feels ill, these bodily sensations influence the way in which the learner arrives at a conclusion. If we as educators embrace each student as a whole being, then we can greatly increase the capacity for transformative learning in our classrooms.

Amann (2003) states that embodied learning include four main areas: kinesthetic, sensory, affective, and spiritual. Kinesthetic learning refers to learning that occurs from body movements. Role-plays and mindfulness activities are examples of kinesthetic learning. Sensory learning is knowledge that results from use of all five of our basic senses. For example, in a practicum course, we address sensory learning by asking questions such as "How does it feel to be sitting in the chair as a counselor for the first time?" "What physical sensations are present?" "What do you see when you enter the counseling room?" "What do you hear?" "Are there any associated smells or tastes?" We ask these questions to increase students' self-awareness.

Amann (2003) describes affective learning as the "result of paying attention to and honoring our feelings and emotions" (p. 29) and states that although we may rationally arrive at a decision, at times our "gut" may lead us in another direction. This is a valuable area of learning for emerging counselors. Often the presence of feelings or emotions within the counselor during a session can lead to questions and understandings that add significant meaning to the discussion. For example, a counselor may experience a deep overwhelming feeling while listening to a client blandly describe her day. The entire feeling of the session may shift if the clinician shares that the events sound overwhelming, thereby inviting the client to begin to discuss her actual feelings. The body may also become aware of distress before the mind. At times our "fight or flight" reflex may be triggered, and we may *feel* a situation is concerning before we fully become aware of why. Counselors, for example, may feel a sense of discomfort just before a client shares that they have been contemplating suicide. Their bodies may be aware of the distress in the room while their conscious minds are working to make sense of the content of the information that is present. Dirkx (2008) writes, "Helping learners understand and make sense of these emotion-laden experiences within the context of the curriculum represents one of the most important and most challenging tasks for adult educators" (p. 9). Having an awareness of the areas for somatic learning can help educators rise to this challenge by understanding the impact of emotions and sensations in the learning process.

The fourth and final area of somatic learning refers to spirituality. Amann (2003) states that spirituality "is basically about making meaning of our lives" (p. 29). Often people describe spirituality as an experience that promotes a mind-body connection. Counselors often ask clients to describe the meaning they attribute to a particular experience. As a counselor educator, I often ask the same of my students by asking questions such as, "How does the experience of becoming a counselor fit in with your meaning schemas?" and "What does it mean to be a counselor?"

While embodied learning is not only constricted to the categories of kinesthetic, sensory, affective, and spiritual learning, these labels do provide a practical understanding that can lead to the inclusion of embodied experiences in coursework. Somatic techniques can help lay the foundation from which transformative learning can occur.

SOCIAL/CONSTRUCTIVIST LEARNING

Now that we have touched upon what students bring to the learning environment by way of narrative learning and that which students experience by way of somatic learning, we now shift to dynamics at play when the individual learner is in relation with other learners in the classroom and supervision settings.

Authors in the helping fields have issued a call for educators to consider and clarify views on learning specific to graduate level helping profession programs (Dollarhide, Smith, & Lemberger, 2007; Fong, 1998; Olguin, 2004). Fong's (1998) "Considerations of a Counseling Pedagogy" underscores the importance of including constructivist and developmental approaches into the counselor education curricula. Fong concluded, "It is time that counselor education focuses in a similar way on how we teach and the theoretical models that guide the curriculum in our programs" (p. 109). Larson (1998) began the process of answering the call by publishing a social-cognitive model for training derived from Bandura's (1986) social cognitive theory. Dollarhide et al. (2007) have also detailed a constructivist classroom approach when teaching counseling theories. These writings influenced the inclusion of social and constructivist approaches as important components of contextual learning when accounting for a student in relationship with self and others.

Social Learning

Bandura's (1986) concept of *reciprocal determinism* informs that which an individual learns is a result of interacting variables or components, categorized as personal, behavioral, and environmental. The personal component includes beliefs and attitudes about one's self that can affect learning. Behavioral components include the responses one makes, or does not make, in a given situation. Environmental components include the influences of parents, teachers, and peers (Bruning, Schraw, Norby, & Ronning, 2004). Reciprocal determinism suggests that each component (personal, behavioral, and environmental) affects the other components. Indeed, the essence of Bandura's theory is the idea of reciprocal determinism (Schunk, 1991).

Bandura's work continues to be influential and calls attention to social conditions that may have an effect on learning among helping profession students (Bandura, 1993). One way that personal factors relate to behaviors and environmental cues is through mediated responses, that is, how one cognitively interprets events prior to responding (Bruning et al., 2004). Exploring personal narratives and somatic responses previously described in this chapter may assist in identifying and understanding unique ways of cognitive interpretation and how the individual experiences interpretations. For example, corrective feedback from a teacher, supervisor, or peers may elicit anxiety in one student while increasing effort in another because the same event (receiving feedback) is interpreted differently (Bruning et al., 2004). Thus, the powerful influence of negative personal interpretations on behavior may hinder students' willingness to engage in active learning environments (Argyis, 1968; Stockton & Morran, 1981; Stockton, Morran, & Harris, 1991). Although an appreciation for an individual's unique experience exists, formal adult learning rarely occurs when a learner is isolated from the influence of others (Bruning et al., 2004). Even with an increase in online programs within the helping professions, classes still have an interactive component, albeit via technology. Nevertheless, if interpersonal interactions around to-be-learned material are important, as Mezirow (1997) suggests in his description of *reflective discourse*, it is essential to have an understanding of what learning theory informs regarding how knowledge is constructed.

Constructivist Approach

Teaching and learning have historically been highly social activities, yet it has only been in the past several decades that researchers have focused on the social processes involved in learning. Bruning et al. (2004) purport, "from the very earliest of interactions between parent and child on up to a graduate student's relationship with a graduate advisor, much of our learning takes place through interactions with adults or peers who have greater knowledge" (p. 193). The theorist who wrote about the appreciation of multiple forces in learning was Russian psychologist Lev Vygotsky (Crain, 2000). The postmortem translation and publication of Vygotsky's (1978) *Mind in Society: The Development of Higher Psychological Processes* helped to bring about a paradigm shift. Vygotsky suggested that social interactions with adults or peers that are more capable strengthen higher mental functions. His ideas on learning speak to the notion of constructivism whereby the learner contributes to knowledge formation and meaning making through individual and social activities (Biggs, 1996). Transformative learning theorists would echo this by highlighting the importance of critical reflection and reflective discourse in classroom settings (Merriam et al., 2007). However, researchers have recognized the importance of classroom discussion, or discourse, as a means to knowledge construction and report that students are not necessarily engaging in classroom discussions that effectively lead to knowledge construction (Chinn, Anderson, & Waggoner, 2001). Thus the question: How *does* one construct knowledge?

Very much a proponent of the influence of social interactions, Vygotsky expanded upon the idea of constructivism and learning with the concept of dialectical constructivism (Bruning et al., 2004). Dialectical constructivism highlights the importance of the learner's social interactions in developing knowledge and thought (Mosham, 1982). The concept of dialectical constructivism also acknowledges the possibility that one must consider multiple meanings when assessing a singular event (Ornstein & Ganzer, 2003). Students and educators mutually build knowledge through accentuated supportive guidance from educators as they enable students to acquire additional clinical skills, understanding, and competence (Applefield, Huber, & Moallem, 2000).

Specific to dialectical constructivism is the interaction of internal and external aspects of learning, as well as influence from one's social environment (Newman, Griffin, & Cole, 1989). Bruning et al. (2004) comment that dialectical constructivism best captures factors that will most likely yield a student's knowledge construction and cognitive growth. The direct application of Vygotsky's assertion that internal, external, and social factors play a role in knowledge acquisition is perhaps best illustrated in his concept of the zone of proximal development (ZPD), "defined as the difference between the difficulty level of a problem that a learner can cope with independently and the level that can be accomplished with the help of a teacher, or more advanced peer" (Bruning et al., 2004, p. 197). "With appropriate instruction in the zone of proximal development, the boundaries of the zone shift" (Driscoll, 2005, p. 254). The shift represents new knowledge and ability on the part of the learner because of the interactions with a teacher or more capable peer. In terms of evaluating learning, the zone of proximal development shifts the traditional focus from evaluating the knowledge a student possesses to a focus on the knowledge a student has the *ability* to possess. Crain (2000) underscores the importance of this shift in focus, writing, "we need to see what happens when the growing child, trying to figure things out by herself, encounters adults who try to teach her things" (p. 240).

In exploring ways in which learners experience transformations, it is important to draw upon foundational learning theorists. Bandura (1986) introduced the concept *reciprocal determinism*, which informs that personal, environmental, and behavioral components are at play within learners. Also of great importance is *dialectical constructivism* (Mosham, 1982) which details how knowledge is constructed when learners' internal experience and understanding interacts with guidance, support, and challenge from educators and peers. Both provide theoretical support for the ideas of *critical reflection* and *reflective discourse* as central to transformative learning.

EXAMPLES OF NARRATIVE, SOMATIC, AND SOCIAL/CONSTRUCTIVIST ACTIVITIES

What follows are three examples that illustrate narrative, somatic, and social/constructivist activities educators can use in classroom or supervision settings. Following each example are steps that demonstrate how each activity relates to the four components of transformative learning: *experience, critical reflection, reflective discourse,* and *action.*

Narrative Learning Example: Transforming Stories Through Genograms

According to Dirkx (1998), "If we want to learn about fostering transformation among our learners, the most important way to begin the work is with this particular, common, and sacred life one has been given. It is a simple and humble yet incredible place to begin" (pp. 11–12). I (Julie Prindle) became interested in the use of stories about a decade ago as I was going through a graduate program in social work. I embarked on a learning journey of my own story and the story of my family. The assignment called on me to produce a personal family genogram based on the structure of McGoldrick, Gerson, & Shellenberger (1999) and the family therapy model of Bowen (as cited in Nichols & Schwartz, 1998). From the genogram, I told the story of the life of my family and, after much reflection, defined meaning around themes that arose.

Laid out before me was meaning I had yet to story. The meticulous process of looking at themes, relationships, and listening to the stories held by my family members allowed me to begin to piece together my own meaning and narrative about my family. I noticed how I began to translate this map and write my own autobiography filled with themes and meaning that empowered me as a young woman. I translated my family story as one that was rich with strong, smart, empowered, courageous, and passionately dedicated women. Working from this story also allowed me to examine more easily difficult, sad stories embedded in my visual family map. The telling and retelling of my story allowed my narrative to become alive with meaning that propelled me as a woman and first-generation graduate student in my family. The sharing of my story with the professor and fellow students opened up an opportunity for others to know me on a deep level, to feel honored and supported in my story, to encourage new stories, and to make reflective connections to my emerging role as a counselor. Table 5.1 illustrates how this experience relates to the components of the transformative learning process as outlined by Mezirow (1997) and others.

TABLE 5.1 Narrative Learning Components

Experience: This experience is presented to students with the following directive: story your life using a self-generated genogram.

Critical Reflection: The process of genogram construction challenged me as a student to explore my own story and the story of my family, to ask questions, to listen to stories held by my family members and to begin to make meaning of themes and stories from this visual map.

Reflective Discourse: The sharing of my story with the professor and students created an opportunity for interpersonal self-understanding and served as a foundation from which reflective connections could be made to my emerging role as a helper. Questions that help in this process include "What sense do you make of your genogram?" "What themes are present?" "What impact does this have on your emerging role as a clinician?"

Action: The opportunity for students to share, explore, and question their stories increased self-understanding and led to new ways of relating in the classroom. Exploring and sharing my own humble and sacred story transformed me as a young woman and graduate student, and ultimately enhanced how I related to, and connected with, my graduate education.

Somatic Learning Example: Somatic Experiencing

As a counselor educator, I (Stacy England) have the honor of supporting students as they step into the role of counselor for the first time during a practicum course. For many, this is a time filled with anxiety. The students typically want to be the best counselors they can be. They come to the field driven by a genuine desire to help others. In those first sessions, many students are fearful that they do not *know* enough to be helpful. They review theories and techniques. They seek guidance on what to do and what to say. Their minds spin with material from classes that they have taken to this point. My job is sometimes to help students momentarily put aside the information spinning in their minds. I refocus the discussion to address active listening skills, relaxation, and attention to how it *feels* to be in the role of counselor. This skill is not only helpful to the supervisory relationship, but it is helpful to the alliance between counselor and client as well. After the establishment of this relationship, the clinicians can freely explore the techniques and theories that will deepen their practice.

The format of practicum is different from other courses. We have the opportunity to learn through a process of group supervision, immediately followed by clinical sessions. If I notice a topic that needs to be addressed (for example, the process of termination or closure), I will pose it as a question to the group such as, "What are you thinking and feeling about the closure process today?" From a basic question such as this, the students will follow up with questions of their own for each other. They discuss what it is like to sit with someone they have a working relationship with but may not see again—the topic of termination. At this point, I become an infrequent participant in the process. The students guide the discussion. I chime in with questions to deepen the dialogue, such as asking the students what they feel in their bodies when they think about the closure process. When a student has an idea of how to approach termination with a client, I may ask for a role-play between students to demonstrate the skill. As closure and the end of the term are often associated with increased anxiety, I also facilitate a relaxation exercise. I begin teaching a process of deep breathing, introducing it as I would in a session. I direct the activity by counting through three long, deep breaths. Students then have the opportunity to guide themselves through 3–5 more. As the students exhale their last breath, I ask again, what they feel in their bodies. We then discuss how this relaxed state can help us to be present and attentive to our clients. The students are also asked if and how this activity might be helpful in their sessions. This generally opens a lengthy discussion among the students about the benefits of relaxation.

After the breathing exercise, the energy in the room is different. Stillness and confidence replaces the anxiety. The students are present in the classroom—mind and body—and they carry this presence into session.

Over the course of a term, the students participate in many discussions and activities that encourage awareness of the mind-body connection. This can build to a very powerful experience for the student. It is exhilarating to watch as an emerging counselor has an "aha" moment in session. This also occurs when the student moves from *thinking* about being a counselor (and being present primarily in their own minds) to *being* a counselor, fully in the room and engaged with the client. Table 5.2 illustrates the components of transformative learning presented in this example.

Social/Constructivist Learning Example: The Great Debate

Over the years, I (Daniel Stroud) have spent quite a bit of time reflecting on the Psychopathology and Diagnostics class I teach as part of a master's

TABLE 5.2   Somatic Learning Components

Experience: In the example of group supervision above, the opportunity for a new experience is created when the students are asked to identify their somatic responses. Role-plays and activities such as the relaxation exercise help deepen this opportunity for learning. Students are asked to focus on how it *feels* to sit in the room as a counselor as opposed to what they *think* about when counseling.

Critical Reflection: Through the opportunities for experience above, we are able to look for discords that may exist between what the student thinks is important to the counseling relationship and what their physical presence conveys in a session. A student may say, "The process of closure may be challenging for clients" and yet in session become nervous and only briefly mention the termination process. As the professor, I attempt to foster critical reflection by asking the students to consider their beliefs and values as well as their body sensations and physical actions. How congruent are the thoughts of the mind with the actions of the body? What are the sensations in our bodies trying to tell us about the situation we are experiencing? The answers to these questions certainly give us much to talk about.

Reflective Discourse: Group supervision is a process of reflective discourse. A topic is raised and students are given the opportunity to dialogue and problem solve. The difference in somatic learning is that we discuss abstract concepts and thoughts as well as sensations in the body. In this example, students are given the opportunity to discuss their thoughts about the termination process. They are asked to consider how termination felt in their body and are able to identify and discuss those feelings and sensations. A breathing exercise is followed by further discussion. It is important to connect the physical experiences to each student's knowledge, beliefs, values, culture, spirituality, and other factors, which creates the context through which new information is then understood.

Action: After experience, reflection, and discourse pertaining to the closure process, the students now have the opportunity to practice new ways of initiating termination in sessions with their clients. Within group supervision, opportunities are created for action by asking students to role-play challenging situations, or by having them participate in activities that may also benefit clients, such as deep breathing and mindfulness. Practice helps shrink the divide between the body and mind and helps students shift, skillfully and intentionally, into their new identity as Counselor.

level counseling program. A theme that seems to continually present is that a number of students enter this class with reservations about diagnosing human beings, oftentimes saying things like, "I don't believe in diagnoses, they are too negative and deterministic." These observations led me to question: How can I honor their reservations, while at the same time challenge them to appreciate an alternative perspective? With a plan in place, I head off to the first class meeting.

I use the initial meeting of the class to highlight and challenge preconceptions some of the students may be bringing to the class. Prior to even covering the syllabus, I split the class into halves and instruct that one half of the students debate why diagnosing is *counterproductive*. The other half make an argument for why diagnosing is *worthwhile*. Both groups have 15 minutes to prepare. The instructions are that while one group presents, the members of the other group are to listen closely and write down points the other group makes that they appreciate, because they will be reflecting those back during the process piece of this activity.

The anti-diagnosing group presents first and make their case that diagnosing is a form of negative labeling and can potentially harm a client in an overly deterministic way, such as referring to someone as "a bipolar" as opposed to referring to that person as "a human being who struggles with bipolar disorder." "Not to mention the prevalence of misdiagnosing and overreliance on psychotropic medications." After listening, the pro-diagnosing group reflects that they too do not want to misdiagnose or label their clients in a way that would be inaccurate or devaluing of that individual.

The next group then presents making the argument that "diagnosing allows a client to better understand that with which he or she is struggling; provides the client with an answer to a difficult unknown that has potentially been the cause of much grief, and in turn allows for effective treatment planning that will ultimately help that individual achieve a higher level of functioning." To this, the anti-diagnosing group reflects that it could be of benefit to provide a client with an answer to a struggle as well as an effective treatment plan that specifically addresses the problem.

Next, I engage both groups by asking, "What was it like for you take part in this activity?" Typically answers are a blend between enthusiasm and appreciation for having heard multiple perspectives, to struggle with trying to be *okay* in one's mind with something that had maybe *not been okay* in the past (for example, the student who is all for diagnosing yet is placed in the anti-diagnosing group).

After processing, I summarize key points made by each group and reflect what I perceive to be the meaning behind them, which has typically been something like, "It sounds like it is very important that the work that each of you do with clients serves to empower, accurately understand, assess, and diagnose in a way that positively contributes to clients' therapeutic outcome." When I sense that a level of agreement exists in relation to that statement, I try to challenge further by asking, "So how will *we* go about incorporating the material this class presents in a way that works *for* the good of the human beings we will be helping?"

Students verbalize that which is important to them, that which they are taking from the activity. Basically, they hope to diagnose in a way that is cautious, holistic, well-informed, and ultimately leads to appropriate interventions that help to empower clients. At this point, I share with the class that it seems as if we as a group have established a framework that will serve as our foundation as we engage in the to-be-learned material specific to this class. Table 5.3 out-

---

TABLE 5.3 Social/Constructivist Learning Components

Experience: In taking a close look at the "Great Debate" activity, we see several components that when combined, create a potentially transformative experience. First, students are given time to formulate an argument as a group. In instructing students to do this, they are catapulted into a situation wherein they have to draw upon their personally held beliefs, more so than new "textbook" information in that the reading for the class has not yet begun. Because of this, information arises that reflects the students' previously held beliefs. Second, students must try to quickly formulate a *solid* rationale based upon their (sometimes underinformed) beliefs. Third, providing the students with instructions that they will be reflecting back salient points the other group makes, increases the likelihood that they will listen more attentively than if they were listening with skepticism. These steps combined place the students in a position of questioning that which they know, or don't know, by way of wrestling with the tasks of creating a solid argument and having to reflect aspects of an alternative perspective with which they actually do agree.

Critical Reflection: What is critical reflection, if not questioning what one believes? As students work to create an argument, they are simultaneously questioning that which they have come to believe about a topic—previous assumptions and biases included—to see if those beliefs actually hold up under scrutiny.

Reflective Discourse: In this activity, the most significant times in which students are engaging in reflective discourse is when they are (a) talking as a group formulating their group's rationale, (b) when they are reflecting back that which they heard the other group argue that resonated with them, and (c) the postdebate processing that led to my reflection, "It sounds like it is very important that the work each of you do with clients serves to empower, accurately understand, assess, and diagnose in a way that positively contributes to clients' therapeutic outcomes."

Action: This step is especially important, and I believe an assumption should not exist that students now *get it*, so to speak, simply as result of taking part in the debate. As an educator, I want to be quite intentional and challenging at this moment and ask an open-ended process question that influences the group such as, "So how will *we* now go about incorporating the material this class presents in a way that works *for* the good of the human beings we will be helping?" The summary of their responses—that they hope to diagnose in a way that is cautious, holistic, well-informed, and ultimately leads to appropriate interventions that help to empower clients—illustrates a degree of buy-in and willingness to approach, with an open mind, the content of this diagnostics class while also lowering apprehension and dissonance. Furthermore, their co-constructed responses very closely resemble the objectives of the class, which serves as a seamless transition to the next phase of their initial Psychodiagnostics class—covering the syllabus.

lines components of transformative learning exemplified in the discussion activities.

SUMMARY AND CONCLUSION

Educators in helping-professions training programs can effectively facilitate students' experience of transformation by way of engaging the complete learner—mind and body—by using narrative, somatic, and social/constructivist learning approaches. Narrative learning approaches are invaluable because of their focus on illuminating personal narratives that are illustrations of personal worldviews as they exist prior to entering a learning environment. Not only do personal narratives serve as a useful baseline, the educator and students may continually assess the narratives to determine movement and growth throughout the learning journey. Taking personal narrative a step further can be done through somatic processing, allowing students to increase awareness and self-understanding by tuning in to that which students physiologically experience in relation with to-be-learned material, perhaps especially useful when learners enter skill-based helping-profession experiences such as practicum and internship. Finally, when students become aware of their personal narratives and the ways in which they experience themselves in relation to new learning experiences, they are well-advised to engage in the type of discourse that has been recommended by learning theorists whose focus is on social and constructivist approaches; approaches that ultimately lead to meaning making and knowledge construction.

In short, educators can honor both the stories and the here-and-now experience of helping-professions students by intentionally tapping into students' self in relation to others and to-be-learned material, ultimately creating a classroom environment that is equal parts supportive and challenging.

REFERENCES

Amann, T. (2003). Creating space for somatic ways of knowing within transformative learning theory. In C. A. Wiessner, S. R. Meyer, N. L. Pfhal, & P. G. Neaman (Eds.), *Proceedings of the Fifth International Conference on Transformative Learning* (pp. 26–32). New York, NY: Teachers College, Columbia University.

Applefield, J., Huber, R., & Moallem, M. (2000). Constructivism in theory and practice: Toward a better understanding. *High School Journal, 84*(2), 35–54.

Argyis, C. (1968). Conditions for competence acquisition and therapy. *Journal of Applied Behavioral Science, 4*, 147–177.

Bandura, A. (1986). *Social foundations of thought and action: A social cognitive theory.* Englewood Cliffs, NJ: Prentice-Hall.

Bandura, A. (1993) Perceived self-efficacy in cognitive development and functioning. *Educational Psychologist, 28,* 117–148.
Beckett, D., & Morris, G. (2001). Ontological performance: Bodies, identities, and learning. *Studies in the Education of Adults, 33*(1), 35–48.
Biggs, J. (1996). Enhancing teaching through constructive alignment. *Higher Education, 32,* 347–364.
Brockman, J. (2001). A somatic epistemology for education. *Educational Forum, 65*(4), 328–334.
Brooks, A. (2001). Narrative dimensions of transformative learning. *Proceedings of the Annual Meeting of the Adult Education Research Conference.* Retrieved from http://www.edst.educ.ubc.ca/aerc/2001/2001brooks.htm
Bruning, R., Schraw, G., Norby, M., & Ronning, R. (2004). *Cognitive psychology and instruction* (4th ed., pp. 119–197). Upper Saddle River, NJ: Pearson.
Chinn, C., Anderson, R., & Waggoner, M. (2001). Patterns of discourse in two kinds of literature discussion. *Reading Research Quarterly, 36,* 378–411.
Clark, M. C. (2001). Off the beaten path: Some creative approaches to adult learning. *New Directions for Adult and Continuing Education, 89,* 83–91.
Clark, M. C., & Dirkx, J. M. (2008). The emotional self in adult learning. *New Directions for Adult and Continuing Education, 120,* 89–95.
Clark, M. C., & Rossiter, M. (2008). Narrative learning in adulthood. *New Directions for Adult and Continuing Education, 119,* 61–70.
Crain, W. (2000). *Theories of development: Concepts and applications* (4th ed., p. 240). Upper Saddle River, NJ: Prentice Hall.
Dollarhide, C. T., Smith, A. T., & Lemberger, M. E. (2007). Counseling made transparent: Pedagogy for a counseling theories course. *Counselor Education and Supervision, 47*(4), 233–248.
Dirkx, J. M. (1998). Transformative learning theory in the practice of adult education: An overview. *PAACE Journal of Lifelong Learning, 7,* 1–14.
Dirkx, J. M. (2008). The meaning and role of emotions in adult learning. *New Directions for Adult and Continuing Education, 120,* 7–39.
Driscoll, M. (2005). *Psychology of learning for instruction* (3rd ed., p. 254). Boston, MA: Pearson.
Fong, M. (1998). Considerations of a counseling pedagogy. *Counselor Education and Supervision, 38*(2), 109.
Goldenberg, J. L., Pyszczynski, T., Greenberg, J., & Solomon, S. (2000). Fleeing the body: A terror management perspective on the problem of human corporeality. *Personality and Social Psychology Review, 4*(3), 200–218.
King, P. K. (2005). *Bringing transformative learning to life.* Malabar, FL: Krieger.
Larson, L. (1998). The social cognitive model of counselor training. *The Counseling Psychologist, 26,* 219–273.
McGoldrick, M., Gerson, R., & Shellenberger, S. (1999). *Genograms: Assessment and intervention* (2nd ed.). New York, NY: W.W. Norton.
Merriam, S., Caffarella, R., & Baumgartner, L. (2007). *Learning in adulthood* (3rd ed.). San Francisco, CA: John Wiley & Sons.
Mezirow, J. (1997). Transformative learning: Theory to practice. *New Directions for Adult and Continuing Education, 74,* 5–12.

Mosham, D. (1982). Exogenous, endogenous, and dialectical constructivism. *Developmental Review, 2,* 371–384.

Newman, D., Griffin, P., & Cole, M. (1989). *The construction zone: Working for cognitive change in school.* Cambridge, England: Cambridge University Press.

Nichols, M. P., & Schwartz, R. C. (1998). *Family therapy: Concepts and methods* (4th ed.). Boston, MA: Allyn and Bacon.

Olguin, D. L. (2004). *Determinants of preparation through perceptions of counseling and teaching self-efficacy among prospective counselor educators* (Doctoral dissertation, University of New Orleans). Dissertation Abstracts International: 65(04), 1266.

Ornstein, E., & Ganzer, C. (2003). Dialectical constructivism in clinical social work: An exploration of Irwin Hoffman's approach to treatment. *Clinical Social Work Journal, 31*(4), 355–369.

Rossiter, M. (1999). Understanding adult development as narrative. *New Directions for Adult and Continuing Education, 84,* 77–85.

Rossiter, M., & Clark, C. (2010). Editor's conclusion. *New Directions for Adult and Continuing Education, 126,* 91.

Schunk, D. (1991). *Learning theories: An educational perspective.* New York, NY: Macmillan.

Stockton, R., & Morran, D. K., (1981). Feedback exchange in personal growth groups: Receiver acceptance as a function of valence, session, and order of delivery. *Journal of Counseling Psychology, 28*(6), 490–497.

Stockton, R., Morran, D. K., & Harris, M. (1991). Delivery of positive and corrective feedback in counseling groups. *Journal of Counseling Psychology, 38*(4), 410–414.

Vygotsky, L. (1978). *Mind in society: The development of higher psychological processes.* Cambridge, MA: Harvard University Press.

Wiessner, C. A., & Mezirow, J. (2000). Theory building and the search for common ground. In J. Mezirow & Associates (Eds.), *Learning as transformation: Critical perspectives on a theory in progress* (pp. 329–358). San Francisco, CA: Jossey-Bass.

CHAPTER 6

IN HOPE OF TRANSFORMATION

Teaching and Learning Through Relational Practice in the Adult Learning Classroom

Teresa J. Carter

When midlife adult learners enter the academic environment, often they have self-doubts about their abilities to succeed (Herman & Mandell, 2004; Kasworm, 2008). This appears to be as true for graduate students reentering the academic environment to earn a master's degree as it is for undergraduates (Schwartz, 2009). Kegan (2000) refers to the mental demands of a hidden curriculum for adult learners who function in the multiple roles of parent, partner, worker, and community member. Simultaneously, however, an often-undefined need for change propels many adult learners to return to school, where they arrive at the educational doorstep ready for a significant developmental experience.

Faculty who seek to foster transformative learning must ask themselves what kind of environment supports epistemological growth and development within their learners. What is required of both teacher and learner to move students forward on an educational journey that results in much more than acquisition of skills and content knowledge—one that educators hope will be transformative in nature? This chapter seeks to answer this question and to directed professionals who have the goal of fostering and promoting transformative learning in their practices as educators. It assumes that an educator seeks more than content acquisition for learners and is interested in a growth experience that will result in an epistemological shift in how learners come to know. Changes in the way that a learner constructs knowledge are likely to challenge previously assimilated beliefs, values, and assumptions (Mezirow, 1991). Many of these have been adopted uncritically through childhood experiences as the right way to think, believe, and act in the world through the influences of parents, caregivers, and other authority figures. Learning to revisit and perhaps to alter these previously assimilated viewpoints and perspectives requires both challenge and support from an educator and courage on the part of the learner who must undergo the discomfort inherent in such challenge.

Inevitably, most learners display some trepidation about the demands of study and evaluation and are concerned about how long it has been since they were in school. Their confidence is guarded, at best, and their fears are usually out of proportion to the reality they soon discover. However, meeting the expressed needs of these learners, teaching in a manner that draws on their life and work experiences, and conducting the classroom in a learning-centered manner are insufficient to foster the type of change that most educators would like to inspire (Taylor, 2006). Well beyond the confidence gained in successful achievement of an academic degree, growth-fostering developmental change asks more from learners as well as their educators by requiring a transformation in perspective (Dirkx, 1998; Kegan, 2000; Schwartz, 2009).

This chapter is about developing relationships between teachers and learners as a way of supporting growth-fostering change for those willing to take the risks involved. In it, I explore the potential for transformative learning in relationship to the higher education environment in which midlife and midcareer professionals return to earn a master's degree in adult learning, drawing on my experience of teaching in the Adult Learning program at Virginia Commonwealth University. Learning in relationship is defined here as *relational practice* according to the concepts of relational cultural theory, or RCT, (Jordan, Kaplan, Miller, Stiver, & Surrey, 1991; Miller & Stiver, 1997) and relational mentoring (Fletcher & Ragins, 2007; Ragins & Verbos, 2007). A small, but growing, body of literature on authenticity in teaching (Cranton, 2006a, 2006b; Cranton & Carusetta, 2004) also contributes to an understanding of the role of relationships in transformative learning theory as described by Mezirow (1991, 2000).

Relational cultural theory is a model of human growth developed by psychologists and psychiatrists at the Stone Center for Developmental Services and Studies at Wellesley College over the past three decades (Fletcher & Ragins, 2007; Jordan et al., 1991; Miller & Stiver, 1997). According to RCT, practices that include authenticity, mutual empathy, and mutual empowerment enhance psychological growth (Jordan et al., 1991; Miller & Stiver, 1997). Schwartz (2009) was among the first to apply RCT to explore the relational practices of teachers acting with developmental intentions toward students in master's level education in the social sciences. My intention is to contribute to the literature about relationships for enhancing transformative learning and add to a perspective that scholars have asserted is underdeveloped in the literature (Taylor, 1998, 2007). I believe that it is through relational practices involved in mutual empathy and mutual empowerment, and the mentoring episodes that characterize relational mentoring, that educators can realize the hope of transformative learning.

TRANSFORMATIVE LEARNING THEORY AND THE NATURE OF ADULT DEVELOPMENT

More than 30 years ago, Jack Mezirow (1978) described a nascent theory of adult learning after researching the experiences of 83 women returning to college during the era of the Women's Movement. Since then, transformative learning theory has evolved to become the most researched and discussed theory in the field of adult learning (Taylor, 2007). Mezirow (1991, 2000) describes the constructivist nature of transformative learning as the epistemology of how adults learn to think for themselves rather than act upon the assimilated beliefs, values, feelings, and judgments of others.

In transformative learning theory, revision to an adult's meaning perspectives, or frames of reference, is the central feature in adult development, a process that is conscious and intentional. Transformative learning occurs through critical reflection and critical self-reflection on the assumptions and expectations that filter sense impressions and involves cognitive, affective, and conative dimensions of learning (Mezirow, 2000). Since a frame of reference provides the context for making meaning and represents cultural paradigms assimilated unintentionally, revising it can often be an emotionally painful, intense, or even disorienting learning experience for many learners (Mezirow, 1991, 2000). Through the years, core concepts inherent in transformative learning theory have remained unchanged. Yet, as scholars continue to research and build upon this theory, new insights have expanded upon the nature of critical reflection and learners' experiences by emphasizing dialogue, relationships, and the importance of emotions in learning (Dirkx, 1998; Taylor, 2007, 2009).

Kegan (2000) implored educators to distinguish between learning that is informative, resulting in an increase in knowledge or change in behavior, and transformative learning that results in a revised perspective or worldview. Expressing a theoretical stance grounded in constructive developmental psychology, Kegan (2000) believes that most of the desirable goals that educators have for their learners—changes in confidence, self-perception, motives for learning, and self-esteem—all occur within existing frames of reference and, as such, take place without a transformation of perspective. Instead, transformative learning requires development in the very way that an adult comes to know—an epistemological shift in how knowledge is constructed.

Kegan (2000) asserts that this developmental shift begins in adolescence with potential to develop through five levels of increasing sophistication. The critical transformation for most adults is movement from the third to fourth level in Kegan's schema, away from other-directed actions, values, and expectations—the dictates of family, friends, and culture—toward development of an internal, self-authorized belief system (p. 59). Such journeys are inherently risky for both learners and their educators since learners must give up some cherished ways of being in the world, and educators must provide the intellectual challenges to their perspectives that enable them to do so (Brookfield, 2006; Kegan, 2000). In hope of fostering transformative learning, educators need to be cognizant of what constitutes appropriate developmental challenge as well as the ethics of teaching for change (Brookfield, 2006; Ettling, 2006). Most importantly, as Dirkx (1998) notes, an educator needs to be sensitive to change that is at work within the individual to support a growth process that has already begun:

> It would be naïve and silly for us as educators to think that we can always foster transformation.... When we seek transformative learning as the aim of what we do, we attend to processes of change already at work within persons.... Some would lead us to believe that transformative learning is or can be a fairly common experience among adult learners, but it is my sense that transformative learning, as it has been defined here, is relatively rare within settings of adult education.... How we consciously and willfully attend to its presence is perhaps the greatest challenge we face as educators and learners. It requires careful, thoughtful, and constant attention to inner work on the parts of both the learner and the educator. (pp. 10–11)

Not all learners are ready for transformative learning, but for those who are, the educator has an ethical responsibility to be self-aware as well as aware of what one is asking of the learner (Ettling, 2006). Scholars have found that authentic relationships with learners hold this potential to foster growth and change (Cranton, 2006a; Cranton & Carusetta, 2004; Frego, 2006).

AUTHENTICITY IN TRANSFORMATIVE LEARNING

Establishing authentic relationships with learners has emerged as a core element of transformative learning theory as it has evolved over the years (Taylor, 2009). What does authenticity look like in practice? In research that explored the nature of authenticity in teaching, Cranton and Carusetta (2004) found that the most often discussed theme among the experiences of 22 faculty members in their study was the relationship between the teacher and student. They came to understand authenticity as a multifaceted concept that was dependent upon the nature of dialogue exchanged. Based on this study, Cranton (2006a) has defined the components of authenticity as (a) having a strong self-awareness of who we are as teachers and as people, (b) being aware of the characteristics and preferences of learners and how these relate to our own characteristics, (c) developing a relationship with learners that fosters genuineness and openness, (d) being aware of the context and constraints of teaching, and (e) engaging in critical reflection and self-reflection to become aware of underlying assumptions about teaching and from where these assumptions originate (pp. 6–7).

Brookfield (2006) also explored authenticity in teaching, describing the necessary tension created by the power differential between teacher and student, asserting that the teacher needs to be both an ally as well as an authority in the classroom. Students, he claims, want to be able to trust that the teacher is an ally who has no hidden agendas or intentions to misuse power within the position, but students also expect the expertise of an authority who has both practical experience as well as scholarly knowledge of the subject matter. According to Brookfield, a teacher expresses authentic behavior through congruent words and actions; she involves full disclosure by making public the criteria, expectations, and assumptions that are guiding her behavior. In his view, teaching for transformation demands responsiveness that demonstrates caring, genuine helpfulness, and behaviors that reveal the teacher as a "flesh and blood human being with a life and identity outside the classroom" (p. 10). It is Brookfield's position that the difficulty of teaching for transformation is embedded in the *appropriate* use of power, which requires that teachers push students to engage with material that challenges them intellectually, often contradicting many of their previously unexamined assumptions about how the world works.

Others who write about transformative learning (Cranton, 2006a; Frego, 2006; Schwartz, 2009) affirm the idea that teaching for development occurs by being in relationship with the learner in a manner that allows intentions, actions, and words to flow from a core of intellectual and emotional honesty. Frego (2006) believes that authenticity emanates from an educator's values and reflects the essence of the person. Relational cultural theory, as espoused by Stone Center scholars (Jordan et al., 1991), explores how who we are as a person can contribute to the development of others in a mutually growth-enhancing process that empowers both individuals in the relationship.

RELATIONAL PRACTICE AND RELATIONAL MENTORING IN FOSTERING DEVELOPMENT

Miller and Stiver (1997) assert that Stone Center researchers originally sought to describe how women grow through relationships with the idea that "certain psychological activities that are vital to the health of all human beings occur in growth-fostering relationships" (p. 21). Over time, RCT has evolved to include contextual, cultural, and sociopolitical issues that are central to healthy human functioning (Jordan, 2000). Building on the seminal works of Jean Baker Miller's (1976) *Toward a New Psychology of Women*; Carol Gilligan's (1982) *In a Different Voice*; and Belenky, Clinchy, Goldberger, and Tarule's (1997) *Women's Ways of Knowing*, RCT has been extended to describe studies of relational practice in the workplace (Fletcher, 1999), relational mentoring (Fletcher & Ragins, 2007; Ragins & Verbos, 2007), and interactions between teachers and their students in higher education (Schwartz, 2009).

Relational cultural theory includes several core tenets. Among them is the idea that people grow through and toward relationship throughout the lifespan, a perspective that contrasts markedly with traditional theories of adult development that assert growth as a process of individuation, separation, and increasing autonomy (Jordan et al., 1991; Miller, 1976). RCT posits that development is an influence process that occurs through mutual empathy and mutual empowerment (Jordan et al., 1991). In this theoretical stance, movement toward mutuality and interdependence rather than toward separation and individuation characterizes mature adult functioning (Jordan, 2000; Jordan et al., 1991; Miller & Stiver, 1997).

Within RCT, mutual empathy is movement in dialogue that occurs when individuals build upon the feelings and thoughts of each other in such a way as to extend ideas beyond what either individual originally expressed (Jordan et al., 1991; Miller & Stiver, 1997). In a study of transformative learning among midcareer professional women, Carter (2002) found developmental relationships that exhibited love and emotional caring for the other person to contain this aspect of enlarging the person as well as the fullness of ideas expressed. The dialogic exchange described as mutual empathy in RCT is not a passive process of listening and responding, but an active engagement of each person in entering the emotional and cognitive world of the other (Jordan, 2000). When this happens, new ideas emerge through the interpersonal exchange (Miller & Stiver, 1997).

Miller and Stiver (1997) assert that mutual empathy brings about mutual empowerment as each person experiences a positive, growth-enhancing connection with the other.

Stone Center scholars (Fletcher & Ragins, 2007; Jordan, 2000; Miller & Stiver, 1997) have elaborated upon the characteristics of mutual empowerment resulting from this empathic engagement with another person: *zest*, the feeling of aliveness and increased vitality that comes from a real sense of connection; *action*, in which individuals both affect and are affected by the other; *knowledge of self*, the self-awareness that results from expression of both thoughts and feelings; enhanced *sense of worth* as a person is recognized and acknowledged by another; and *desire for more connection*, which occurs as the exchange generates motivation and energy to expand connections to others (Fletcher & Ragins, 2007, p. 386). As a consequence of being in a mutually empowering relationship, Jordan (2000) claims that people "come into their own wholeness" as they begin to appreciate the gifts they have to offer, further enhancing their capacity for empathy (p. 1015).

This concept of mutuality in RCT differs from the reciprocity, equality, or disclosure often present in most helping relationships (Jordan, 2000; Schein, 1999). It reflects the quality of engagement in the relationship and an attitude of being real and authentic with the other person (Jordan, 2000). As Jordan notes, there are no special techniques or strategies for relational practice in therapy or in life other than a constant awareness of the impact that one has on the other person and a way of being that is authentic, open, and trusting (p. 1015).

Relational practice, as described in RCT, has also become a way of thinking about what occurs in the specific moment-to-moment interactions termed "mentoring episodes" in a mentoring relationship, whether this occurs in the workplace (Fletcher & Ragins, 2007; Ragins & Verbos, 2007) or in an educational setting (Schwartz, 2009). Schwartz's (2009) study of 10 matched pairs of recent master's degree graduates and their teachers revealed brief, meaningful interactions that contained all of the elements of mutual empowerment: increased vitality and zest, motivation and action, an increased sense of self-worth, and a desire for further connection. She found that these transpired in typical classroom and advising situations and were not necessarily embedded in a long-term student-teacher mentoring relationship.

Fletcher and Ragins (2007) define the skills needed for *relational mentoring*: *authenticity*, the ability to access and describe one's own thoughts and feelings; *fluid expertise*, the ability to acknowledge help and give credit to others with no loss of self-esteem, moving easily from expert to nonexpert roles; *empathic competence*, the ability to understand another's experience and perspectives; *emotional competence*, the ability to understand, interpret, and use emotional data; *vulnerability*, the ability to admit "not knowing" and to seek help when needed; *holistic thinking*, the ability to join thinking with feeling and acting; and *response-ability*, the ability to hold one's own perspective while at the same time permitting mutual influence (p. 384). To express mutual empathy requires these interpersonal skills as well as a high degree of self-awareness and sense of presence on the part of mentors as well as the mentees. At its core, relational practice appears to be about making meaning of experiences in such a way that the dialogue that occurs between individuals is growth enhancing, whether this occurs in an ongoing relationship between teacher and student or in the multitude of brief interactions that a teacher has with any learner encountered during the day.

DEVELOPING RELATIONAL PRACTICE IN THE ADULT LEARNING CLASSROOM

How do I as a teacher intentionally attempt to engage in relational practice with learners? For me, relational practice enacts a deeply held philosophy of practice about working with adult learners. This philosophy includes values, beliefs, and attitudes that have developed over many years as I have reflected on what makes for a stimulating learning environment and what contributes to the feeling of aliveness that I have when I am in the presence of those who want to learn with me. The theoretical model of RCT has given me a new way to think about what I do, however, so that I am now more self-aware of the potential for mutual influence and how it occurs. It also provides me with a vocabulary and the conceptual framework for understanding the intersecting dimensions of authenticity, mentoring, and the role of relationships in transformative learning. RCT expresses the influence I believe I have on my students' development as learners and the mutually empowering influence that they have on me. Schwartz (2009) attributes this to the bidirectional nature of teaching and learning with master's level students who bring a wealth of professional knowledge that energizes and helps keep their professors current in their fields.

My experiences occur in the graduate classroom, teaching, advising, and interacting with primarily midlife and midcareer learners. Most of these students are also adult educators, or aspiring ones, in a variety of contexts in corporate, nonprofit, higher education, and community-based settings. Cranton (2006a) describes three relational stances that an educator can take with regard to learners: respectful distance (focusing on the subject matter and learning goals), collaborative and collegial (viewing learners as current or future colleagues who have expertise to share), and closeness (coming to know each other as people outside of the classroom). My own approach falls somewhere between the second and third relational stance that Cranton describes. Students have been in my home for year-end graduation celebrations, they know something about my life and family, and I am aware of many aspects of their personal lives. We also engage as collaborators; I view them as potential (and some are actual) colleagues with each of us having expertise that benefits the other. This does not negate at all our mutual awareness of the differing roles we occupy in higher education. Instead, the traditional power distance between student and teacher, always operating tacitly as subtext, infuses our learning with respect for the nature of the contribution that each of us brings. When the atmosphere in the classroom is one of collegiality, I have found that my challenges are not personal affronts, but they become the impetus for further dialogue. Challenge comes not only from me to learners in the form of questioning assumptions, but learners also provide alternative viewpoints for each other's consideration. I know that they take seriously these challenges to their thinking because they write about them and the effect they have had on their thinking when engaging in reflective practice.

Reflective practice is the mainstay of our master's degree program, and learners express this in many different ways, including through blogs kept as learning journals. In one of the first courses in the program on adult learning theories, students write educational autobiographies as histories of informal and formal learning and describe the significant role other people have played in their learning experiences. They reflect on their chosen professions and the sometimes circuitous route by which they arrived where they are today, and they consider the nature of adult development across the lifespan. They know ahead of time that they will share these with their classmates, so they write only what they are comfortable in disclosing. Students post these biographies on a class wiki, a collaboratively authored Web site, open only to class members. The class as a whole then engages in collective meaning-making about what constitutes learning in adulthood. It is an eye-opening experience for all of us to see the ebb and flow of learning trajectories, with poignant moments infused with emotions of hurt, challenge, and joy. This is the first of many opportunities that they will have in the program to get to know each other as individuals with unique backgrounds, building authentic relationships with each other, and viewing theory through the lenses of personal and collective experience.

Another class in Learning in Groups and Teams has a first-night experience in which each student brings a small box of personal artifacts to describe to the group members who will be part of the student's project team for the semester. While each learner has the freedom to choose what to include and what to reveal about the artifacts and their personal meaning, the effect is one of building community so that project team members begin to develop group cohesion and understand its importance for productive teamwork. As learners advance through the program, they take on more of the facilitation role, leading class dialogues and presenting content as they experiment with different learning strategies, design exercises, and solicit peer feedback. At the end of the program, learners have the option of writing a paper or creating a digital story to reflect on a significant learning experience or a revised perspective that has been personally meaningful. Digital stories are a form of narrative storytelling created with images, voice narration, and music to convey an emotionally intense experience in a 3- to 5- minute multimedia vignette (Rossiter & Garcia, 2010). Although our roles in the classroom are different, we all share in the response-ability (Fletcher & Ragins, 2007) for learning that engages, challenges, supports, and enlarges individual perspectives. The fluidity of expertise in our roles means that sometimes my students know more than I do about a given topic. On these occasions, I find it takes discipline to relinquish traditional teacher expectations and get out of the way so that learning can occur.

When I see resistance to what we are learning, whether it results from a reaction to assigned readings or to the dialogue in class, I know we have touched on a point of view or perspective that a learner holds dearly. It is an indicator that we are doing what we should be doing to create the potential for transformation by engaging in the struggle of conflicting ideas, feelings, or emotions that may ultimately enlarge both individual and collective thinking. To achieve this, as Mezirow (1991, 2000) has stated, learners must be free from coercion to participate in informed discourse. This requires that the classroom be a sacred space in which learners feel safe enough to trust each other and to trust me as their teacher so that they risk saying what might otherwise be too embarrassing or threatening to express. Many powerful stories emerge when learners have the courage to say what they believe and also recognize where their understanding falls short.

If we are fortunate and committed to the hard work of considering alternative ways of thinking, feeling, and acting in the world, for some the learning is transformative, resulting in the type of epistemological shift that Kegan (2000) has so aptly described as developmental. I see such learning occurring more often through dialogue rather than rational discourse, however. It builds upon the foundation of authentic relationships in an environment characterized by mutual empathy in which each person contributes feelings and thoughts to generate a new or revised understanding. When this happens, the dialogue among teacher and learners becomes mutually empowering.

A RESEARCH AGENDA FOR RELATIONAL PRACTICE IN PROMOTING TRANSFORMATIVE LEARNING

Particularly noteworthy when considering the potential of relational practice to foster transformative learning is Mezirow's (2000) assertion that development in adulthood is a learning process that occurs through "expanded awareness, critical reflection, validating discourse, and reflective action as one moves toward a fuller realization of agency" (p. 25). This conception of agency, aligned with traditional concepts of adult development and conceived as separation, individuation, and increased autonomy, occurs throughout adult life either at particular ages and stages or through transition periods (Merriam, 2005). While Mezirow (2000) has responded to critics' assertion that the role of relationships is underdeveloped in transformative learning theory, and Taylor (2009) claims relational learning as an emerging core concept within the theory, there is a need for more research that examines the role of relationships.

An extensive body of literature has developed on mentoring relationships during the past two decades (Daloz, 1999; Kram, 1988; Ragins & Kram, 2007). The concept of relational mentoring (Fletcher & Ragins, 2007) now offers a bridge for connecting transformative learning theory to the power of relational practice to explore learning that results in a developmental shift in perspective. The concepts of mutual empathy and mutual empowerment inherent in RCT can add to what transformative learning scholars (Brookfield, 2006; Cranton, 2006a, 2006b; Cranton & Carusetta, 2004) have discovered through research and practice about authenticity in teaching, but these have yet to be examined through research on relational practice. This presents an opportunity for exploring relational practice and the outcomes of relational mentoring as outlined by Fletcher and Ragins (2007) vis-à-vis the literature on authenticity and the role of relationships in fostering transformative learning.

CONCLUDING THOUGHTS

Relational practice is a conscious, intentional effort on the part of an educator to embody a developmental stance in the classroom, grounded in RCT and concepts of authenticity in teaching, but it is not without challenges for both educators and learners. As learners, students must be mature enough to accept the challenges of their own growth-in-relationship, which can mean relinquishing past behaviors and adopting new ones. They must do the hard work of learning in graduate education by coming prepared, ready to engage with their teachers and fellow learners as peers, unafraid to venture into uncertain territory to contribute meaning-making that is in transition (Schwartz, 2009). When adults experience mutual empathy and mutual empowerment, they are making authentic connections through their abilities to access and express both feelings and thoughts in a manner that enlarges the connection between individuals as well as the ideas expressed (Fletcher & Ragins, 2007; Jordan et al., 1991; Miller & Stiver, 1997).

This requires intentional effort and insight into the emotional and affective processes at work within individuals.

Brookfield (2006), Cranton (2006a, 2006b), Dirkx (1998), and Taylor (2006) have all identified the self-awareness needed by an educator who wishes to teach for change and the openness and trusting environment necessary for learners to feel safe and extend themselves into new or unknown territory. For students who do experience learning that is transformative, the difference between the student who begins a program of study seeking content knowledge and the one who walks across the stage at graduation can be profound. Clark (1993) describes it poignantly with the statement that "transformational learning shapes people; they are different afterward, in ways both they and others can recognize" (p. 47).

Relational practice holds potential to foster growth for teachers and learners through mutual empowerment as co-learners. Thus, the transformative potential of relational practice merits consideration by educators for their own personal development as well as the development of their students. Institutions of higher education, like other workplace settings, often undervalue relational practice (Fletcher, 1999; Schwartz, 2009). Faculty labor under competing priorities, and the demands of teaching, research, and service often pull in directions other than toward time invested in relationships with learners. Subtle (and not-so-subtle) pressures inherent within institutional systems of higher education—student evaluations of faculty performance, promotion and tenure policies, grading policies, and in some situations, expectations for grade distributions—present challenges to the teacher who wants to teach for transformation (Hunt, 2006). As Brookfield (2006) and Hunt (2006) have noted, engaging in behaviors and teaching strategies that challenge a learner's thinking can be risky business for educators when student satisfaction is a measure of performance. Transformative learning can also be a disquieting experience for a learner at the time it occurs. Ultimately, however, such growth yields rewards that extend far beyond the classroom for those who are willing to take the journey.

REFERENCES

Belenky, M. F., Clinchy, B. M., Goldberger, N. R., & Tarule, J. M. (1997). *Women's ways of knowing: The development of self, voice, and mind*. New York, NY: Basic. (Original work published 1986)

Brookfield, S. D. (2006, Fall). Authenticity and power. *New Directions for Adult and Continuing Education, 111*, 5–16. doi:10.1002/ace.223

Carter, T. J. (2002). The importance of talk to midcareer women's development: A collaborative inquiry. *Journal of Business Communication, 39*, 55–91.

Clark, M. C. (1993, Spring). Transformational learning. *New Directions for Adult and Continuing Education, 57*, 47–57. doi:10.1002/ace.36719935707

Cranton, P. (2006a, Spring). Fostering authentic relationships in the transformative classroom. *New Directions for Adult and Continuing Education, 109,* 5–13. doi:10.1002/ace.203

Cranton, P. (2006b, Fall). Integrating perspectives on authenticity. *New Directions for Adult and Continuing Education, 111,* 83–87. doi:10.1002/ace.230

Cranton, P., & Carusetta, E. (2004). Developing authenticity as a transformative process. *Journal of Transformative Education, 2*(4), 276–293. doi:10.117/1541344604267898

Daloz, L. A. (1999). *Mentor: Guiding the journey of adult learners.* San Francisco, CA: Jossey-Bass.

Dirkx, J. M. (1998). Transformative learning theory in the practice of adult education: An overview. *PAACE Journal of Lifelong Learning, 7,* 1–14.

Ettling, D. (2006, Spring). Ethical demands of transformative learning. *New Directions for Adult and Continuing Education, 109,* 59–67. doi:10.1002.ace.208

Fletcher, J. K. (1999). *Disappearing acts: Gender, power, and relational practice at work.* Cambridge, MA: MIT Press.

Fletcher, J. K., & Ragins, B. R. (2007). Stone Center relational cultural theory: A window on relational mentoring. In B. R. Ragins & K. E. Kram (Eds.), *The handbook of mentoring at work: Theory, research, and practice* (pp. 373–399). Thousand Oaks, CA: Sage.

Frego, K. A. (2006, Fall). Authenticity and relationships with students. *New Directions for Adult and Continuing Education, 111,* 41–50. doi:10.1002/ace.226

Gilligan, C. (1982). *In a different voice.* Cambridge, MA: Harvard University Press.

Herman, L., & Mandell, A. (2004). *From teaching to mentoring: Principle and practice, dialogue and life in adult education.* New York, NY: RoutledgeFalmer.

Hunt, R. (2006, Fall). Institutional constraints on authenticity in teaching. *New Directions for Adult and Continuing Education, 111,* 51–62. doi:10.1002/ace.227

Jordan, J. V. (2000, August). The role of mutual empathy in relational-cultural therapy. *Journal of Clinical Psychology, 56*(8), 1005–1016.

Jordan, J. V., Kaplan, A., Miller, J. B., Stiver, I., & Surrey, J. (1991). *Women's growth in connection.* New York, NY: Guilford.

Kasworm, C. E. (2008, Winter). Emotional challenges of adult learners in higher education. *New Directions for Adult and Continuing Education, 120,* 27–34. doi:10.1002/ace.313

Kegan, R. (2000). What "form" transforms? A constructive-developmental approach to transformative learning. In J. Mezirow & Associates (Eds.), *Learning as transformation: Critical perspectives on a theory in progress* (pp. 35–69). San Francisco, CA: Jossey-Bass.

Kram, K. E. (1988). *Mentoring at work: Developmental relationships in organizational life.* Lanham, MD: University Press.

Merriam, S. B. (2005). How adult life transitions foster learning and development. *New Directions for Adult and Continuing Education, 108,* 3–13. doi:10.1002/ace.193

Mezirow, J. (1978). Perspective transformation. *Adult Education, 28,* 100–110.

Mezirow, J. (1991). *Transformative dimensions of adult learning.* San Francisco, CA: Jossey-Bass.

Mezirow, J. (2000). Learning to think like an adult: Core concepts of transformation theory. In J. Mezirow & Associates (Eds.), *Learning as transformation: Critical perspectives on a theory in progress* (pp. 3–33). San Francisco, CA: Jossey-Bass.

Miller, J. B. (1976). *Toward a new psychology of women.* Boston, MA: Beacon.

Miller, J. B., & Stiver, I. P. (1997). *The healing connection: How women form relationships in therapy and in life.* Boston, MA: Beacon.

Ragins, B. R., & Kram, K. E. (Eds.). (2007). *The handbook of mentoring at work: Theory, research, and practice.* Thousand Oaks, CA: Sage.

Ragins, B. R., & Verbos, A. K. (2007). Positive relationships in action: Relational mentoring and mentoring schemas in the workplace. In J. E. Dutton & B. R. Ragins (Eds.), *Exploring positive relationships at work: Building a theoretical and research foundation* (pp. 91–116). Mahwah, NJ: Lawrence Erlbaum.

Rossiter, M., & Garcia, P. A. (2010, Summer). Digital storytelling: A new player on the narrative field. *New Directions for Adult and Continuing Education, 126*, 37–48. doi:10.1002/ace.370

Schein, E. H. (1999). *Process consultation revisited: Building the helping relationship.* Reading, MA: Addison-Wesley.

Schwartz, H. L. (2009). *Thankful learning: A grounded theory study of relational practice between master's students and professors* (Unpublished doctoral dissertation). Antioch University, Yellow Springs, OH. (AAT3367777)

Taylor, E. W. (1998). *The theory and practice of transformative learning: A critical review* (Information Series No. 374). Washington, DC: Office of Educational Research and Improvement (ERIC Document Reproduction Service No. ED423422). Retrieved from http://www.eric.ed.gov:80/ERICWebPortal/detail?accno=ED423422

Taylor, E. W. (2006, Spring). The challenge of teaching for change. *New Directions for Adult and Continuing Education, 109*, 91–95. doi:10/1002/ace.211

Taylor, E. W. (2007). An update of transformative learning theory: A critical review of the empirical research (1999–2005). *International Journal of Lifelong Education, 26*(2), 173–191. doi:10.1080/02601370701219475

Taylor, E. W. (2009). Fostering transformative learning. In J. Mezirow, E. W. Taylor, & Associates (Eds.), *Transformative learning in practice: Insights from community, workplace, and higher education* (pp. 3–17). San Francisco, CA: Jossey-Bass.

CHAPTER 7

SPIRITUAL AUTOBIOGRAPHY

A Transformative Journey for a Counselor in Training

Michelle Kelley Shuler and Katrina Cook

Transformative pedagogy refers to the interactions between teacher and student that foster collaborative efforts resulting in emotional and educational growth. The transformative educator operates as a guide to the student whose journey is to explore, investigate, and challenge personal values, beliefs, and assumptions (Scofield, Saginak, Reljic, & Harper, 2009; Tisdell, 2003). The nurturing guide, whose purpose is to help students transform previous self-concepts into newer understandings of the self, closely watches over students' experiences during this journey. The processes involved in the transformation open our hearts and minds to deeper meanings and encourage ongoing development of and integration of the self with others and the community.

Transformative learning theory emerged from the adult education literature. Its origins stem from the works of Jack Mezirow (1978, 1991, 1995a, 1995b) and provide a framework of the need for human beings to understand the meaning of their experiences. According to Cranton, transforma-

---

Pathways to Transformation, pages 97–110
Copyright © 2012 by Information Age Publishing
All rights of reproduction in any form reserved.

tive learning has evolved "into a comprehensive and complex description of how learners construe, validate, and reformulate the meaning of their experience" (1994, p. 22). Central to this process of reformulation of meaning is the concept of critical reflection (Taylor, 1998). When students engage in critical reflection, they are closely examining their past life experiences which, according to Mezirow (1991), allows for a transformation of perspectives. "Perspective transformation is the process of becoming critically aware of how and why our assumptions have come to constrain the way we perceive, understand, and feel about our world" (p. 167). When students participate in critical reflection, they have the opportunity to free themselves from such constraints, through transformative learning, and develop perspectives that are much more inclusive, discriminating, and integrated.

Facilitators in adult education contexts use transformative learning to foster learners' confidence in thinking independently. Mezirow (2000) considers the capacity or state of acting out of individual power to be a key goal of transformational work; however, achievement of this goal does not occur without reframing of the assumptions actively constructed by the individual that give meaning to situations. Brookfield (2000) states that assumptions in need of examination might include those about power and dominant ideologies that shape our everyday relationships and practices. Transformational Learning, therefore, argues "failure to reflect on one's beliefs and understanding about the world ensures that they will continue to exert undue influence on one's thinking and behavior during social interactions" (Forster, McColl, & Fardella, 2007, p. 41).

Although transformational learning theory is not a theory of counseling, it does have relevance for counselor education and the training of counselors. Scofield et al. (2009) recognize transformative pedagogy in counselor education as possibly having profound implications for instructors, supervisors, students, and clients. They suggest that the inclusion of transformative learning in counselor training increases the co-construction of knowledge between the instructor and student, which in turn leads to increased student empowerment and self-efficacy. Self-efficacy is a prevalent theme in counselor development and has profound implications for counselors' clinical functioning in the areas of cognitive, affective, and behavioral responses during counseling sessions (Hanson, 2006; Larson, 1998; Larson & Daniels, 1998; Lent, Hill, & Hoffman, 2003). Such findings suggest counselor trainees with reasonably high self-efficacy tend to feel calmer and remain more flexible. They also report less anxiety, greater positive affect, and more favorable skill usage. Incorporating aspects of transformative learning in counselor education, as suggested by Scofield et al. (2009), facilitates the personal and professional development of counseling students. Basic student outcomes in counselor training include the capacity for critical thinking and self-reflection (Hoshmand, 2004), as well as the affective and deeply personal aspects of transformative learning (Hansman, Jackson, Grant, & Spencer, 1999). Although there is little research reported on observed deep personal shifts as a result of transformative education efforts in counselor training (Hoshmand, 2004), some have suggested change in a frame of reference as change in worldview (Trevino, 1996). Examination of narrative data from student self-reflective journals about their learning experiences is a potential means of exploring such changes in worldview (Coleman, 1996; Halen-Faber, 1997).

THE ROLE OF SPIRITUALITY IN TRANSFORMATIVE EDUCATION

Recently, several scholars have supported the expansion of Mezirow's concept of critical reflection to go beyond the cognitive realm to include spiritual dimensions, as well as emotional and situational dimensions (English, 2005; English, Fenwick, & Parsons, 2003; Forster et al., 2007; Kovan & Dirkx, 2003; Kroth & Boverie, 2000; Tisdell, 2000; Vanier, 1997). When referring to the relationship between social worker and client, Vanier (1997) argues that spirituality is fundamental to the transformational process. Vanier also speaks to the importance of the individual process, stating that those who had engaged in the transformational process were more likely to provide appropriate support for their clients. Perhaps Tisdell (2003) best stated the importance of spirituality in the lives of adult learners when she wrote "Spirituality is a major organizing principle in the lives [of learners], and perhaps in the lives of many who are trying to attend to cultural issues in learners' lives in adult education" (p. 3).

How students see themselves and others in relation to spiritual beliefs can be likened to a frame of reference that Mezirow (1991, 1995b) states encompasses cognitive, conative, and emotional components. According to Mezirow (1995a), we transform our frames of reference through critical reflection on those assumptions, which form the basis of our beliefs and values.

THE ROLE OF SPIRITUALITY IN COUNSELOR EDUCATION

Parallel to the recent interest in the incorporation of spirituality in transformative learning is the increased infusion of spirituality in counselor education (Cashwell & Young, 2005; Curtis & Glass, 2002; Faiver, Ingersoll, O'Brien, & McNally, 2001; Hammer, 2006; Myers & Willard, 2003; Rose, Westfeld, & Ansley, 2001). Self-awareness of one's own spirituality is critical to the process of counselor training and competence (Cashwell & Young, 2005; Curtis & Glass, 2002; Faiver et al., 2001). A counselor's awareness of his or her own belief system and values allows for the opportunity to examine how these systems might affect personal and professional development as well as the development of the client. Furthermore, gaining insight into one's own belief system creates the possibility of recognizing similarities and differences between the counselor and that of the client. Lack of self-knowledge in this area may create transference or countertransference to arise within the counseling process (Faiver et al., 2001). The integration of spiritual development exercises could enhance the counselor-in-training's spiritual self-awareness. According to McLennan, Rochow, and Arthur (2001), spiritual self-awareness for counselors is a developmental process across four integrated areas. Spiritual self-awareness includes reflection on the development of one's value system across the life span and self-exploration of one's biases, fears, and prejudices. This awareness also incorporates investigations of how one integrates spirituality or religion into the counseling process and an ongoing self-assessment of how counselors understand their similarities and differences from the client's spiritual and religious values and beliefs (McLennan et al., 2001). Similar to Mezirow's (1995a) transformative learning theory, which recognizes the "process of effecting change in a *frame of reference*" (p. 5, emphasis in original), McLennan et al. (2001) suggest that as counselors progress through the developmental process, they form new perspectives, derive meaning from old perspectives, and increase understanding of how personal beliefs and values affect their work with clients (Hagadorn, 2005).

Curtis and Glass (2002) explored the effectiveness of increasing counseling students' confidence to manage issues related to spirituality in counseling through course instruction. Objectives of their course included expanding students' awareness of spirituality, increasing students' self-awareness of their own spirituality, and increasing counseling students' confidence in addressing spiritual issues through course instruction. Course activities designed to achieve these objectives included an in-class presentation on a related topic, engagement in specific techniques used to address spiritual issues with clients, keeping a journal, and a spiritual autobiography. To assess whether this counseling class that specifically focused on spirituality reached its objectives, students completed a short, four-item questionnaire related to the course content and overall effectiveness of the course. Results indicate participation in this course effectively increased confidence in participants' ability to address spiritual issues with clients. Furthermore, class content seemed to decrease counseling students' judgmental thoughts related to clients who hold differing beliefs or values than the student. Because self-awareness is an important component in counselor development and growth, the authors imply that this additional time is necessary to allow for adequate processing and discussion related to spiritual self-awareness (Curtis & Glass, 2002).

In terms of increasing self-awareness, students seemed to indicate that more class time should be devoted to the spiritual autobiography exercise. Using a spiritual autobiography as experiential coursework is an example of an intervention designed to include spiritual self-reflection in the counselor training process. The spiritual autobiography is a semistructured self-assessment tool with the purpose of encouraging a "free-association response" (Faiver et al., 2001, p. 152) to questions about life experiences that influence spiritual development. Use of the spiritual autobiography engages students in a process of recalling events and experiences from their history. The process encourages students to contemplate how these events or circumstances influenced how they see themselves and others in relation to spiritual beliefs and values.

Incorporation of the spiritual autobiography in coursework provides an opportunity for counselors-in-training, at any level of development, to reflect upon and explore areas of development possibly previously unknown (Erwin, 2001). The review of personal history, which takes place during the writing of a spiritual autobiography, increases the opportunity for self-reflective assessment of one's own ideas and beliefs, which might result in gained insight into how and why beliefs exist as well as how beliefs may influence personal and professional choices. Mezirow (1995b) indicates that "self-reflection can lead to significant personal transformations" (p. 7).

Self-exploration of themes taken from a spiritual autobiography may help a counseling student to recognize personal characteristics, which could influence choices in personal and professional development. For example, themes such as "self" and "relation to others" represent characteristics important to the domain of attributes considered important for counselors to possess (Jennings & Skovholt, 1999).

RECOLLECTIONS OF MY SPIRITUAL AUTOBIOGRAPHY

As a doctoral student enrolled in a counselor education and supervision program, I (Michelle Shuler) recognized the importance of spiritual self-awareness in my development as a counselor. However, very few counselor education programs, including the one I enrolled in, offer courses in spirituality and religion, or provide course components or learning activities related to this area (Kelly, 1994). In response to the absence of available courses, a mentor professor and I developed an independent study course entitled, "Spiritual Interventions in Counseling," which would fulfill the needs of the university as well as meet my interests in exploring how my spirituality impacts my work as a counselor.

In the spirit of transformative learning (Mezirow, 1995b), one of the goals of the course was to increase my spiritual self-awareness through self-reflective practice. The course assignment of completing my own spiritual autobiography and identifying significant themes in that autobiography supported the goal of self-reflection. The purpose of the spiritual autobiography assignment was to provide a way to explore not only my immediate feelings but also explore how my spirituality has developed over the course of my lifetime. We chose to use a spiritual autobiography format suggested by Cashwell and Young (2005) to facilitate this exercise. This particular spiritual autobiography is a revised version of the format first suggested by Faiver et al. (2001), and included five content areas: (a) introductory statement, (b) spiritual themes, (c) spiritual influences, (d) life's lessons and, (e) personal conclusions.

The personal nature of this project brought up feelings of apprehension related to expressing significant circumstances and events from my life. Self-examination of these areas proved to be challenging and stressful. Much of the challenge and stress seemed based in fear of examining areas of consciousness that might be unknown. Furthermore, I experienced a significant amount of fear related to the ambiguity of working through an experiential exercise and discovering unexpected results. Therefore, a supportive emotional climate was essential for exploration of significant life circumstances to take place. In transformative learning, the responsibility of helping students become aware and critical of their own assumptions is a delicate and sensitive task placed on the teacher. The success of such tasks requires the establishment of situations free from judgment and coercion (Mezirow, 1995a) so that the student feels safe to explore potentially personal and sensitive content. Similarly, in counselor training, nurturing and supportive supervision is necessary to provide a balance between the challenge of bringing up personal and sensitive circumstances and working through meaning that has come from them. In my case, my instructor provided the challenge and nurturing support necessary to facilitate maximum growth and development for transformational learning to occur.

As discussed previously, transformative learning is the process of critically examining ones' beliefs, assumptions, and values, igniting a process of personal change known as *reframing* in perspective transformation (Mezirow, 1990). This transformation often follows some variation of 10 phases or stages beginning with a "disorienting dilemma" followed by "critical assessment of assumptions," and resulting in a reintegration into ones' life dictated by ones' "new perspective" (Mezirow, 2000). Such self-reflection is at the heart of counselor training, in particular the incorporation of spirituality in counseling. Therefore, for the purpose of this writing, Mezirow's (2000) transformative learning theory characterizes the process of writing the spiritual autobiography and identifying themes revealed through critical self-reflection. What follows is an exploration of my spiritual autobiography.

including excerpts from the autobiography, to give voice to my transformative experience as a counselor-in-training completing this assignment.

SPIRITUAL AUTOBIOGRAPHY TRANSFORMATIONS

The idea to write this autobiography developed from an independent study course entitled, "Spiritual Interventions in Counseling," supervised by Christine Lumadue, in which I (Michelle Shuler) was enrolled during my doctoral program in 2007. As part of the coursework, my instructor asked me to describe my spiritual experience. This is the first time someone asked me such a question, and it seemed to pose an interesting and disorienting dilemma as suggested by Mezirow's (2000) initial stage of transformation. As I rolled the question around in my head for a few minutes, my focus shifted quickly from my intellect to my heart. I wrote,

> My emotions stirred, and I felt a bit of reluctance to speak. But as the words began to flow from my thoughts, I felt a sense of importance and urgency in the need to explore this question. The feelings of apprehension seemed to come from the strength of the emotion behind the words. I wondered why, at this point in my life, I would become so emotional at the thought of expressing this aspect of my life. But intuitively I knew I was in a safe place to begin this process of exploration.

As the writing process continued throughout the semester, I noticed major themes emerging from my writing. My instructor suggested that once the autobiography was completed, reflection upon the themes that emerged could help me identify how certain themes might play important roles in my personal and professional development. After reflection upon the autobiography, I discovered four main themes. These were (a) moving beyond and reframing, (b) spirituality as a force, (c) finding peace in daily practice, and (d) spirituality as a reflection of self in the world.

Moving Beyond and Reframing

The first main theme identified was "moving beyond and reframing" childhood experiences and messages received from family about religion and spirituality. Reflection upon parental perspectives and influences characterized Mezirow's (2000) stage three, which is a critical assessment of assumptions. Self-reflection that related to previously held assumptions brought into awareness the power family and culture can have on the individuals' belief system. In my case, family influences led to a lack of connection with and disregard for the value of spirituality in my life. As a young adult, it became clear that old family belief systems no longer seemed appropriate, and change was necessary. I wrote,

> I have never thought before about how my parents' lives might have been different if they had been connected to some spiritual belief or practice. Instead they struggled to survive without the support and comfort provided by a spiritual community. What I do know is the message passed on to us was that "god couldn't help." How could God allow such horrible things to happen to us? I had nothing to even wonder about. I had no frame of reference to base any assumptions on. All I knew came from listening to my father criticize the intellect of anyone who based their meaning of life on an entity who's existence could be argued away with rational thought, and my mother who seemed to loath anything remotely related to someone else's happiness. This combination, added to my own hate and rage, led me to declare myself an atheist.

In addition to recognizing childhood influences and their impact on my values and beliefs, it became clear that along my spiritual journey, a confrontation with these old beliefs was necessary in order to reframe and move on. Looking back, it appears as if this "confrontation" finds representation in Mezirow's (2000) fifth stage, referred to as exploration of options for new roles, relationships, and actions. In retrospect, it is clear that moving beyond my parental influences was necessary for me to live a purposeful and happy life. The opportunity to reframe old belief systems into a personal sense of spirituality opened new doors for growth and development.

Spirituality as a Force

To me, miracles are forces of the universe that intervene in a person's life path, changing the course of events at just the right moment. In my spiritual autobiography, I wrote,

> As a self-declared atheist, I continued on the path of anger and cynicism established in my childhood. Shame and sadness permeated my life. I sunk deeper and deeper into depression not knowing what would happen to me. Then one day in 1988, a miracle happened. Today, I call it a miracle. At the time I just remember having hope for the first time in my life.

Sometimes I call these forces synchronicity. Synchronicity occurs when the universe aligns itself at just the right moment bringing about a message of how life could be. Self-insight comes from being open to receiving the delivery of this message. Following a spiritual force provided opportunity for professional growth. During this time, I received instruction from professors who introduced me to dream analysis, the writings of Carl Jung, and

Spiritual Autobiography ■ 105

the power of guided imagery. Each of these experiences led me to explore and analyze individual behavior and subsequently led to enhanced curiosity of my own behavior. Why do I behave the way I do? What were the events of my life that shape who I am today? For the first time, I began to examine who I was and what my beliefs were. I began to question things my family taught me and looked for new meaning in my life. Just as importantly, it appears as if I was "acquiring knowledge and skills for implementing one's plans" (stage 7) (Mezirow, 2000, p. 22).

Finding Peace in Daily Practice

The reflection of "Building competence and self-confidence in new roles and relationships" (stage 9) (Mezirow, 2000, p. 22) is evident in living my new life with compassion and empathy toward others. In my spiritual autobiography I wrote,

> In 1992, I moved to Lake City, Colorado. High in the San Juan mountain range, this little city is still pristine. Nestled in between two mountain passes, there is plenty of hiking, mountain biking, and outdoor play. This place would be my reconnection to the spiritual world of my childhood. As I explored the mountains, I experienced, for the first time in many years, a feeling of comfort and calmness. I felt centered, like I belonged there. I began to discover a calming of the mind allowing me to practice methods of meditation and guided imagery. I began to accept myself as a spiritual person who was connected to the earth and could draw energy and guidance from its spirit.

During this time, a sense of inner peace and confidence enriched my spiritual life with time to strengthen and solidify my beliefs and practices. Positive physical and mental health are by-products of this daily spiritual practice. Now, my daily practice continues to consist of exercise, attention to meditation and prayer, and willingness to recognize the need to let go of thought that might clutter the mind.

Spirituality as a Reflection of Self in the World

As stated in stage 10, "a reintegration into one's life on the basis of conditions dictated by one's new perspective" (Mezirow, 2000, p. 20), my experience of this stage is in the following words from my spiritual autobiography.

> Today as my spiritual life grows, I can see the significant changes that have taken place in my life. How I am as a person is different from how I was in the past. I don't think my spiritual life has changed who I am, but it has sig-

nificantly changed how I am in the world. I am far less cynical about life, and treat myself and others with much more respect. I am more capable of seeing others as people who are doing the best they can, given whatever their situation is. I approach life from a place of compassion and love, instead of blame and resentment.

My belief is that our spirit and soul are one and the same, and our souls connect to the world of spirit around us. We are a part of a much larger community of spiritual beings all traversing this universe on the path of healing.

REFLECTIONS ON THE SPIRITUAL AUTOBIOGRAPHY

The stages of transformation provided by Mezirow (2000) provided a structure to the process of examining the themes presented in my spiritual autobiography. This examination, through the lens of transformative learning, provided an opportunity to explore personal circumstances, relationships, and life events that significantly influenced my spiritual and religious development. Consistent with objectives of transformative learning, Bishop (1992) described how personal values influence every phase of therapy. According to Bishop, personal beliefs, values, biases, and prejudices that result from a personal developmental process can become a part of how professional counselors express themselves in clinical practice. Therefore, self-exploration is imperative for counselors who wish to integrate spirituality in the counseling process.

Similarly, my own exercise in self-reflection through the spiritual autobiography assignment helped me gain insight into how childhood events sparked a lifelong journey of seeking knowledge and understanding from a higher power. Prior to this time of self-reflection and exploration, I was unclear as to how my personal circumstances, relationships, and life events might influence my professional development. Exploration of the experiences that contributed to my spiritual development deepened my understanding of how those experiences influenced my choice to pursue a career in a helping profession. Through this insight, I have a deeper understanding of my personal and professional goals as an individual who seeks to help others. I have a better understanding of the counseling relationship and my role as an authentic partner within that relationship.

RECOMMENDATIONS AND CONCLUSIONS

Counselor education programs must begin to be more effective in addressing the integration of spirituality into counselor training and core curriculum. Use of the spiritual autobiography as a training tool in counselor education programs could prove to be very beneficial when used to enhance counselor development and increase awareness of characteristics identified as being integral with master counselors. Furthermore, transformative learning theory (Mezirow, 2000) provides a foundation for the pivotal role that learning experiences involving critical self-reflection can play in counselor training. Critical thinking skills and self-reflection, encouraged by counselor training programs, can ignite perspective transformational experiences, enhancing the affective and deeply personal experiences (Hoshmand, 2004) of counseling students.

Self-exploration and reflection of the themes presented in their spiritual autobiography can help students recognize how significant life events, certain personal beliefs and values, and past relationships have influenced their own spiritual development. Deeper understanding of these aspects may increase awareness of areas in which the client and counselor possess similarities and differences as well as areas in which the counselor may hold personal biases and judgments.

Use of the spiritual autobiography during counselor training coursework provides an opportunity for counselors-in-training, at any level of development, to reflect upon and explore areas of development possibly previously unknown. An informal exploration of my (Michelle Shuler's) experience with a spiritual autobiography provides anecdotal support that the use of spiritual autobiographies can benefit the critical reflection development of counselors-in-training. Self-exploration of themes taken from the spiritual autobiography may help counselors-in-training to recognize personal characteristics that could influence choices in personal and professional development.

AUTHOR NOTE

I (Michelle Shuler) would like to thank Christine Lumadue, who is now in private practice in San Antonio, Texas. Her supervision as the faculty of record for the Independent Study course taken during my doctoral program in the Department of Counseling, University of Texas at San Antonio supported the writing of the original spiritual autobiography.

REFERENCES

Bishop, D. R. (1992). Religious values as cross-cultural issues in counseling. *Counseling and Values, 36*(3), 179–191. doi: 10.1002/j.2161-007X.1992.tb00786.x

Brookfield, S. D. (2000). Adult cognition as a dimension of lifelong learning. In J. Field & M. Leicester (Eds.), *Lifelong learning: Education across the lifespan* (pp. 89–101). Philadelphia, PA: Falmer.

Cashwell, C. S., & Young, J. S. (2005). *Integrating spirituality and religion into counseling*. Alexandria, VA: American Counseling Association.
Coleman, H. L. K. (1996). Portfolio assessment of multicultural counseling competency. *The Counseling Psychologist, 24,* 216–229. doi:10.1177/0011000096242003
Cranton, P. (1994). *Understanding and promoting transformative learning: A guide for educators of adults.* San Francisco, CA: Jossey-Bass.
Curtis, R. C., & Glass, J. S. (2002). Spirituality and counseling class: A teaching model. *Counseling and Values, 47*(1), 3–12. doi: 10.1002/j.2161-007X.2002.tb00219.x
English, L. (2005). Historical and contemporary explorations of the social change and spiritual directions of adult education. *Teachers College Record, 107*(6), 1169–1192. doi:10.1111/j.1467-9620.2005.00509.x
English, L., Fenwick, T., & Parsons, J. (2003). *Spirituality of adult education and training.* Malabar, FL: Krieger.
Erwin, T. M. (2001). Encouraging the spiritual development of counseling students and supervisees: Using Fowler's stages of faith development. *The Educational Resources Information Center.* Retrieved from http://?/?edres.org/?eric.ED457473.htm
Faiver, C. F., Ingersoll, R. E., O'Brian, E., & McNally, C. (2001). *Explorations in counseling and spirituality.* Belmont, CA: Brooks/Cole.
Forster, D., McColl, M. A., & Fardella, J. (2007). Spiritual transformations in clinical relationships between social workers and individuals living with disabilities. *Journal of Religion and Social Work, 26,* 35–51. doi:10.1300/J377v26n01_03
Hagadorn, W. B. (2005). Counselor self-awareness and self-exploration of religious and spiritual beliefs: Know thyself. In C. S. Cashwell & J. S. Young (Eds.), *Integrating spirituality and religion into counseling: A guide to competent practice* (pp. 63–84). Alexandria, VA: American Counseling Association.
Halen-Faber, C. (1997). Encouraging critical reflection in preservice teacher education: A narrative of a personal learning journal. *New Directions in Adult and Continuing Education, 74,* 51–60.
Hammer, C. M. (2006). A phenomenological study of psychologists' experience of spiritual development as it relates to therapy practice. *Dissertation Abstracts International, 67*(10). (UMI No. 3238280)
Hansman, C. A., Jackson, M. H, Grant, D. F., & Spencer, D. E. (1999). Assessing graduate students' sensitivity to gender, race, equality, and diversity: Implications for curricular development. *College Student Journal, 33*(2), 261–268.
Hanson, M. G. (2006). *Counselor self-efficacy: Supervision contributions, impact on performance, and mediation of the relationship between supervision and performance.* Unpublished doctoral dissertation, Southern Illinois University, Carbondale.
Hoshmand, L. T. (2004). The transformative potential of counselor education. *Journal of Humanistic Counseling, Education and Development, 43,* 82–90.
Jennings, L., & Skovholt, T. M. (1999). The cognitive, emotional, and relational characteristics of master therapists. *Journal of Counseling Psychology, 46*(1), 3–11. doi:10.1037//0022-0167.46.1.3

Kelly, E. W. (1994). The role of religion and spirituality in counselor education: A national survey. *Counselor Education and Supervision, 33*(4), 227–237. doi:10.1002/j.1556-6978.1994.tb00290.x

Kovan, J. T., & Dirkx, J. M. (2003). "Being called awake": The role of transformative learning in the lives of environmental activists. *Adult Education Quarterly, 53*(3), 99–118. doi:10.1177/0741713602238906

Kroth, M., & Boverie, P. (2000). Life mission and adult learning. *Adult Education Quarterly, 50*(2), 134–149. doi:10.1177/07417130022086955

Larson, L. M. (1998). The social cognitive model of counselor training. *The Counseling Psychologist, 26,* 219–273. doi:10.1177/0011000098262002

Larson, L. M., & Daniels, J. A. (1998). Review of the counseling self-efficacy literature. *The Counseling Psychologist, 26,* 179–218. doi:10.1177/0011000098262001

Lent, R. W., Hill, C. E., & Hoffman, M. A. (2003). Development and validity of the counselor activity self-efficacy scales. *Journal of Counseling Psychology, 50,* 97–108. doi:10.1037//0022-0167.50.1.97

McLennan, N. A., Rochow, S., & Arthur, N. (2001). Religious and spiritual diversity in counseling. *Guidance and Counseling, 16*(4), 132–137.

Mezirow, J. (1978). Perspective transformation. *Adult Education, 28,* 100–110. doi:10.1177/074171367802800292

Mezirow, J. (1990). *Fostering critical reflection in adulthood.* San Francisco, CA: Jossey-Bass.

Mezirow, J. (1991). *Transformative dimensions of adult learning.* San Francisco, CA: Jossey-Bass.

Mezirow, J. (1995a). Transformation theory of adult learning. In M. R. Welton (Ed.), *In defense of the lifeworld* (pp. 39–70). New York, NY: SUNY Press.

Mezirow, J. (1995b). Transformative learning: Theory to practice. *New Directions for Adult and Continuing Education, 74,* 5–12. doi:10.1002/ace.7401

Mezirow, J. (2000). Learning to think like an adult. In J. Mezirow & Associates (Eds.), *Learning as transformation: Critical perspectives on a theory in progress* (pp. 3–34). San Francisco, CA: Jossey-Bass.

Myers, J. E., & Williard, K. (2003). Integrating spirituality into counselor preparation: A developmental, wellness approach. *Counseling and Values, 47*(2), 142–155. doi:10.1002/j.2161-007X.2003.tb00231.x

Rose, E. M., Westfeld, J. S., & Ansley, T. N. (2001). Spiritual issues in counseling: Client's beliefs and preferences. *Journal of Counseling Psychology, 48*(1), 61–71.

Scofield, T., Saginak, K., Reljic, R., & Harper, A. (2009). *Transformative practices in counselor education: Creating transparent connections* (ACAPCD-28). Alexandria, VA: American Counseling Association.

Taylor, E. (1998). *The theory and practice of transformative learning: A critical review.* (Information Series No. 374). Columbus: ERIC. Clearinghouse on Adult, Career, and Vocational Education, Center on Education and Training for Employment, College of Education, The Ohio State University.

Tisdell, E. (2000). Spirituality and emancipatory adult education in women adult educators for social change. *Adult Education Quarterly, 50*(4), 308–335. doi:10.1177/07417130022087062

Tisdell, E. J. (2003). *Exploring spirituality and culture in adult and higher education.* San Francisco, CA: Jossey-Bass.

Trevino, J. G. (1996). Worldview and change in cross-cultural counseling. *The Counseling Psychologist, 24,* 198–215

Vanier, J. (1997). *Our journey home: Rediscovering a common humanity beyond our differences* (M. Parham, Trans.). Toronto, Ontario, Canada: Novalis.

CHAPTER 8

DEVELOPING SCHOLARSHIP THROUGH MENTORING AND REFLECTION

A Transformative Process for Doctoral Students

Brandé Flamez, Javier Cavazos Jr., Varunee Faii Sangganjanavanich, and Joshua C. Watson

In this chapter, we describe the process of scholarship development through mentoring and reflection. First, we provide a literature review concerning mentoring experiences of graduate and doctoral students, as well as an overview of the literature related to transformative learning. Second, we provide two case studies to illustrate the impact of negative and positive mentoring experiences. In the first case, we outline how transformative growth may occur as a result of a negative mentoring experience. In the second case, we illustrate how transformative growth may occur from a positive mentoring experience. We also offer a five-step process of scholarship development including selecting mentors, becoming involved in research with supportive faculty, collaborating with others on research projects, examining assumptions on research and publication, and engaging in reflection. Finally, we provide implications for practice in graduate and doctoral programs as well as strategies that faculty can use to provide students with transformative learning experiences.

MENTORING EXPERIENCES IN GRADUATE EDUCATION

Graduate faculty, more so than their undergraduate faculty peers, serve in the informal role of gatekeeper for their professions. This responsibility includes preparing students to become competent, fully functioning members of the profession. A significant part of this preparation involves the establishment of mentoring relationships. Black, Suarez, and Medina (2004) conducted a review of the extant literature on mentoring relationships and pieced together a definition that describes mentoring as

> A nurturing, complex, long-term, developmental process in which a more skilled and experienced person serves as a role model, teacher, sponsor, and coach who encourages, counsels, befriends a less skilled person for the purpose of promoting the latter's professional and/or personal development. (p. 46)

When conceptualizing mentoring, it is important to keep in mind that that there are a number of dimensions or domains of mentoring including (a) research (Briggs & Pehrsson, 2008), (b) personal (Gilbert & Rossman, 1992), (c) professional (Liebenberg, 2010), or (d) peer-to-peer (Watson, Clement, Blom, & Grindley, 2009). First, research mentorship fosters academic productivity (Briggs & Pehrsson, 2008). Second, the personal domain of mentoring focuses on interpersonal factors such as self-esteem and self-confidence (Gilbert & Rossman, 1992). Third, the professional domain focuses on a protégé's career including networking and coaching (Liebenberg, 2010). Finally, peer mentoring is a relationship between a more advanced and a less advanced graduate student (Watson et al., 2009).

In the literature, myriad benefits of establishing mentoring relationships are noted. Among these many benefits are more positive levels of self-efficacy (Rheineck & Roland, 2008), increased overall satisfaction with graduate school (Tenenbaum, Crosby, & Gilner, 2001), the opportunity to learn about unwritten rules and understand the importance of giving back by mentoring others (Casto, Caldwell, & Salazar, 2005), networking (Chao, 2009), support (Schwille, 2008), and encouragement (Rheineck & Roland, 2008). For example, Casto et al. (2005) provided personal reflections on their experiences with mentoring in their counselor education programs. They commented that an important benefit of their mentoring relationships included the realization that they wanted to give back by mentoring others. Roberts and Plakhotnik (2009) echoed the same notion that the role of mentors extends beyond academic support. They reported that mentors listened to their concerns and feelings which, in their opinions, was an important part of the mentoring experience.

In terms of peer mentoring in graduate school, Watson et al. (2009) revealed that 25% of the 104 graduate students in their study had experience with a formal or informal peer mentoring program. These participants indicated that although peer mentoring had its disadvantages (e.g., their peer mentor lacked experience), there were a number of benefits including the openness of the relationship and learning about the student perspective. It also is important to note that 46% of the participants commented that peer mentoring "was equally or more effective than professional mentoring" (p. 242). Additionally, researchers also have found that peer mentoring generates benefits to students with diverse backgrounds such as African American (Patton & Harper, 2003) and Latina/o (Castellanos, Gloria, & Kamimura, 2006).

Based on the mentoring literature, it appears that many graduate and doctoral students have benefited from mentoring relationships (Briggs & Pehrsson, 2008; Sherman, 2009). In these studies, researchers suggest that students have seen an increase in their self-efficacy, overall experience in graduate school, and research productivity because of a mentoring relationship. Conversely, Clark, Harden, and Johnson (2000) documented negative effects of relationships between mentees and mentors. As a result of such experiences, it is important that students have guidelines and information regarding the selection of a mentor. To establish an effective mentoring relationship, Casto et al. (2005) noted that students should initiate the mentoring relationship. This recommendation is supported by Clark et al. (2000), who noted that "students who initiate mentor relationships are most likely to be mentored" (p. 267) and Watson et al. (2009), who found that approximately 41% of participants in their study ($n = 104$) actively sought out mentoring relationships with faculty.

The Role of a Supportive Environment

To create a supportive environment that helps graduate and doctoral students increase their research productivity, faculty should identify a model on which to structure this environment and any other resources needed to maintain it. First, Gelso (1993) recommended a number of theoretical propositions to produce a research training environment (RTE). Using these theoretical propositions to produce a supportive environment can influence students' attitudes toward research and therefore increase students' involvement in research. These theoretical propositions are as follows: (a) faculty must model positive behavior and attitudes with regard to research; (b) faculty should positively enforce students' involvement in research; (c) students' involvement in research should be nonthreatening to them; (d) faculty should introduce students to the notion that each study has at least one limitation; (e) faculty should teach multiple methodological approaches; and (f) graduate programs should illustrate how science and practice are complementary (Gelso, 1993). Faculty and programs can use many of these ideas to facilitate self-reflection and transformative learning in mentoring relationships.

Using RTE as a theoretical framework, professors are encouraged to model "appropriate scientific behavior and attitudes" such as enthusiasm and excitement about a research project to their students (Gelso, 1993, p. 6). Second, program coordinators and professors should reinforce students' research efforts and productivity. To increase student productivity and provide them with the motivation to attend conferences or submit manuscripts to professional journals, departments can allocate travel money to students and develop a department- or college-wide newsletter focusing on student publications (Gelso, 1993). Third, students should become involved in research early in their doctoral training. Such an experience will allow students to become familiar with research in a minimally threatening way. For example, faculty can task students with searching for relevant literature, distributing surveys, entering data into a statistical software package, or transcribing face-to-face interviews. Fourth, faculty should communicate to students the notion that every research study contains flaws. According to Gelso's (1979) bubble hypothesis, for every methodological solution there is a price paid elsewhere in the study design. Helping students learn to accept this inevitability will allow them to come to the realization that they do not have to design the perfect study. In addition, graduate programs could structure curricula around multiple research approaches. Preparing students to become well-rounded scholars and methodologists will allow them to gain confidence in their ability to tackle a number of varied research designs. Finally, it is important that graduate programs emphasize the connection between practice and research (Gelso, 1993). Throughout their program, students should have opportunities to learn about important ideas and theories, as well as ways to apply these ideas to real-world situations to increase their self-efficacy in their chosen field of study (Szymanski, Ozegovis, Phillips, & Briggs-Phillips, 2007).

In addition to establishing an environment that supports and facilitates student-research, it is important to develop a student-led organization with this objective in mind. The Counselor Education Research Consortium (CERC) is an example of one such organization. The purpose of CERC is to promote scholarly productivity of research and facilitate the professional development of counselors and counselor educators in a safe learning environment (Devlin, Flamez, & Garza, 2008). CERC is a student-led organization and has faculty advisors to help mentor the officers and fellow students. CERC works collaboratively with faculty, doctoral, and master's students. CERC members meet once a month, and during this time members discuss research ideas, write conference proposals, solicit someone to edit their work, practice a presentation, or listen to a guest speaker. Students who become involved in organizations such as CERC have the benefit of developing creative research interests, participating in healthy mentoring relationships, developing professional identities, and collaborating with other graduate students and faculty members.

Collaboration

There are a number of important factors to consider when collaborating with professors on research projects. First, graduate students must become familiar with guidelines concerning authorship of manuscripts. There are organizations such as the American Counseling Association (ACA) that provide guidelines on authorship in order to protect students from unethical research behavior (see the ACA Code of Ethics, 2005). Given that some doctoral students have reported unethical behavior (e.g., taking credit for one's work; Gonzalez, 2007) on the part of their professors, it is important that graduate students find out about those professors who engage in this behavior and therefore avoid collaborating with these individuals. Second, graduate students should seek out faculty who appear to be encouraging and supportive of their academic and research potential. Roberts and Plakhotnik (2009) have indicated that protégés enjoy their mentoring relationships when they perceive their mentors as supportive and encouraging. In addition, they noted that it is important to collaborate with professors who not only provide academic but also emotional support. Third, graduate students should read narratives of graduate students who have had successful relationships with professors or other students (Casto et al., 2005; Roberts & Plakhotnik, 2009). Understanding the factors involved in successful collaborations will provide students with an improved understanding of those factors that can lead to successful outcomes. While collaborating with professors can often result in a positive and productive experience, graduate students should keep in mind that a power differential still exists in these relationships.

In relationships between students and faculty members, a power differential almost always exists. The source of this power typically stems from the faculty member holding an evaluative role in academic settings. Although an evaluative role may not be a part of the mentoring relationship between students and faculty members, a power differential between the two parties remains (Sangganjanavanich & Magnuson, 2009). In addition, when faculty members are involved with students beyond their role as an educator (i.e., serving as a course instructor while writing a manuscript for publication with a student), they put themselves in dual or multiple relationships with students. That is, the faculty members are not only course instructors who are responsible to educate and evaluate, but also mentors who help students navigate their professional journey. Students, then, are not only students in the classroom, but also mentees who rely on professional guidance and support from the faculty members. It is unavoidable that individuals engaged in multiple relationships experience role confusion. The confusion can potentially lead to vulnerability and conflict within one relationship that influences an individual's judgment in other closely related relationships. For example, a student decides to withdraw from the research team led by course instructor, dissertation advisor, and mentor. The student's decision may potentially bring complications to the multiple relationships, which at times seems like only one relationship, she/he has with that faculty member. Although both parties are aware and use caution in those relationships, boundaries between them become blurred, and it is difficult for both parties to remain objective.

Bowman and Hatley (1995) emphasized students' vulnerability and inability to voluntarily give consent to engage in diverse platonic relationships with faculty. Results of this research drew attention to inconsistent opinions regarding decision making related to multiple relationships. Kolbert, Morgan, and Brendel (2002) investigated faculty and student perceptions of dual relationships within counselor education. Based on their findings, they indicated that students viewed dual relationships as more negative than beneficial. Conversely, faculty views indicated that such relationships had more benefits than negative consequences to students. The authors emphasized the importance of considering students' perceptions when assessing the appropriateness of extracurricular relationships. The cases in this chapter include examples of collaboration and power differentials between students and faculty.

TRANSFORMATIVE LEARNING

Transformative learning theory focuses on how adults make meaning in their lives. According to the theory, transformative learning occurs when people alter how they make meaning of the world by critically reflecting on their assumptions and taking action to create new ways of defining their worlds (Imel, 1998). As such, transformative learning is the process by which individuals effect change in their own frame of reference (Brock, 2010;

Cranton, 1994, 1996; Mezirow, 1991, 1995, 1996a). Originally developed by Mezirow (1978) as an approach to adult learning, transformative learning includes 10 steps learners undergo in changing their world view (as cited in Brock, 2010). Included in these 10 steps are variations of the following: (a) an initial distorting dilemma, such as returning to graduate school; (b) self-examination with feelings of guilt and shame; (c) recognition that one's discontent and the process of transformation are shared and that others have gone through a similar change; (d) exploration of options for new roles; (e) a critical assessment of assumptions; (f) trying out new roles; (g) planning a course of action; (h) acquisition of knowledge and skills for implementing one's plan; (i) building competence and self-confidence in new roles and relationships; and (j) a reintegration into one's life on the basis of conditions dictated by one's new perspective (Mezirow, 2000).

As mentioned, an integral part of transformative learning is reflection. Mezirow (1991) defined reflection as "the process of critically assessing the content, process, or premise(s) of our efforts to interpret and find meaning to an experience" (p.104). Based on this definition, critical reflection is a catalyst for perspective transformation. Mezirow goes on to describe perspective transformation as follows:

> Perspective transformation is the process of becoming critically aware of how and why our assumptions have come to constrain the way we perceive, understand, and feel about our world; changing these structures of habitual expectation to make possible a more inclusive, discriminating, and integrative perspective; and, finally, making choices or otherwise acting upon these new understandings. (p. 167)

In addition to the role in perspective transformation, researchers have noted the importance of reflection in helping students navigate their doctoral studies (Castellanos et al., 2006; Kamimura, 2006). In a personal account of his own experiences as a doctoral student, Kamimura (2006) commented that he made meaning out of his experiences by engaging in the following stages: (a) open-mindedness and self-awareness, (b) culture mismatch and dissonance, (c) rebellion and self-distancing, (d) self-reflection, (e) re-integration, and (f) navigation/control/power. Kamimura further explained that this time of self-reflection provided an opportunity to examine any value conflicts, understand the sacrifices required in order to pursue an advanced degree, and discover the motivation needed to continue with the program. Given the importance of Mezirow's (1996b) concept of self-reflection and the literature supporting its role in helping students persist in graduate school (Castellanos et al., 2006), it is vital to create an environment that helps students engage in self-reflection about their experiences, beliefs, and perspectives as related to graduate education. Mentoring relationships between faculty and students have the potential to help students engage in self-reflection and transformative learning.

CASE STUDY 1: TRANSFORMATION THOUGH A NEGATIVE MENTORING EXPERIENCE

Rose is a first-year doctoral student enrolled in a cohort system in which a group of people starts classes together and continues taking the same courses together until they finish all of their coursework requirements. John is two cohorts ahead of Rose and is almost finished with his dissertation. John approached Rose to work on an article with two other professors, Drs. Jones and Farrell. Dr. Jones is a professor to both Rose and John; however, Dr. Farrell teaches at another university, and Rose has never met Dr. Farrell.

John informed Rose that the article would be about Dr. Jones' dissertation. They would use some of the data from Dr. Jones' dissertation to create an assessment. John had already provided some directions to guide Rose, but he informed her that her responsibility was to do the literature review and write the introduction. He told her that she would be third author. He further explained that Dr. Jones would be first author because she had done the previous research and that he (John) would be second author because he initiated the idea to turn Dr. Jones' dissertation into an article. Dr. Farrell, who was responsible for the editing, would be fourth author.

Although John had provided some directions to develop the introduction, Rose soon discovered after doing a literature review that his sources were outdated. She realized she would need to rewrite the introduction from scratch. After writing the introduction, she met with Dr. Jones and showed her the manuscript. Dr. Jones explained to Rose that she was having a hard time completing her part. Rose was confused because she thought Dr. Jones had already collected the data. Dr. Jones asked Rose to conduct the statistical analyses. Because Dr. Jones was Rose's teacher, Rose said she did not mind.

Rose began to feel that she was doing more than her assigned parts. She soon became discouraged and felt that her co-authors were not properly acknowledging her contributions to the project. Frustrated, she tried to call John several times to speak to him about her role, but he would not return her calls. Soon thereafter, Dr. Farrell called and reminded Dr. Jones and Rose that he needed the article soon so he could edit it. Dr. Jones tried to call John and also was unable to reach him. When Rose finally was able to get a hold of John, she explained her reasoning for wanting to move up on authorship. John's reply to Rose was, "No way, no how! If it wasn't for me, you would not even be an author on a book chapter!" Dr. Jones then replied to Rose, "Well, I guess we will just keep you as third author."

The above case presented Rose with an excellent opportunity to engage in transformative learning. When she realized that her contributions would be much greater than the original agreement, she decided to contact John to express her concern. The response she received seems to imply that she should be grateful for even being included in the project in the first place. For Rose, this situation provided her with a disorienting dilemma that was the impetus for her questioning her understanding of the collaborative research of which she was supposed to be a part. Was she really in a position to demand additional recognition for her work? Should she, as John intimated, be grateful for the opportunity to publish regardless of her position in the author hierarchy? The following section describes an approach Rose could follow to handle the situation and make meaning of the situation so that she could be better prepared to handle similar situations in the future.

In this scenario, the disorienting dilemma for Rose was clear. The way her faculty co-researchers treated her was not in accord with how she envisioned the collaborative process unfolding. As a result, she began to question her understanding of the research process to see if she might have been mistaken in her understanding. Was her understanding of the process of collaborative research and the policy for the ethical attribution of credit accurate? Realizing that she is not the first student to experience such a dilemma, she can begin to find clarity in the situation by acquiring the knowledge that will allow her to reexamine her previous assumptions as to what her role should be as a junior researcher and discern exactly what it is she should and should not be doing.

To handle the current situation in a professional manner, and to help her make meaning of it so that she is prepared to handle similar situations in the future, Rose will need to educate herself more on professional standards of practice germane to the area of research and scholarship. In so doing, she will be able to develop a cogent plan of action that will guide her interactions with her senior colleagues moving forward. Since she is new to the practice of research, she should make a concerted effort to explore her rights and responsibilities as a researcher. Among counselors and counselor educators, there are organizations (e.g., ACA; National Board for Certified Counselors) that provide guidelines on authorship to protect students from unethical research behavior (National Board for Certified Counselors, 2005). The ACA *Code of Ethics* (2005) clearly state that "the principal contributor is listed first and minor technical or professional contributions are acknowledged in notes," and furthermore, "students who have been the primary contributors, they are listed as principal authors" (p. 18). Counselors who conduct research with students are supposed to establish agreements in advance regarding tasks and publication credit (ACA, 2005).

Equipped with this new knowledge of the professional standards governing research and scholarship in her field, Rose can now try out her new role as a professional and ethical researcher, and she can approach her colleagues to discuss her concerns regarding the way she believes she is being treated. If her attempts to communicate directly with the primary and secondary author prove unproductive, her next step would be to seek consultation. According to the ACA *Code of Ethics* (2005), "counselors strive to resolve ethical dilemmas with direct and open communication among all parties involved and consult with colleagues and supervisors when necessary" (p. 18). If the issue is not properly resolved, the *Code of Ethics* recommends further action such as "referral to... state licensing boards or to appropriate institutional authorities" (p. 18).

While the *Code of Ethics* outlines the course of action Rose should take, it does not account for the dissonance she feels in this particular situation. For Rose, it would be impossible to ignore the fact that she is in a power differential with her professor. Her actions, as much as we would like to believe they would not, could have serious negative consequences. When engaged in writing for publications or developing manuscripts in the future, Rose might consider having a written agreement that indicates expectations of all parties. Contracts not only communicate expectations and help avoid confusion but also protect parties that have less power in the relationship (Sangganjanavanich & Magnuson, 2009). Whereas she might have thought such a formal arrangement was not necessary given her familiarity with the two principle authors, her experiences in this situation have transformed her way of thinking and highlighted for her the importance of following professional protocol. As a result, she is likely to be more assertive in future collaborations to ensure that equity of workload is maintained and proper credit for work completed distributed accordingly.

CASE 2: TRANSFORMATION THROUGH A POSITIVE MENTORING EXPERIENCE AND A MODEL OF SCHOLARSHIP DEVELOPMENT

On April's first day of class, the professor walked in and communicated to the class that their careers do not solely depend on their GPAs, but the students must shift gears and begin to focus on writing, research, and publication. The professor then placed on the table a proposal for an upcoming conference and stated that he wanted the students to submit a proposal and present. Present? Submit a proposal? April had no idea where to start. It was only the first day of class, and students were supposed to be experts on something to present to an audience? Immediately April felt the anxiety in the room as the class all looked at each other asking, "Where do we start?" April was lost and needed direction.

The idea of starting from scratch and seeing a project to its finish is intimidating. Similar to other graduate students, April felt confused, incompetent, and anxious when the faculty member told her that doctoral education was not about completing a degree, rather it was about developing one's scholarship. April always wondered where to find a recipe for developing a successful research agenda. There were many questions in mind in seeking to understand, for example, "Who should I talk to about my research interests? How do I know which interests have the potential to be a study? How many hours per week do I need to put into my research besides working full time and going to school full time?" April implemented various strategies in developing scholarship such as reading professional journals, talking to professors, joining a research group, and attending conferences. Similar to other students, April listened to these suggestions with no clue as to what to do in order to take the first step toward developing a line of scholarship. As a result, April continued to be lost in this academic journey until one day inspiration and clarity was found in an unlikely source.

During the doctoral internship, April found an answer. While watching a cooking program on television, a baker demonstrated how to make blueberry muffins from several recipes. At the end of the program, the baker said "Baking is an art. Do not lock yourself into these recipes. You have to make them however you want. If you like sweet, you add more sugar. If you like strawberries in your muffins, you put them there." April's first reaction was, "Who would want strawberries in their muffins? It is bizarre!" It was then she realized that an answer had been found—scholarship is an individualized process. Although there are various suggestions and recommendations for graduate students on how to develop their scholarship, individuals are responsible to seek means to construct such lines of research through their personal reflection processes. An internal process helps individuals to envision the objectives and goals of their scholarship. Therefore, April found that spending time contemplating and reflecting on professional development and scholarship was helpful.

In terms of selecting a mentor, there were a number of factors that influenced April's choice. First, she chose a specific professor to be her mentor due to the professor's belief in April's academic and research potential. For April, it was important to select a mentor who would provide unconditional support and encouragement. Second, as a prospective doctoral student, April knew it was important to write for publication but was unsure of how to become proficient at writing. Professors discussed the importance for undergraduate students of writing articles and presenting at conferences to pursue a graduate degree, but at the time the message did not resonate with April. As a result, April had several conflicting messages about what constituted good writing and how the process should unfold. April relied heavily on the mentor to help to gain clarity in this area.

In addition to pointing out myths about writing (e.g., writing is an innate ability or revision is not necessary), April's mentor also extended an invitation to participate in the entire publication process from start to finish. This included reading and responding to an editor's decision, and presenting on the publication at a professional conference. The mentor suggested that April begin reading journals. As April began to read more journal articles, she became familiar with the writing style which these journal editors found acceptable. The professor also taught April that it was important to have an idea in mind about journals that are of interest in submitting written work and familiarizing herself with their requirements for submission. After April had chosen the appropriate journal to submit an article to, a literature review was undertaken. April made sure to be familiar with the research on the specific topic of interest in the journal as well as drafting an outline describing what was to be included in the article and how the article would add to the existing literature. April now was ready to begin writing.

After she wrote the article and edited several drafts, April took her article to the writing center on campus for review. She submitted the article and waited anxiously for a response. The response from the counselor at the writing center was positive, so April submitted the article to the journal she had previously selected. To April's surprise, the journal accepted her article with minimal revisions. However, this was not the case with other articles she had written and submitted. Having an article rejected is a part of the process. Early on, after getting many rejections, April began to question whether she could really write. April's mentor reminded her that not every editor would like her work. Likewise, some feedback will make sense and other feedback will be confusing and undecipherable. The important thing is to remember that if a journal rejects an article in the initial attempt, it is possible that another journal will accept the article. As noted by her mentor and in previous research by Silvia (2007), a good article always will find a home.

As a result of reflecting on her experiences and the important factors that go into writing for publication, April came to a number of conclusions. First, she found that it is important for mentors to create research environments that provide self-reflection opportunities for their students. As a research assistant under the mentorship of a prolific professor, April had many opportunities to reflect on her goals, values, and writing style. Second, April realized that learning could not occur in a mentoring relationship without unconditional positive regard, genuineness, and empathy (Rogers, 1957). If her mentor did not communicate his respect for her ideas, hard work, and efforts, then April would not have been motivated to engage in self-reflection. In other words, establishing a safe environment for sharing and exchanging ideas preceded learning in her mentoring relationship. Finally, self-reflection allowed April to recognize that she was involved in a nonlinear relationship in which a mentor and protégé exchanged ideas. Whereas a linear mentoring relationship involves an expert and novice (Quijada, 2006), April was engaged in a relationship in which her professor valued and appreciated her ideas and contributions. This feeling left her with the impression that she was not working *for* her professor but *with* him to create scholarly works.

As April reflected on the entire experience, she can say that her interactions with her mentor definitely changed her perceptions of the scholarly role doctoral students, and future professors, undertake. Initially, April did not give much thought to the writing process and as a result was completely unprepared to conduct the scholarly work expected of her. In working with her mentor and learning more about the writing and publishing processes, April came to realize that she had the ability to be a productive writer. Gradually, she changed her approach to writing and learned how to interpret editor feedback in a way that allowed her to improve her manuscripts and ultimately find a place to publish them. These successes have helped April feel more confident in her writing. As she looked back on her earlier experiences, she could truly see where she has grown and her perspectives have changed.

In this case, a five-step model of scholarship development was very effective (see Figure 8.1). April was able to establish her own research agenda by

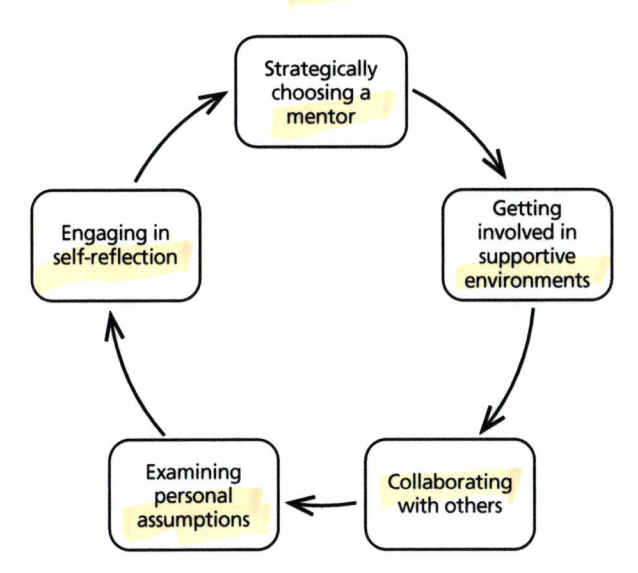

Figure 8.1 Five-step model for scholastic development.

(a) strategically choosing a mentor that provided her with what she needed at that stage of her career, (b) getting involved in supportive environments, (c) collaborating with others who would model for her successful writing strategies, (d) examining her assumptions on research and writing, and (e) engaging in self-reflection. Based on this mentoring experience, April had an opportunity to critically assess her assumptions on writing and research. With new knowledge gained from her mentor, she understood that revision was important in the research process and writing was not an innate ability. Finally, April appeared to be transformed with new knowledge and insight related to developing her scholarship because of self-reflection. By reflecting on her goals, values, and writing style, she gained insight into her motivation to conduct research and publish scholarly articles. In summary, through this process of a five-step model for scholarship development, she has gained success in her first publishing experience and thus will feel confident in her future research and writing endeavors.

IMPLICATIONS FOR COUNSELOR EDUCATION PROGRAMS AND FACULTY

The aforementioned examples and insights could broaden to include programs in education and the social sciences. Scholarship development is an individualized process. As Lambie, Sias, Davis, Lawson, and Akos (2008) noted, "scholarly writing is a personal process within a structured framework" (p. 23). Individuals encounter different processes and implement diverse strategies to facilitate their scholarship development. Even though individuals all develop in different ways, the one constant that endures is that scholarly writing is a developmental process that needs to be both supported and nurtured (Lambie et al., 2008). As such, educators are in an excellent position to foster scholarship development of their graduate students by providing positive conditions and learning environments. The following examples illustrate strategies for fostering scholarship development.

First, graduate programs in education and the social sciences can provide useful resources that benefit students, such as research interests of the faculty members, the availability of peer mentoring programs, opportunities to participate in student research groups, and an introduction to resources that could help improve student writing. Second, counselor educators can encourage students to initiate their research interests and work collaboratively with them while letting the students take the lead on these research projects. Faculty members can also play a supportive role in facilitating the development of scholarship in students. It is important to note that although a student-faculty relationship is hierarchical, an egalitarian relationship between both parties can create a supportive environment rather than an evaluative atmosphere. For example, rather than acting as an expert, faculty members foster the relationship in such a way that students understand they are working *with* rather than *for* faculty. To ensure that a successful relationship develops, it is important that faculty help students understand the nature and expectations of the relationship to avoid confusion and conflicts (Sangganjanavanich & Magnuson, 2009).

Consider for a moment a situation in which a student is a teaching assistant for a professor. The professor might ask the student to help create the course syllabus. Furthermore, the professor could ask the student which topics he or she is interested in teaching rather than assigning the student to specific topics or dates. In *The Power of Myth*, Campbell (1988) stated, "A good coach doesn't tell a runner exactly how to hold his arms or anything like that. He watches him run, then helps him to correct his own natural mode" (p. 143). This means that instead of evaluating the students' presentations as good or bad, faculty can actively encourage students to self-reflect on his or her presentation.

Third, as many researchers suggest, faculty members can create an impact on student's scholarship development and professional identity development (Sangganjanavanich & Magnuson, 2009; Schlosser & Gelso, 2001, 2005; Schlosser & Kahn, 2007). Therefore, faculty members can act as role models for students. These activities include (a) maintaining a strong professional identity; (b) participating and taking leadership roles in professional organizations on local, state, regional, and national levels; (c) publishing scholarly works in professional journals; (d) attending and presenting at state and national conferences; and (e) inviting students to collaborate on research projects. By fostering a professional and scholarly identity through role modeling, faculty can provide students with a vicarious learning experience.

Fourth, it is important that counselor educators debunk common myths about writing for publication. As described earlier, Rose had impressions from her educators that (a) a specific number of publications are necessary for success in graduate school; (b) writing is an innate ability; and (c) revision is unnecessary (Silvia, 2007). When these and other myths are not debunked in graduate education, students may be left with inaccurate information and develop unrealistic expectations about their doctoral studies. These unrealistic expectations, if left unchecked, could result in poor performance or even worse, student withdrawal from the program. Therefore, myths about writing for publication (e.g., every article is accepted for publication) must be demystified in order to provide students with accurate information.

Finally, it is important to invite graduate students to reflect on their experiences, beliefs, values, research interests, and motivation. It is our contention that some mentoring relationships and assignments have potential to help students engage in self-reflection and transformative learning. Sample assignments could include questions that focus on students' (a) research interests; (b) career aspirations; (c) reasons for pursuing graduate degrees; and (d) motivation to persevere. When students reflect on these areas, they are in a better position to engage in transformative learning by examining their beliefs, perspectives, and goals.

CONCLUSION

Given the importance of Mezirow's (1996b) concept of self-reflection, it is imperative that professors create an environment that helps graduate students engage in self-reflection about their experiences, beliefs, and perspectives as related to graduate education. This type of environment creates a safe zone for students to critically assess their previously held beliefs and explore new ways of acting based on this assessment. Doctoral students often feel pressure to develop a line of scholarship. In the first case study presented in this chapter, it became evident that even a negative mentoring experience can lead to transformation and wisdom. Likewise, the second case illustrates that positive mentoring experiences can result in increased self-efficacy and new knowledge and insight with regard to research and publication. In conclusion, we believe that graduate students who enter into relationships with others (i.e., mentoring, supportive environments, and collaborating) are more likely to engage in self-reflection and transformative learning as part of their graduate education. As a result, these students will have a greater opportunity to increase and enhance their development as researchers.

REFERENCES

American Counseling Association. (2005). *Code of ethics.* Alexandria, VA: Author. Retrieved from http://www.counseling.org/Resources/CodeOfEthics/TP/Home/CT2.aspx

Black, L. L., Suarez, E. C., & Medina, S. (2004). Helping students find themselves: Strategies for successful mentoring relationships. *Counselor Education and Supervision, 44,* 44–55.

Bowman, B. E., & Hatley, L. D. (1995). Faculty-student relationships: The dual role controversy. *Counselor Education and Supervision, 34,* 11–35.

Briggs, C. A., & Pehrsson, D. E. (2008). Research mentorship in counselor education. *Counselor Education and Supervision, 48,* 101–113.

Brock, S. E. (2010). Measuring the importance of precursor steps to transformative learning. *Adult Education Quarterly, 60,* 122–142. doi:10.1177/0741713609333084

Campbell, J. (1988). *The power of the myth.* New York, NY: Doubleday.

Castellanos, J., Gloria, A. M., & Kamimura, M. (2006). Enderezendo el camino/Straightening the path: Dispelling myths and providing directions for Latina/o doctoral students. In J. Castellanos, A. M. Gloria, & M. Kamimura (Eds.), *The Latina/o pathway to the Ph.D.* (pp. 191–200). Sterling, VA: Stylus.

Casto, C., Caldwell, C., & Salazar, C. F. (2005). Creating mentoring relationships between female faculty and students in counselor education: Guidelines for potential mentees and mentors. *Journal of Counseling and Development, 83,* 331–336.

Chao, G. T. (2009). Formal mentoring: Lessons learned from past practice. *Professional Psychology: Research and Practice, 40,* 314–320. doi:10.1037/a0012658

Clark, R. A., Harden, S. L., & Johnson, W. B. (2000). Mentor relationships in clinical psychology doctoral training: Results of a national survey. *Teaching of Psychology, 27,* 262–268. doi:10.1207/S15328023TOP2704_04

Cranton, P. (1994). *Understanding and promoting transformative learning: A guide for educators of adults.* San Francisco, CA: Jossey-Bass.

Cranton, P. (1996). *Authenticity in teaching.* San Francisco, CA: Jossey-Bass.

Devlin, J., Flamez, B., & Garza, K. (2008, May). Bridging the gap between counseling and research. *Fifth Annual CS3 Symposium: Action Research in Education and Leadership.* Symposium conducted at the meeting of University of San Diego, San Diego, CA.

Gelso, C. J. (1979). Research in counseling: Methodological and professional issues. *The Counseling Psychologist, 8*(3), 7–35. doi:10.1177/001100007900800303

Gelso, C. J. (1993). On the making of a scientist-practitioner: A theory of research training in professional psychology. *Professional Psychology: Research and Practice, 24,* 468–476. doi:10.1037/0735-7028.24.4.468

Gilbert, L. A., & Rossman, K. M. (1992). Gender and the mentoring process for women: Implications for professional development. *Professional Psychology: Research and Practice, 23,* 233–238. doi:10.1037/0735-7028.23.3.233

Gonzalez, J. C. (2007). Surviving the doctorate and thriving as faculty: Latina junior faculty reflecting on their doctoral studies experiences. *Equity in Education, 40,* 291–300. doi:10.1080/10665680701578613

Imel, S. (1998). *Transformative learning in adulthood.* (Report No. EDO-CE-98-200). Columbus, OH: Adult, Career, and Vocational Education. (ERIC Document Reproduction Service No. ED423426)

Kamimura, M. (2006). Finding my way: Enculturation to the Ph.D. In J. Castellanos, A. M. Gloria, & M. Kamimura (Eds.), *The Latina/o pathway to the Ph.D.* (pp. 191–200). Sterling, VA: Stylus.

Kolbert, J. B., Morgan, B., & Brendel, J. M. (2002). Faculty and student perceptions of dual relationships within counselor education: A qualitative analysis. *Counselor Education and Supervision, 41,* 193–206.

Lambie, G. W., Sias, S. M., Davis, K. M., Lawson, G., & Akos, P. (2008). A scholarly writing resource for counselor educators and their students. *Journal of Counseling & Development, 86,* 18–25.

Liebenberg, E. (2010). Mentoring matters: Linking with a professional network. *English Journal, 99,* 86–88.

Mezirow, J. (1978). Perspective transformation. *Adult Education, 28,* 100–110. doi:10.1177/074171367802800202

Mezirow, J. (1991). *Transformative dimensions of adult learning*. San Francisco, CA: Jossey-Bass.
Mezirow, J. (1995). A transformation theory of adult learning. In M. Welton (Ed.), *In defense of the lifeworld: Critical perspectives on adult learning* (pp. 39–70). Albany: State University of New York Press.
Mezirow, J. (1996a). Contemporary paradigms of learning. *Adult Education Quarterly, 46*, 158–172. doi:10.1177/074171369604600303
Mezirow, J. (1996b). Toward a learning theory of adult literacy. *Adult Basic Education and Literacy Journal, 6*, 115–126.
Mezirow, J. (2000). Learning to think like an adult. In J. Mezirow and Associates (Eds.), *Learning as transformation* (pp. 3–33). San Francisco, CA: Jossey-Bass.
National Board for Certified Counselors. (2005). *Code of ethics*. Greensboro, NC: Author.
Patton, L. D., & Harper, S. R. (2003). Mentoring relationships among African American women in graduate and professional school. *New Direction for Student Services, 104*, 67–77. doi:10.1002/ss.108
Quijada, D. A. (2006). Collegial alliances? Exploring one Chicano's perspective on mentoring in research and academia. In J. Castellanos, A. M. Gloria, & M. Kamimura (Eds.), *The Latina/o pathway to the Ph.D.* (pp. 255–268). Sterling, VA: Stylus.
Rheineck, J. E., & Roland, C. B. (2008). The developmental mentoring relationship between academic women. *Adultspan Journal, 7*, 80–93.
Roberts, N. A., & Plakhotnik, M. S. (2009, Summer). Building social capital in the academy: The nature and function of support systems in graduate adult education. *New Directions for Adult and Continuing Education, 122*, 43–52. doi:10.1002/ace.333
Rogers, C. R. (1957). The necessary and sufficient conditions of therapeutic personality change. *Journal of Consulting Psychology, 21*, 95–103. doi:10.1037/h0045357
Sangganjanavanich, V. F., & Magnuson, S. (2009). Averting role confusion between doctoral students and major advisers: Adviser disclosure statements. *Counselor Education and Supervision, 48*, 194–200.
Schlosser, L. Z., & Gelso, C. J. (2001). Measuring the working alliance in advisor-advisee relationships in graduate school. *Journal of Counseling Psychology, 48*, 157–167. doi:10.1037/0022-0167.48.2.157
Schlosser, L. Z., & Gelso, C. J. (2005). The Advisory Working Alliance Inventory—Advisor version: Scale development and validation. *Journal of Counseling Psychology, 52*, 650–654. doi:10.1037/0022-0167.52.4.650
Schlosser, L. Z., & Kahn, J. K. (2007). Dyadic perspectives on advisor-advisee relationships in counseling psychology doctoral programs. *Journal of Counseling Psychology, 54*, 211–217. doi:10.1037/0022-0167.54.2.211
Schwille, S. A. (2008). The professional practice of mentoring. *American Journal of Education, 115*, 139–167. doi:10.1086/590678
Sherman, N. (2009). Mentoring graduate students' career development. *Revista Romana de Comunicare si Relatii Publice, 11*(3), 87–92.
Silvia, P. (2007). *How to write a lot: A practical guide to productive academic writing*. Washington, DC: American Psychological Association.

Szymanski, D. M., Ozegovis, J. J., Phillips, J. C., & Briggs-Phillips, M. (2007). Fostering scholarly productivity through academic and internship research training environments. *Training and Education in Professional Psychology, 1,* 135–146. doi:10.1037/1931-3918.1.2.135

Tenenbaum, H. R., Crosby, F. J., & Gilner, M. D. (2001). Mentoring relationships in graduate school. *Journal of Vocational Behavior, 59,* 326–341. doi:10.1006/jvbe.2001.1804

Watson, J. C., Clement, D., Blom, L. C., & Grindley, E. (2009). Mentoring: Processes and perceptions of sport and exercise psychology graduate students. *Journal of Applied Sport Psychology, 21,* 231–246. doi:10.1080/10413200902777297

CHAPTER 9

THE TRANSFORMATIVE RELATIONSHIP WITHIN TEACHING COUNSELING SKILLS AND METHODS

Implications for Training and Practice

Laura J. Fazio-Griffith

Since its inception, the counseling profession has included foundational elements from other disciplines, such as education, and often borrows from various learning theories and models. One theory that has been in the forefront in the educational field is transformative learning, which has been a significant part of the literature in adult education. However, the concepts from the theories and models of transformative learning do not only relate to the field of adult education; they can be applied to the field of counseling and, more specifically, to teaching counseling skills and methods. This chapter will examine the potential for transformative relationships to emerge during the process of counseling graduate students who are learning counseling skills and methods. The definition of transformative relationship is how one demonstrates counseling skills, such as developing rapport and the relationship during the counseling session, when working with students in the classroom. Counseling methods such as clinical supervision, feedback, and case conceptualization are included with the concept of the transformative relationship. Additionally, this chapter will examine some theoretical perspectives of counseling and the relationship including the humanistic, or person-centered, theory of psychotherapy espoused by Carl Rogers (Corey, 1996). The theory is significant in terms of how its constructs influence the counseling relationship.

The building of the relationship during the counseling process is at the crux of helping. According to Young (2009), "at the center of the helping process is the therapeutic relationship, which provides the core conditions or supports for the other activities of the helper. The relationship is the glue or the hub of the helping process" (p. 43). The building of the relationship is crucial to the effectiveness of the counseling process, as is the learning relationship crucial to the classroom environment. The definition of the learning relationship for the purpose of this chapter is the environment that the instructor creates within the classroom to foster a community of scholars in which students share resources and learn the counseling techniques more effectively based on their relationship with others.

This chapter will discuss the learning relationship and the relationship to others, specifically masters' level counseling students enrolled in a basic counseling techniques course. An examination of the learning relationship relative to how relationships foster the learning environment, allow students the freedom to express their views on specific techniques, and facilitate a more effective counselor based on their experiences in this course will follow. Finally, the chapter offers a discussion of salient concepts from the transformative learning literature, including Mezirow's (1991) theory, which includes reference to reflection, feedback, and the process of learning to make meaning of our experiences, and blends these concepts with those of teaching counseling skills and methods to graduate students.

REVIEW OF RELATED LITERATURE

The research on transformative learning and the relationship to others is abundant in the educational field. A gap in the literature exists in applying the transformative learning model to the human services field, specifically counseling and human development. This literature review will begin with a theoretical overview of the theory of transformative learning. Following the discussion of transformative learning theory, it is imperative to narrow the discussion of the literature review to the humanistic theory. A discussion will follow of how this theory pertains to the relationship between counselor and client during the counseling process as well as an examination of the relationship between instructor and students in the classroom during a basic counseling techniques course. A discussion of the humanistic/existential theory of psychotherapy as it applies to students as they learn the counseling skills over the course of a semester will conclude the section.

The theory of transformative learning developed by Mezirow during the past two decades has greatly evolved "into a comprehensive and complex description of how learners construe, validate, and reformulate the meaning of their experience" (Cranton, 1994, p. 22). Centrality of experience, critical reflection, and rational discourse are three common themes in Mezirow's theory (Taylor, 1998), which is based on psychoanalytic theory and critical social theory. For learners to change their "meaning schemes (specifically beliefs, attitudes, and emotional reactions)," they must engage in critical reflection of their experiences, which in turn leads to a perspective transformation (Mezirow, 1991, p. 167). Many empirical studies have supported Mezirow's theory, but some contend that the critical reflection has too much importance, and the process can be too rationally driven (Taylor, 1998, pp. 33–34).

A new approach of transformative learning is beginning to emerge in the current literature. This approach looks at transformative learning as the process by which intuition, creativity, and emotion are integral pieces of how adults learn. Boyd and Meyers (1988) discuss how transformation is a "fundamental change in one's personality involving (together) the resolution of a personal dilemma and the expression of consciousness resulting in greater personality integration (p. 459). Transformative education draws on the realm of the individual's experiences, the rationale being expressed through insight, judgment, and decision; the other being expressed through symbols, images, and feelings" (p. 459). The framework of Boyd and Meyers (1988) moves beyond the ego and the emphasis on reason and logic to a definition of transformative learning that is more psychosocial in nature, which pertains to the human service professions, specifically counseling.

The person-centered therapeutic approach, based on concepts from humanistic psychology, is a branch of the existential perspective. Humanistic psychology was an alternative to the psychoanalytical and behavioral approaches. The humanistic approach grew out of the philosophical background of the existential tradition. The major concept of humanistic psychology including freedom, choice, value, personal responsibility, autonomy, purpose, and meaning are all-important to the person-centered approach (Corey, 1996). Carl Rogers is the founder of the person-centered approach, which works under the basic assumption that people are essentially trustworthy, that they have a vast potential for understanding themselves and resolving their own problems without direct intervention on the therapist's part, and that they are capable of self-directed growth if they are involved in a therapeutic relationship (Corey, 1996). For Rogers, the attitudes and personal characteristics of the therapist and the quality of the client/counselor relationship are the most important aspects in determining the outcome of the therapeutic process. Considered secondary by Rogers are the therapist's knowledge of theory and counseling interventions, as he believed that without a solid relationship, the client would be unable to progress during therapy. In 1961, Rogers published *On Becoming a Person*, which focused on the approach of "becoming the self that one truly is." Rogers characterized the process of "becoming one's experience" as an openness to experience, a trust in one's experience, an internal locus of evaluation, and a willingness to be a process. The opportunity and optimism of early American culture were undoubtedly an influence for Rogers's framework and approach of person-centered school of psychotherapy. Rogers's thinking on human personality, learning, and individual and social development is an extension of European existentialism (Walters, 2008, p. 112). Rogers's person-centered approach to the counseling and therapy process paved the way for the existential model of counseling.

The humanistic and existential approaches both share a respect for the client's subjective experience and a trust in the capacity of the client to make positive constructive choices. Each approach has in common an emphasis on concepts such as freedom, choice, values, personal responsibility, autonomy, purpose, and meaning. The major difference between the two approaches is that existentialists take the position that individuals have the anxiety of choosing to create an identity in a world that lacks an intrinsic meaning (Corey, 1996). The humanistic approach takes a less anxiety-evoking position, referencing that each individual has within by nature a potential that we can actualize and through which we can assign meaning (Corey, 1996, pp. 199–200).

The humanistic and existential approaches of counseling and psychotherapy are relevant to teaching and how students learn through the art of the relationship with the professor and each other. Rogers believed that the relationship between teacher and learner should partake of such qualities as freedom, choice, values, personal responsibility, autonomy, purpose, and meaning, and that there was huge merit in developing educational relationships that promote both therapeutic and transformational ends (Kirschenbaum & Henderson, 1989, p. 108). This philosophy espoused by Rogers was present over 100 years ago through the great existential thinker Soren Kierkegaard, who observed that the main duty of a teacher is not that of simply providing facts or delivering a lecture:

> No, to be a teacher in the right sense is to be a learner. Instruction begins with you, the teacher, learn from the learner, put yourself in his place so that

you may understand what he understands and in the way he understands it. (Kierkegaard as cited in Bretall, 1946, p. 335)

The learning relationship for Kierkegaard involves a mutual relationship, which fosters an exchange such as the active sharing of views between the learner and facilitator as a way of knowledge. For Kierkegaard and Rogers, a difference between facilitator, teacher, and educator held slight nuances, which was important for facilitating learning goals and objectives.

According to Taylor (2000), educators refer to "relational ways of learning" as holding the promise of transformation, both personal and social. Transformational learning requires trust, friendship, and support, which are all necessary for learning goals and objectives to be completed. As the learning relationship develops, Rogers would argue for the essence of the relationship between teacher and learner, regardless of the setting. The relationship between the learner and teacher should be continually committed to notions of personal worth and to one's destiny as an individual (Walters, 2008). Additionally, Rogers espoused that education must offer more than instruction, more than an offering of facts. New learners encounter an entirely different situation in the classroom, one in which the goal is that of effecting personal change through transformative learning, that is, "where only the process of seeking knowledge provides any legitimate foundation for future security" (Rogers, 1967, p. 1). As the teacher fosters the relationship, learners transform into individuals who become motivated, are open to feedback, and open to questions as well as exploration. The building of a truly authentic relationship between learner and teacher helps to foster the kind of individuals who can live a delicate but ever-changing balance between the here-and-now and face a future of working with a very diverse population of clientele. According to Dirkx (1998), the teacher facilitates change in an individual when he or she is already at work, balancing life and connecting to others while building a relationship.

According to Kahn (1991, p. 38), Rogers stated that it is the essential quality of relationship that makes a difference in achieving deep levels of learning. The qualities of genuineness, empathy, and unconditional positive regard define not only the therapeutic relationship but also the transformative learning fostered. A genuineness or congruence is essential for students learning the basic counseling skills and methods. A teacher who is not self-aware or receptive to feedback concerning his or her own thoughts and feelings would be inept at assisting students in becoming aware of their own. Rogers believed that transparency is another dimension of genuineness. Transparency indicates that the teacher does not knowingly conceal information from the student in relation to the learning process. For example, in a basic counseling techniques class, the teacher discusses with the students that some of the topics during the role-play sessions may elicit feelings and emotions that the students were unaware of prior to entering the course. The teacher should prepare the students for the potential of examining their thoughts and feelings related to a particular topic and how these feelings and thoughts may assist them in becoming a more effective counselor or hinder them in the learning process.

Rogers refers to empathy as a second quality necessary for the transformative relationship as it pertains to learning. Empathy is the sensitive way in which the teacher comes to understand and express his or her awareness of the inner experience of the learner. The teacher should attempt to experience the students' worldview but without getting lost in their world (Kahn, 1991, p. 41). As one looks at group learning in the classroom setting, the qualities of the relationship between students and teacher as well as students and students will allow for a more meaningful person-to-person encounter, hence, the anxiety of the students will decrease and the students will feel comfortable experiencing the instruction in a basic counseling techniques course.

LEARNING RELATIONSHIPS

The transformative relationship provides for a plethora of learning opportunities for graduate counseling students. One may apply the framework of Carl Rogers's theory and major tenets to the learning relationships between the teacher and the students as well as between the students themselves. If one believes the theory espoused by Boyd and Meyers (1988), then learning becomes the framework for the learner to explore alternate expressions of meaning. In order to explore these alternate expressions of meaning, the learner has to be open to receiving feedback and the authenticity of the feedback. The learner must be willing to explore new ways of learning and integrating old patterns into new meaning. The relationship developed by the teacher can greatly enhance or hinder the transformative learning process.

The role of the teacher and relationship development is paramount to this process. According to Imel (1998), the teacher's role in establishing an environment that builds trust and care and facilitates the development of sensitive relationships among learners is a fundamental principle of fostering transformative learning. Loughlin (1993) discusses the responsibility of the teacher to create a "community of knowers," individuals who are united in a shared experience of trying to make meaning of their life experience" (pp. 320–321). As a member of that community, the teacher also sets the stage for transformative learning by serving as a role model and demonstrating a willingness to learn and change by expanding and deepening the understanding of and perspectives about both subject matter and teaching (Cranton, 1994).

These concepts relate to the field of counseling as an overall premise of how teachers instruct students to become effective counselors. For example, in a graduate counseling Introduction to Techniques course, teachers and students spent the first two class meetings developing a relationship between the teacher and students as well as between students. Much time is devoted to developing rapport and a safe environment where students will feel comfortable to demonstrate the counseling skills by utilizing life situations during the role-play sessions. In order for students to execute the counseling skills successfully, they need to feel safe, respected, and have a sense of purpose or meaning for the task at hand. The teacher creates a "community of scholars" and allows the students to take ownership of their learning by developing a consensus for attendance and participation over the course of the semester. This is only possible once the relationship between teacher and student is secure and each student feels safe and willing to give and receive feedback about skills. The feedback will enhance the meaning assigned to the events that occur throughout the learning process. The role of the teacher is as the facilitator of the learning process. It would be unfair not to include the role of the learner in this process.

Taylor (1998) argues that often we place too much emphasis on the role of the teacher at the expense of the role of the learner. Although it can be very difficult for transformative learning to occur without the teacher playing a defined role, the learner also has a responsibility for creating the learning environment. As part of a community of knowers, learners share the responsibility for constructing and creating the conditions under which transformative learning can occur. The student in the Introduction to Counseling Techniques course has to decide how much of a risk she is willing to take in becoming an active participant in developing a relationship where learning can be effective.

Counseling skills, if taught effectively, can increase the student's ability to feel confident and develop a relationship with his or her clients based upon the relationship developed through transformative learning. Several learning points can ensure effective skill levels when working with clients, based on the experiences the student has in the basic counseling techniques course. First, the teacher cannot impose learning on the student. Each student needs to be able to develop and explore his own personhood and create his own style of counseling. Second, very little learning takes place unless the student and teacher invest in the process, which is inclusive of the relationship. The context of the skills and the way in which the teacher executes the course has to have some personal meaning for the student or the student will shut it out of her worldview. Third, the student will decide what is relevant and meaningful based on his or her experiences in the course.

USE OF BEST PRACTICES

This section demonstrates a model of transformative learning that takes place in a graduate counseling course. The model used will be the one espoused by Jack Mezirow (2000) in *Learning is Transformation*. Mezirow's model identifies the following steps:

- A Disorienting Dilemma—loss of job, divorce, marriage, back to school, or moving to a new culture
- Self-examination with feelings of fear, anger, guilt, or shame
- A critical assessment of assumptions
- Recognition that one's discontent and the process of transformation are shared
- Exploration of options for new roles, relationships, and actions
- Planning a course of action
- Acquiring knowledge and skills for implementing one's plans
- Provisional trying of new roles
- Building competence and self-confidence in new roles and relationships
- A reintegration into one's life on the basis of conditions dictated by one's new perspective (Mezirow, 2000, p. 22).

One way to demonstrate transformative learning in an Introduction to Counseling Techniques course is by utilizing the "fish bowl" technique in building and developing counseling skills. The fish bowl technique begins by having two students in the middle of the classroom conduct a mock counseling session using personal data from the perspective of the student who is portraying the client. While around the perimeter of the room, the other students and the teacher are observing the "client's" behaviors as well as the counseling skills exhibited by the student in the counselor role. Once the role-play is completed, the students around the perimeter of the room, as well as the teacher, provide feedback (Hulse-Killacky, 1996) to the "counselor" in terms of effective skill delivery, personal issues that were present for the "counselor," and skills that were utilized that were not appropriate considering the "client" issue. In order for the fish bowl technique to be effective, the teacher needs to facilitate a building block for a relationship between the teacher and students, as well as the students with each other. The teacher may use several techniques to develop rapport and ensure a safe and effective learning environment (see Appendix A for relationship-building activities).

In order for the process of feedback to be effective, it is important for students to process their past experiences with feedback. How does the student assign meaning to the feedback they have received in the past? Is this how the student will interpret the feedback provided by the teacher and peers after each role-play? Some of the questions that teachers and students may ask include (a) When someone says to you, "I'd like to give you some feedback," what do you think? What do you feel? What do you do? What is your worst fear? (b) When you need to give someone corrective feedback, what do you think? What do you feel? What do you do? What is your worst fear? (c) Reflect for a moment on the following phrase and then complete this sentence: "Receiving feedback as a child meant for me ____" (Hulse-Killacky, 1996). This microlab designed by Diana Hulse-Killacky can be utilized to determine how students can engage in critical reflection to understand how they can transform their past feelings and present ways of conceptualizing the process of feedback into new patterns of learning and behaviors. Teachers and students revisit the establishment of the relationship during the course of the semester when during each class a personal growth activity is used to enhance the safety and unconditional positive regard that the teacher has for the students and the students for each other. Transformative learning does not end once the relationship is established but continues throughout the learners' exposure to the classroom. Transformative learning provides the opportunity for the learners to explore their previous assumptions and look at different ways of action and relating to others (Mezirow, 2000). One can relate this directly to counseling clients, as the relationship between counselor and client is present throughout the duration of the counseling process, in which the counselor is constantly exploring assumptions and biases and exploring options for a new way of interacting with the client.

An additional technique that can demonstrate transformative learning is the use of the case study (see Appendix B). A case study is a narrative of a client who presents with specific mental health and psychosocial issues. The teacher asks the students to conceptualize and use their critical thinking skills to formulate interventions for the client. Having the students work in small groups and discuss their own worldview of the client further develops the transformative relationship. Students answer several reflection questions (see Appendix B) that will stimulate how or why their assumptions of the client may hinder the way in which they perceive, understand, and feel about the client's world. Once the students have discussed their own perceptions of the case, they share their perceptions with their peers and the teacher. The feedback exchange between students and teacher helps continue to foster the "community of scholars" or "community of knowers." As the students process the case study, they are able to share experiences and assign meaning to their experiences while assisting the client in the case study. This process relates to Mezirow's (2000) Transformational Learning Model by having the students examine self and the feelings, thoughts, and behaviors related to the case study. The beginning of the process is a disorienting dilemma, which for the students is assisting a client who may have a very different value system or live in a very different cultural context. The students become "disorientated" as they struggle with where to begin in assisting the client. The students, with the assistance of the teacher, will need to examine their assumptions about the client and the way in which the client behaves in order to counsel this client. The transformation occurs when the students and teacher recognize that their discourse will lead them to exploring new roles, relationships, and actions not only with the client presented in the case study but with each other in the classroom environment. The students can explore a course of action with the client, and they can work on acquiring the skills and knowledge needed to implement the plan. The teacher facilitates building competence and self-confidence as the students move into the role of counselor and develop new collaborative relationships with the teacher and each other within the classroom.

Teachers can include transformative learning in the classroom through a variety of techniques. I have outlined some of the techniques in this section. These techniques are not exhaustive, but they provide a framework for developing learning relationships as well as transferring this relationship from the teacher to the counseling student to working with clients. The teacher can use the case study as a dual technique for continuing the learning relationship as well as having the students examine their assumptions, beliefs, values, and how they would integrate their old patterns of thinking with new patterns to assist the client while conceptualizing the case.

DISCUSSION

The literature discussed views transformative learning as a concept applied to adult education in a formalized classroom environment. The literature seldom specifically addresses how this concept transfers to the human services field and working outside the classroom with clients. The relationship is of utmost importance to transformative learning, and this is precisely true for the counseling process (Dirkx, 1998). The relationship is essential during the counseling process, and without the relationship between the counselor and client, the process is stagnant at best. There are several commonalities in transformative learning and teaching students how to be effective counselors; it is imperative in both ventures to form relationships, use critical thinking skills and conceptualization skills, examine beliefs and value systems, and look at assumptions and worldviews. Students may experience transformative learning in an introduction to counseling skills class and then transfer this experience again into work with clients. One may easily fold transformative learning theory into several theories of counseling including the humanistic/existential schools of thought. Carl Rogers, the founder of the person-centered therapeutic approach in counseling clients, extended the theory to include aspects of teaching how to be effective with clients using some of the concepts from the transformative learning theory. Rogers' (1967) focus is on the relationship, which provides a transition to how the learning relationship can benefit students studying to be effective counselors.

Future research on this topic could take many forms. Researchers, using a qualitative inquiry, could examine transformative theory and the learning benefits for students enrolled in a basic counseling techniques course. A qualitative inquiry could help determine if students are more prepared for advanced clinical work based on the implementation of transformative theory in their basic counseling techniques course. Additionally, future research could examine students' perceptions of the counseling techniques courses that utilize transformative learning theory. Future research could also explore the basic counseling skills modeled by the teacher in a basic techniques course. Some of these skills could include attending behaviors, developing rapport, asking open-ended questions, paraphrasing, summarizing, and reframing. The researcher could analyze these skills using some qualitative research methods in exploring how students perceive their progression of the skills based on the learning environment and their own perceptions regarding their skill level.

Additionally, transformative learning theory is easily applicable to several counseling courses, such as introduction to counseling techniques, advanced counseling techniques, group work, and family counseling. Educators should consider applying transformative learning theory to courses such as research, analysis of the individual, basic statistics, and basic theories of counseling. If counselor educators incorporate transformative learning theory into the counseling curriculum, students may have a greater chance of examining their assumptions and reorganizing their old patterns of thinking and integrating them with new thinking patterns, hence making them more effective clinicians.

CONCLUSION

This chapter examines the transformative relationships during the process of developing students counseling skills during an Introduction to Counseling Techniques course. The chapter defines the transformative relationship in conjunction with the examination of several theories of counseling that specifically target developing a relationship. The humanistic and existential theories are particularly important in relation to developing a transformative learning relationship in the classroom. The chapter defines the learning relationship and how this relationship is relevant to transformative learning and the teaching of counseling skills and methods. The chapter includes best practices for incorporating transformative learning theory and explores the learning relationship. The goal of this chapter is to link the learning relationships and transformative learning theory to the development and demonstration of basic counseling skills by students in an Introduction to Counseling Techniques course. In exploring the link between learning and relationships, the modeling and development of counseling skills can enhance students' ability to conceptualize, think critically, and explore their own worldviews and perceptions, which will make them a more effective counselor in their work with clients.

A learning point of this chapter for educators is that transformative learning may not always be the goal in the classroom, but educators should not overlook the importance and impact of learning and relationships. Counselor educators may choose not to incorporate transformative learning theory in their approach to teaching but should strive to understand the theory and how effective the transformative process can be for the students and the educator when choosing whether to implement the art of the relationship in the teaching and training of counseling students.

APPENDIX A

Learning Relationship Activities

The goal of each activity is to develop learning relationships between the students. Each activity fosters a sense of genuineness and the ability to develop a safe learning environment where students can share their perceptions and worldviews and how these perceptions and worldviews may relate to counseling clients.

SAMPLE CLASS OUTLINE

1. Getting acquainted: Provide students with index cards and have them write their first names and three characteristics related to their personalities. Have the students walk around the classroom, meet everyone, and share their characteristics. Once they have met everyone, they can sit down and share their name and characteristics with the teacher.
2. Ask the students to find a partner and discuss the following: What do you find most exciting about individual counseling? What do you

find most challenging about individual counseling? Each student will introduce their partner to the class and share their thoughts.
3. Provide the students with colored paper and markers. On one side of the paper, have the students draw a picture of how they perceive self. On the other side of the paper, have the students draw how they think others perceive them. Have them find a partner that they have not already paired up with and share his or her drawing. As a large group, have the students discuss how this activity can inform their work with clients.
4. Bring a box of crayons to class and have each student choose a crayon from the box. Give the students a colored piece of paper and have them write down some adjectives about the color they selected and how they might be like the color they selected. Have the students find a partner that they have not previously worked with to share their activity. Discussion points would include, How could you apply your perception or assumption about your color to your work with clients?
5. Bring some modeling clay to class and have each student sculpt how they see self and how they see self as a counselor. Pair the students with someone they have not yet worked with to share their sculptures. Discussion points include, How is your perception of self modified with your perception of self as a counselor? Or does it? How does your worldview of self accommodate becoming a counselor? How might this activity inform your work with clients?

APPENDIX B: CASE STUDY EXAMPLE

"Amanda"

"Amanda" is a 24-year-old Caucasian female with multiple sclerosis (MS) who received the diagnosis when she was 15 years old. Amanda has been able to hide her disability until recently when she began using a cane to walk. Her doctors have told her she will continue to deteriorate until she becomes wheelchair bound. Amanda works as an intake specialist at a community mental health center. A co-worker who has noticed that her job performance is not as effective as it was several months ago referred Amanda. Amanda reports she is having difficulty making friends and dating. She states that she wants friends and a boyfriend more than anything, but she thinks a boyfriend will abandon her and she will be alone forever. She regrets telling her last boyfriend that she loved him after their fourth date, but he hung in there with her for a while. She reports that she does not feel like she belongs anywhere, even in her "perfect" family. She had a very serious boyfriend in college, but when she began using the cane, he broke up with her stating that he did not think he could handle such a serious disability and was doing her a favor, as he was not the man he thought he was. Amanda does not like going to bars as she cannot dance, and she does not want to attend an MS disability group to meet someone. She states that MS is enough for one person to handle; she does not want a relationship in which her partner has MS as well.

Amanda reports that she grew up in an upper-middle-class household. Her father is a physician and her mother has a PhD in biomedical engineering. Amanda is the youngest child and has an older brother who is a surgical resident and a sister who is an attorney. She states that her father and mother feel they have failed, as they can help everyone but their daughter. Amanda attended Catholic high school and a Jesuit college where she graduated with a degree in psychology. She would like to pursue her PhD in psychology but states, "What is the point, I cannot very well see clients in the state I will become."

She has requested that you help her with making friends and dating. Amanda tells you that she has really grown fond of you and would like for you to go to dinner with her. She thinks it will help her if you attend a social situation with her.

She tells you that if you do not want to, she thinks you are probably embarrassed to go with her because of her disability. You decline because of the potential dual relationship and your ethical code. Amanda talks about having thoughts of ending her life because you are going to abandon her as well, but tells you she would never act on it as long as you remain her therapist. During her next couple of sessions, Amanda discloses that she has begun going to bars alone, drinking to get drunk, and trying cocaine. She admits that she does not like the alcohol, but likes the high cocaine gives her. She tells you that when she is doing cocaine, she has friends who do not care about her disability.

REFLECTION QUESTIONS

1. How might the counselor develop rapport with Amanda? What are some techniques that the counselor could use to facilitate the counseling relationship?
2. How might the counselor integrate his/her own beliefs and assumptions into the counseling process?
3. How could the counselor assign meaning to the issues that the client has presented?
4. What skills could the counselor use to assist the client with her issues?

REFERENCES

Bretall, R. (Ed.). (1946). *A Kierkegaard anthology*. Princeton, NJ: Princeton University Press.
Boyd, R. D., & Myers, J. G. (1988). Transformative education. *International Journal of Lifelong Education, 7*(4), 261–284.
Corey, G. (1996). *Theory and practice of counseling and psychotherapy* (5th ed). Pacific Grove, CA: Brooks/Cole.
Cranton, P. (1994). *Understanding and promoting transformative learning: A guide for educators of adults*. San Francisco, CA: Jossey-Bass.
Dirkx, J. M. (1998). Transformative learning theory in the practice of adult education: An overview. *PAACE Journal of Lifelong Learning, 7*, 1–14.
Hulse-Killacky, D. (1996). *Microlab on feedback exchange* (Unpublished document).
Imel, S. (1998). *Transformative learning in adulthood*. (Report No. EDO-CE-98-200). Columbus, OH: Adult, Career, and Vocational Education. (ERIC Document Reproduction Service No. ED423426)
Kahn, M. (1991). *Between therapist and client*. New York, NY: W. H. Freeman.
Kirschenbaum, H., & Henderson, V. L., (Eds.). (1989). *The Carl Rogers reader*. New York, NY: Houghton Mifflin.
Loughlin, K. (1993). *A women's perceptions of transformative learning experiences within consciousness-raising*. San Francisco, CA: Mellen Research University Press.
Mezirow, J. (1991). *Transformative dimensions of adult learning*. San Francisco CA: Jossey-Bass.
Mezirow, J. (2000). *Learning as transformation*. San Francisco, CA: Jossey-Bass.
Rogers, C. (1961). *On becoming a person*. Boston, MA: Houghton Mifflin.
Rogers, C. R. (1967). The interpersonal relationship in the facilitation of learning. In R. Leeper (Ed.), *Humanizing education* (pp. 1–18). Alexandria, VA: Association for Supervision and Curriculum Development.
Taylor, E. W. (1998). *The theory and practice of transformative learning: A critical review*. (Contract No. RR93002001). Columbus, OH: Center on Education and Training for Employment. (ERIC Document Reproduction Service No. ED423422).
Taylor, E. W. (2000). Analyzing research on transformative learning theory. In J. Mezirow & Associates (Eds.), *Learning as transformation: Critical perspectives on a theory in progress* (pp. 285–328). San Francisco, CA: Jossey-Bass.
Walters, D. A. (2008). Existential being as transformative learning. *Pastoral Care in Education, 26*(2), 111–118.
Young, M. E. (2009). *Learning the art of helping: Building blocks and techniques* (4th ed.). Upper Saddle River, NJ: Pearson.

CHAPTER 10

THE ROLE OF FACULTY IN DISPOSITIONAL DEVELOPMENT OF TEACHER CANDIDATES

A Neglected Voice in Teacher Preparation

Janet Filer, Candice Dowd Barnes, and Mark Cooper

Faculty members across many university campuses are becoming increasingly perplexed and concerned about teacher candidates who compromise their learning with dispositional deficits (Jung & Rhodes, 2008; Misco, 2007; Shiveley & Misco, 2010). They often put forth minimal effort and expect maximum reward. This is a major concern within teacher education programs. The compromise in excellence is not only a detriment to the candidates, but also to their future students. Teacher candidates who engage in undesirable dispositions in the university classroom often bring those same undesirable dispositions into their teaching classrooms. This is a growing concern of faculty members responsible for teacher preparation.

Dispositions are habits of mind displayed in behaviors of an individual (Katz, 1993; Mezirow, 1997), described in the literature with terms such as "tendency," "temperament," "trait," "characteristic," or "attitude" (Damon, 2007; Splitter, 2010). More specifically, Sockett (2009) defines dispositions by three characteristics. "First, a disposition is a disposition to act (friendliness), not merely to 'be' (closed to experience). Second, a disposition to act implies awareness of what one is doing (e.g., being friendly). Third, acting with awareness implies that a person acts with intention" (p. 294). Using Sockett's definition of disposition, Mezirow (1991), and Krathwohl, Bloom, and Masia (1964) offer two theories that when combined, we propose, offer an approach that faculty members can apply to developing dispositions within university candidates. A brief review of the theories follows with synthesis later in the chapter.

TRANSFORMATIVE LEARNING

Mezirow's transformative learning theory, founded on many constructivist ideas and developed over several decades of research (Cranton, 1994; Dirkx, 1997; Mezirow, 1991), includes influences such as the works of Freire, Gould, Habermas, and Siegal. Another building block for the theory was his wife's transformative experience (Mezirow, 2009) to explain how learners build knowledge-based constructs from various experiences and information. Self-empowerment, understanding how culture and relationship shape one's life, and taking action by using various strategies and resources are essential to this theory. There are four main components of transformative learning: experience, critical reflection, reflective discourse, and action (Merriam, Caffarella, & Baumgartner, 2007). Transformative learning represents the achievement of a heightened awareness of one's own strengths, beliefs, and feelings that often leads to a paradigm shift in the learner's thinking that affects future experiences. Such learning cannot take place in isolation; it requires relatively intense discourse with others who challenge the learner's way of thinking (Mezirow, 2003).

According to Mezirow (as cited in Cooper, n.d.), one's worldview, termed the "meaning perspective," is typically acquired passively through childhood by accumulating "meaning schemes." These schemes are composed of "specific knowledge, values, and beliefs about one's experiences" (Cooper, n.d., para. 5). Together these schemes form a filter one uses when assimilating new information or experiences. As long as incoming information easily fits within a person's meaning perspective, transformative learning does not occur. It is not until an event strongly challenges one's current meaning perspective, thus forcing an accommodation, that transformative learning begins to occur.

Transformative learning (Mezirow, 1991) often begins when an individual is faced with a disorienting dilemma not easily explained by an individual's reference point, which includes one's background, culture, and prior learning. Once the individual acknowledges, analyzes, and reflects upon this dilemma and a suitable action put in place, the individual has a new reference point for future reflection. It is not simply an accumulation of additional information that indicates transformative learning, but rather it is the internalization of a new perspective through which one will view and judge future experiences. It is at this point that transformative learning occurs (Curran & Murray, 2008). At the core of Mezirow's theory is critical reflection and discourse with others in forming the new perspective (Cranton, 1994; van Halen-Faber, 1997).

KRATHWOHL'S AFFECTIVE TAXONOMY: RECEIVING TO INTERNALIZATION

Krathwohl's theory of affective development is a hierarchy that characterizes how one moves along a continuum of internalizing various schemes, constructs, ideas, and experiences (Krathwohl et al., 1964; Wilkerson & Lang, 2007). The hierarchical stages include attending, responding, valuing, organizing, and characterizing. In each stage, candidates invest more in the learning. For instance, there are three characteristics of receiving: awareness, willingness to receive, and acceptance. Krathwohl et al. (1964) are right to suggest that when candidates fail to receive or attend to teaching they compromise the learning process.

The second stage of Krathwohl et al.'s (1964) hierarchy involves responding. Compliance represents the lowest level of responding followed by two additional levels: a willingness to consider new perspectives and an emotional response to the new information. Candidates may accept information while in the first stage of the hierarchy; however, such acceptance may represent no more than blind acceptance of that information. On the other hand, the higher stage of responding involves the candidates' propensity to know not only the facts but also to experience the facts taught.

As the candidates begin to experience the facts outlined by faculty members, a third stage of Krathwohl et al.'s (1964) hierarchy emerges: valuing. In the beginning of this stage, the candidates consider the information as a new idea or perspective without any great commitment to the idea or perspective. The candidates move from this lukewarm view of the information taught to a view that represents a higher level of understanding and even a commitment to such understanding as a belief. Commitment entails an enormous amount of conviction. The candidates have a deeper level of confidence that their new perspective, ideas, knowledge, or phenomena are true. At this level, the candidates also recognize that there may be various instances in which this new idea is relevant. Therefore, the candidates have to organize these new values, which is the beginning of a value system.

The fourth stage of Krathwohl et al.'s (1964) hierarchy involves the organization of a value system. In this case, the candidates see how the values relate to those they hold or ones that they are coming to hold. It is not until the candidates begin to develop this value system that they reach the peak of this internalization hierarchy called characterization. Candidates' actions based solely on the value system they have internalized characterize this final and highest level in Krathwohl's hierarchy. The candidates' beliefs, ideas, perspectives, and attitudes now greatly influence their lives (Villegas, 2007).

UNDERSTANDING TEACHER CANDIDATES

Mezirow (1991) and Krathwohl et al.'s (1964) theoretical foundations help faculty members better understand their role for developing productive dispositions among teacher candidates. While necessary, such understanding is not sufficient to help the candidates maximize learning. High quality instruction requires that faculty members know the "who" of teacher candidates. Most candidates attending teacher education programs of study are from the Millennial Generation, also referred to as Generation Y. These are candidates born between 1982 and 2002. The first members of this generation began entering universities and colleges in 2000. Of course, overgeneralization about any category of candidates misleads faculty members to use a one-size-fits-all mentality. Yet there are some common denominators among the Millennial Generation important for consideration in instructional preparation.

There are seven unique characteristics of the millennial candidates that may help or hinder academic success in the university classroom. The seven descriptors include being special, team-oriented, sheltered, confident, pressured, conventional, and achievers (Howe & Strauss, 2000, 2003; Monoco & Martin, 2007; Wilson, 2004). These descriptors reflect the values, ideas, morals, ethics, and common messages received from parents and society. While the millennial candidates' sense of *being special* can be a wonderful quality, it can also translate into a sense of entitlement; a sense that A's should come more easily rather than hard. *Sheltered* was a second characteristic Howe and Strauss (2000), and others outlined. These authors explained that parents were often the source of such thinking, and such insulation from challenge often impaired the teacher candidates from dispositions involving self-advocacy, initiative, and self-sufficiency, enormous impediments to candidates' propensity to grasp beyond their reach (Howe

& Strauss, 2000; 2003; Monoco & Martin, 2007; Murray, 1997; Wilson, 2004). The "No Child Left Behind" era introduced a third characteristic of the millennial candidates: *pressure to achieve*. Such pressure leads teacher candidates down a slippery slope to academic misconduct often found in candidates' inability to discriminate between plagiarism and originality (Howe & Strauss, 2003; Wilson, 2004). Subsequently, academic honesty and knowledge of the behaviors that constitute cheating and misrepresentation of original work are dispositional constructs that faculty members must promote. The teacher candidates' propensity to *work in teams* is a fourth quality addressed by Howe and Strauss (2000, 2003) and other authors, which combine admirable and potential undesirable qualities. It is admirable for candidates to work in cooperative groups. Yet some of those same candidates find difficulty working independently and reflecting privately. They often fail to think for themselves, process information in-depth, and analyze information critically. A fifth characteristic of the millennial candidates involves a *sense of confidence*. The sense of confidence is like a two-edged sword. On one hand, confidence bolsters the message, "I am unique and distinguished." On the other hand, the message is, "I feel paralyzed by potential failure due to my achievement orientation." A bosom buddy of feeling special and the pressure to succeed is a sixth characteristic that influences the teacher candidates: *drive to achieve*. This explains the findings in a recent report on the millennials that millennial candidates are on target to become the most educated generation in American history (Pew Research Center, 2010). The fact that the teacher candidates have a drive to achieve does not ensure they have a desire to demonstrate the dispositions that promote achievement. Subsequently, faculty members may find highly driven candidates who act like a ship without a rudder. They tend to go forward but with too little direction. Finally, the millennial researchers describe candidates as *conventional*. In this respect, they believe more than prior generations that social rules are acceptable and important (Monoco & Martin, 2007; Wilson, 2004). In the classroom, these candidates challenge faculty assumptions that some things are just "understood." For example, for most, professors forbid texting during class. This generation is highly engrossed in technology and may not perceive texting in class as a distraction to the learning process. However, if no texting during class becomes a class policy, it brings attention to an undesirable behavior in the classroom.

These seven characteristics certainly present some positive qualities in the university classroom, but they also present challenges that complicate the candidates' propensity to be good collaborators, problem solvers, and reflective decision-makers. Thus, faculty members must first understand who their teacher candidates are and use this information to develop desirable dispositions in candidates; dispositions that will not only increase their engagement in the learning process, but will translate into dispositions they impart to future generations of learners.

DISPOSITIONAL DEVELOPMENT IN TEACHER PREPARATION

We propose that faculty members who engage in a transformative learning process are better equipped to help candidates understand the dispositional challenge, analyze it, reflect on it, and take action. We also believe that Krathwohl et al.'s (1964) affective hierarchy provides faculty members the help necessary for them to assess candidates' level of attention, responsiveness, valuing, internalization, and characterization of information taught in the university classroom. How does Mezirow's (1991) transformative learning theory in combination with Krathwohl's affective domain hierarchy apply to dispositional development within teacher education programs? The following scenario represents a conversation between two faculty members regarding teacher candidates' dispositions in the classroom:

> "I just don't know what to do with my students anymore!" the junior professor exclaimed to a more experienced colleague. The colleague was not surprised by such an expression. The professor's demeanor reflected more defeat than victory. "You're working harder than the students," the colleague retorted. "Yes, how did you know?" the junior professor asked. The colleague almost seemed anesthetized to such a reality when she lamented, "Well, many of today's students lack particular dispositions important to learning; dispositions like initiative, critical reflection, and such." "That's it! That's it!" the junior professor exclaimed. The professor continued, "Many of my students appear to come to class ill-prepared or distracted."

As in this scenario, faculty members must face teacher candidates who are ill-prepared for classroom work. Such a lack of preparation compromises teacher preparation and ultimately teacher excellence. Subsequently, the faculty members must assume some level of responsibility for not only the knowledge building and skill enhancement among the teacher candidates, but also the dispositional development required to maximize learning in the university classroom. Faculty members must initially engage in a transformative learning process composed of five steps: (a) an acknowledgement of the dilemma; (b) critiquing their own assumptions about disposition development in teacher candidates; (c) critically reviewing new ideas or perspectives to reconcile the dilemma of ill-prepared candidates; (d) making a decision on how to incorporate the newly acquired skills, knowledge, or perspectives in place of old ones; and (e) taking action. This

The Role of Faculty in Dispositional Development of Teacher Candidates ▪ 153

level of action includes implementing strategies, methods, and approaches used to develop the dispositions in candidates.

For teacher educators who acknowledge dispositions as a growing challenge, transformative learning theory (Mezirow, 1997, 2003, 2009) can be utilized to emphasize a paradigm shift from simply inferring or assuming that teacher candidates have the dispositions (values, beliefs, and attitudes) to be good teachers to providing candidates with a healthy learning environment in which they are supported in the acquisition of such dispositions in the university classroom (Nelson, 2006; Splitter, 2010). These candidates come to the university classroom with preset ideas, values, attitudes, and beliefs. Faculty members, who require the candidates to reflect on their knowledge and assess alternative perspectives, make decisions to accept or deny the new perspectives, and take action to fit the newly acquired information or experience into the broader context of their life, challenge this prior learning. Faculty members must then facilitate transformative learning in the classroom to support teacher candidates who will then internalize these dispositions into their own learning and the future teaching practices (see Figure 10.1).

According to Mezirow (1991), the movement from reflection to intentional action is the most integral part of transformative learning. In the scenario, faculty members are initiating the first phase of transformative learning by acknowledging that a dispositional challenge exists. They must then continue until they engage in an action to change their assumption that

Changing our thinking and actions

Desirable dispositions are **innate** in teacher candidates → **Transformative Process** → **Developing** desirable dispositions in teacher candidates

Faculty must internalize and value a new perspective and take action on that new thinking to effectively strengthen desirable dispositions in teacher candidates.

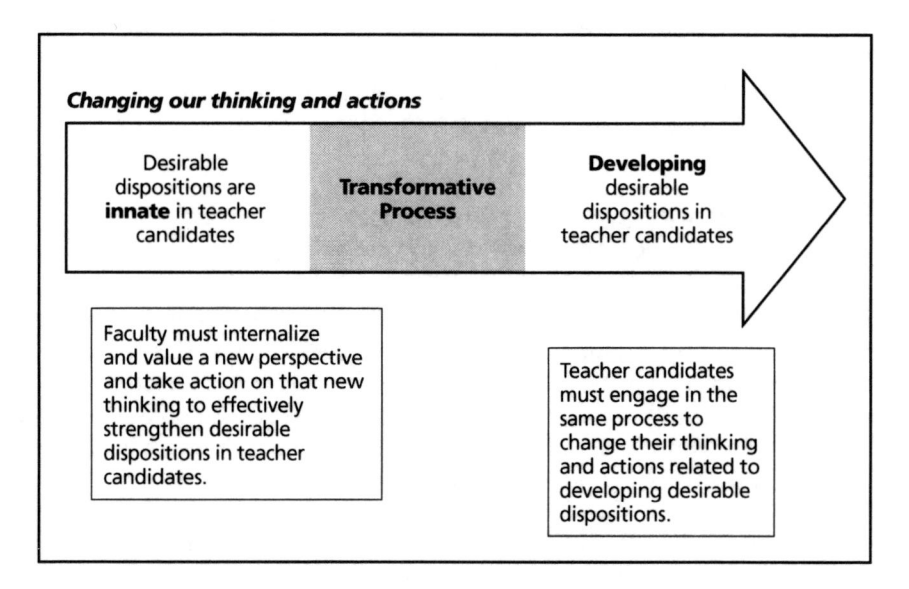

Teacher candidates must engage in the same process to change their thinking and actions related to developing desirable dispositions.

Figure 10.1 Paradigm shift for faculty and candidates.

candidates come with the prerequisite dispositions to achieve success in the college classroom. This is a continual process that can occur when new situations arise or when one encounters new information. This paradigm shift in the thinking and actions of both faculty and candidates is necessary to develop desired dispositions, as shown above in Figure 10.1.

The identification of productive or counterproductive dispositions is often a moving target. There must be dozens of dispositions that may qualify as important to the pursuit of excellence among teacher preparation candidates. Dispositional deficits in diligence, determination, initiative, patience, risk-taking, graceful mistake-making, self-discipline, responsibility, internal locus of control, and flexibility are all great qualifiers for interfering with learning in the university classroom. The ability for faculty members to help teacher candidates overcome those dispositional deficits is vital to candidates' success in the university classroom. However, faculty members must go beyond helping candidates simply identify the dispositions that need improvement or strengthening (Diez, 2007). They must create and facilitate opportunities for candidates to internalize the dispositions and transfer them successfully into their teaching pedagogy. By internalizing dispositions, teacher candidates are more likely to transfer those skills, attitudes, behaviors, and values to their students (Villegas, 2007). Key to achieving internalization for faculty and teacher candidates is an understanding that internalization does not magically happen. It requires an individual to connect both the affective and the cognitive domains in order to achieve the highest level of internalization-characterization of the value system. As demonstrated in Figure 10.2, the affective domains coincide with the transformative learning process. It is by integrating Krathwohl et al.'s (1964) hierarchy into the classroom experiences that will solidify the transformative learning process in candidates.

FACULTY ROLE IN DISPOSITIONAL DEVELOPMENT: A NEGLECTED VOICE NO MORE

It is important that an emphasis on dispositional development among teacher education candidates becomes more evident within the university classroom. Dispositional development should no longer be a silent partner in teaching, a hidden agenda, and/or a neglected voice. Faculty must clearly identify, define, demonstrate, rehearse, monitor, and yes, affirm candidates' dispositional development. There must be open and honest discussions among faculty members and teacher candidates as well as attempts to teach dispositions through a variety of instructional modalities—formal, informal, incidental, and modeling. An integral part of such lessons requires that teacher candidates become strong and high func-

The Role of Faculty in Dispositional Development of Teacher Candidates ▪ **155**

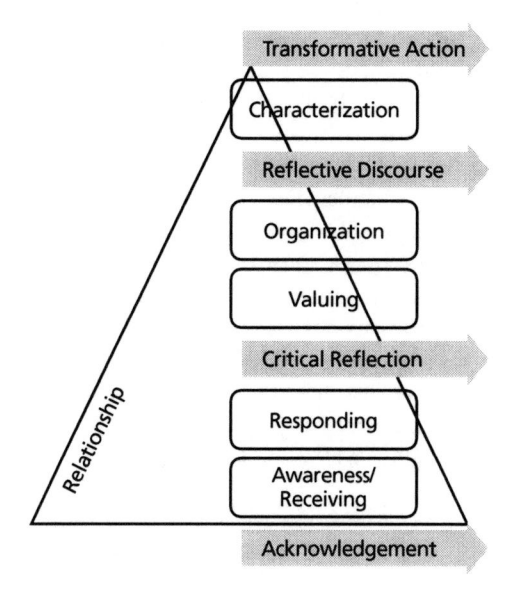

Figure 10.2 Relationship between Transformative Learning and the Affective Hierarchy.

tioning. Candidates who fail to demonstrate particular dispositions fail to pursue excellence at an optimal level and stunt their potential while also reducing their understanding of knowledge and skills important to teacher effectiveness.

Therefore, if faculty members believe teacher candidates compromise learning due to dispositional deficits, they must become proactive and ask two questions, "What explains such deficiencies?" and "What must be done to develop dispositions?" While faculty members cannot make teacher candidates change, they can create a climate for change. They can provide instruction designed to promote the development of those dispositions such as diligence, determination, self-acceptance, patience, risk-taking, and graceful mistake-making. In other words, teacher educators must carve out a path for teacher candidates to follow and resist taking for granted mastery in dispositional development. There must be closer attention paid to reducing those dispositions that profoundly impede learning as well as producing those dispositions that enhance learning. If the goal is to have highly effective teachers, then there must be more attention paid to the development of highly effective candidates as learners. The development of knowledge and skills of teaching effectiveness are necessary but not sufficient. There must also be a third component of learning: dispositional development. A better understanding of the candidates makes such a proposition an instructional imperative. A primary goal is to ensure that candidates become active and empowered learners capable of thinking critically and capable of showing sensitivity to all learners, including themselves.

Faculty members need to focus on changing the behaviors that inherently shape these dispositions in our candidates (Diez, 2007). While there is no consensus on the best way to promote productive dispositions and demote counterproductive dispositions, Taylor (2007) suggests that authentic and genuine relationships between faculty members and teacher education candidates is an essential factor in this transformative learning experience. Cranton (2006) corroborates such an assertion by stating, "Fostering transformative learning opportunities depends to a large extent on establishing meaningful, genuine relationships with candidates" (p. 5). This lack of consensus should not dissuade faculty members from organizing and developing an action plan for dispositional development. The following section represents possibilities for such development.

HOW TO GET STARTED

The aforementioned scenario most likely occurs in many institutions across the nation. Lengthy conversations must occur regarding strategies useful to help faculty members influence teacher candidates to maximize learning and strive for their personal best. The first step is for faculty members to stop complaining about dispositional deficits among teacher candidates and take action that includes an application of transformative learning. Faculty members should not stop short of applying the steps of transformative learning outlined by Merriam et al. (2007). They need to recognize the experience, reflect upon it, have discourse, and take action. A faculty team charged with reviewing the literature about dispositional development and defining dispositional deficits that impinge on teacher candidates' learning as well as those dispositions that maximize learning can facilitate this process of transformative learning. It is at this time that faculty members share examples of dispositional deficits found in classrooms. Common deficits might include inattention, lack of class preparation, lack of study, overconfidence in understanding, punctuality with assignment submissions, and so forth. Following such discussions, faculty members should elaborate on the three primary questions:

1. How should faculty members introduce information to teacher candidates about dispositional development?
2. How can faculty embed dispositional expectations into teacher candidates' program of study?
3. How do faculty members hold students accountable for demonstrating dispositions?

How Should Faculty Members Introduce Information to Teacher Candidates About Dispositional Development?

There is no single answer to the question about the introduction of dispositional development to teacher candidates. High quality orientation of candidates should include consideration of candidates' background and characteristics by a team of faculty members. In all cases, expectations must become increasingly explicit and transparent. Such explicitness and transparency emerges from discussions between faculty members and teacher candidates (Diez, 2007; Henderson & Gornik, 2007). In fact, faculty members might survey graduates or conduct focus groups designed to solicit feedback about dispositional development in hindsight. Once faculty members have organized enough information about dispositional needs, they can begin developing and implementing some preliminary activities designed to introduce the development of dispositions at the beginning of the program of study. It is very likely that the faculty team will have many ideas that might include some of the following:

- Conduct class discussions with teacher candidates participating in strategically placed introductory classes about the meaning of dispositions and those dispositions that help or hinder learning in the university classroom (Imel, 1998).
- Share dispositional development information during program and field orientations.
- Create visual cues or bulletin board displays throughout the building and in classrooms that highlight the importance of dispositional development. There is the old adage, "Visualization reinforces vocalization." The visuals or bulletin board displays can help reinforce discussions about dispositions and achieving personal bests.
- Create an online instructional module for all incoming students to review and discuss on dispositional development.
- Conduct focus groups on the importance of dispositional development and strategies for promoting such dispositions.

A key aspect of a dispositional development plan is to take the plan out of hiding and let teacher candidates know its importance.

How Can Faculty Embed Dispositional Expectations Into Teacher Candidates' Program of Study?

Introductory activities designed to increase awareness about dispositional development are necessary but not sufficient. Faculty members must also develop and implement strategies that represent more breadth and depth for knowledge building and skill enhancement. Candidates' immersion in dispositional development must occur during the program of study. Such immersion might include the following activities:

- The faculty team must model explicitly the dispositions considered important to the pursuit of excellence among teacher candidates. It is helpful for faculty members to discuss ways they resist dispositional deficits and how the development of dispositions like persistence helps them maximize learning. Faculty members who expect teacher candidates to attend class prepared must also demonstrate the same preparedness.
- There are few documents that represent the course better than the course syllabi. The faculty team should include in the course syllabi a consistent statement about dispositional development. Consistency communicates an organized effort and highlights more clearly the consensus among faculty members about the importance of dispositional development.
- Case analyses can be effective activities for helping teacher candidates move from a superficial understanding of dispositional development to one that represents internalization. Such analyses are significant strategies for promoting reflective decision-making. Teacher candidates can create role-playing activities designed to represent the different cases germane to the particular candidates.
- One idea that has great appeal involves contract development. Teacher candidates can be encouraged to share among classmates dispositional deficits to overcome followed by strategies to overcome those deficiencies. They can conclude this activity with a statement of intent designed as a commitment to strengthen particular dispositions.

How Do Faculty Members Hold Candidates Accountable for Demonstrating Dispositions?

Educators, family members, and students understand high-stakes testing. Teacher candidates are well-aware of the many accountability systems designed to assess academic progress. An accountability system for evaluating dispositions is entirely different. Most faculty members pay less attention to grading dispositions, such as persistence, initiative, and cooperation, and responsibility, yet those are factors that influence grades in particular university classes. In some instances, course and assignment grades represent the demonstration of those dispositions. The presumption is that an emphasis on such disposition assessment makes clearer faculty members' aspirations to help teacher candidates strengthen dispositions. In doing so, teacher candidates maximize learning considering the correlation between work ethic and learning. The following activities may encourage the development of an accountability system:

- Provide candidates with a dispositional rubric designed to help teacher candidates more fully understand the appropriate level of dispositional development that maximizes learning in the university classroom.
- Encourage faculty members to conduct staff meetings for the purpose of reviewing teacher candidates' dispositional development. Faculty and staff should identify needs among teacher candidates as well as to develop action plans designed to help candidates meet those needs.
- Develop and implement remediation plans when necessary. Such plans represent responses to candidates who exhibit dispositional deficits that impair learning at a level detrimental to future teaching. Candidates who graduate and have a habit of procrastinating may need a remediation plan. The perfectionist may be a good candidate for remediation if the perfectionism causes undue duress and emotional outbursts among teacher candidates. Teachers learn that children in the class are capable of compromising the best lesson plan in the world. The perfectionist must learn to cope with such a reality without thinking, "I am worthless as a teacher."
- Organize activities for professional development/inservicing, coaching, and fidelity checks. It is important to have instructional activities, workshops, and/or seminars designed for dispositional development. Coaching and fidelity checks should be integral to those activities. Short-lived activities without follow-up and assessment usually fall far short of mastery or even proficiency.

Through such explicit attention to dispositional development, teacher candidates will evaluate newly developed dispositions and embrace such dispositions as a fundamental part of teaching.

CONCLUSION: INFLUENCERS OF DISPOSITIONAL DEVELOPMENT

The question of how best to provide opportunities to develop dispositions and assist candidates in maximizing their learning, which will in turn influence their future teaching, is an important one. The development of dispositions is not an easy task. It is deeply rooted in the candidates' background knowledge and experiences, prejudices, personalities, and temperaments. Those characteristics become increasingly evident when the candidates reach the university classroom. They have acquired a unique and distinctive way of viewing the world and interpreting new knowledge, skills, and experiences. They now have the task of integrating their previous knowledge from their K–12 experiences with new ideas and experiences that likely contradict their beliefs. This integration of prior and present knowledge requires reflection, revision, and even rejection of prior learning, a difficult task for many candidates. Thus, it is necessary for faculty members to provide candidates with opportunities to reflect critically on their work, pursue academic excellence and informed decision-making, and guide them through a transformative learning process. Fostering transformation is a process that requires significant resolve among faculty members.

Faculty members very often see themselves as teachers rather than influencers. It may be that teacher preparation requires the faculty team to teach content knowledge while also influencing dispositions. Patterson, Grenny, Maxfield, McMillan, and Switzler (2008) stated,

> The fact that many of us don't realize that it's our duty to become good at exerting influence causes us a great deal of grief. Instead of owning up to our responsibility of becoming effective agents of change and then going about the task of improving our influence repertoire, we grumble, threaten, ridicule, and, more often than not, find ways to cope. (p. 9)

The application of the serenity prayer should not replace a proactive position to influence teacher candidates to practice dispositions that help them maximize learning.

Faculty members who see themselves as influencers will better empower teacher candidates to change their perspective based on newly acquired information. These changes will require carefully constructed experiences within the university classroom. During this process, faculty members will guide teacher candidates through a transformative learning process wherein dispositions they develop will support their success and achievement. More importantly, this process of change will affect the 20+ students the teacher candidates teach once graduated from their teacher preparation program of study.

Henry David Thoreau once stated, "If you have built castles in the air, your work need not be lost; that is where they should be. Now put the foundation under them" (as cited in Edelman, 2005, p. 21). The foundation for teacher candidates reaching their optimal level of learning involves their dispositional development. Candidates who show determination, confidence, initiative, patience, risk-taking, responsibility, cooperation, and so forth maximize learning. Faculty members must not be complacent about dispositional development. Such development must not be a hidden part of the academic agenda. The previously neglected voices of faculty members across the country must be silent no longer—the teaching of content knowledge should include the voice of reason. It is the teaching of dispositions that can very possibly transform learning and keep those castles built in the air airborne.

ACKNOWLEDGMENT

The authors would like to acknowledge the contributions made in the "How to Get Started" section of the chapter by the Department of Early Childhood and Special Education faculty members and the department's Disposition Committee.

REFERENCES

Cooper, S. (n.d.). *Theories of learning in educational psychology*. Retrieved from http://www.lifecircles-inc.com/Learningtheories/humanist/mezirow.html

Cranton, P. (1994). *Understanding and promoting transformative learning: A guide for educators of adults*. San Francisco, CA: Jossey-Bass.

Cranton, P. (2006). *Understanding and promoting transformative learning*. San Francisco, CA: Jossey-Bass.

Curran, E., & Murray, M. (2008). Transformative learning in teacher education: Building competencies and changing dispositions. *Journal of the Scholarship of Teaching and Learning, 8*(3), 103–118.

Damon, W. (2007). Dispositions and teacher assessment: The need for a more rigorous definition. *Journal of Teacher Education, 58*, 365–369.

Diez, M. E. (2007). Looking back and moving forward: Three tensions in the teacher dispositions discourse. *Journal of Teacher Education, 58*, 388–396.

Dirkx, J. (1997). Nurturing soul in adult learning. In P. Cranton (Ed.), *Transformative learning inaction: Insights from practice* (pp. 79–88). San Francisco, CA: Jossey-Bass.

Edelman, M. W. (2005). *I can make a difference*. New York, NY: Harper Collins.

Henderson, J. G., & Gornik, R. (2007). *Transformative curriculum leadership*. Upper Saddle River, NJ: Pearson.

Howe, N., & Strauss, W. (2000). *Millennials rising. The next greatest generation*. New York, NY: Vintage Books.

Howe, N., & Strauss, W. (2003). *Millennials go to college. Strategies for a new generation on campus: Recruiting and admissions, campus life, and the classroom*. New York, NY: LifeCourse.

Imel, S. (1998). *Transformative learning in adulthood*. Retrieved from http://bern.library.nenu.edu.cn/upload/soft/0-article/025/25003.pdf

Jung, E., & Rhodes, D. M. (2008). Revisiting disposition assessment in teacher education: Broadening the focus. *Assessment & Evaluation in Higher Education, 33*(6), 647–660.

Katz, L. G. (1993). *Dispositions as educational goals.* ERIC Clearinghouse on Elementary and Early Childhood Education, University of Illinois-Urbana. Retrieved October 22, 2009, from www.ericdigests.org/1994/goals.htm

Krathwohl, D., Bloom, B., & Masia, B. (1964). *Taxonomy of educational objectives, Book 2: Affective domain.* New York, NY: Longman.

Merriam, S. B., Caffarella, R. C., & Baumgartner, L. M. (2007). *Learning in adulthood: A comprehensive guide* (3rd ed., pp. 130–158). San Francisco, CA: Jossey Bass.

Mezirow, J. (1991). *Transformative dimensions of adult learning.* San Franciso, CA: Jossey-Bass.

Mezirow, J. (1997). Transformative learning: Theory to practice. *New Directions for Adult and Continuing Education, 74,* 5–12.

Mezirow, J. (2003). *Epistemology of transformative learning.* Retrieved from http://transformativelearning.org/index_files/Mezirow_EpistemologyTLC.pdf

Mezirow, J. (2009). Transformative learning theory. In J. Mezirow, E. W. Taylor, & Associates (Eds.), *Transformative learning in practice: Insights from community, workplace, and higher education.* San Francisco, CA: Jossey-Bass.

Misco, T. (2007). Did I forget about dispositions? Preparing high school graduates for moral life. *The Clearing House: A Journal of Educational Strategies, Issues, and Ideas, 80*(6), 267–270.

Monoco, M., & Martin, M. (2007, April–June). The millennial student: A new generation of learners. *Athletic Training Education Journal, 2,* 42–46.

Murray, N. D. (1997). Welcome to the future: The Millennial Generation. *Journal of Career Planning and Employment, 57*(3), 36–40.

Nelson, D. B. (2006). *The emotionally intelligent teacher: A transformative learning model.* Retrieved from www.21stcenturysociety.org/Darwin_Nelson.html

Patterson, K., Grenny, J., Maxfield, D., McMillan, R., & Switzler, A. (2008). *The power to change anything.* New York, NY: McGraw-Hill.

Pew Research Center. (2010). *Millennials, a portrait of generation next: Confidence, connected, open to change. Pew Research Center.* Retrieved from http://pewsocialtrends.org/files/2010/10/millennials-confident-connected-open-to-change.pdf

Shiveley, J., & Misco, T. (2010). "But how do I know about beliefs?": A four-step process for integrating and assessing dispositions in teacher education. *The Clearing House: A Journal of Educational Strategies, Issues, and Ideas, 83*(1), 9–14.

Sockett, H. (2009). Dispositions as virtues: The complexity of the construct. *Journal of Teacher Education, 60*(3), 291–303.

Splitter, L. J. (2010). Dispositions in education: Nonentities worth talking about. *Educational Theory, 60*(2), 203–230.

Taylor, E. W. (2007). An update of transformative learning theory: A critical review of the empirical research (1999–2005). *International Journal of Lifelong Education, 26,* 173–191.

van Halen-Faber, C. V. (1997). Encouraging critical reflection in preservice teacher education: A narrative of a personal learning journey. In P. Cranton (Ed.), *Transformative learning in action: Insights from practice* (pp. 51–60). San Francisco, CA: Jossey-Bass.

Villegas, A. M. (2007). Dispositions in teacher education: A look at social justice. *Journal of Teacher Education, 58,* 370–380.

Wilkerson, J., & Lang, W.(2007). *Assessing teacher dispositions.* Thousand Oaks, CA: Corwin.
Wilson, M. (2004, Summer). Teaching, learning and millennial students. *New Directors for Student Services,* (106), 59–71.

RELATIONSHIP WITH CULTURE, CONTEXT, AND TECHNOLOGY

PART I

TRANSFORMATIVE LEARNING IN MULTICULTURAL, CROSS-CULTURAL, AND INTERCULTURAL CONTEXTS

CHAPTER 11

EASING TEACHER CANDIDATES TOWARD CULTURAL COMPETENCE THROUGH THE MULTICULTURAL STEP OUT

Freddie A. Bowles and Nancy P. Gallavan

Becoming a classroom teacher in the 21st century requires teacher candidates to demonstrate proficiencies with the appropriate knowledge, skills, and dispositions in ever-changing sociocultural contexts to ensure educational efficacy with all students (Association of Teacher Educators, 2008; Interstate New Teacher Assessment and Support Consortium, 1999; National Council for the Accreditation of Teacher Education, 2007; Teacher Education Accreditation Council, 2009). Striving for educational efficacy necessitates incorporating multiple domains of learning, types of intelligences, forms of expressions, and points of view. Today's candidates must broaden their teaching styles and optimize their learning experiences for students to develop profound cultural comprehension and powerful individual connections.

To this end, teacher educators must guide and support their candidates to understand these concepts and practices by involving candidates in purposeful investigations related to their distinctive backgrounds, beliefs, behaviors, and bequests or legacies (Gallavan & Webster-Smith, 2010). This process, called navigating cultural competence, encompasses understanding and accepting oneself, one another, and all of society—locally and globally—demonstrated through thoughts, words, actions, and interactions (Gallavan, 2011a). "Understand(ing) the meaning of our experience" (Mezirow, 1997, p. 5) as individuals and as members of many different ever-changing groups and environments encompasses a common human experience; equipping candidates with a compass to help them guide their paths is essential.

The authors detail the Multicultural Step Out (MC Step Out) conducted in an introductory education course, guiding candidates in navigating cultural competence. Grounded on the Gallavan Cultural Competence Compass (GCCC; see Figure 11.1), the MC Step Out presents an inclusive model. Each of the eight steps aligns with each of the eight directions of the GCCC, providing direction throughout candidates' transformational process.

The GCCC provides educators with a physical representation of the eight essential elements of cultural competence for enhancing efficacy. Arranged as the directions on a compass, the points communicate the nature

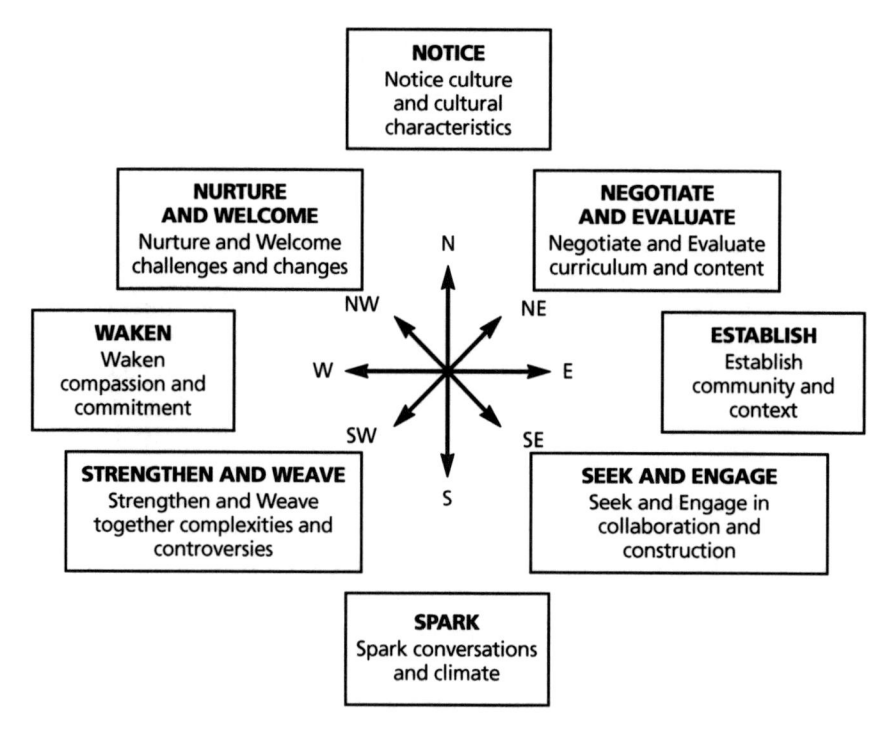

Figure 11.1 Gallavan Cultural Competence Compass (Gallavan, 2011b).

of education as a journey and the importance for navigating it within the milieu of one's career path. Achieving a balance of the eight elements allows educators to assess their own abilities and attitudes, guide their curriculum and instruction, equip them with tools and techniques, open their hearts and minds, and reflect upon their personal growth and professional development, all essential elements of educational efficacy.

The MC Step Out and the GCCC incorporate three common elements central to Mezirow's concept of transformative learning: centrality of experience, critical reflection, and rational discourse (Taylor, 1998). The themes unifying this chapter illuminate the importance of developing relationships with culture and context as candidates individually experience transformative learning exemplifying centrality of experience and as group members as they share their accounts with one another in class, demonstrating rational discourse.

The majority of candidates, Caucasian and middle class, bring limited experiences of other cultures into their education classes. In Multicultural Issues, candidates begin an intense process of self-reflection to examine their perspectives on issues involving identity of self and others. From guest speakers to reading circles, candidates explore their interpretations of events and actions related to cultural and linguistic diversity. Individual candidates nurture one another through transformative relationships as they share experiences and transfer their discoveries to their educational efficacy exemplifying critical reflection.

TEACHER EDUCATION PROGRAM AND COURSE CONTEXT

The multicultural education course at this mid-south university is a required 3-credit-hour course featured in a fifth-year Master of Arts in Teaching (MAT) cohort graduate teacher education program culminating in initial licensure. Over the course of a calendar year, candidates attend courses in a specific sequence, scaffolding the content and practices taught during the previous semester. Each candidate observes three different classrooms at the middle, junior, and senior levels in area schools within a 40-mile radius. The candidate progresses from observing the teacher to teaching full time, with mentorship and supervision provided by both the classroom teacher and MAT faculty.

The multicultural education course occurs during the third and last semester. The curriculum helps candidates explore and understand the sociocultural context of communities, families, schools, classrooms, and students in relationship to society, education, and themselves. Candidates have matured and become more comfortable in their roles as educators as they delve into topics, issues, rights, and responsibilities.

The multicultural education course caters to middle/secondary school environments and is in candidates' content areas and educational contexts. Partnerships with participating school administrators and teachers provide the appropriate guidance and collaborative support necessary to fulfill the expectations of the multicultural education course.

The demographic composition of this group of candidates in this MAT program reflects contemporary new teachers: young adult, Caucasian, middle-class females. The goal of the course is to prepare these candidates to practice efficacy with culturally and linguistically diverse students, the definition of today's P–12 learners. Research reveals mixed results in candidates' abilities to transform their attitudes and beliefs regarding cultural/racial differences (Sleeter, 2001; Weisman & Garza, 2002). Yet despite encountering disequilibrium, teacher educators remain dedicated to offering opportunities for change with their candidates so they will model and reinforce change among their own future students (Bergeon, 2008).

REVIEW OF THE LITERATURE

U.S. students in P–16 classrooms need a wide range of content and practices strengthened with productive models and positive reinforcements to become knowledgeable, active, responsible, and contributing citizens in the interdependent global society (National Council for the Social Studies, 1994). Just as no learning occurs in a vacuum, curriculum for every academic subject area, whether taught in isolation or via an integrated focus, entails knowledge, skills, and dispositions placed within a multitude of sociocultural contexts. To reach the nucleus of learning, it is the teacher's obligation to enable each student to activate prior experiences, incorporate new learning, broaden connections within the classroom and community, and take ownership of outcomes.

As a young learner matures, sociocultural contexts expand engaging student's peers, family members, and communities while encountering the sociocultural contexts of people who are like and unlike the learner. Teachers must realize the powerful role of one's sociocultural context influencing the developmentally appropriate cognitive, physical, affective, and social growth of individuals and groups. In order to achieve efficacy, it is essential for teachers to demonstrate cultural competence within the curriculum and classroom at all times and with all students (Bruce, Esmond, Ross, Dookie, & Beatty, 2010; Putney & Broughton, 2011).

Although education programs are framed by standards that call for cultural competence (ATE, 2008; INTASC, 1999; NCATE, 2007; TEAC, 2009), not all candidates are prepared to understand and demonstrate cultural competence and educational efficacy. Today's candidates bring limited knowledge and experience; learning about cultural competence is foreign to them. Gay states, "educators who have only superficial knowledge of cultural, racial, and ethnic differences cannot address them sufficiently in instructional programs and policies" (Gay, 2000, p. xvi). She elaborates on the complex issues deeply ingrained in society and suggests that multicultural education scholars create "systematic mechanisms to make these analyses [of these issues], and their related instructional practices, more manageable" (p. xvi).

Candidates may or may not have been raised or educated in environments that understand, practice, and/or value multicultural education. According to the U.S. Department of Education, National Center for Education Statistics (2006), 84% of teachers are European American and 75% are female. By chance and by choice, cultural competence may or may not occur in their courses and/or field placements; the quality of navigating cultural competence differs across programs. Additionally, candidates exhibit varying degrees of acceptance or resistance to cultural competence (Garmon, 1996; McGeehan, 1982); they may or may not be motivated to learn for themselves or teach their students responsively.

Multicultural education courses aim to equip candidates with the tools that Mezirow (1997) deems important for cultural competence to "move toward a frame of reference that is more inclusive, discriminating, self-reflective, and integrative of experience" (p. 5). Thus, as candidates gain cultural competence, they transform from an exclusive ethnocentric frame of reference to a more holistic and flexible frame.

Dedicated teacher educators have developed multicultural education courses with assorted activities and assignments to meet the standards, fulfill the goals, equip candidates, and demonstrate efficacy through methodologies that reflect Vygotsky's Social Development Theory (Vygotsky, 1978). Serving as a facilitator or the More Knowledgeable Other with whom students interact and collaborate to construct their own meaning (Vygotsky, 1978.), the teacher balances the range of variables influencing cultural competence.

Studies have examined multicultural education reform (Banks, 2008) and variables associated with cross-cultural change (Pohan, 1996). Surveying 492 teacher candidates, Pohan found that cross-cultural experiences positively affect personal and professional beliefs about diverse learners. Experiential learning in diverse cultural contexts provides candidates with unlimited opportunities to learn by participating in first-person activities such as field trips or multicultural excursions (Farmer, Knapp, & Benton, 2007). Through carefully designed field trips, candidates are more likely to experience the lives of misunderstood and marginalized people who have become victims of society, stereotyped with labels of cultural deficiencies; from their reflectivity, candidates transfer discoveries and learning into their teaching, transforming into agents of change (Schön, 1987; Zeichner et al., 1998).

Candidates become advocates for all students in their schools and classrooms; they understand how to design and implement instruction and assessment for diverse learners; they seek ways to utilize the cultural capital of all students in creating effective learning environments; and they provide leadership and examples of culturally responsive teaching for their colleagues. According to Gay, change agents are committed to "create equality, justice, and power balances among ethnic groups" (2000, p. 34). Gay also states that change agents accomplish these outcomes by "confronting and transcending the cultural hegemony nested in much of the curriculum content and classroom instruction of traditional education" (p. 34).

The MC Step Out assignment, based on Gallavan's Cultural Competence Compass (GCCC), takes the reader through a journey of transformation. Each direction of the GCCC tracks the steps of the assignment as candidates move from exposure to a cultural event outside their realm of experience to enlightenment as they share and reflect on their perspectives.

Mezirow's themes of transformative learning—centrality of experience, critical reflection, and rational discourse—connect to the assignment. Imel describes Mezirow's theory as manifested "when individuals change their frames of reference by critically reflecting on their assumptions and beliefs and consciously making and implementing plans that bring about new ways of defining their worlds" (1998, para. 8). Candidates begin this process by analyzing cultural knowledge and perspectives about themselves and their students. The MC Step Out assignment takes the candidates into the community to discover how other people, particularly middle and secondary school students, define their worlds. Candidates use this information to make plans for transforming their personal, professional, and pedagogical lives that "validates, facilitates, liberates and empowers ethnically diverse students by simultaneously cultivating their cultural integrity, individual abilities, and academic success" (Gay, 2000, p. 44).

THE GALLAVAN CULTURAL COMPETENCE COMPASS

The Multicultural Step Out

Capitalizing upon the accessible resources of the immediate geographic area (Black, 2000), the instructor designed a combination of in-class activities and out-of-class assignments that involves conducting a field trip or cultural excursion. The instructor devoted the first four class sessions to Gallavan's compass directions "N" and "NE." Candidates examine their unique cultural identities by composing an *ABC: Who Are We?* poem, explore their cultural competence through a Human Cultural Bingo game, delved into their cultural competence about their students, and brainstormed lists and locations for them to "step out." The instructor and candidates collaborated in the creation of a protocol for conducting the Step Out. Class sessions 1 and 2 connected to Mezirow's (1997) theme of centrality of experience; class sessions 3 and 4 linked with his theme of rational discourse.

Class sessions 5 through 9 focused on Gallavan's compass directions "E" and "SE" and connected to all of Mezirow's (1997) themes including critical reflection. Candidates chose an event and location for their MC Step Out, recording their experiences and reflections. Candidates worked independently during this time, but the instructor allowed class time for questions and feedback.

Class sessions 10 through 12 completed the journey with compass points "S," "SW," "W," and "NW," providing more connections to Mezirow's (1997) themes of critical reflection and rational discourse. Candidates shared final drafts in small group settings during class session 10. In class session 11, candidates drew connections to the concepts of cultural competence, summarizing with ways to infuse their personal, professional, and pedagogical lives with these new concepts. During class sessions 12 and 13, candidates presented a synopsis of their MC Step Out, with peers providing valuable feedback. Candidates uploaded their reports to their electronic portfolios as the final project.

Some candidates are enthusiastic about this project; other candidates are less interested in the project and/or resistant to multicultural education in general. Instructors should be aware of candidates' attitudes and participation to intercede appropriately when necessary.

MC Step Out Goals and Purposes

The MC Step Out has highlighted the MAT multicultural education course for two years with candidates visiting approximately 50 locations enhancing their personal, professional, and pedagogical efficacy. The instructor starts the in-class activity by asking candidates to focus on one of their middle or high school students with whom the candidate seems to possess little knowledge of or identification with the students' life away from school. This first activity showcases one of the common themes in transformative learning—centrality of experience. Then candidates are led through a sequence of four instructions for completing a 2-T table.

The table helps candidates isolate specific qualities or descriptive aspects about one student, aligning the information identified in each column in a succinct graphic organizer. First, candidates write phrases that describe the student in every way possible in the left column of the table. Second, candidates write phrases about what they do not know about the student in the center column. Third, candidates identify in the right column locations where this student might go when not in school. Fourth, candidates discuss their papers with other candidates.

This activity initiates conversations relating to the course goals and the purposes previewing the MC Step Out. By approaching the course as a teacher trying to reach one student, the course has established a meaningful and manageable context. Rather than looking at multicultural education in its entirety or a whole class collectively, concentrating on one student gives each candidate an immediate and relevant purpose for the course curriculum. In addition, by telling other candidates about one student, the candidate's focus on this particular student has intensified and initiated the candidate's transformation.

The instructor delineates the expectations of the MC Step Out assignment. Each candidate is required to select a location in the geographic area that is new or different to the candidate. The candidate conducts the MC Step Out by visiting the location (making advance arrangements when necessary), observing all facets, taking notes, collecting artifacts, and writing a summary of the visit to be shared in class.

The assignment is scored through both self-assessment and instructor assessment. Candidates are encouraged to connect their MC Step Out with the student they identified in the in-class activity and share their MC Step Out experience at the end of the semester. Stepping out of their comfort zones broadens candidates' zones of proximal development so that teaching and learning are inclusive.

The class generates a list of possible locations built upon previous class lists. Candidates report to the instructor their chosen locations within 2 weeks, so the instructor can provide guidance, reinforce candidates' commitment to the assignment, and ensure that no two candidates have chosen the same location.

The Gallavan Cultural Competence Compass Alignment with the MC Step Out

Gallavan's Cultural Competence Compass (GCCC) provides the framework for the semester-long multicultural journey essential for candidates to comprehend efficacy (Bandura, 1977). The MC Step Out activities and assignments pave the route for candidates as they travel through their processes of transformation. Table 11.1 illustrates alignment.

Easing Teacher Candidates Toward Cultural Competence ▪ 177

TABLE 11.1 Alignment of Cultural Competence, MC Transformation, Activity/Assignment Objectives, and Learning Outcomes with the MC Step Out

Cultural Competence Compass Directions	MC Step Transformation	Activity/Assignment Objectives	Learning Outcomes
N = Notice culture cultural and characteristics	1. Event	Become aware of cultural locations in immediate geographic area appropriate for conducting MC Step Out.	Survey choices and report intended location for conducting the MC Step Out.
NE = Negotiate and **Evaluate** curriculum and content	2. Experience	Arrange and conduct an MC Step Out on own referencing protocol.	Co-construct protocol for conducting MC Step Out.
E = Establish community and context	3. Evidence	Journal observations and collect documentation during MC Step Out.	Conduct MC Step Out. Collect documents.
SE = Seek and Engage collaboration and construction	4. Expression	Formalize report by talking with peers.	Synthesize notes through member checking.
S = Spark conversations and climate	5. Exchange	Share report and ask questions of peers.	Participate in class discussions.
SW = Strengthen and Weave together complexities and controversies	6. Expand	Connect discoveries with concepts of cultural competence.	Identify themes and unique phenomena in relationship to research.
W = Waken compassion and commitment	7. Evolve	Decide mechanisms for infusing cultural competence into personal, professional, and pedagogical life.	Plan aspects of report and record future goals in one's own life, as a career educator, and in the classroom.
NW = Nurture and Welcome challenges and changes	8. Enlighten	Advance awareness, involvement, and reflection of cultural competence especially in schools and classrooms	Make class presentation and submit final with feedback for growth and development.

Step 1: N = Notice Culture and Cultural Characteristics

Starting with "N" for North, candidates begin by examining themselves individually, noting who they are, how they identify themselves, why they have chosen particular identifiers, and where they place themselves within the dominant culture by using the *ABC: Who Are We?* activity as the focal point for discussion. Understanding oneself is requisite before understanding one another and other people in society. As teachers, candidates must be attuned to themselves in order to demonstrate educational efficacy and cultural competence for and with all of their students. Noticing culture and cultural characteristics reveals the locations that people visit regularly and find comfortable

The MC Step Out begins with the in-class activity focusing on one particular student, so candidates can begin to explore how their students may think, believe, and behave. Candidates have already begun to explore their own values, codes, standards, worldviews, and beliefs throughout the MAT program. The goal of the student exploration is to offer candidates consideration of other perspectives. From this in-class *encounter* and small group discussions, candidates' awareness of similarities and differences within and among the cultures and characteristics of teacher candidates and students is stimulated. The absence of information about the students in the T-chart allows candidates to contemplate gaps in their cultural competence. The candidate is ready to consider the various events and locations where the student might visit and select one to attend.

Step 2: NE = Negotiate and Evaluate Curriculum and Content

Moving clockwise around the compass, the candidates encounter the necessity to negotiate and evaluate curriculum and content. Classroom teachers not only need to know their required curriculum, including the standards and expectations, teachers must have in-depth understanding of their content (ATE, 2008; INTASC, 1999; NCATE, 2007; TEAC, 2009). Cultural competence includes placing the knowledge, skills, and dispositions in a sociocultural context so all students have ample opportunities to comprehend and connect with the curriculum. Teachers must provide developmentally appropriate instruction aligned with ongoing assessments so students learn about all people, near and far. Teachers must be well-informed and fully prepared to make wise decisions regarding students' learning experiences.

For the MC Step Out, once candidates notice the culture of their selected students, candidates are encouraged to see and *experience* their shared surroundings as their students see the world. The instructor poses questions provoking candidates to consider how students connect with and experience their learning, especially in relationship to their future learning and living.

Step 3: E = Establish Community and Context

Establishing community is essential for all students to feel safe, welcome, and wanted. To increase attendance in class, motivation to learn, and ownership of one's progress, candidates must create a sense of place where all students engage, participate, contribute, and grow. The community must reflect the students in the classroom, school, city, and world through the textbooks, assignments, decorations, and other indicators.

In order to understand all of their students' cultures and communities, candidates benefit from investigating communities that are foreign to their comfort zone and regular routines. The candidates record their observations, thoughts, and feelings; then they analyze and share their insights through class conversations and written papers supplemented with *evidence* and artifacts documenting their experience. Candidates' new insights will enrich their future classrooms and connections with all of their students.

Step 4: SE = Seek and Engage Collaboration and Construction

Many teachers who strive for efficacy co-construct the learning with their students. These teachers talk with and listen to their students to help the students make meaningful individual connections. Holistic learning experiences result from honest collaboration that models positive and productive techniques for the students to use in the future (Gallavan, 2011b).

For the MC Step Out, candidates are encouraged to participate with the community that they visit and to be ready to prepare an *expression* communicating their thoughts and feelings and to co-construct new meaning for them to apply in their own classrooms.

Step 5: S = Spark Conversations and Climate

From their firsthand experiences connecting learning with life, students are prompted to delve into their observations, thoughts, and feelings in ways to spark comfortable conversations. Students tend to learn more from their peers, so teachers expand their efficacy by facilitating conversations for students to make their own discoveries rather than telling their students the targeted outcomes.

As candidates reflect upon their MC Step Out experiences and *exchange* discoveries, the same guidelines apply to the instructor, who also shares a transformative experience with the students and reflects upon how the instructor used that experience in the classroom. At this juncture, the instructor leads the candidates in support of their transformative processes.

Step 6: SW = Strengthen and Weave Together Complexities and Controversies

Steps 6, 7, and 8 transform and strengthen candidates' relationships with culture and one another through reflectivity as they build upon their cultural foundations. Viewing all learning from multiple perspectives raises candidates' critical thinking skills and broadens their imaginations.

These same outcomes occur as candidates reflect upon their MC Step Out experiences, noting the expansion of their observations, thoughts, and feelings. The instructor weaves the candidates' discoveries into the candidates' classrooms to *expand* and fortify their curriculum and communities of learning by including a section in their report on how they would infuse their content and context with the information they have discovered in the MC Step Out assignment.

Step 7: W = Waken Compassion and Commitment

This direction on the GCCC presents the most difficult step, and the candidates can only try to instill a sense of compassion and commitment in their students. It may not be possible for the candidate to assess each student's awakening, as the change may be visible only outside of class or into the future. However, the knowledge and skills of cultural competence are not complete without the relevant dispositions linked with compassion and commitment. Similarly, the instructor facilitating the MC Step Out strives to inspire candidates to acknowledge, *evolve*, and adopt the importance of and value for teaching and modeling care and concern for all students.

Step 8: NW = Nurture and Welcome Challenges and Changes

Most likely candidates agree that challenges and changes will occur frequently in their classrooms and careers. Some candidates actually nurture and welcome these events. These candidates are enlightened and want to attain efficacy with all students. By designing a semester-long, multistep series of in-class activities and out-of-class assignments, candidates are most likely to develop cultural competence as they enlighten one another and ease themselves out of their comfort zones.

As the candidates maximize all eight directions of the GCCC, they not only find satisfaction and reward for themselves, but they also find that their joy emanates among their students, the students' families, and their peers. Visiting locations previously unknown and foreign to them and exchanging their discoveries will motivate and assure each candidate to expand and enrich resource repertoire and cultural competence.

CANDIDATES' REVELATIONS FROM THE MC STEP OUT

The eight-step processes detailed in this chapter provide the description, justification, and significance vital for understanding and applying transformative learning in one multicultural education course in a mid-south university that can be applied in both higher education courses and P–12 classrooms. Creating cross-cultural experiences to learn about cultural competence requires instructors to consider carefully each step of the process and monitor mindfully as candidates are engaged in the process. Easing toward cultural competence involves continuous conversations that are honest, natural, authentic, and holistic (Gallavan, 2011b). Candidates begin their journeys through self-examination of who they are, based on their own frames of reference. By looking at their own students' cultural foundations and exchanging the insights gained by their peers, candidates continue the transformative processes.

Throughout the MC Step Out activities and assignments, the instructor facilitated conversations and modeled documentation to promote critical reflection and rational discourse. Comments were categorized according to each of the eight compass directions of the GCCC. Although the eight steps of the MC Step Out are sequenced in a clockwise rotation around the GCCC, using the compass is not a linear experience. One can begin the journey at any point on the compass. Some steps may and need to be repeated, some steps can be skipped, and some steps may be omitted depending on the situation.

Evidence of each of these possibilities was realized in the candidates' conversations and papers. Reflective comments from the final papers are included in each of the following steps. Comments include candidates' connections to their text by Gollnick and Chinn (2009) and to the Pathwise observation protocol used in this particular MAT Program.

Step 1: Encounter Disequilibrium and Curiosity

Most candidates reacted to the MC Step assignment exhibiting discomfort, apprehension, hesitancy, and reluctance. Candidates expressed orally and in writing that the MC Step Out assignment instilled nervousness, embarrassment, anxiety, and awkwardness. Only a few candidates appeared to accept the assignment with a slight degree of excitement. One candidate, Aimee, stated, "I never expected to experience the perfect merging of enjoyment and discomfort, but that is exactly what I found."

Noting their immediate disequilibrium and anticipating their reactions, the instructor reassured the candidates that visiting locations outside of their comfort zones replicates the same feelings that many of their own students experience with their teachers and schools, especially the one student they had identified during the first in-class activity. This keen insight opened the first class conversation related to privilege. After conducting the MC Step Out, candidates remarked that visiting a location outside of their comfort zones was one of the most transformative events of their lives. Not only did they notice culture all around them, they were aware of how their own culture influences their students.

Step 2: Experience Discomfort and Surprise

During the second class session, candidates shared that they were beginning to observe all of their physical and educational surroundings more attentively. From the conversation about privilege, some candidates voiced the realization that the world around them did not reflect the lives of all people living in the area, the United States, or the world. Likewise, they reported that the course content in their internship placements did not include every student's story and that the instructional strategies did not vary enough to ensure success for every student's learning style. Another candidate, Nathan, observed that "some students may have a language of communication that is different from that to which we are accustomed, but as effective professionals, we must be willing to value and adapt to their needs." After the candidates conducted their MC Step Outs, their remarks punctuated their surprise at the availability of content at the various locations and the easy access of technology for connecting the location with their classrooms.

Step 3: Evidence Hesitancy and Participation

Candidates started to transfer the concepts and importance of community and context to their own classrooms, which piqued their curiosity about the upcoming MC Step Out. Comments related to this step revealed that the candidates were oblivious to the many different cultural communities that existed in their geographic area. Jenny observed that "It was interesting to observe the stereotypes based on class and language that exist within Hispanic culture. This observation reminded me that subcultures exist within all cultures, not just the one I live in" (Gollnick & Chinn, 2009).

Some of the candidates voiced their newfound appreciation for the diversity and the opportunity to increase their knowledge. As candidates visited the various communities, some were willing to participate in the event, making the experience more meaningful and transformative. Candidates were eager to collect their evidence to share with each other. They identified their responses as the cultural markers, and they emphasized the value of integrating these markers into the classroom naturally and authentically. At this step, candidates exhibited a growing ease with their processes of transformation.

Step 4: Express Reluctance and Discovery

This step represents an important transition in the process of transformation. After the MC Step Out, many candidates shared that they had remained silent observers at their various locations. Being strangers and not knowing the routines increased their concerns about making inappropriate actions or saying the wrong words. Although some of the candidates revealed reluctance to construct new knowledge through social interaction (Bandura, 1977), other candidates realized the power of participating in new and different experiences outside of school in order to transfer their discoveries into school. Lindsey wrote, "It is important also to be willing to try new things without having a mind that is turned only towards the things to which we have used effectively in the past." Navigating cultural competence entailed expanding their abilities to collaborate with community members and educational colleagues to construct a range of opportunities for all students to express their learning and teach one another.

Step 5: Exchange Distress and Reward

During their MC Step Out experiences, few candidates sparked conversations in their selected locations. Most candidates reported that they felt they were viewed skeptically, and they seemed unprepared to talk with community members with whom they believed (falsely) that they held nothing in common. The candidates who engaged in conversations shared that their visits were held in people's homes and were more personal. Melissa described her encounter at a birthday party attended by her and her young daughter:

> Soon two young men, friends of the eldest sister, arrived and were requested, by the sister, to sit and eat beside me (integration?). Apparently, she had noticed my "alienation" as I made an attempt to smile and listen to the Spanish-speaking group while eating alone (Gollnick & Chinn, 2009, p. 26). They obliged and began a conversation with me in English. This was a wonderful relief.

Once the candidates introduced themselves, the community members urged them to become a part of their group. However, in the multicultural education classroom, conversations raged, and the climate glowed. The candidates who had crossed the thresholds and begun their transformative journeys were eager to exchange their travels with the other candidates, again underscoring the application to the conversations and climate in classrooms and supporting Mezirow's (1997) theme of centrality of experience.

Step 6: Expand Anxiety and Comfort

This step capitalized upon writing prompts, asking candidates to explain their observations, thoughts, and feelings about each step of the MC Step Out and how the experience contributes to their growth and development as an emerging professional. The assessment rubric stipulated that the candidates needed to make connections with the textbook (Gollnick & Chinn, 2009) and the Pathwise protocol (Danielson, 2007) used to prepare candidates for passing the Praxis III, a state requirement for a standard 5-year license. Even without explicit interaction with other participants during the MC Step Out, many candidates successfully drew upon their prior knowledge to construct meaning. At this point in their MAT courses and internships, the candidates have acquired the abilities to reflect thoughtfully (Mezirow's theme of critical reflection) and make meaningful connections to their careers (Howard, 1999). Ryan expressed self-realization when he recorded, "This observation reminded me that subcultures exist within all cultures, not just the one I live in. Forcing myself to face my own racial and religious issues and being willing to risk rejection have both helped me better understand the authors' positions."

Mae focused on students in general when she explained that

> Teachers should attempt to become familiar with relevant aspects of their students' background knowledge and experiences. Establishing and maintaining rapport with students and these students especially, who I often had noticed were removed from the majority of the group and have even spoken about being bullied in the past, is extremely important.

Likewise, Rhett noted,

> The information I gathered affect my teacher professionalism of Domain D, more specifically, teacher efficacy and parental communication. If I know there is a single parent or one that works odd hours, I can be more flexible in creating time to communicate with that parent.

The instructor shared an analysis of the candidates' transformative comments associated with complexities and controversies of cultural competence along with research from the text which indicated that "long-term cultural experiences are probably the most effective means for overcoming fear and misconceptions about a group" (Gollnick & Chin, 2009, p. 397). The instructor also highlighted from the text that "Not only are these [English language learner] students faced with having to learn new subject matter, but they must also learn a new language and often a new culture" (p. 221).

Step 7: Evolve Limitations and Possibilities

Many of the candidates' comments showed their compassion for and commitment to developing cultural competence with words such as "building rapport" and "staying flexible." Other remarks revealing their compassion and commitment were communicated through their plans to infuse their own future classrooms with evidence of cultural competence to help their students evolve individually and as members of various groups. Change was evident and growing, reflecting Mezirow's third theme of transformative learning—rational discourse. Kelly stated,

> I will ensure that no student in my class is prohibited from engaging in my instruction due to funding. I can think of more creative or engaging ways to assess their learning. By knowing more about what is important to them, I can design both formative and summative assessments that will be a true depiction of what they know and have learned.

Step 8: Enlighten Skepticism and Competency

This step aspires for candidates to achieve enlightenment. Ashton wrote,

> In understanding that one's students may not share the same interpretation of an event, a teacher can work to offer a wide selection of resources that explore alternative explanations to what is commonly taught in a classroom in the United States.

Other candidates exposed their deeper levels of commitment to social justice. Elizabeth accounted, "Because many new teachers do not understand cultural dynamics in their classrooms, they choose to not engage students who present problems, which are not easily identifiable." And Patricia reported, "Ignorance has the same effect as bigotry, which is something I will strive to keep out of my classroom. When students are experiencing alienation due to language or cultural differences, it is my responsibility to find inclusive opportunities."

FURTHER USE, ADDITIONAL POSSIBILITIES, AND FUTURE RESEARCH

As the demographics of the United States continue to change, so do the demographics of schools and classrooms. Teacher candidates benefit greatly from cross-cultural experiences that guide and support them toward educational efficacy and cultural competence. However, the path is not linear, and the journey is without end. Gallavan's Cultural Competence Compass offers educators another perspective on the endless journey of transformation. It is recursive, interwoven, continuous, and revealing. The model provides administrators with a framework for insightful and practical professional development. It gives classroom teachers a visual representation of a complex process that is modified easily to make their own curricular changes.

LIMITATIONS

Using the GCCC to guide the MC Step Out is accompanied with four limitations associated with motivation, implementation, negotiation, and disposition (Gallavan, 2011b). Infusing cultural competence into a candidate's personal existence, professional efficacy, and pedagogical experiences relies first upon the candidate's motivation. Motivation involves reason and rationale for pursuing an endeavor, revealing why particular actions are significant to the individual (Ostroff, 1992). If the candidate is open and eager to see and ensure cultural competence for all learners, and if the candidate is provided guidance and support personally, professionally, and pedagogically, more likely the candidate will be willing to conduct the self-assessment of one's beliefs and behaviors to begin the transformation. If the candidate is required to infuse cultural competence and report to instructors without appropriate guidance and support, then the candidate is less likely to display motivation to initiate or sustain changes in the teaching, learning, or schooling.

The second limitation relates to implementation. Implementation entails preparation and facilitation of practice, describing the actions that are occurring or have occurred accompanied by issues of quality (Fenstermacher & Richardson, 2005). Every candidate demonstrates a unique teaching style, and infusing cultural competence determines the priorities related to the importance and frequency of infusing culture competence into that candidate's repertoire. As emphasized throughout this chapter, implementation must be honest, natural, authentic, and holistic. If a candidate chooses to diminish the importance or frequency of infusing cultural competence, then most likely efficacy of practice declines.

The third limitation pertains to the candidate's abilities to navigate and negotiate all elements of the Gallavan Cultural Competence Compass by actively engaging in critical thinking, problem solving, and decision making. Infusing cultural competence involves assessing all people and priorities carefully to determine one's path (Mewborn & Stinson, 2007). Candidates must be aware of their senses, sensibilities (thoughts), and sensitivities (feelings) while interacting with each student and situation. Without experience and reflection, candidates may navigate poorly and find themselves encountering unwanted results.

The fourth limitation concerns candidates' dispositions, their attitudes, intentions, and characteristics applied to explain and justify their actions to themselves (Ostroff, 1992) as well as everyone around them. Candidates must "believe it to see it" rather than "see it to believe it." Unless candidates want to optimize each of the eight directions of the Gallavan Cultural Competence Compass, more likely cultural competence will not occur, students will be limited in their learning experiences, and teachers will not achieve efficacy in their practices.

CONCLUSION: EASE INTO TRANSFORMATION

Jeremy stated, "It is important to experience different aspects of other cultures so educators remember that there is more than one way to see the world." This candidate's comment reinforces the fundamental issue of diversity: each culture views the world through a unique perspective. The responsibility of believing that perception rests with each individual and varies depending on one's background. Teacher educators offer myriad techniques, theories, and strategies to guide candidates through the pedagogical journey toward efficacy and cultural competence.

Teacher educators recognize that the impact of multicultural education courses has mixed results in changing candidates' knowledge, skills, and dispositions about diversity (Sheets, 2005; Sleeter, 2001; Weisman & Garza, 2002). However, it is essential for teacher educators to push candidates out of their comfort zones within their own geographic communities (Spalding, Savage, & Garcia, 2009) and experience empathy (McAllister & Irvine, 2002).

All teacher candidates, classroom teachers, and thus their students, benefit and transform by navigating their own journeys of cultural competence.

REFERENCES

Association of Teacher Educators. (2008). *Standards for teacher educators*. Retrieved from http://www.ate1.org/pubs/uploads/tchredstds0308.pdf

Bandura, A. (1977). *Social learning theory*. New York, NY: General Learning.

Banks, J. A. (2008). *An introduction to multicultural education* (4th ed.). Boston, MA: Pearson Education.

Bergeon, B. S. (2008). Enacting a culturally response curriculum in a novice teacher's classroom: Encountering disequilibrium. *Urban Education, 43*(1), 4–28.

Black, M. S. (2000). Using your city as a multicultural classroom. *Teaching Education, 11*(3), 343–351.

Bruce, C. D., Esmonde, I., Ross, J., Dookie, L., & Beatty, R. (2010). The effects of sustained classroom-embedded teacher professional learning on teacher efficacy and related student achievement. *Teaching and Teacher Education, 26*(8), 1598–1608.

Danielson, C. (2007). *Enhancing professional practice: A framework for teaching* (2nd ed.). Alexandria, VA: Association for Supervision and Curriculum Development.

Farmer, J., Knapp, D., & Benton, G. M. (2007). The effects of primary sources and field trip experience on the knowledge retention in multicultural education. *Multicultural Education, 14*(3), 27–31.

Fenstermacher, G. D., & Richardson, V. (2005). On making determinations of quality in teaching. *Teachers College Record, 107*(1), 186–212.

Gallavan, N. P. (2011a). Old dogs, new tricks: A self-study investigating my online instruction. In S. Huffman, S. Albritton, W. Rickman, & B. Wilmes (Eds.), *Cases on building quality distance delivery programs: Strategies and experiences* (pp. 247–267). Hershey, PA: IGI Global.

Gallavan, N. P. (2011b). *Navigating cultural competence: A compass for teachers*. Thousand Oaks, CA: Corwin.

Gallavan, N. P., & Webster-Smith, A. (2010). Navigating teachers' reactions, responses, and reflections in self-assessment and decision-making. In E. G. Pultorak (Ed.), *The purposes, practices, and professionalism of teacher reflectivity: Insights for twenty-first-century teachers and students* (pp. 191–209). Lanham, MD: Rowman & Littlefield.

Garmon, M. A. (1996). Missed messages: How prospective teachers' racial attitudes mediate what they learn from a course on diversity. (Doctoral dissertation, Michigan State University, 1996). *Dissertation Abstracts International, 57*(9), 3896A.

Gay, G. (2000). *Culturally responsive teaching: Theory, research, & practice*. New York, NY: Teachers College Press.

Gollnick, D. M., & Chinn, P. C. (2009). *Multicultural education in a pluralistic society* (8th ed.). Upper Saddle River, NJ: Pearson.

Howard, G. R. (1999). *You can't teach what you don't know.* New York, NY: Teachers College Press.

Imel, S. (1998). *Transformative learning in adulthood.* Retrieved from ERIC database. (ERIC Document Reproduction Service No. ED423426)

Interstate New Teacher Assessment and Support Consortium. (1999). *INTASC standards for beginning teachers.* Retrieved from http://www.wresa.org/Pbl/The%20INTASC%20Standards%20overheads.htm

McAllister, G., & Irvine, J. J. (2002). The role of empathy in teaching culturally diverse students: A qualitative study of teachers' beliefs. *Journal of Teacher Education, 53*(5), 433–443.

McGeehan, R. (1982). The *relationship of selected antecedents to outcomes to training in multicultural education for preservice teachers.* Unpublished doctoral dissertation, Indiana University, Bloomington.

Mewborn, D. W., & Stinson, D. W. (2007). Learning to teach as assisted performance. *Teachers College Record, 109*(6), 1457–1487.

Mezirow, J. (1997). Transformative learning: Theory to practice. In P. Cranton (Ed.), *Transformative learning in action: Insights from practice* (pp. 5–12). San Francisco, CA: Jossey-Bass.

National Council for the Accreditation of Teacher Education. (2007). *Professional standards for the accreditation of teacher preparation institutions.* Washington, DC: NCATE.

National Council for the Social Studies. (1994). *Curriculum standards for social studies.* Washington, DC: NCSS.

Ostroff, C. (1992). The relationship between satisfaction, attitudes, and performance: An organizational level analysis. *Journal of Applied Psychology, 77,* 963–974.

Pohan, C. A. (1996). Preservice teachers' beliefs about diversity: Uncovering factors leading to multicultural responsiveness. *Equity and Excellence in Education, 29*(3), 62–69.

Putney, L. G., & Broughton, S. H. (2011). Developing collective classroom efficacy: The teacher's role as community organizer. *Journal of Teacher Education, 62*(1), 93–105.

Schön, D. A. (1987, April 20–24). *Educating the reflective practitioner.* Paper presented at the annual meeting of the American Educational Research Association, Washington, DC.

Sheets, R. H. (2005). *Diversity pedagogy: Examining the role of culture in the teaching-learning process.* Upper Saddle River, NJ: Pearson.

Sleeter, C. E. (2001). Preparing teachers for culturally diverse schools: Research and the overwhelming presence of Whiteness. *Journal of Teacher Education, 52*(2), 94–106.

Spalding, E., Savage, T. A., & Garcia, J. (2009). The march and remembrance of hope: The teaching and learning about diversity and social justice through the Holocaust. *Teachers College Record, 109*(6), 1423–1456.

Taylor, E. W. (1998). *The theory and practice of transformative learning: A critical review.* Retrieved from ERIC database (ERIC Document Reproduction Service No. ED423422).

Teacher Education Accreditation Council. (2009). *TEAC principles and standards for teacher education programs*. Retrieved from http://www.teac.org/wp-content/uploads/2009/03/quality-principles-for-teacher-education-programs.pdf

U.S. Department of Education; National Center for Education Statistics. (2006). *The condition of education 2006* (NCES 2006-071). Washington, DC: U.S. Government Printing Office.

Vygotsky, L. S. (1978). *Mind and society: The development of higher mental processes*. Cambridge, MA: Harvard University Press.

Weisman, E. M., & Garza, S. A. (2002). Preservice teacher attitudes toward diversity: Can one class make a difference? *Equity and Excellence in Education, 35*(1), 28–34.

Zeichner, K., Grant, C., Gay, G., Gillette, M., Valli, L., & Villegas, A. (1998). A research informed vision of good practice in multicultural teacher education: Design principles. *Theory Into Practice, 37*(2), 163–171.

CHAPTER 12

THE TRANSFORMATIVE PATH OF LOCAL, CROSS-CULTURAL RELATIONSHIPS

Ellen L. Marmon

If you always look in the same direction, your neck will grow stiff.
—Kenyan Proverb

During my senior year of college, I agreed to be the swimming part of a mini-triathlon team. It was a ridiculous promise, seeing as how I was not an athlete and hated competition. Our team's captain was, in fact, a real triathlete, so he started showing up at the campus pool and offering unsolicited pointers. "Bilateral breathing," he said. "You've got to breathe every third stroke for a good rhythm; start turning your head left as well as right." No problem, I thought. I had been swimming since grade school and those instructors at the local YWCA were top notch. Pushing off from the wall, I counted my strokes: one, two, three—turn head right and breathe; one, two, three—turn head left—and swallow half the pool. I surfaced gasping and snorting in disbelief. My friend laughed, "It's all about muscle memory. You'll have to train your neck muscles to turn left; otherwise, you'll drown." I was not amused. "Just sleep on your stomach with your neck turned to the left at night," he suggested nonchalantly, "and maybe when you're laying out in the sun too. You'll get used to it eventually." He left and I continued swimming laps the *correct* way, turning my head every fourth stroke to the right.

Over two decades later, I now interpret learning how to breathe bilaterally (and having a near-death experience in the pool) as a parable of sorts. I challenge adults to see things from a different perspective than their own; they confront mental, emotional, and spiritual muscles that have never before turned at those angles. The process of adults making room for new ideas, values, and beliefs is not unlike turning our heads in a different direction for the very first time. It is awkward, unfamiliar, and quite frankly, a real pain. Life itself offers adults multiple opportunities to question their views of how the world works. When adults experience something that does not match up with their mental map, they can hurl headlong (or in some cases crawl reluctantly) into what Jack Mezirow (1975, 1991, 2000) calls a "disorienting dilemma." That dilemma can lead to transformative learning.

While the process of Mezirow's transformative learning is not strictly linear, his model does propose the following phases:

1. A disorienting dilemma (trigger event or developing process);
2. Self-examination with feelings of fear, anger, guilt, shame [I would add surprise];
3. A critical assessment of assumption (within a community);
4. Recognition that one's discontent and the process of transformation are shared;
5. Exploration of options for new roles, relationships, and actions;
6. Planning a course of action;
7. Acquiring knowledge and skills for implementing one's plans;
8. Provisional trying of new roles;
9. Building competence and self-confidence in new roles and relationships;
10. A reintegration into one's life on the basis of conditions dictated by one's new perspective. (2000, p. 22)

Cross-cultural encounters serve as one source of personal disorientation for adults in the United States (race, ethnicity, gender, age, socioeconomics, physical and/or mental ability). In 1994, Kegan argued, "Diversity of cultural experience may once have been the province of the adventurous, the open-minded, and those too poor to live where they wished. Tomorrow it will be the province of all" (p. 208). The Census Bureau projects that by 2042, minorities, currently about one third of the U.S. population, will become a majority (Aizenman, 2008). Kegan's prediction has become our present reality. Instead of the few who travel overseas or people who live in big cities, most adults in suburban and rural settings now cross paths with the world locally. These intersections can be troubling, yet they often lead to new and enhanced ways of seeing (or breathing, as the case may be).

FOUNDATIONS

Initially, Piaget's disequilibration (1952) and Festinger's cognitive dissonance (1957) described what happened in a learner's head when previously constructed reality and new information did not add up. For adults, Peter Jarvis (1987, 2004) prefers to call these moments of "creative disjuncture," unsettling breaks between the person's biography and present situation. Both Jarvis and Mezirow are particularly interested in the role this disjuncture or dilemma plays in the meaning-making process for adults. When formerly held values and beliefs are insufficient to interpret an experience, learners benefit from both self-examination and corporate (group) reflection. Unfortunately, because grownups are quick to justify their current point of view, they often dismiss the new information/experience as ridiculous, random, or just plain wrong (Cranton, 1994, 2006).

Cognitive, emotional, and spiritual dilemmas lead adults to various responses. Jarvis (1987) identifies three:

1. Non-Learning: presumption, non-consideration and rejection;
2. Nonreflective Learning: preconscious, practice and memorize;
3. Reflective Learning: contemplation, reflective practice, transformative experimental learning, and different outcomes. (p. 63)

Mezirow (2000) refers to adults' assumptions as "habits of mind, broad, generalized, orienting predispositions that act as a filter for interpreting the meaning of experience" (p. 17). He identifies three levels of transformation regarding these assumptions:

1. Meanings (basic content can be changed by modifying knowledge, skills);
2. Premises, assumptions, or habits of mind (processes of learning; how we come to know; why we value what we do; meaning schemes);
3. Meaning perspectives (general framework of meanings and cultural understandings underlying assumptions, premises, or habits of mind; pp. 10–11).

The last levels of "reflective learning" and "meaning perspective transformation" involve consciousness raising, self- and group reflection, and critical thinking. These practices create an awareness of the constraints within which one's personal model of reality was developed and is now operating.

Mackeracher (2004) argues, "perspective transformation requires both a critical reappraisal of the supporting assumptions and the development of new assumptions as well as a transformed model of reality." (p. 16) When an adult does embrace a new way of seeing the world (or even just a small part of it), Mezirow believes that he or she has experienced transformative learning:

> The process of becoming critically aware of how and why our assumptions have come to constrain the way we perceive, understand, and feel about our world; changing these structures of habitual expectation to make possible a more inclusive, discriminating, and integrative perspective; and, finally, making choices or otherwise acting upon these new understandings. (1991, p. 167)

Transformative learning then, is a holistic process engaging the adult's mind, emotions, and behavior.

Mezirow, Jarvis, and other adult learning theorists/practitioners value people processing their experiences together. A reflection group can be a place in which men and women break away from insufficient or inaccurate assumptions. The facilitator, whether a church leader, counselor, or classroom teacher, must host this process thoughtfully and respectfully. This person orchestrates a safe and challenging space (Nouwen, 1991; Vella, 2002), an evolutionary "holding environment" (Kegan, 1994, p. 53) in which adults can grow. The reflection facilitator also knowingly takes the risk of discovering his/her own limited perspectives and of considering some personal changes as a result (Cranton, 2006; Taylor, 2006).

Over the last 30 years, researchers and educators alike have identified hundreds of possible triggers for transformative learning, culture shock being one example (Taylor, 1994). However, few have explored the potentially transformative impact of *local* cross-cultural relationships; in particular, the impact of these relationships on White/Anglo people. In North America, and in the United States especially, "it's fairly unusual to call attention to the fact that someone is white" (Harris & Schaupp, 2004, p. 13). If White/Anglo adults think of racial identity at all, it relates to others, not to them (Helms, 1990; Sue & Sue, 2007; Tatum, 1997). White adults rarely consider the implication of their race on the opportunities and unearned privileges they have in life (Hess & Brookfield, 2008; McIntosh, 1989; Rothenberg, 2007). Therefore, when they experience cultural diversity, not as a seminar topic but through a personal relationship, they can move from dilemma to discovery. If White adults are willing to turn their heads in a different direction and participate in a supportive process, perspective transformation is possible.

DATA COLLECTION, ANALYSIS, AND DISCUSSION

Getting used to curry isn't the same thing as getting used to people who eat curry.
—Storti, 2001, p. 23

Encountering different cultures locally can occur in numerous contexts. My continuing qualitative research with White graduate students in a theological seminary traces the process of transformative learning (or lack of it) through their stories about local, cross-cultural ministry (Marmon, 2007, 2010). Seidman argues that it is the "process of selecting constitutive details of experience, reflecting on them, giving them order, and thereby making sense of them that makes telling stories a meaning-making experience" (1998, p. 1). Open-ended questions invite people to tell their stories; narrative analysis gives the researcher a tool to interpret them (Glesne, 1999; Riessman, 1993).

During 2006–2007, I conducted semistructured interviews with White students before, during, and after their semester-long, cross-cultural ministry experience (Seidman, 1998). The stories they told revealed how they were making sense of specific ministry contexts and their reactions to them. Using Labov's (1972) method of narrative analysis, I identified not only the structure of each story within the interviews, but also recorded words and phrases that reflected some aspect of the transformative learning process (Mezirow, 1991, 2000). Document analysis of students' case studies and the faculty's syllabi, as well as interviews with each student's mentor, enhanced the data for a fuller picture of their local, cross-cultural experiences.

During a semester-long course, seminary students served in a cross-cultural ministry setting for 8 hours each week. In addition, they participated weekly in a 2-hour theological reflection group with other students and a faculty member. For most students, serving with people different from themselves, talking things through with a mentor, and reflecting with other students created pathways to transformed perspectives. For others, learning to turn their heads in new directions would have to wait for another day.

Student Surprises and Stories

Dan

Dan, a pseudonym, described his wife and himself as "city people, middle class, professional, all my life." So tutoring in an afterschool program for White, African American, and Hispanic American at-risk students was a stretch for him. He struggled with communication. One of his responsibilities was to teach a Bible story to the children. However, he wondered about talking to them about God the Father, when most of them did not have a father at home. After 4 weeks of tutoring, Dan felt frustrated. His assignments became routine, and the children had terrible behavior problems. His mentor did not understand his ministry context, and his reflection group offered what he thought were "artificial" case studies. In the absence of any meaningful connections, he assessed his cross-cultural experience as "probably a good thing." While Dan did think about the differences between his home life and those of the children in the program, he never questioned the beliefs and values that influenced his personal responses to the children. Nor did he actively engage in critical reflection with the discussion group. Jarvis (1987) would qualify Dan's overall response as "nonreflective learning."

Nell and Joanna

Nell, a pseudonym, also worked at a church that offered after-school tutoring for the neighborhood children (mostly Hispanic and African American). But her surprise came on a ride home "through the hood."

> As I passed one house, there was a group of [African American] people standing, sitting, just probably like a group of friends talking. As my car went by, eyes stared. They—were—just—tracking—me [drawn out and whispered]. And there was hostility and anger and suspicion in those looks, like, "What are YOU doing here?" Just like, "You don't belong here! WHAT ARE YOU DOING HERE?"

The experience was so unnerving, Nell avoided that street the rest of the semester. "I don't know if I want to take that same drive home or not! It's like [whisper], cause how do you answer that? How do you answer that suspicion and hostility?"

In a previous seminary course that Nell had taken, the professor raised the issue of "White privilege" (McIntosh, 1989; Rothenberg, 2007). Nell rejected the validity of this concept at that time. Using an exercise to increase awareness, the same professor lined up all the students and asked them to take one step back or forward if the statements she read applied to them. For example, "If you had to use public transportation when you were growing up, take one step back. If you were told you could do anything you wanted to by parents and teachers, take one step forward." Nell recalled how the line separated: "At the front you had young, White males; at the back, Blacks, and I pretty much stayed close to the center. WHOA." More class discussions and reading revealed a different reality than she had imagined for her African American and Hispanic fellow students. Her perspective on power in personal relationships and institutional systems began to change. Consequently, she processed her cross-cultural ministry experiences through a lens that was already in the midst of being transformed (Brookfield, 2008; Harris & Schaupp, 2004; Hess & Brookfield, 2008; Kegan, 2000; Mackeracher, 2004).

Now when she reflected on her unsettling drive home, Nell saw herself as the "oppressor," a member of "the dominant societal group," who was met with suspicion and anger that day. As she served in the after-school program, issues of power became very important to Nell. She asked herself how many times people had experienced ethnically/racially based suspicion from her eyes, tone of voice, and words. When a Hispanic parent ignored Nell until she learned of Nell's Cuban grandfather, Nell shared, "Now I was accepted because I had some Spanish background? It was just weird. I hadn't really thought about it, but I kind of wonder if there are people that get that from me from time to time too. You know it works both ways." These long-standing power issues make building trust an essential element of cross-cultural ministry. Nell learned, "There is no quick fix because you've GOT to start with relationships."

Joanna, a pseudonym, led a recovery group for addicts that met in a local church. White/Anglo, Hispanic American, and African American women gathered once each week to encourage each other on their journey toward sobriety. She spoke of surprise and guilt as she reflected on her initial reaction to the women:

> I was uncomfortable being in there with people who openly admitted, you know, they were drug addicts, and some of them were still in the middle of relapsing. I was OK until they talked about leaving their kids alone, and that really bothered me a lot. It was hard not to judge. How could you leave your kid? Even though I knew a lot about addiction, still, when it came down to somebody leaving their kid so they could go on some drug binge, you know, that was hard.

The initial culture Joanna saw herself struggling with was primarily behavioral, not ethnic or racial. Joanna's unanswered questions kept her uncomfortable during the first few weeks of recovery meetings with the women. Later she wondered about her own culture and the origins of her beliefs and values. "Am I just making this assumption [addicts create all their own problems] because of my WASP world that I came from and the ivory tower that I've lived in?"

Goleman (1985) posits that we protect ourselves from anxiety by selective perception. This response creates psychological, social, and behavioral "blind spots" that hinder our growth as adults. Kegan argues that this is the price we pay when we construct our own realities. "Being active in our seeing and hearing can mean being actively blind to what we do not see and deaf to what we do not hear" (1994, p. 204). Both Nell and Joanna encountered personal blind spots and paid attention to them. In paying attention to their disoriented thoughts and feelings, they turned their heads in a different direction and created the possibility for transformative learning to unfold. For example, over time, the nature of Joanna's relationships with the women changed.

> I've come to love these women as a supporter of their recovery. It's much more comfortable, and it has probably removed, I don't know, sanctimonious, self-righteousness, whatever. Watching what they're going through and empathizing, realizing, you know, we're all in the same boat. So it has gotten easier to relate to them and their struggle than it was when I started. Seeing it from the addict's side is different. It's changed my heart.

During our final conversation, Joanna mentioned her surprise at how soon she came to love the women in her group. "I didn't think I'd get to that point, at least not this quickly. I guess that's why they have you get in the trenches with them, because it does change you." The relationships that formed within the group led Joanna on a path of transformation.

Thomas

Thomas, a pseudonym, has no illusions that he emerged from this class with all assumptions corrected. Toward the end of the semester, Thomas shared that he had an opportunity to counter a racial slur, but failed to speak up. Still, he believes that he will keep thinking about "changing his attitude and trying not to exert power over people." His personal emancipation is ongoing, as is his commitment to taking his discoveries into ministry.

Thomas grew up in the deep South and worried that his current church would feel "betrayed" by his involvement with a Black church of a different denomination. A big part of what stretched Thomas was his reaction to adults in the African American congregation calling him "Mr. Thomas." He expected it from the children, but not from their parents and other adult ministry volunteers. This was the subject of the case study he brought to his reflection group.

> Individually, the depth of this dilemma cuts to the core of my being. I'm struggling with it, whether that's authority because of the given position as pastor, or if there is some cultural things there. But it's just striking to me; there's a tension in me. Is it a power issue? Do they see me as somebody with power? I mean, that self-reflection just makes me wonder. Is this an expression of respect or perceived power? Is it a cultural misunderstanding or is it a behavioral pattern of power by myself?

Thomas talked his concerns over with a mentor who asked him helpful questions. "He [mentor] allows me to deal with my own internal struggle, mostly embedded prejudices coming from a small rural town. My mentor does a great job of making me think, of turning things around on me."

Thomas was surprised at how much he learned about himself and other cultures. "Liberating" was how he described the process of being able to confront his upbringing in light of a hands-on experience where he was unconditionally accepted. "I'm starting to see people outside of my frame of reference." In spite of Thomas's initial reservations, cognition, emotion, relationships, and environment worked together to create a situation ripe for discovery and change. "It's really been a transforming time for me because of the impact of the ministry setting [African American church] and being able to deal with my own prejudices."

Moments of Insight

The four stories above emerged from a series of in-depth interviews over one semester. At the end of each semester, all students in local, cross-cultural ministry write a narrative of an encounter or situation that impressed them. These stories reveal more White students who are learning to turn their heads in new directions. One man working in a neighborhood of generational poverty (Payne, 2005) made an important discovery.

> Prior to this experience, I had many (unintended) preconceived notions about the poor and how they arrived in their situations in life. One hard working couple attempted to save for the future and spent money wisely, but they were still poor. They shattered all my stereotypes and taught me the importance of seeing people as individuals and withholding judgment.

A relationship with one couple helped this student choose a new pathway to understanding others and himself.

In a conversation with a White church member and a Hispanic pastor, one student recalled a revealing and potentially hurtful comment. The pastor suggested introducing various flags in the worship center for the Hispanic service.

> "You mean the Mexican flag?" the white man asked. The pastor responded, "Yes! And a Puerto Rican, Honduran, El Salvadorian, Costa Rican, and Guatemalan flag, and anywhere else where our congregants come from." The only difference between me and the other guy was that he said out loud what I was thinking—"a Mexican flag." I wonder how many would be insulted by the lack of distinction. At worst they would feel like second-class citizens hosted by an uncaring church. I resolved to remember that we are all very different, and to understand people as individuals, not as groups. I relearned a valuable lesson that day.

Not everyone intentionally chooses to connect with others and step onto a transformative pathway. However, many of those who do develop cross-cultural relationships understand that their world has not only grown bigger, but also deeper and richer.

IMPLICATIONS

Since developing local, cross-cultural relationships can open up pathways for transformation, what are the implications for educators, mentors, and counselors in the potentially life-changing contexts that we encounter every day? Admittedly, we could answer this question in hundreds of ways. However, three essential commitments warrant our consideration: (a) embracing and modeling the role of life-long learner; (b) discovering what it means to be "good hosts" to other adult learners (employees, students, clients); (c) taking steps professionally that encourage others to turn their heads in new directions.

A Lifelong Learner

As much as we would wish it so, none of us are exempt from unexamined assumptions and limited perspectives. Therefore, our first commitment is a personal one. We must dedicate ourselves to holistic, lifelong learning. The trouble with a label like "terminal degree" is that it conveys a "finishedness" about learning. To the contrary, Taylor asks, "Are we willing to transform ourselves in the process of helping our students transform? One could therefore take the position that without developing a deeper awareness of our own frames of reference and how they shape our practice, there is little likelihood that we can foster change in others" (2006, p. 92). Identifying unknown presuppositions often allows us to discover additional blind spots, leading us along a pathway of ongoing transformation.

Adopting the posture of a learner means we relinquish any ideas of self-importance or self-sufficiency (Nouwen, 1975; Palmer 1998). We replace those myths with an expectation that all people and experiences have something to teach us. Noticing personal blind spots is not possible alone, so we acknowledge our limitations and join students, clients, and employees on the pathway of lifelong growth. Once I was relating a time when I apologized to my seminary students. It was my first attempt at teaching online, and my instructions were not only unclear, they were just plain wrong. A veteran university professor objected, "I wouldn't be comfortable with that. You are the authority in that classroom, and you don't ever apologize." Quite frankly, I was not *comfortable* with apologizing, but it was the appropriate thing to do in my situation. In addition, "being comfortable" cannot be the goal of an educator, or of anyone else in a service-oriented profession. Being a learner and an authentic guide for others on the learning path are my goals. They sometimes lead me into awkward situations; thankfully, awkward moments often lead to significant discovery.

A Good Host

Most adults need someone to walk with them through the dissonance that can lead to holistic shifts in their thinking, feeling, and behaving. Daloz (1999) argues that mentors need to look for "a fundamental shift in stance" from their students (p. 135). This shift can be scary for adults:

> Much of the fear we experience at such times is a consequence of our inability to see the larger frame, is rooted in our unwillingness to let go, to risk a transformation that at the moment may feel like disintegration. At such time we need experienced travelers to tell us that it is safe to go that way, to trust in our own contrary movement toward the source. (p. 140)

Nouwen calls this job of walking alongside adults who are learning something new "hosting" (1975, p. 84). If we see ourselves as hosts and think of the students, clients, or trainees as "guests," then learning will not be a unilateral, competitive, or disrespectful experience. A good host believes that "students are not just the poor, needy, ignorant beggars who come to the man or woman of knowledge, but that they are indeed like guests who honor the house with their visit and will not leave it without having made their own contribution" (p. 89).

Rather than function as detached disseminators of information, we become authentic facilitators who create space for meaningful experiences to unfold. While inviting honest dialog and posing challenging questions, good hosts also practice and encourage critical reflection. Along with cognitive engagement, they welcome intuitive, affective, and spiritual contributions (Cranton, 2006; Hess & Brookfield, 2008; Tolliver & Tisdell, 2006). Good hosts champion the holistic development of their guests. Perhaps I should call this a commitment to "messiness" in our professions. Rather than a prescribed, one-size-fits-all content to deliver, we discover insights together, and we do that within a multifaceted cultural context.

Practical Steps

As members of a highly literate culture, we have incredible resources at our disposal. We need to read broadly and deeply. I used to think this meant learning about a wide variety of topics. Now I research issues in my particular area of study/practice written by people from a variety of backgrounds. Intentionally seeking resources by authors from different cultures, races, ethnicities, ages, socioeconomic experience, and genders opens new worlds of understanding in our respective fields. Moving beyond my North American, White/Anglo, upper-middle-class perspective personally motivates me to evaluate my required reading lists for the classes I teach. What will my students read that challenges their current "mental maps" and offers them a more global view on this topic? Just stopping to ask that question is a step forward for me, or maybe a turn of the head in a new direction.

The downside of living in a literate culture is that we can rely too easily on printed resources alone to provide cross-cultural insights and stimulate personal change. Movies, art, worship, dance, storytelling, and music all communicate a great deal about culture. Exposing others and ourselves to these expressions of worldview can be a "safe" way for some people to begin encountering and appreciating differences. However, nothing can take the place of personal experience and relationships.

The women and men I have interviewed point to the people and the actual ministry setting as the sources of their growth. Because we generally gravitate toward environments and people who are like us, another step for us to consider is accountability. We would all benefit from a friend who occasionally asks, "What are you learning from others these days?" or "When was the last time you put yourself in an uncomfortable setting?" Giving that person permission to speak gentle reminders into our lives (and possibly laugh at us when we swallow the pool water), adds depth and integrity to our practice, whatever that practice may be.

CONCLUSION

The woman who never leaves her village thinks only her mother's cooking tastes sweet.
—Kenyan Proverb

I never swam in the mini-triathlon years ago; the cyclist sprained his ankle one week before the competition (thankfully). However, during that summer, I did train my neck to turn left as well as right, a practice I do now without thinking. Changing my frames of reference as a White, educated, North American woman requires so much more of me than 3 months of sleeping with my neck turned to the left. Mental, emotional, spiritual, and volitional muscles are involved in perspective transformation. This holistic process calls into question the very framework of our values and beliefs as adults. Instead of thinking about *what* we believe (content) or *how* we came to believe it (process), we evaluate *why* we believe what we do. In addition, men and women engaged in premise reflection decide, based on their current context, whether or not the former "whys" in their lives hold up. Shifting our premises causes us to see differently—not because of new glasses on the outside, but because of new lenses on the inside.

If Kegan (1994) is right and life itself serves as our ongoing curriculum, then adults will encounter continual opportunities to discover new ways of seeing, responding, and making sense of the world. Local, cross-cultural relationships offer a pathway to transformation, that is, "a more expansive understanding of the world regarding how one sees and experiences both others and one's self...grounded in one's entire being" (Tolliver & Tisdell, 2006, p. 37). Educators, researchers, counselors, and leaders who pay attention to the curriculum of diverse relationships in their places of influence can host meaningful experiences for others. These experiences have the power to develop enhanced understanding in us all. As a result, we will not just be better at doing something like swimming, we will be better at being human.

REFERENCES

Aizenman, N. (2008, August 14). U.S. to grow grayer, more diverse. *The Washington Post*, Metro p. 1.

Brookfield, S. (2008). How do we invite students into conversation? Teaching dialogically. In M. Hess & S. Brookfield (Eds.), *Teaching reflectively in theological contexts: Promises and contradictions* (pp. 32–47). Malabar, FL: Krieger.

Cranton, P. (1994). *Understanding and promoting transformative learning.* San Francisco, CA: Jossey-Bass.

Cranton, P. (2006). Fostering authentic relationships in the transformative classroom. *New Directions for Adult and Continuing Education, 109,* 5–13.

Daloz, L. (1999). *Mentor: Guiding the journey of adult learners* (2nd ed.). San Francisco, CA: Jossey-Bass.

Festinger, T. (1957). *A theory of cognitive dissonance.* Stanford, CA: Stanford University Press.

Glesne, C. (1999). *Becoming qualitative researchers: An introduction* (2nd ed.). New York, NY: Addison Wesley Longman.

Goleman, D. (1985). *Vital lies, simple truths: The psychology of self-deception.* New York, NY: Simon & Schuster.

Harris, P., & Schaupp, D. (2004). *Being White: Finding our place in a multiethnic world.* Downers Grove, IL: InterVarsity Press.

Helms, J. (1990). *Black and White racial identity: Theory, research, and practice.* New York, NY: Greenwood.

Hess, M., & Brookfield, S. (2008). "How can White teachers recognize and challenge racism?" Acknowledging collusion and learning an aggressive humility. In M. Hess & S. Brookfield (Eds.), *Teaching reflectively in theological contexts: Promises and contradictions* (pp. 162–189). Malabar, FL: Krieger.

Jarvis, P. (1987). *Adult learning in the social context.* New York, NY: Croom Helm.
Jarvis, P. (2004). *Adult education and lifelong learning: Theory and practice* (3rd ed.). New York, NY: Routledge/Falmer.
Kegan, R. (1994). *In over our heads: The mental demands of modern life.* Cambridge, MA: Harvard University Press.
Kegan, R. (2000). What "form" transforms? A constructive-developmental perspective on transformational learning. In J. Mezirow & Associates (Eds.), *Learning as transformation: Critical perspectives on a theory in progress* (pp. 35–69). San Francisco, CA: Jossey-Bass.
Labov, W. (1972). The transformation of experience in narrative syntax. In W. Labov (Ed.), *Language in the inner city: Studies in the Black English venacular* (pp. 354–396). Philadelphia: University of Pennsylvania Press.
Mackeracher, D. (2004). *Making sense of adult learning.* Toronto, Ontario, Canada: The University of Toronto Press.
Marmon, E. (2007). *Transformative learning in local, cross-cultural situations: Surprising dilemmas, reflections, and stories.* Unpublished doctoral dissertation, University of Kentucky, Lexington.
Marmon, E. (2010). Cross-cultural field education: A transformative learning experience. *Christian Education Journal, 7*(10), 70–83.
McIntosh, P. (1989 July/August). White privilege: Unpacking the invisible knapsack. *Peace and Freedom,* 8–10.
Mezirow, J. (1975). *Education for perspective transformation: Women's re-entry programs in community colleges.* New York, NY: Center for Adult Education, Teachers College, Columbia University.
Mezirow, J. (1991). *Transformative dimensions of adult learning.* San Francisco, CA: Jossey-Bass.
Mezirow, J., & Associates. (Eds.). (2000). *Learning as transformation: Critical perspectives on a theory in progress.* San Francisco, CA: Jossey-Bass.
Nouwen, H. (1975). *Reaching out: Three movements of the spiritual life.* New York, NY: Doubleday.
Nouwen, H. (1991). *Creative ministry.* New York, NY: Doubleday.
Palmer, P. (1998). *The courage to teach: Exploring the inner landscape of a teacher's life.* San Francisco, CA: Jossey Bass.
Payne, R. (2005). *A framework for understanding poverty.* Highlands, TX: aha! Process.
Piaget, J. (1952). *The origins of intelligence in children.* New York, NY: International Universities Press.
Riessman, C. (1993). *Narrative analysis.* Newbury Park, CA: Sage.
Rothenberg, P. (2007). *White privilege: Essential readings on the other side of racism* (3rd ed.). New York, NY: Worth.
Seidman, I. (1998). *Interviewing as qualitative research: A guide for researchers in education and the social sciences* (2nd ed.). New York, NY: Teachers College Press.
Storti, C. (2001). *The art of crossing cultures.* Yarmouth, ME: Intercultural.
Sue, D. W., & Sue, D. (2007). *Counseling the culturally diverse: Theory and practice* (5th ed.). New York, NY: John Wiley & Sons.
Tatum, B. (1997). *"Why are all the Black kids sitting together in the cafeteria?" And other conversations about race.* New York, NY: Basic.

Taylor, E. (1994). Intercultural competency: A transformative learning process. *Adult Education Quarterly, 44,* 154–174.
Taylor, E. (2006). The challenge of teaching for change. *New Directions for Adult and Continuing Education, 109,* 91–96.
Tolliver, D., & Tisdell, E. (2006). Engaging spirituality in the transformative higher education classroom. *New Directions for Adult and Continuing Education, 109,* 37–47.
Vella, J. (2002). Learning to listen, learning to teach: The power of dialogue in educating adults (Rev. ed.). San Francisco, CA: Jossey-Bass.

CHAPTER 13

IN BLACK AND WHITE

Transformation Through Examined Selves

Gabriele Strohschen

This chapter offers up a concept for facilitating awareness of self for adults in the context of education programs as a first step toward functioning within today's cross-cultural environments. Within a liberatory education and critical pedagogy praxis, this concept crystallizes basic reflection and action practices that are based on phenomenology. The chapter presents vignettes that are focused on learning in intersubjective relationship and analyzed to identify principles and steps in this process. The hope is that this chapter spurs discussion among diverse practitioners and students in the field of adult education to open pathways to transformation of self and communities across differences by means of adult education.

ORIGINS

Freire told us, "The educator must not be ignorant of, underestimate, or reject any of the 'knowledge of living experience' with which educands [students] come to school." (2004, p. 58). All too often, educators have not critically examined their own knowledge of living experience, giving us opportunity to investigate our self and inquire into the goals and subject of our profession in relationship with one another.

Illumination of one's own pathways and passages clarifies the process of one's moving from the known to the unknown; a concept that runs deeply through the ideas and work of Freire and many other writers who purport critical reflection as a means for self-awareness raising (e.g., Aronowitz & Giroux, 1986; Brookfield 1995; Daloz, 1999; Stanage, 1987; Vygotsky, 1978). Self-awareness is a simple concept, the importance of which we can readily accept in the practice of teaching and learning. This concept is a precursor to delineating and strengthening one's professional identity and group belonging. Freire's concept of conscientization speaks to awareness, action, and organization (2001, p. 19) and shows a straightforward movement from individual change to communal change. Can individuals support communal (or social) change without having completed critical self-examination on their values and assumptions? Surely we will answer, "no." However, just how do we approach this personal, ego-transcending self-awareness raising in the moments we are challenged with understanding a greater, shared, or maybe even universal truth—a truth or reality that includes that of those "other" from ourselves? What principles might guide this process? How do we become what Aronowitz and Giroux (1986) first termed a "transformative intellectual?"

In 1975, Krishnamurti opened a vast panorama for considering such thoughts on transformation: "To understand oneself there must be the intention to understand—and that is where our difficulty comes in" (p. 43). Although he agrees that for transformation of the world, transformation of the self is necessary (p. 44), he claims,

> The fundamental understanding of oneself does not come through knowledge or through the accumulation of experiences, which is merely the cultivation of memory. The understanding of oneself is from moment to moment; if we merely accumulate knowledge of the self, that very knowledge prevents further understanding, because accumulated knowledge and experience becomes the centre through which thought focuses and has its being. (p. 46)

The difficulty in our training, schooling, and socializing into mind-centered thinking is that it strengthens the existing "me." Krishnamurti would explain that we do so through the projection of desires, which we then manifest in our experiences. In other words, when we consciously and cognitively, with our knowing mind, seek peace, inner stillness, justice, understanding, altruism, knowledge or any other such valued ideals, which are a part of what is typically considered important in individual and social transformation, we are actually strengthening the existing self in its now-heightened awareness. Yet this awareness is centered on the self and not on those ideals. And although this awareness of the self is an important step in the direction of transformation toward such ideals of interdependency in *Gemeinschaft* (Fechner, 2008), we get caught up in a circular movement of experiencing only what we have already projected to be or to become our truth.

The possibility for a "moment-to-moment" creation, or *trans*-formation, is therewith thwarted. When we seek a sort of one-approach-fits-every-moment model to self-awareness, we fall short of creating awareness of our self within myriad contexts in which we find a need for grasping the whole of a situation; one that includes more than one's own reality. At the same time, I suggest there are some fundamentals we might follow. The philosophical frameworks of constitutive phenomenology and liberatory education delineate principles for both reflection and action. When applied, those principles form a model that scaffolds our moment-to-moment creation of self in community. This chapter attempts to expose these principles and steps in the process by way of vignettes, reflection, and analysis of the meaning of each of the narratives.

Originating

An essay by an adult educator on self-awareness as a precursor for individual and social transformation ought to begin with a simple chronicling of significant life passages, as such narratives (i.e., what is termed here "vignettes") allow the readers a glimpse into this educator's "truth" while being nudged to reflect on their own. This brings about sound possibilities for examination, analyses, and syntheses of experience for common threads, or what we may call "universals." With those common threads, we may eventually be able to weave a matrix of intersubjective and intercultural (and any other "inter" category we hold for people) relationships within the teaching/learning context of adult education. Therefore, with Vignette 1, I examine the feeling phase (Stanage, 1987) of the phenomenological approach to identifying self-awareness as a first step in considering, reflecting, and relating to the teaching and learning practice at the intuitive level.

VIGNETTE 1: HOW MY ORIGINS BECAME THE GENESIS OF MY EDUCATIONAL CREDO

A child of survivors of World War II, I grew up in an environment that held more questions than answers. Mine was a child's lifeworld that saw the aftermath of violence and hate; that saw adults struggle with physical and psychological damages inflicted upon them during the war. It was a world struggling in the wake of hegemonic oppression and the results of individuals' and countries' ethnocentric and expansionist goals. These adults were born in the 1920s and had followed their elders and their leadership's propaganda, basically, without asking questions. Few questioned the greed for power, the quest for forced territorial acquisition, the desire for riches, or the need for self-aggrandizement and righteousness. These survivors of WWII had grown up to become my family members. This generation surrounded me during my formative years. My parents, aunts, and uncles had gone along with what they had been taught since childhood. Yet the horrors of war, the violence of imprisonment, the rapes and tortures during the occupation of Germany, and the realization of truths that emerged during the war and after the fall of the Third Reich put questions to them that they continued to deal with into their adult years. They dealt with these questions, if not openly with actions, then internally with agony.

As a child in the 1950s in Germany, I, too, began to live with questions. They shaped my beliefs and values. Mine had been a childhood in utter flux. We lived among destruction and poverty in a postwar and Cold War world in Berlin. Around us we witnessed assassinations, political unrest, the building of walls, and the further division of the world into East and West. Division among people was not just created with barbed wire and concrete walls; with handheld weapons, mines, and automatic shooting devices. Division also cocooned minds within the invisibility of unexamined ideology. Behind the invisible and visible walls, among the tangibles and intangibles, questions remained. In our schools, I was introduced to the atrocities of war in a matter-of-fact, historical context. We learned what our elders had created. And we were taught to question it all.

Coming of age during the era of revolts and protests in Europe, I was introduced to the leadership of individuals who risked, and often lost, their lives, in the pursuit of peace and love for humankind and for a sustainable lifeworld. My heroes then, of course, were the presented global leaders like Gandhi and Martin Luther King Jr.; but far less famous figures, too, like Ms. Rapp and Mr. Geiger. She was a Lutheran social worker who led my Girl Scout troop, not an easy task given our teenage rebelliousness and her physical restrictions due to childhood polio. He was the minister of our church; his left arm long lost in a war injury; his spirit held together with the righteous hand of religion. Their actions spoke of peace, compassion, and lifelong learning as the ways to make an impact on our world. They, too, continued to question. And with that, they instilled in us the urgency for creating community by, with, and for others.

Reflection

My early life experiences continue to beckon me to look beyond what appears. I am always reminded of the multiple realities that exist because the contradictions and incongruence in my childhood world sensitized me to this. The practice I deem appropriate for educators of adults and the processes for such a practice are grounded in respect and love for my sister and fellow human beings. Somehow that lesson was learned early by way of simply seeing the will and perseverance of the adults around me and in my relationships with those surrounding me (Buber, 1979). In spite of their physical and emotional wounds and scars, they acted, moved forward, and went on. As a child, physical deformity among adults was normal; we did not find it all too odd or scary. I also knew not about posttraumatic stress syndrome then. I learned to accept "wacky" behavior exhibited by the adults around us from time to time. Living within the context of such realities of our elders somehow guided me to acknowledge "otherness" as normal and to comprehend interdependence in its rich wholeness of communal survival.

These origins that bounded my early moral development and values clarification are pivotal in the development of my eventual education credo. It was precisely my childhood that formed the lens through which I analyze and set the goals and roles I expect to manage in my profession. The questioning that began in my childhood continues but with more definite premises: I do not see life as dichotomized into personal, professional, and vocational content areas. I see my life and work as an interdependent process of being in this world.

Therefore, my teaching and my learning are shaped by the belief in interdependency (Strohschen, 2009). If I am to be and to contribute in any setting, I had better be willing to be open toward learning with those in that setting, irrespective of particular roles, positionalities, perspectives, or consequences. I must continue to be open to learning and to growth; and learning and growing happens in relationship with the world. If we are, as we often claim in the field of education, to create a "better world" for everyone, then our mindfully considered, critically examined, and clearly stated beliefs and values must form the foundation from which we act and serve. I have an obligation to myself to engage in reflection, research, study, and dialogue with my sister and fellow human beings for rigorous question-posing if we are to find solutions together and move to action for transformation—of self and community. Such a stance is swiftly undermined because of the risk-taking it calls forth. Risk-taking is not generally an action rewarded in institutional settings such as education organizations. Without the strength that comes from clarity of self and values, one surely falters in those contexts.

From Awareness to Commitment: Posing the Questions

I practice within the field of adult education within this set of beliefs and values that was essentially shaped by processing the feelings about my upbringing in *der Nachkriegszeit* (postwar period) in Germany. I did not seek out critical pedagogy or the liberatory education praxis of adult education; it found me. I did seek self-awareness, and it is an arduous process from those origins in my childhood to the clarification of how I had learned to question what Brookfield termed paradigmatic assumptions (1995). Liberatory education pivots on the development of critical consciousness, which enables learners to recognize connections between their individual problems and experiences and the social contexts in which they are embedded. Coming to consciousness (e.g., Freire's conscientization [2001]) is the necessary first step of praxis; wherein praxis is an ongoing, reflective approach to taking action. Praxis involves engaging in a cycle of theory, application, evaluation, reflection, then back to theory. Social transformation is the product of praxis at the collective level. Clearly, one's praxis includes a whole lot of questioning. My praxis began with asking myself how my beliefs and values were shaped and with examining what I had felt/feel about my experiences. Bringing this to consciousness was the pivotal first step.

VIGNETTE 2: DON'T YOU AGREE?

Another telephone call from one of my advisees—she calls often. Most of the time, we discuss her recent course. Often, she shares annoyance at her classmates' behavior. It is difficult to diplomatically maneuver such conversations. This time, she lamented about one particular classmate. And, gee whiz, he is always late. And, sigh, he comes back late from breaks. And he makes statements in class that confuse her. And he makes them very loudly, very loudly, and so emphatically. And those comments are threatening to her because they are not politely offered. And his perspective is way out there, over the top. He also texts on his cell phone in class. Most annoying, and it so hinders her learning, indeed. And what could she do because this is ruining her educational experience. It was not the first time that she had made comments to me about this particular classmate. I listened. I did not respond with any judgment on his behavior, of course. I reinforced how she could focus on her studies during and after group instruction and benefit from incidental learning about her ability to listen, or to communicate her thoughts and feelings constructively in a group setting. In spite of this support from me, I sensed that this conversation left her frustrated. I did not know why—at first.

Reflection

This call puzzled me because she had lamented about this particular classmate's behavior before—during class sessions, to others, and on the telephone to me. For the reason that one ought not discuss one student's behavior with another student, I did not comment; however, I suddenly felt that there was something else here, something intangible but very real. I sensed that I was receiving a veiled message of sorts in this exchange. What she detailed and how she detailed it was something I had not grasped during several of the past conversations with this student about the male, Black student about whom she was talking.

I tuned in to what I felt: Discomfort. Incongruence. Growing slightly angry at her. What was she telling me? What was I internally, emotionally responding to during this phone call? What was different about her comments about this student from our other conversations? I listened. I listened to my own feeling reaction. I imagined her in the classroom and the student she was talking about and how their interaction had felt to me then. I recalled what she looked like; how she looked at me; and how I interacted with her.

And then it hit me. She, a middle-aged, middle-class, White, U.S.-born woman had apparently certain expectations about how to discuss a young, middle-class, Black, U.S.-born man with another middle-aged, middle-class, White woman. I did not know sufficiently what such expectations were to recognize this kind of invisible winking, this veiled code language of the U.S. brand of racism. Born and raised in Germany, I had not been socialized into the range of behaviors and cross-color expectations and norms of how a middle-aged, middle-class North American White woman is to view Black North American males. Most importantly, even though I might be cognizant of this sort of *ism*, I had not internalized it emotionally. I had no clue about the steps in the dance I was to dance to the silently playing music of institutionalized racism with its subtle discrimination (Rowe, 1990) with this seeming counterpart of mine. In addition, my nonresponse to her code language confused her as much as her conspiratorial conversation was consternation to me because I did not emotionally understand it. This inability of mine to filter the conversation through the expected social norms and feelings, I think, caused a rift between her and me because I could not and did not readily offer her sought-after agreement or chimed in to her lamenting about *those people*. I felt like I had failed both students in my support of them.

Once I grasped the enormity of what I deemed an insight into the reality of my North American, White, middle-aged, middle-class woman counterpart, I was faced with several decision points. I could consider it a teachable moment and discuss what had come to my mind with the woman student. It was a moment during which a flash of insight illuminated many other such conversations I had had in the past. I could check with her if my insight had any meaning to her, if she would understand my different perspective. My awareness of a possible disconnect on several levels would guide me in bringing this issue to the forefront. I was keenly aware of what I saw through my lens; however, how could I manage to peer through hers, and how open might I be to inform my understanding by grasping hers? Would my values prevent me from listening to hers? Most importantly, how could I remain true to my credo and collaboratively move toward change that would be beneficial to her, to her classmate, and to me?

From Awareness to Commitment: Striving to Transform

Broadly put, developmental psychology focuses on how persons become their true self. The process of individuation includes the integration of elements of personality, experiences of one's life, and aspects of one's psyche into a whole. Clarity and awareness of this wholeness of one's self, then, is said to make for a stable person with consistent behavior. In the field of adult education, much of Mezirow's work is grounded in this perspective on human development (1991, 2000).

But transformation is tricky. Given the socialization one experiences throughout a lifetime and our social mandate to fit into society, somewhere, even our deliberate efforts to be/become aware of this "true" self are fraught with fear. We readily accept values, such as those espoused in my credo, within a liberatory praxis; however, do we examine and reexamine our assumptions from moment to moment; from situation to situation? As educators, to question our self, our motives, and true feelings clearly, authentically, and in good faith can be a most painful and disconcerting undertaking. Doing this publicly means taking risks that mightily threaten our professional relationships because it lays bare our self for others to judge. Hence, our self-directed undertaking may fall prey to the trickster that prefers to deliver the kind of messages to our consciousness, which are soft to the touch.

Who is the trickster? Applying Krishnamurti's (1975) take on it, it is our ego-self. Why does she (the ego-self) succeed? In our efforts to manage and survive the risks and challenges in our human interactions, particularly within the context of the politically enmeshed work environments of educators, and to remain connected to the group, our Trickster Self adapts defenses that prevent us from becoming ostracized from the herd. In the context of Vignette 2, I had selected the softer message that North American society had socialized this woman in a way different from my socialization; she had accepted and internalized beliefs about Black males; she did not understand why I did not chime in with her laments; and I would simply have to make sure that interactions in the classroom follow a consistent, nondiscriminatory process. I would have to make sure that I remained true to my values of liberatory education and subsequent stance toward all students. I would simply have to follow the proper processes and keep things fair, equitable, and within the policies of the university and EEOC rules. Certainly.

What has to be added is that my feelings and perceptions would have to be kept in check-and-balance, achieved through critical examination of my assumptions and preferences so that I would not compensate for "her" behavior by simply supporting him, for example, based on the message I had given myself. The riskier approach loomed in my awareness. All too often in the higher education context I have come to know, students of color do receive different treatment than their White counterparts, or vice versa. Instead of addressing the given issue at hand, situations take a turn because interactions, allegedly about an issue, become personalized and rooted in the very institutionalized racism that is an integral part of this North American culture. So one student focuses on the other's behavior as the issue, in this vignette "his loudness," for example. And this behavior is ascribed to the stereotypes of "his culture" or to those of socioeconomic status associated with "his culture." Surely, norms may differ from group to group; certain norms are reinforced due to institutionalized isms; however, in the context of an instructional setting, unexamined motives and assumptions for accusing those who are "other from self" must be mitigated. As facilitators of learning, particularly within the values of liberatory and transformative learning, we have the obligation to uphold our values and operationalize the guiding principles of transformation. We also have the most earnest responsibility to be accountable to the best possible practice of managing a classroom and creating safe spaces for everyone in it. We most certainly have the rhetoric down for this. Why do we falter?

It is so very disconcerting and difficult to bracket our Self—our thinking and our feeling—in the moment and to make transparent the values or ideals we deem important. Were we able to do this with clarity, authenticity, and in good faith with our self, we may "lose" because we would have to recognize how the ego-self is fooling us and that we, most of the time, choose a path that is least harmful to our self. We survive. We strengthen the ego-self when we continue to use the language and action of that which oppresses our transformation; in this case, it was institutionalized racism.

VIGNETTE 3: WRESTLING WITH WHOSE REALITY?

My long-time colleague was upset. One of our advisees was "stupid," she claimed, because he was not producing the kind of work she expected of him as a graduate program student. After four semesters in the program, without prior warning, and without any indication that his work was substandard hitherto, my colleague suddenly wished to dismiss him from the program and was going to let the student know during the committee meeting tomorrow.

My decision process to assist the student was an arduous one. Letting the student know of this forthcoming action and breaking rank with my colleagues was most definitely not accepted in the academy; not standing with the student went against my credo as a liberatory educator. Discussion with the colleague and program director yielded no solution. This one was on me.

Reflection

At the time I wrestled with the conflicting realities inherent in the U.S. brand of race politics, power, and positionality correlations in the student-teacher and teacher-teacher relationships, and my colleagues' attitudes. I harshly questioned how I could possibly make any difference in this situation? I considered walking away from the entire debacle, allowing the powers-that-be and the education system to play out its rules, albeit skewed toward supporting an elitist institutional formal structure I deemed them. I could have helped a "little," by mitigating the impact and arguing for a probationary period instead of dismissal. With that, I would have seemed the politically correct, concerned academic and stayed safely out of the quagmire of race and other politics. But this whole mess was simply wrong. And a student cannot be told he is incompetent after all of his academic work had been accepted over several terms by the same team of professors, one of whom only now balked at the quality of the work.

This was one of my hardest soul-wrestling moments that would define my praxis. I had a choice whether I would remain an accepted member in the group of colleagues or stand outside of it. In the aftermath of my eventual decision to support the student, who is a Black man, I essentially lost that job and have been labeled by some a race traitor, uncollegial, a maverick, and, as a White woman, even worse names. The student told me later, "I thank you because you didn't have to do this." He was wrong. I had to.

That decision permanently altered the realities of three people: the colleague's, the student's, and mine. The colleague seems to harbor anger toward me, discontinuing our work together. The student graduated and is contributing to the field of adult education based on his research that explored critical race theory in the practice of institutions of higher education. And I solidified my stance on liberatory education, having lost a position and reputation among some colleagues, but having survived in the long run in good faith and congruence with my values.

The problem that remains is that this stance of mine is wrapped up in many moments of ostracism and my sadness for it. In my reality, I can now no longer pacify self-ego with acknowledgement and rewards given by others, but I need to reinforce myself for standing for those values and ideals by means of continuing individuation. I still believe in the choiceless awareness that I must follow what I so early on in my life learned about humans, humans in community, and intersubjective relations: the unequivocal urgency to co-create just and sustainable community by, with, and for one another based on fairness, justness, and equity. These values must be upheld no matter the social price one has to pay for it. I am not presenting this in a romanticized manner, seeking validation and applause for such ideals. I am expressing in these considerations an age-old wisdom that is traced back to the saying of Hillel the Elder (Kolatch, 1985), "If not now, when?" In many lands by many people, the meaning of "If not now, when? If not I, who?" has been a battle cry of transformative leaders, to adapt Giroux's term to this context.

From Awareness to Commitment: Standing as Person

In his landmark treatise on a theory for adult education, my mentor, Sherman Stanage (1987), reasoned a comprehensive analysis of how, within the context of our adult education praxis, we engage in the quest of answering four fundamental questions: Who am I? What can I know? What ought I to do? What may I hope? These four questions, he posited, are what "characterize the study of philosophy" (1987, p. 3). Bringing together his thoughts and teachings, Stanage penned his book over one brief Chicago summer back in 1986 (Figure 13.1). He had been writing it throughout his lifetime. The orientation toward becoming <u>person</u> is fundamental in Stanage's take on adult education seen from within a phenomenological research paradigm. "Adult education does indeed have a clear and distinct subject matter, one which literally stares us in the face" (1987, p. 53), Stanage wrote, as he dedicates a most thorough application of principles

PERSON

Consiouscing ....
Experiencing ....
Feeling ....

Figure 13.1 Model of <u>Person</u> (Stanage, 1987). Graphically adapted by Strohschen.

of constitutive phenomenology to the investigation into adult education. The subject matter of adult education is the adult, indeed. The full "eduction" (p. 37) of a person to become <u>person</u> is at the heart of our praxis. It is what we ought to do. <u>Person</u>, as Stanage explores, is the transformed self that is capable of communicating, or being in relationship with others "on the basis of intersubjectivity within co-existence" (p. 37). Stanage thus sees transformation of self and communities possible in the pathways of adult education.

"CONSCIOUSING" AND CONSTITUTION

The Insights

This chapter flowed along the lines of the model (Figure 13.1) Stanage created for the "eduction" of <u>person</u> through feeling, experiencing, and "consciousing" (1987, p. 328).

The three vignettes and my reflections and analyses of them give a framework for constituting the basic steps in phenomenological and critical reflection approaches in a praxis of adult education that seeks personal and community change for the mutual benefit of all across differences. The focus in these vignettes is on Black-White differences, given the North American context of differences among people as played out within institutionalized racism that is rooted in the origins of this nation (USA). (Note: It is beyond the scope of this chapter to explore the U.S. history of slavery to arrive at an analysis of the systems hence created. It ought to be explored more widely). For an adult education praxis that seeks to "educe" or bring forth liberated adults, self-awareness is a pivotal element in practicing education for transformation.

Vignette 1 speaks to the obligation to one's Self to engage in reflection and dialogue with others about one's own felt origins. In order to engage in rigorous question-posing and if we are to find solutions together and move to action for transformation—of self and community—clarity about one's values is essential. It answers the "Who Am I?" question. Vignette 2 elucidates how we actually strengthen an ego-self when we continue to use the thinking and language of that which oppresses our transformation and reinforces prevailing values without critical examination of our assumptions. It deals with the "What Can I Know?" question. Vignette 3 brings clarity to what adult education is and what we should do based on our examined values and experiences. It addresses dilemmas that come about when our practice calls upon us to answer the "What Should I Do?" question.

Put together, the three vignettes lead us to seek answers to the "What May I Hope?" question. I have disclosed the premises for a definition of adult education with my credo that firmly grounds adult education praxis in the tradition of liberatory education. Irrespective of the particular goals of formal or nonformal education for adults, the freeing of the human spirit (Strohschen, 1999) and the co-creation of contexts for empowerment of self with adult students is at the heart of such praxis. Empowerment, of course, takes many forms, and its outcomes are not for the educator to determine but for the student. Moreover, empowerment happens when we are capable of making meaning of our reality, interdependently with grasping the reality of those "other" from self, and are able to transform our self from an ego-centeredness toward an issue-centeredness.

Krishnamurti's (1975) comments on this first and last freedom of a self dovetail with the phenomenological techniques of bracketing (Stanage, 1987), which asks for an absence of self; an unprojected stilling of thought and mindful considerations. This remains a massive challenge "for educators to be poor in knowledge and beliefs," as Krishnamurti phrased it (p. 82). The grasping of one's own processes of becoming and of becoming aware of the cognitive, affective, and spirit-ful (or metacognitive) changes we experience in our life is essential to letting go of external and internal constraints, such as described in Vignette 2. The consciousing of such processes and one's action in them leads us to making meaning of our world and our relationships within it.

Sharing this understanding, then, is particularly important for educators of adults; not only to become aware of self, and congruently so, with our head, heart, and hands; but also to fulfill our roles of teacher, guide, coach, consultant, and learning process facilitator appropriately, which, paradoxically, ought to mean we accept and dismiss these very roles, take on what appears appropriate at the moment, and disclose what we are doing every step of the way.

LIBERATORY EDUCATION AND PHENOMENOLOGY: AN APPROACH TO TRANSFORMING SELF AND OTHERS

Liberatory praxis of adult education benefits from viewing it from the vantage point of phenomenology. Krishnamurti's (1975) point that "without understanding yourself, you have no basis for thought; without self-knowledge, what you think is not true" (p. 12) underscores this approach of examining transformative learning. This theme of inner freedom of creative reality (p. 17) is reiterated by Huxley (1964) when he describes as a "choiceless awareness" that which Krishnamurti sees as, "a state of being, as silence, in which there is no becoming, in which there is completeness" (p. 17); one that is to be found "where thought frees itself from worldliness and personal craving to be" (pp. 17–18).

Educators can find a path for participating in transformative learning, that is, in the liberation from manifested, internalized, and externally reinforced desires, which includes the judging of self against others. Perhaps, simply put, I learned most about how to become a teacher by being taught, as a child, as a student, and as a teacher by those who seemed to love who they are and show real affection toward me. The very process of teaching, or the leading forth of others through facilitating their learning process, starts with clarity of self, of one's beliefs and values, and of one's credo. Teaching always includes passion and unequivocal commitment to examine self, values, and credo and then to move to action. As Freire told us (1997, p. 93), "I cannot be a teacher if I do not perceive with ever greater clarity that my practice demands of me a definition about where I stand."

My early observations of my childhood's family members and my studies later with my mentors taught me that, in critical pedagogy, one ought to ethically and courageously defend the very essence of liberation. It puzzles me to this day to enter a room of self-proclaimed liberatory educators who do not caringly reach out to a newcomer or who rant warrior-like about social injustices, silencing any voice that does not agree with their ideology. None of the originators (if you will allow this word) of liberatory education would agree with such dogmatism, or the creation of a paralleling universe of oppression based on unexamined ideology.

I suggest that constitutive phenomenology offers a fitting approach to learning about self and other selves. Its principles and processes guide us in finding truth and universalities within intersubjective vantage points and aid in understanding how things appear in our feel*ing*, experienc*ing*, and conscious*ing*. As Freire exclaimed, "I refuse to add my voice to that of the 'peacemakers' who call upon the wretched of the earth to be resigned to their fate. My voice is in tune with a different language, another kind of music. It speaks of resistance, indignation, the just anger of those who are deceived and betrayed" (1997, p. 93). With a mutually understood "language," we can communicate across differences and work for self and communal transformation.

REFERENCES

Aronowitz, S., & Giroux, H. (1986). *Education under siege: The conservative, liberal, and radical debate over schooling*. London, England: Routledge & Kegan Paul.

Brookfield, S. (1995). *Becoming a critically reflective teacher*. San Francisco, CA: Jossey-Bass.

Buber, M. (1979). Ich und du. In *Das dialogische Prinzip* (4th ed.). Heidelberg, Germany: Verlag Lambert Schneider.

Daloz, L. (1999). *Mentoring: Guiding the journey of adult learners* (1st ed.). Hoboken, NJ: John Wiley & Sons.

Fechner, R. (2008). Ferdinand Tönnies (1855–1936). In S. Gosepath, W. Hinsch, & B. Rössler (Eds.), *Handbuch der politischen Philosophieund Sozialphilosophie* (pp. 1347–1348.) Berlin, Germany/New York, NY: Walter de Gruyter.

Freire, P. (1997). *Pedagogy of freedom.* Lanham, MA: Rowman & Littlefield.

Freire, P. (2001). *Pedagogy of the oppressed* (30th anniv. ed.). New York, NY: Continuum International.

Freire, P. (2004). *Pedagogy of hope: Reliving pedagogy of the oppressed.* New York, NY: Continuum International.

Huxley, J. (1964). *Evolutionary humanism.* Buffalo, NY: Prometheus Press.

Kolatch, A. J. (1985). *The second Jewish book of why.* Middle Village, NY: Jonathan David.

Krishnamurti, J. (1975). *The first and the last freedom.* San Francisco, CA: HarperSanFrancisco.

Mezirow, J. (1991). *Transformative dimensions of adult learning.* San Francisco, CA: Jossey-Bass.

Mezirow. J. (2000). *Learning as transformation: Critical perspectives on a theory in progress.* San Francisco, CA: Jossey-Bass.

Rowe, M. P. (1990). Barriers to equality: The power of subtle discrimination to maintain unequal opportunity. *Employee Responsibilities and Rights Journal, 3*(2), 153–163.

Stanage, S. M. (1987). *Adult education and phenomenological research: New directions for theory, practice, and research.* Malabar, FL: Krieger.

Strohschen, G. (1999). *Toward the freedom of the human spirit: A study of the impact of the wisdom traditions on the praxes of adult education.* Unpublished dissertation. Northern Illinois University.

Strohschen, G. (2009). *Handbook of blended shore education: Adult program development and delivery.* New York, NY: Springer Verlag.

Vygotsky, L. S. (1978). *Mind in society: The development of higher psychological processes.* Cambridge, MA: Harvard University Press.

CHAPTER 14

DEVELOPING INTERCULTURAL EFFECTIVENESS COMPETENCIES

The Journey of Transformative Learning and Cross-Cultural Learning for Foreign-Born Faculty in American Higher Education

Pi-Chi Han

The demands of globalization are transforming the boundaries of the world and the relationship of people with other cultures and contexts. Globalization has provided new opportunities for global mobility, and it especially has fundamental implications for the mobility of people across geographical boundaries. Due to the internationalization of higher education and the growing need for international activity between universities, more and more academics are taking overseas appointments (Altbach, 1996; Welch, 1997). Thus, the United States has traditionally benefited from the intellect and the broad experience of foreign-born individuals.

Foreign-born faculty have helped promote campus internationalization as they represent educational and cultural resources (Kuhlman, 1992). They have enriched the learning experience, remained a largely untapped international resource for higher education, offered firsthand intercultural learning opportunities to the students, and added diversity to campus life (Basti, 1996). In reality, foreign-born faculty are like the stranger without attention on a strange campus (Helms, 2005). Much research indicates that foreign-born faculty have faced a huge cultural adjustment, and it has made their life tremendously difficult in the host country (Hser, 2005; Manrique & Manrique, 1999; Marvasti, 2005; Ngwainmbi, 2006). Therefore, they must provide themselves with a profound level of intercultural competence (Haeger, 2007).

The process of intercultural competence is seen as a transformative learning experience (Kim & Ruben, 1988; Taylor, 1994). In effect, scholars suggest that intercultural competence is a transformative process in which the learner develops adaptation skills that, over time, allow the learner to effectively understand other cultures. Therefore the learning relationship includes the connection of culture and context. The existence of foreign-born faculty in the American culture of higher education has provided a great resource for adult educators and international educators to explore what profound level of intercultural competence they have developed even though this rarely has been studied. In this chapter, the author, as one of foreign-born faculty, will discuss personal transformative learning journey as a resource for adult educators and international educators.

BACKGROUND AND LITERATURE REVIEW

In America, the immigrant laborers have long been the underpinning of the country's economic success. The rapid changes in the population are widely affecting the demographics of schools, societies, and workplaces. In 2005, immigrants composed over 12% of U.S. residents and 15% of the workforce (Migration Policy Institute, 2007). Richmond (1988) also suggests that there is a growing demand for importing highly qualified immigrant talents in the U.S. workplace.

The *Open Doors* (Institute of International Education, 2009) reports that in 2008–2009, some 113,494 international scholars were teaching or conducting research at U.S. campuses, which is an increase of 7% from the previous year. In addition, the United States has traditionally depended heavily on foreign-born talent in the field of science and engineering (No & Walsh, 2010), and the need for highly qualified faculty in engineering and other related fields has grown dramatically (Madhavan, 2001). Thus, in order to fulfill that need, many universities and colleges have recruited more highly competent foreign-born faculty (Madhavan, 2001).

Although the foreign-born faculty have made contributions in the United States, many students, parents, legislators, and policymakers are concerned about their impact on students' educational achievement. The perception of foreign-born faculty has been focused on their linguistic problems creating instructional ineffectiveness (Marvasti, 2005; Walker & Bodycott, 2000). They have reported many cross-cultural, legal issues and other concerns that have challenged foreign-born faculty and scholars as they work in the United States (Bonetta, 2007; Foote, Li, Monk, & Theobald, 2008; Ngwainmbi, 2006; No & Walsh, 2010). Han (2008) has recommended a five-competence model of Intercultural Effectiveness Competencies (ICE) as a coping strategy for foreign-born faculty to function successfully in the intercultural interactions.

According to the international education and cross-cultural communication literature, there was no consensus regarding the definition of cross-cultural competence (Baxter Magolda, 2000; Lustig & Koester, 2003). Intercultural competence as a concept has been explored and researched under different terms, such as cross-cultural adjustment (Benson, 1978), cross-cultural competence (Ruben, 1989), intercultural effectiveness (Cui & van den Berg, 1991; Han, 1997, 2008), intercultural competence (Dinges, 1983), and intercultural communication competence (Spitzberg, 2000). The process of achieving intercultural competence involves awareness, understanding, acceptance, respect, appreciation, and developing new attitudes, skills, and behaviors in reaction across cultural boundaries (Deardorff, 2004). Han (1997, 2008) has proposed a model with five competencies to conceptualize intercultural competence as a whole: (a) the ability to handle psychological stress, (b) the ability to effectively communicate, (c) the ability to establish interpersonal relationships, (d) the ability to have cross-cultural awareness, and (e) the ability to have cultural empathy. In her studies, ICE has referred to the multiple measurable abilities allowing one to interact effectively and appropriately across cultures. The measurement of ICE has been developed and validated in the quantitative instrument applied to various demographic groups for investigating ICE competencies and developing ICE baseline data (Han, 1997, 2008). Understanding the dynamic relationships of five ICE competencies will help to learn how to develop ICE.

Psychological Stress and ICE

Many researchers have cited the negative emotional reactions experienced by individuals in new cultures (Church, 1982; Oberg, 1960; Searle & Ward, 1990; Ward & Searle, 1991) and have emphasized the importance of coping with stress as a component of achieving ICE (Abe & Wiseman, 1983; Church, 1982; Kealey, 1989). To maintain a healthy emotional stability and psychological well-being in a stressful situation is an important dimension for overseas success (Tung, 1981; van Oudenhoven, Mol & van der Zee, 2003). Kim (1988) has proposed a model of stress-adaptation-growth that outlines how psychologically stressful experiences help sojourners' adaptation and personal growth.

Communication Competence and ICE

Hall (1976) has emphasized that culture is communication and communication is culture. Intercultural communication competence is the overall internal capability of an individual to manage important challenges in the intercultural interactions (Kim, 1991). Kim has proposed that the positive correlation between sojourner adjustment and communication with host nationals, that is, a high level of interaction yields a higher degree of satisfaction in the host country. Moreover, Byram (1997) stresses the importance of language (linguistic competence), includes identity and cultural understanding in his conceptualization, and urges that a comprehensive definition of intercultural communication should include the social context and nonverbal dimensions of communication. Intercultural communication may be necessary for ICE, yet it cannot guarantee ICE (Hannigan, 1990).

Relationship Building and ICE

Kim (1988) has pointed out that the relational networks of sojourners serves as an important function in facilitating their adaptation. Wilson (1994) suggests that international friendships and membership help sojourners gain in intercultural effectiveness competence. Researchers have confirmed that positive social interaction with host nationals is a necessary condition for effective sojourner adjustment (Klineberg & Hull, 1979; Oberg, 1960). Van Oudenhoven et al. (2003) argue that communication skills and the ability to establish interpersonal relationships as social initiative are a crucial dimension to intercultural effectiveness.

Cross-Cultural Awareness and ICE

In cross-cultural study, self-awareness and cultural awareness are inseparable. Cultural awareness refers to an individual's knowledge of specific cultural material (e.g., language, values, history, art, foods, etc.) of the cultural group of origin and/or the host culture. Cultural awareness involves the degree to which an individual is aware of the history, institutions, rituals, and everyday practices of a given culture. It facilitates a world mindset for the sojourners. The culturally competent person requires an acceptance of a particular culture's basic worldview and the ability to act within the constraints of that worldview when interacting with members of that culture.

Cultural Empathy and ICE

Cultural empathy is also referred to as sensitivity (Hawes & Kealy, 1981; van Oudenhoven et al., 2003). Empathy is defined by Bennett (1993) as "the ability to experience some aspect of reality differently from what is given by one's own culture" (p. 53). Bennett means that empathy needs to involve a frame of reference shift in being able to understand another's perspective. Ruben (1976) defines cultural empathy as the capacity to be interested in others and to obtain and to reflect an accurate sense of another's thoughts, feelings, and/or experiences. It includes the ability to empathize with feelings, thoughts, and behaviors of different cultural groups. Shear (1993) concludes that cultural empathy is the most found behavioral characteristic among successful international assignees.

Literature has linked intercultural competence to cross-cultural learning. Cross-cultural learning is the process of adapting to a new environment and its requirements through obtaining necessary knowledge, skills, and attitudes (Hannigan, 1990). Scholars assert that acquiring intercultural competence is the result of cross-cultural learning (Bartel-Radic, 2006; Hannigan, 1990). In reality, effective cross-cultural learning does not always come from a positive experience but from effective reflection. The reflection is a cognitive process based on the learner's personal level of maturity regarding their current level of cognitive development.

Learning in another country is a process of learning that involves constructing a new or reviewed interpretation for guiding action. Bartel-Radic (2006) has defined intercultural learning as "the acquisition or modification of the representations of intercultural situations" (p. 652). Intercultural learning does not mean to change one's own culture but to understand other ways of seeing and finding the world. During the period of interacting with others, the modification process starts to happen. In the assumption of intercultural learning, representations are the learning outcome, while acquisition and modification are the learning process. Mezirow (1991) has stated that the change or modification from cross-cultural learning is viewed as an integrative and transformative process.

Transformative learning in acquiring intercultural competence is an ongoing process of the individual's internal system. Taylor (1994) views intercultural competence as an adaptive capacity that allows individuals to integrate their worldview and to function effectively in another culture. McPhatter and Ganaway (2003) indicate that cultural competence is the ability that allows learners to transform knowledge and awareness. Kim and Ruben (1988) confirm that the process of acquiring intercultural competence is transformational and a learning and growth process that allows individuals to function effectively across cultural and national boundaries.

Furthermore, Mezirow (1996) states that learning is a process of making meaning and how adult learners make sense of their own lives. The transformative learning process begins with an experience of a disorientating dilemma for learners. He asserts that

> The process by which we transform our taken-for-granted frames of reference (meaning schemes, habits of mind, and mindsets) to make them more inclusive, discriminating, open, emotionally capable of change, and reflective so that they may generate beliefs and options that will prove more true or justified to guide action. (Mezirow, 2000, p. 8)

Transformation is a deep and structural shift in one's thoughts, feelings, and actions that represents and explains the world around oneself. Not all learning is transformative, and effective cross-cultural learning does not always come from a positive experience. According to Mezirow's (1991) work, there are four components in transformative learning: (a) experience, (b) critical reflection, (c) reflective discourse, and (d) action. First, learning begins with the learner's experiences. Second, the self-examined interpretation follows. Third, after testing the new meanings, learners engage in the discoursing dialogue in order to obtain a new and empathic understanding that allows assessment of the interpretation. Fourth, the learner takes "immediate action, delayed action or reasoned reaffirmation of an existing pattern of action" (Mezirow, 2000, p. 24).

The process of acquiring intercultural competence starts from the need to change, and the outcome of the process is transformative learning. Taylor (1994) has implied that a personal transformation becomes the outcome of intercultural learning for sojourners to function across cultural borders. Although Taylor has argued a significant link between becoming interculturally competent based on Mezirow's (1991) theory of transformative learning, he has not provided a specific explanation of how intercultural competencies can be acquired or trained. In this chapter, based on the conceptual exploration and literature review, an integrative ICE model (see Figure 14.1), the author proposes a mode of inquiry to help foreign-born faculty obtain ICE competencies.

Developing Intercultural Effectiveness Competencies ▪ **229**

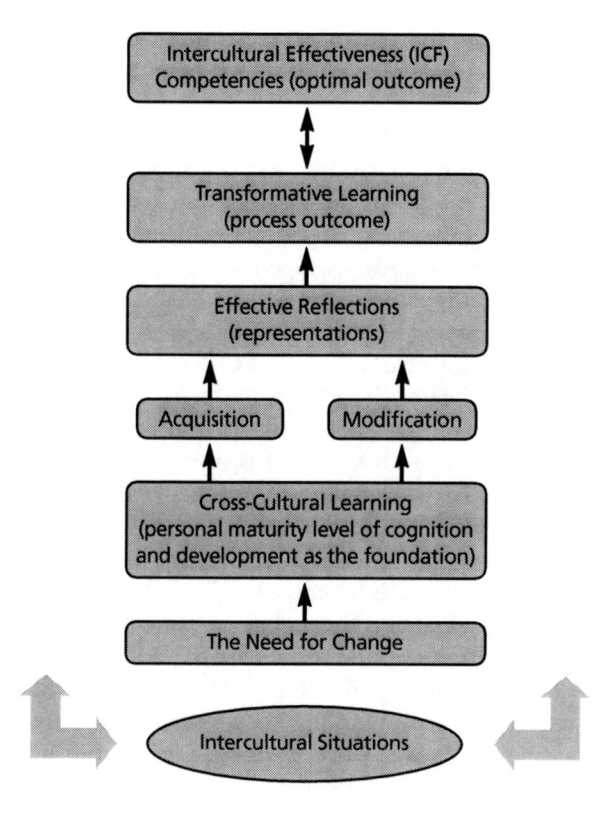

Figure 14.1 Integrative model of ICE.

DISCUSSIONS FOR INTEGRATIVE MODEL OF ICE

Switching from one culture to another means not only a change of time, climate, and living conditions, but also a change in daily life and social norms. "Change, however positive, may still be stressful" (Carneale, Gainer, & Meltzer, 1990, p. 220). This chapter provides the opportunity to explain and better understand how I have gone through transformative learning and cross-cultural learning in my life and what I have learned in order to achieve the level of maturity that I seek in my academic and personal lives. I wrote this chapter to promote a broader cross-cultural understanding.

In the United States, many Asian foreign-born students and faculty have chosen to inhabit large metropolitan areas. I have chosen a midwestern state with few international residents to start my transformative journey. It was the right decision for my cross-cultural learning, as I was able to have more opportunities to learn American culture than just being with homogeneous ethnic groups. In retrospect, it provided the perfect space and time in which to review my own culture and help me attain my personal level of growth.

My journey of acquiring ICE competencies in the United States has echoed Figure 14.1. I grew up within a very traditional Chinese family unit. Before beginning my studies in the United States, I was molded by a homogenous culture in Taiwan. At that time, studying abroad, especially in the United States, was a trendy intellectual pursuit. In addition, it was a prestigious honor for my ancestors and immediate family. I came to the United States with a strong spiritual foundation in Confucianism, which focuses on self-discipline of one's intellect. Before I started my learning journey in the United States, I had never noticed the tremendous difference between Chinese and American culture in practice.

My story started from the first day of communication with the staff of the graduate school. I had struggled with the realization of my limited understanding of the American culture and language proficiency. Initially, I recognized that there was an intercultural situation I encountered, and immediately I felt there was a call for me to make a change. Coping with the resistance of change was always there. Life became challenging for me to learn cross-cultural differences on a daily basis. Along the way, a personal maturity level of cognition and development rooted in Confucianism was the foundation for my learning. In the process of acquisition and modification, I have learned to express and represent myself in different learning settings in an appropriate and reflective way.

Notably, it became clear for me to identify the change process I experienced when I went back to Taiwan after I accomplished my advanced degree. I have recognized my change and been able to have reflective dialogues with my acquaintances in Taiwan. The dialogue has helped me to know how the transformative learning has taken place and evolved along with the intercultural learning as a process outcome. Most importantly, I have been able to perform ICE competencies as the optimal outcome for my cross-cultural learning.

I still can recall the time when I sat on a bench at the busy college campus in the United States with a blank mind. The only thing I grasped was a call for change. Without any support system, I abided by the strong voice that requested me to make a change without hesitation. In retrospect, my ability to persevere and find the courage I needed to succeed came from the foundation of personal maturity molded in Chinese culture, which provided the solid foundation I needed to open my heart and move forward fearlessly.

In addition, I remember many times when I sat in front of my computer attempting to write my dissertation while tears streamed from my eyes, as that was the year I also lost my father. Again in 2009, the devastating family losses during my new teaching journey in the United States transformed me with strength by reinforcing my personal maturity level. A striving to understand the meaning of life's occurrences has provided a route in which I receive my strength. In essence, my journey of cross-cultural learning has not been an easy one. With hard-earned sweat and many tears, I continue to search my personal maturity with acquisition and modification from the cross-cultural learning. By having an effective reflection and searching for the inner self, I have moved across the cultural border with learned ICE competencies.

Due to the travel back and forth between Chinese and American cultures, my cross-cultural learning experience offered me opportunities in which I was exposed to a new culture, and I learned necessary lessons in order to obtain the desired knowledge, skills, and attitudes of my peers. Although it was not always pleasant and positive, these learning opportunities have given me time to have effective reflections and representations from the cross-cultural learning process of modification and acquisition. During this time, my personal maturity level of cognition and development has evolved. My life experiences have contributed to my own transformative learning experiences.

Experience can be life's textbook for every adult learner. Kolb (1984) asserted that "Learning is a continuous process grounded in experience. Knowledge is continuously derived and tested out in the experience of the learner" (p. 27). My experiences of cross-cultural learning started from the quest of change and disorientation. By meeting different encounters and having intercultural interactions, I have engaged myself in a change process, and the process has inspired me in many different perspectives, which have helped me to search the transformative learning and ICE.

Transformative learning theory has provided a theoretical framework for me to understand my cross-cultural journey. The change process has echoed the theory of transformative learning. I started to interpret the issues of intercultural interactions with self-examination. When I was unable to successfully solve issues, I tried to search for the discourse through effective dialogues with trusted others who had deeper understandings in both American culture and my culture to acquire the new meanings or to obtain an empathic understanding to support my meaning-making process. Trusted friendship is necessary for one to form rational discourse for transformative learning (Taylor, 2000). Based on the meaningful discourse, I took a suggested action that I analyzed through my meaning-making process. The representations became the outcomes of acquisition and modification in the intercultural situations (Bartel-Radic, 2006; Mezirow, 1991).

BEST PRACTICES

Learning in a new culture is a prerequisite to obtaining intercultural competence. The most challenging effort of my cross-cultural learning was to be able to acquire and modify the representations of intercultural interactions without losing my own cultural identity and heritage. It is very easy to be trapped in the mode of ethnocentrism with the baggage of cultural bias and prejudice during the journey of intercultural learning. The more cross-cultural awareness and cultural empathy we have, the better cross-cultural understanding we may acquire (Bennett, 1993). As an Asian faculty member, I have experienced tremendous cultural differences between the East and the West. In America, Asian Americans have been treated as the model minority and yet perpetual foreigners (Ng, Lee, & Pak, 2007). Ng et al. also report that Asian women faculty encounter additional stereotypes and barriers.

I have tried hard to release myself from the stereotyped perspectives and make a difference by how I present myself in every intercultural interaction. I have acquired and modified cross-cultural notions and have come out with my own representation. The most powerful notion I have been able to modify and acquire in the American culture is to be myself. Therefore I have given up the melting pot metaphor and turned to support the salad bowl metaphor, because it reflects what I perceive to be a realistic status quo in the United States. Although there is a great deal of differences between Chinese culture and the American culture, I have found the basic belief that practices in the human beings' societies are the same. People believe in good virtues and ethics no matter where they are. This was the common ground for me to be able to open a dialogue with each encounter during my journey of intercultural interactions.

In addition to improving my English linguistic proficiency, I have focused my discussions on those who might be interested in my observations of the United States. This action has helped broaden my understanding of American perspectives and experiences, and I have learned to modify those perspectives over time. My acceptance of the differences between American culture and mine has evolved as the cross-cultural awareness that has helped me build solid personal relationships with my American friends. As a result, I have had more opportunities to share intercultural differences.

To be interculturally competent is an ongoing evolution. In the professional setting, as the opportunity arises, I strive to understand current issues in the United States and share my non-Western perspectives in formal gatherings, meetings, and classes. I have also invited guest speakers to act as panels in my seminar class in order to initiate an open forum of intercultural dialogue with broader cross-cultural speakers and participants. Furthermore, I have focused my research agenda on exploring intercultural competence and with the intention of developing my own ICE competencies in order to be an interculturally well-rounded professional. I have been a change agent for my own transformative learning journey. Hofstede (1994) concludes that only when the individual has passed through the realization of the impact of cultural differences, critical reflections, and practical experiences does cross-cultural learning occur.

DISCUSSIONS FOR FURTHER USE, POSSIBILITIES, AND FUTURE RESEARCH

Over three decades, the demographic shift of importing more foreign-born faculty, scholars, and researchers has impacted the United States academic institutions dramatically (Marvasti, 2005). Simultaneously, the increasing complexity and diversity of culture in the U.S. society has launched a challenge of cross-cultural learning for immigrants to acquire ICE competencies in the intercultural interactions. The autoethnological reflections have provided the following implications for the future:

Further Use

As a Resource

The autoethnological reflections in developing ICE based on the real practices and the theories of transformative learning and cross-cultural learning will provide applicable information for adult educators, Human Resource Development (HRD) practitioners, and policymakers to analyze and develop training and education programs for immigrants, international students, foreign-born faculty, and business expatriates in the international settings.

As a Reference for Developing Global Talent

The demand for global talent development is on the rise (Kramer, 2005). These autoethnological reflections provide a reference resource for organizations in selecting and recruiting global talent and in planning, designing, and conducting programs for developing the global talent.

Possibilities

An Integrative Model of ICE

As the foreign-born faculty have a strong impact on their students, campuses, and the U.S. higher education institutions at-large, the study of ICE for foreign-born faculty based on their cross-cultural learning and transformative learning experiences can serve as an instructional resource. Based on my own autoethnological reflections, I have linked cross-cultural learning, transformative learning, and ICE competencies in the ICE model. I recommend educators take a proactive attitude to recognize the factors in cross-cultural learning and the process of acquiring ICE. Based on my current autoethnological reflections, transformative learning is the process outcome, while the ICE is the optimal outcome of acquiring ICE. I recommend researchers explore the relationships between ICE, transformative learning, and cross-cultural learning by an integrative model of ICE.

Higher Education

In order to have successful transformative learning for foreign-born faculty, the higher educational institution needs to value foreign-born faculty and their experiences as an important asset. It is necessary to provide the mentorship and cross-cultural training and development programs to help foreign-born faculty during their cross-cultural adaptations in the United States (Han, 2008).

Non-Western Culture

Increasing cultural hegemony by one-way assimilation and accommodation of culture will no longer suffice in this century. Understanding the different values between West and East will be helpful in managing the multicultural and multinational world. A call for a non-Western perspective is on the rise in the U.S. public and private settings.

Future Research

The Empirical Study for the Integrative ICE Model

It is necessary to apply quantitative and qualitative research methods to explore the relationship between transformative learning (process outcome), ICE (optimal outcome), and cross-cultural learning.

Developing ICE Baseline Data

Comparing the foreign-born faculty from non-Western countries to those who are from Western countries in the performance of ICE competencies as they worked in the United States or other countries will help establish the baseline data of ICE for foreign-born faculty. It will also help to understand the current ICE competencies for foreign-born faculty in the United States.

CONCLUSION

The most crucial resource in the global knowledge economy is talent (Hart, 2006). Attracting talent in a global market has been the hallmark of the most competitive economies. Douglass and Edelstein (2009) have reported that higher education in the United States has hosted the greatest numbers of world-class talent, although it has been changed because emerging competitors have attracted some of that talent in the market share over time. Although the number of foreign-born scholars has decreased because of the rigid immigration policy in the United States, the demand for importing talent is even greater (Marvasti, 2005; Richmond, 1988).

In retrospect, I have taken a proactive role in my transformative learning and cross-cultural learning. I have acted as a change agent for promoting cross-cultural understanding in the academic setting. By receiving the different feedback and determining implications from my personal experiences and practices, I have figured out that it is not enough to use personal experience as the means to acquire ICE. Future research could explore the dynamic relationship between transformative learning and ICE competencies and the affecting factors that influence transformative learning and ICE. Transformative learning in the cross-cultural setting is an ongoing learning process based on personal experience followed by critical reflection and reflective discourse. With this understanding, the learners are able to take appropriate action.

In the integrated ICE model, developing ICE competencies should come from cross-cultural learning and evolve into transformative learning. As time goes by, the process outcome is ongoing transformative learning. Developing ICE competencies has become the optimal outcome for me in the cross-cultural learning journey. Transformative learning theory has provided a profound theoretical framework for me to understand the change process in cross-cultural learning and intercultural situations. In the integrative ICE model, ICE competencies have facilitated transformative learning and vice versa. It is an ongoing learning process.

In higher education, it is clear that facilitating the success of internationalization efforts has to involve the recognition of foreign-born faculty (Basti, 1996; Deardorff, 2004). However, the successful academic experiences of foreign-born faculty cannot be accomplished without the support and commitment of the institution (Hser, 2005). Policymakers, adult learning, and HRD professionals in public, private, and nonprofit organizations should pay more attention to applying transformative learning and cross-cultural learning theories for developing ICE competencies. A call for professionals in the fields of international education, cross-cultural learning and training, international HRD, international business, and adult education is needed to work together as the call for developing intercultural competence is on the rise.

REFERENCES

Abe, H., & Wiseman, R. L. (1983). A cross-cultural confirmation of the dimension of intercultural effectiveness. *International Journal of Intercultural Relations, 7,* 53–67.

Altbach, P. G. (Ed.). (1996). *The international academic profession: Portraits of fourteen countries.* Princeton, NJ: Carnegie Foundation for the Advancement of Teaching.

Bartel-Radic, A. (2006). Intercultural learning in global teams. *Management International Review, 46*(6), 647–677.

Basti, C. F. (1996). *A study of the professorate from the perspective of selective foreign-born faculty.* (Unpublished doctoral dissertation). Northern Illinois University, Dekalb.

Baxter Magolda, M. B. (Ed.). (2000). *Teaching to promote intellectual and personal maturity: Incorporating students' worldviews and identities into the learning process.* San Francisco, CA: Jossey-Bass.

Benson, P. G. (1978). Measuring cross-cultural adjustment: The problem of criteria. *International Journal of Intercultural Relations, 2,* 21–37.

Bennett, M. J. (1993). Towards ethnorelativism: A developmental model of intercultural sensitivity. In R. M. Paige (Ed.), *Education for the intercultural experience* (2nd ed., pp. 21–71). Yarmouth, ME: Intercultural.

Bonetta, L. (2007, February). *Foreign faculty face challenges.* Retrieved from http://sciencecareers.sciencemag.org/career_magazine/previous_issues/articles/2007_02_02/science.opms.r0700027

Byram, M. (1997). *Teaching and assessing intercultural communication competence.* Clevedon, England: Multilingual Matters.

Carnevale, A. P., Gainer, L. J., & Meltzer, A. S. (1990). *Workplace basics.* San Francisco, CA: Jossey-Bass.

Church, A. T. (1982) Sojourner adjustment. *Psychological Bulletin, 91*(3), 540–572.

Cui, G., & van den Berg, S. (1991). Testing the construct validity of intercultural effectiveness. *International Journal of Intercultural Relations, 15*(2), 227–241.

Deardorff, D. K. (2004). *The identification and assessment of intercultural competence as a student outcome of international education at institutions of higher education in the United States.* (Unpublished doctoral dissertation). North Carolina State University, Raleigh.

Dinges, N. (1983). Intercultural competence. In D. Landis & R. W. Brislin (Eds.), *Handbook of intercultural training* (Vol. 1, pp. 176–202). New York, NY: Pergamon.

Douglass, J. A., & Edelstein, R. (2009). *The global competition for talent: The rapidly changing market for international students and the need for a strategic approach in the U.S.* Center for Studies in Higher Education, Research & Occasional Paper Series: CSHE.8.09.

Foote, K. E., Li, W., Monk, J., & Theobald, R. (2008). Foreign-born scholars in U.S. universities: Issues, concerns, and strategies. *Journal of Geography in Higher Education, 32*(2), 167–178.

Haeger, L. (2007). *Intercultural competence: An investigation of strategies employed by transnational faculty members.* (Unpublished doctoral dissertation). Capella University, Minneapolis, MN.

Hall, E. T. (1976). *Beyond culture.* Garden City, NY: Anchor.

Han, P. C. (1997). *An investigation of intercultural effectiveness of international university students with implications for human resource development.* (Unpublished doctoral dissertation). University of Arkansas, Fayetteville.

Han, P. C. (2008). An investigation of intercultural effectiveness for foreign-born faculty in Taiwan. *The International Journal of Learning, 15*(10), 165–174.

Hannigan, T. (1990). Traits, attitudes, and skills that are related to intercultural effectiveness and their implications for cross-cultural training: A review of the literature. *International Journal of Intercultural Relations, 14,* 89–111.

Hart, D. M. (2006, November 17). Global flows of talent: Benchmarking the United States. *The Information Technology and Innovation Foundation.* Retrieved from http://www.itif.org/files/Hart-GlobalFlowsofTalent.pdf

Hawes, F., & Kealey, D. (1981). An empirical study of Canadian technical assistance. *Intercultural Relations, 4,* 239–258.

Helms, R. M. (2005). *Inhabiting the borders: The experience of foreign language faculty in American colleges and universities.* (Unpublished doctoral dissertation). Boston College, Boston, MA.

Hofstede, G. (1994). *Vivre dans un monde multiculturel.* Paris, France: Les Editions d'Organisation.

Hser, M. P. (2005, Fall). Campus internationalization: A study of American universities' internationalization efforts. *International Education, 35*(1), 35–48.

Institute of International Education. (2009). *Open doors.*

Kealey, D. J. (1989). A study of cross-cultural effectiveness: Theoretical issues, practical applications. *International Journal of Intercultural Relations, 13,* 387–428.

Kim, Y. Y. (1988). *Communication and cross-cultural adaptation: An integrative theory.* Clevedon, England: Multilingual Matters.

Kim, Y. Y. (1991). Intercultural communication competence: A systems-theoretic view. In S. Ting-Toomey & F. Korzenny (Eds.), *Cross-cultural interpersonal communication* (pp. 259–275). Newbury Park, CA: Sage.

Kim, Y. Y., & Ruben. B. D. (1988). Intercultural transformation. In Y. Y. Kim & W. B. Gudykunst (Eds.), *Theories in intercultural communication* (pp. 299–321). London, England: Sage.

Klineberg, O., & Hull, W. F. (1979). *At a foreign university.* New York, NY: Praeger.

Kolb, D. A. (1984). *Experiential learning: Experience as the source of learning and development.* Englewood Cliffs, NJ: Prentice Hall.

Kramer, R. (2005). *Developing global leaders.* New York, NY: Conference Board.

Kuhlman, A. (1992). Foreign students and scholars. In C. Klasek, B. Garavlia, & K. Kellerman (Eds.), *Bridges to the future: Strategies for internationalizing higher education* (pp. 22–38). Carbondale: University of Illinois.

Lustig, M. W., & Koester, J. (2003). *Intercultural competence: Interpersonal communication across cultures* (4th ed.). Boston, MA: Allyn & Bacon.

Madhavan, S. M. (2001). *The job satisfaction level of Chinese- and Indian-born engineering faculty at a research university*. (Unpublished doctoral dissertation). West Virginia University, Morgantown.

Manrique, C., & Manrique, G. G. (1999). *The multicultural or immigrant faculty in American society*. Lewiston, NY: Edwin Mellen.

Marvasti, A. (2005, March). U.S. academic institutions and perceived effectiveness of foreign-born faculty. *Journal of Economic Issues, 39*(1), 151–177.

McPhatter, A. R., & Ganaway, T. L. (2003). Beyond the rhetoric: Strategies for implementing culturally effective practice with children, families, and communities. *Child Welfare, 82*(2), 103–125.

Mezirow, J. (1991). *Transformative dimensions of adult learning*. San Francisco, CA: Jossey-Bass.

Mezirow, J. (1996). Contemporary paradigms of learning. *Adult Education Quarterly, 46*(30), 158–172.

Mezirow, J. (2000). Learning to think like an adult: Core concepts of transformation theory. In J. Mezirow & Associates (Eds.), *Learning as transformation: Critical perspectives on a theory in progress* (pp. 3–33). San Francisco, CA: Jossey-Bass.

Migration Policy Institute. (2007). *2005 American community survey and census data on the foreign born by state*. Washington, DC: Author. Retrieved from http://findarticles.com/p/articles/mi_qu4052/is_200301/ai_n9223188/print

Ng, J., Lee, S. S., & Pak, Y. K. (2007). Contesting the model minority and perpetual foreigner stereotypes: A critical review of literature on Asian Americans in education. *Review of Research in Education, 31*, 95–130.

Ngwainmbi, E. K. (2006). The struggles of foreign-born faculty. *Diverse Issues in Higher Education, 23*(10), 28–29.

No, Y., & Walsh, J. (2010). The importance of foreign-born talent for US innovation. *Nature Biotechnology, 28*, 289–291.

Oberg, K. (1960). Culture shock: Adjustment to new cultural environments. *Practical Anthropology, 7*, 177–182.

Richmond, A. H. (1988). *Immigration and ethnic conflict*. New York, NY: St. Martin's.

Ruben, B. D. (1989). The study of cross-cultural competence: Traditions and contemporary issues. *International Journal of Intercultural Relations, 13*, 229–240.

Searle, W., & Ward, C. (1990). The prediction of psychological and sociocultural adjustment during cross-cultural transitions. *International Journal of Intercultural Relations, 14*, 449–464.

Shear, E. B. (1993). *Strange encounters: A communication model for cross-cultural adaptation and training*. (Unpublished doctoral dissertation). University of Kentucky, Lexington.

Spitzberg, B. H. (2000). What is good communication? *Journal of the Association for Communication Administration, 29*, 103–119.

Taylor, E. W. (1994). Intercultural competency: A transformative learning process. *Adult Education Quarterly, 44*(3), 154–174.

Taylor, E. W. (2000). Analyzing research on transformative learning theory. In J. Mezirow & Associates (Eds.), *Learning as transformation: Critical perspectives on a theory in progress* (pp. 285–28). San Francisco, CA: Jossey-Bass.

Tung, R. L. (1981) Selection and training of personnel for overseas assignments. *Columbia Journal of World Business, 15,* 68–78.

van Oudenhoven, J. P., Mol, S., & van der Zee, K. (2003). Study of the adjustment of Western expatriates in Taiwan ROC with the multicultural personality questionnaire. *Asian Journal of Social Psychology, 6,* 159–170.

Walker, P., & Bodycott, A. (2000). Teaching abroad: Lessons learned about intercultural understanding for teachers in higher education. *Teaching in Higher Education, 5*(1), 79–94.

Ward, C., & Searle, W. (1991). The impact of value discrepancies and cultural identity on psychological and sociocultural adjustment of sojourners. *International Journal of Intercultural Relations, 15,* 209–225.

Welch, A. (1997). The peripatetic professor: The internationalization of the academic professor. *Higher Education, 34*(6), 323–345.

Wilson, A. H. (1994). The attributes and tasks of global competence. In R. D. Lambert (Ed.), *Educational exchange and global competence* (pp. 37–50). New York, NY: Council on International Educational Exchange.

CHAPTER 15

TRANSFORMATIONAL LEARNING EXPERIENCE OF HAITIAN AMERICANS IN RESPONSE TO THE EARTHQUAKE IN HAITI

Emmanuel Jean Francois and William H. Young III

The purpose of this chapter is to explore and analyze the transformative learning experience of Haitian Americans in response to the Haiti earthquake in relationship with culture and context. The earthquake that hit in Haiti on January 12, 2010, has forever changed the lives of many Haitian Americans. Although the devastating earthquake caused posttraumatic pain and suffering, it also provided opportunities to develop resilience and transformative growth. The co-author of this chapter lost two brothers, one sister, and a baby nephew during the earthquake. Other Haitian Americans in the Tampa Bay, Florida, area are experiencing life-changing learning experiences due to the terrible catastrophe in Haiti. Given the intercultural implications of natural disasters with respect to the human response after extreme trauma situations, an understanding of the transformational learning experience of Haitian Americans may inform practitioners addressing facets of transformative learning in relationship with culture and context. The following research questions guided the analysis: "What are the perceived transformative learning effects of the earthquake in Haiti on the consciousness, reflective discourse, and perspective to actions of Haitian Americans?" and "How can the transformative learning experience of Haitian Americans in response to the earthquake in Haiti inform practitioners addressing facets of transformative learning in relationship with culture and context?"

TRANSFORMATIVE LEARNING THEORY

The theoretical framework of this chapter comes from transformative learning theory (Mezirow, 1991, 2000) and other literature relating to the process of transformation; more specifically, the three major transformative learning dimensions: critical reflection, reflective discourse, and perspective to actions (Merriam, Caffarella, & Baumgartner, 2007). Mezirow defined transformative learning as a process:

> [Whereby] we transform our taken-for-granted frames of reference (meaning perspectives, habits of mind, mind-sets) to make them more inclusive, discriminating, open [changeable], and reflective so that they may generate beliefs and opinions that will prove more true or justified to guide action. (Mezirow, 2000, pp. 5–8)

Mezirow (1991) previously indicated that critical reflection of personal experience can change "the beliefs, attitudes, and emotional reactions" (p. 167) of the learner. Similarly, Feinstein (2004) argued that reflexive discourse and critical reflection are two major catalysts of the transformative learning experience.

Mezirow (2000) asserted that transformative learning occurs through 10 phases. It starts with a disorienting dilemma (internal or external personal crises). Then it evolves through self-examination (feelings of fear, anger, guilt, or shame), critical assessment of assumptions, recognition that others share one's discontent and the process of transformation, exploration of alternatives (options for new roles, relationships, and actions), course of action planning, acquisition of new knowledge, trying of new roles, competence building and self-confidence, and reintegration.

In addition to Mezirow, Freire (2000) has developed a sociocultural perspective of transformative learning. According to Freire, transformative learning is a process of empowerment and social transformation. Rather than using the concept of critical reflection suggested by Mezirow (2000), Freire refers to that of conscientization as a catalyst for transformational learning. The reality is, both critical reflection and conscientization involve problem posing and dialogue with others as part of the process that helps an individual or a learner develop awareness of long-held assumptions, beliefs, and values. This increased awareness leads to a transformational experience (Freire, 2000; Mezirow, 2000). In that context, Taylor (2000) presented the transformative learning experience as a developmental process in five dimensions, encompassing (a) knowing as a dialogical process, (b) dialogical relationship with oneself, (c) continuing learning, (d) self-agency and authorship, (e) and connections with others.

Critics have argued that Mezirow's (1991) view of transformative learning is acontextual (Clark & Wilson, 1991). Taylor (2000) asserted that some biographical and social cultural factors influence a transformative learning experience. Other critics have questioned Mezirow's neglect of the role of relationship in the transformative learning process (Taylor, 2000), and the overreliance on rationality (Dirkx, 1998). Nevertheless, most scholars agree on some of the key concepts of transformative learning: experience, critical reflection, and development (Merriam et al., 2007).

This chapter focuses particularly on transformative learning after life-changing events. It builds upon existing literature on the transformative learning theory by investigating the transformational experience of individuals after life-changing events not only in the light of Mezirow's (1991, 2000) concepts, but also in exploring other aspects of transformative learning related to context, culture, and affect. Additional analysis in this chapter emphasizes the implications for practitioners addressing facets of transformative learning in relationship with culture and context.

METHOD

The design of this chapter involved a phenomenological research approach (van Manen, 2001; Wolcott, 2001). Phenomenology allows the researchers to conduct qualitative research and analysis based on the lived experience of the participants (van Manen, 2001). Haitian Americans are reaching out to people and organizations unknown to them before the earthquake. How are these entities doing this very important work for the people in Haiti? Often Haitian Americans feel caught between their Haitian culture and the American context in which they now live. The need for cultural understanding between the two countries is critical to help the people in Haiti. This chapter addresses the following research questions:

- How do Haitian Americans' unique position as immigrants to the United States affect their reactions to a natural disaster in their country of origin?

- What meaning do Haitian Americans make out of the earthquake disaster, and what transformations occur?

To answer the questions stated above, the authors of this chapter engaged selected Haitian Americans in the Tampa Bay, Florida, area in individual interviews. To understand the transformative learning experiences, a total of 12 individuals (seven women and five men, including one of the co-authors of this chapter) volunteered to participate in the interviews. The researchers selected participants through purposive sampling and contacted participants by telephone. The researchers explained the purpose of the call and requested their participation in the study, which provided the data to write this chapter. All the participants interviewed were Haitian American professionals working in the Tampa Bay area as schoolteachers ($n = 4$), organization or company managers ($n = 5$), realtors ($n = 2$), and one college professor ($n = 1$). Each participant signed an informed consent form, which indicated the purpose of the study as well as a statement of voluntary participation and confidentiality. The questionnaire included items on cultural and immigration experience, meaning of the earthquake, critical reflection, and transformational experience. Prior to conducting the formal interviews for the study, the questionnaire was field tested with three Haitian professionals who live in New York and were visiting the Tampa Bay area. This enabled the co-authors to make minor changes and refinements to the questionnaire.

The recorded interviews lasted between 30 and 45 minutes. A research assistant transcribed the interviews, and the researchers shared the transcripts with the participants for member-checking purposes. However, the co-authors did not conduct two rounds of interviews. Then the researchers analyzed the data through thematic coding (LeComte & Schensul, 1999) and constant analysis (Strauss & Corbin, 1998) for emerging themes. The themes developed from the research questions, concepts from the Mezirow's (1991, 2000) model, and emerging patterns from successive transcripts. Two scholars in qualitative research reviewed the transcripts and coding. To preserve the anonymity of the participants, the researchers used aliases in quoting from the interviews.

THE IMMIGRATION AND CULTURAL EXPERIENCE

In relation with culture and context, the immigration experience of Haitians in the United States is part of the broader African American experience in the American hemisphere. Haitian immigration in the United States dates from the 18th century when hundreds of Haitians migrated to Louisiana, especially after fire destroyed the entire city of Cap Français (now Cap Haitian) in 1793 (Brasseaux & Glenn, 1992). Since that time,

Haitians have made and continue to make significant contributions in American life through sports, music, literature, politics, and the economy (Bell, 1997; Christian, 1965; Hall, 1992; Kein, 2000). Estimates indicate that almost one million Haitians live in the United States (Miller, 2004).

When asked about their immigration and culture, almost all the participants described their lives as an improbable journey for being in the United States. They shared their incredible stories in terms of pursuit of economic opportunities, political persecutions, family network, scholarship/study opportunities, and luck (lottery green card). Haitians come to the United States to pursue various economic opportunities. Almost all the participants considered their opportunity to live in the United States a miracle that they are still trying to understand. Not all the Haitian immigrants came illegally to the United States. Some explained that they benefited from their parents who have been living as legal residents in the United States. However, some participants indicated that they emigrated in the United States as a result of political persecution, scholarship/study opportunities, or some luck.

The type of contact that Haitians living in the United States maintain with Haiti varies from one individual to another. The themes that emerged with respect to the contact that participants maintain with their country of Haiti are money transfer to relatives in Haiti, real estate/business investment for retirement in Haiti, love-hate relationships, and activist involvement through grassroots or political organizations. Table 15.1 illustrates the key themes and supporting quotations related to the participants' immigration experience.

Participants in our interviews said that their lived immigration and cultural experience in the United States has been painful and nostalgic at times. Some participants shared their lifelong learning experience. Others expressed concerns for their complete acculturation. The interviews also revealed many conspiracy theory beliefs that characterized the history of relations between Haiti and the United States.

MEANING OF THE EARTHQUAKE

The earthquake that hit Haiti had shaken the traditional pessimistic assumptions about Haiti in relation to the world made by Haitians living both in the country and abroad. The state of poverty of Haiti, the poor quality of the structures, and the heartbreaking images showing the brutal development of the painful days after the earthquake have probably challenged the beliefs, assumptions, value judgments, and emotions of people around the world. The intensity of emotions expressed through tears from individuals who have heard about a country for the first time and of those who participated in candlelight vigils and fundraising events, have reminded us about what Mezirow (1991) called "meaning perspectives," which is "a way

TABLE 15.1 Key Themes and Supporting Quotations Related Participants' Immigration Experience

Themes	Supporting Quotations
Pursuit of economic opportunities	My presence in the United States is a miracle. I was on my way home, back from school when a friend told me "There is a trip right now for Miami. Let's go!" I was hesitant. And he said, "I know the captain. You will pay me when you get settled." I ended up being in Miami, went to a refugee camp, got released, went to college, and now I am an elementary school teacher. I never even dreamed being in the U.S. (Sylvia, elementary school teacher)
Political persecutions	I arrived in the U.S. at the age of 16 months. That's what my parents told me at least. My mom had to flee the country after my dad was killed by the Duvalier regime. (Mark, restaurant manager)
Family network	My dad came to the U.S. as a boat people when the U.S. used to encourage people to take the sea. At that time, there was a need for factory workers. In the process, my dad obtained his green card and brought all our family (my mom, my brothers, and my sisters) to the U.S. (Harold, realtor)
Scholarship/study opportunities	I came here on a student visa during the 1980s. Things went bad after Duvalier lost power in 1986. I decided to stay. (Ed, store manager)
Money transfer to relatives in Haiti	I am working here to take care of my mom, my dad, my brothers, my sisters, and my cousins. I regularly transfer money for them, especially to pay for their school tuition fees, pay for their rent and their food. (Bill, restaurant manager)
Real estate/business investment	Haiti is my country and I love it despite what people are saying. I made a lot of real estate investment in my native city of Saint Marc. This is how I plan my retirement. (Anita, realtor)
Love-hate relationship	To tell you the truth, I used to go to Haiti for Christmas, Carnival, and the summer. There was a time, I could not wait to travel and enjoyed the country. When the insecurity situation became intolerable, I really started to hate the country. I mean, I hate the people in the government, their corruption, and also the fact that people still vote for them to put them in power. (Jenna, elementary schoolteacher)
Activist involvement	I am always involved in what is going on in Haiti. Sometimes I am more involved... I always tried to remain current with the news and my friends in the grassroots and popular movements. (Romel, college professor)

of seeing the world, that is the perspective or view through which meaning emerges from experience" (Cranton, 1994, p. 42). Obviously, the meaning perspective in the context of this chapter refers to Haitian American participants in the interviews. For them, the earthquake signifies the death of a nation-state, irresponsibility, self-guiltiness, helplessness, personal loss, and financial loss.

Almost all the participants believed that the earthquake means the death of a nation-state once called Haiti, and that the earthquake destroyed everything that symbolized the pride of the Republic of Haiti. Participants interpreted the heavy consequences of the earthquake and the management of its aftermath as a result of the irresponsibility of past and current Haitian governments. Some participants said that they felt personally guilty about the heavy consequences of the earthquake. They said that the earthquake helped them realize how worthless they can be when others need their assistance the most. For some participants, the earthquake simply meant "personal loss" and financial loss. Table 15.2 summarizes the key themes and supporting quotations related to the participants' meaning of earthquake.

TABLE 15.2   Key Themes and Supporting Quotations Related to the Participants' Meaning of Earthquake

Themes	Supporting Quotations
Death of a nation-state	The national palace symbolizing the executive power has flattened. The judicial palace symbolizing the judicial power has flattened with judges and lawyers. The legislative palace has flattened with senators and congressmen. Universities and schools collapsed with students and professors. Churches collapsed with priests, ministers, and believers. Hospitals have collapsed with patients, physicians, and nurses. Police and security buildings have collapsed.... What else do you want to hear as evidence that the nation is symbolically dead? (Romel, college professor)
Irresponsibility	I was very angry, very frustrated. I was angry at the government, at God, at the people who did not care about how they built their house. (Harold, realtor)
Self-guiltiness	I felt like I was somehow responsible for what happened. I don't know why, but this is how I really felt when I saw the images on TV. (Anita, realtor)
Helplessness	I sat there, watching people dying and could not help. I felt worthless. I felt helpless. That augmented to my pain. (Paul, high school teacher)
Personal loss	I drove my mom to the airport Saturday morning to go to Haiti. The morning of the day that the earthquake hit, I was talking to her on the phone. She was so happy that she was back home. She was telling me how she was having a good time and wanted me to change the date on her ticket even if that was going to cost her some bucks. She did not come back! She will never be back! She will never be back! I will not see my mom again, my friend, my hero [started crying] ... I felt I lost myself in the process. I lost my soul. I lost my faith. I lost myself. I am still lost. I am still wondering what's going on? How could that happen to us? How could that happen to me? I don't know [tears]. (Ed, store manager)
Financial loss	I was in Haiti three weeks before the earthquake. I built my retirement house where I was supposed to travel to leave in February. Some of my friends were planning to go with me to see the Haitian carnival. I literally lost all my financial investments in Haiti. This is terrible, man! This is terrible! (Bill, restaurant manager)

CRITICAL REFLECTION

According to Mezirow (2000), critical reflection is essential to the transformation process. In this study, critical reflection does not refer to a problem-solving perspective; rather, it refers to an ability to question the assumptions related to a disturbing event. Mezirow distinguished content reflection (examination of the content of a problem in order to understand what happened), process reflection (the questioning of assumptions or beliefs that one holds regarding a problem), and premise reflection (questioning of the relevance of assumptions and beliefs that one has long held about a problem). Haitian Americans were engaged in critical reflection, process reflection, and premise reflection after the earthquake through self-reported challenges of their assumptions and beliefs, spirituality, personal identity, personal self-reflection, virtual reflection, and community-based reflection.

Assumptions and Beliefs Challenged

The experience of the earthquake has challenged several assumptions and beliefs that some Haitians held regarding the hostility of the international community toward real social and economic changes in Haiti. They said that they came to the realization that Haiti is not a neglected nation as they thought. They realized that many foreigners are aware of the struggles of the Haitian people and what the history of Haiti means for the history of a free world. Harold, a realtor, remarked, "I never thought that humanity could be so sensitive about the sufferings of other human beings in a poor country like Haiti."

Spirituality Challenged

Some participants said that the earthquake has put their spirituality to test, and they have been through deep spiritual reflection since the earthquake hit. They said that they have been asking themselves all kinds of spiritual questions. They felt like the earthquake seriously attacked their faith in God or any spiritual being. Paul, a high school teacher, said, "To be honest with you, I asked very challenging questions about the existence of God."

Personal Identity Challenged

Most participants said they have been hard on themselves for their hopelessness, helplessness, and sense of irresponsibility and accountability vis-à-vis the situation of Haiti after the earthquake. Ed, a store manager, pointed out that

Things were going so bad in Haiti that I was not always excited to identify myself as Haitian. The earthquake really put me to a different place in that regard. I felt like my Haitian identity was strongly challenged in my personal reflection on what happened and my interactions with other people, and the excitement that I saw in the news, in communities, and in churches.

Personal Self-Reflection

Participants confessed that they had to halt for a while to let the emotion go because they felt like they were about to lose their mind. They said that they had to take a moment with themselves to think about what they could personally do in the situation. Sylvia, an elementary school teacher, pointed out,

> I had a lot of doubts about my people despite our glorious past. The doubt was probably my own doubt about myself. I traveled far away inside myself during the earthquake. When I saw the people chanting on CNN the Sunday after the earthquake, I could not feel more empowered than that. Their chant exhibited resilience and fed my strength

Virtual Reflection

There was a recurrent theme of reflections about the earthquake using various virtual means of communication. Participants cited Myspace, Facebook, Skype, Twitter, blogs, and teleconferencing as examples of support they used to have all types of discussions about the earthquake. Romel, a college professor, said,

> After the earthquake, I contributed to several blogs, gave my opinions about what can be done for Haiti, the role of the international community, the roles of Haitians in Haiti and abroad. I also participated in teleconference meetings with former classmates who live in France, Canada, Mexico, Dominican Republic, and in other places in the U.S. like New York, Miami, Chicago, Boston, Atlanta, etc. We shared great ideas that we passed on to friends who are participating in conference on the rebuilding of Haiti.

Community-Based Reflection

Participants' critical reflection also materialized through their participation in various community events or community gatherings, involving reflection, planning, or fundraising or collection of items to send to Haiti. Jenna, an elementary school teacher, shared,

> I participated in many community events where people shared their emotions and ideas about what is going on in Haiti. I was always cynical about some community events. Now, wherever they invite me, here I am. I felt like I could not be the passive woman that I was before. And you can see that the community has changed in the way they think about Haiti.

TRANSFORMATION

Transformative learning is a process. It can unfold when one questions uncritically internalized or assimilated assumptions, beliefs, values, and perspectives through content reflection, process reflection, and premise reflection (Mezirow, 2000). The narrative discourses of the participants in our interviews suggest that most of them have revised some assumptions that they held prior to the earthquake. They self-reported increased appreciation for humanity, increased resilience and spirituality, liberation from long-held conspiracy theories, enhanced national identity, reevaluation of contact with Haiti, and development of advocacy skills.

Increased Appreciation for Humanity

Participants believed that regardless of race or nationality, a genuine human being is the same everywhere when witnessing heartbroken suffering. They said that they no longer believe that people in industrialized countries are insensitive to the pain of other human beings in poor countries. Harold said,

> I always saw myself as an individual because of many unfortunate events in my life. I probably lost the notion of humanity until after the earthquake. I mostly saw people through their greed and selfishness. Now I treasure humanity and see people with their heart and their compassion for folks that they don't even know.

Increased Resilience and Spirituality

Some participants confessed that they were skeptical about the idea of a God, but the earthquakes in Haiti, Japan, and Chile have made them believe that at least a higher being exists somewhere. They believe that something is going on, that a higher being is shaking the order of things. Paul revealed,

> The first week of the earthquake, I probably stopped to believe there is a God. I have been comforted by stories of survival and the fragility of human life. I feel like I became a stronger and more spiritual person. I go to church and I pray [to] God now!

The increase in resilience and spirituality was observed in both those participants who regularly attend church (religious) and those who do not (nonreligious). For the religious participants, the experience was influenced by their involvement in spiritual gatherings. The nonreligious group explained the relied-on spirituality by witnessing the resilience of the victims of the earthquake in Haiti with which they were in direct contact.

Liberation From Conspiracy Theories

Almost half of the participants acknowledged that the aftermath of the earthquake contributed to help them free themselves from some long-held conspiracy theory assumptions about the United States. Jenna pointed out,

> People say all kinds of stupid things about a conspiracy from the U.S. to take over Haiti. Thank God I am free from some conspiracy theories about Haiti and the U.S. that I used to believe in. I mean, every country tries to defend its interests, but I think there are people in the U.S. who really want to help Haiti.

Enhanced National Identity

Participants indicated that they feel more proud to identify themselves as Haitians, contrary to the sense of embarrassment that they used to have prior to the earthquake. Harold said, "I never felt so proud of being Haitian. I hope the new perception about Haiti could help transform the economic and social realities of the country!"

Reevaluation of Contact with Haiti

All the participants said that the earthquake has made them reevaluate their contact with Haiti, whether to reestablish or reinforce their relationships with Haiti. Mark pointed out, "I have been living in the U.S. for over 20 years. I never wanted to travel back to Haiti. I was disgusted by what was going on. Since the earthquake, I have already did two missionary trips in Haiti."

Development of Advocacy Skills

All the participants said they have developed advocacy skills that they used to help in the relief effort, and that can help them academically and professionally as well, especially in activities and projects related to rebuilding Haiti. Jenna said,

> There are a lot of skills that I have developed over the course of the past months, which I was not aware of about myself [sic]. Usually I am a bad advocate even for myself. I have been a good advocate for victims of the earthquake brought to Tampa. I did my homework and help[ed] a lot of victims find assistance through social service agencies in the Tampa Bay area. I challenged people to do missionary trips in Haiti.

IMPLICATIONS FOR PRACTITIONERS

The earthquake that hit Haiti represented a disorienting dilemma for all the participants interviewed in the context of writing this chapter. They all revealed that this terrible event brought them to a strange emotional place that they have never been before. In this strange place, they felt induced to question some assumptions, beliefs, feelings, and perspectives about Haiti, the United States, and the world, which they have accumulated over the course of their lived cross-cultural and immigration experience in the United States. Therefore, this disorienting dilemma is not acontextual. There is a cross-cultural and immigration context that triggered the external and internal crises that participants were facing. Without the context, the disorienting dilemma might not be enough to serve as potential for transformative learning and change. In that sense, an understanding of the implications of context and culture is essential for practitioners addressing facets of transformative learning. Haiti and the United States have two different cultures. Therefore the experience of a Haitian in the United States may involve issues of cultural shock and/or cultural adaptation. It is not just for Haitians living in the United States. This is a reality inherent in any cross-cultural experience. However the meaning of a cross-cultural experience depends in large part on individual experiences and social, cultural, economic, and political factors that contextualize such experiences.

There was a strong reliance on emotion and spirituality and less on rationality in the transformative learning experience revealed by the participants, although rationality played a role. Not all the participants experienced a perspective transformation based on critical reflection. Most of the participants confirmed that they had a transformative learning experience based on the intensity of their emotion and their spirituality. For some others, the transformation occurred through their involvement in virtual discussions (technology) and community-based activities (social interactions). In that regard, practitioners addressing facets of transformative learning should be aware that transformative learning does not exclusively occur in classroom (formal or nonformal) training or activities, but also can be triggered by emotional and traumatic events, virtual interactions, and community involvement.

This chapter has explored and analyzed the transformative learning experience of Haitian Americans in response to the Haiti earthquake in relationship with culture and context. The immigration and cultural experience, and the meaning attached to such experience, put the process of transformative learning exploration into a cross-cultural context. This is the context of one's contact with a new cultural reality and the adaptation to a new cultural environment while carrying old cultural habits, practices, and experiences. The critical reflection of the individuals living such dual cultural experiences exposed them to surprising information and observations during and after the earthquake, which challenged or contradicted some previously unquestioned assumptions, beliefs, and perspectives. Participants were challenged to ask tough questions about themselves, their country, and the world as a result of the earthquake. Their critical reflection, combined with their emotion and spirituality, helped them develop a deeper understanding of their personal and cultural identity. This combination of critical reflection, emotion, and spirituality has led to a transformation from a form of relative ethnocentrism to ethnorelativism, a more inclusive and integrative understanding of humanity, identity, and self.

What are the implications of the transformative learning experience of Haitian Americans in response to the earthquake in Haiti for practitioners addressing facets of transformative learning in relationship with culture and context? The findings from participants' narrative discourses have several implications for practitioners addressing facets of transformative learning in relationship with culture and context. One of the major implications resides in the fact that the cross-cultural experiences of an individual or a learner carry the potential for meaningful contribution toward personal growth and possibly professional growth. These implications confirm the findings of previous studies, which suggested that cross-cultural experiences can facilitate change in meaning perspectives, motivations, and attitudes (Savicki, 2008) or positively affect the intellectual and personal lives of individuals (Dolby, 2004).

The existence and the strength of historically based assumptions in reference to context and culture is another implication that practitioners addressing facets of transformative learning should take into account. The historical relationships of colonialism, interstate wars, ethnic wars, or other religious or cultural conflicts between countries from the center (industrialized countries) and countries from the periphery (developing countries) or between countries sharing borders tend to leave an intergenerational imprint of mutual bitterness and resentment in the mind, judgment, and meaning perspectives of individuals based on their country of origin. Of course, the strength of the historically based assumptions will vary with an individual level of ethnic identity. Regardless of the level, historically based assumptions can strongly affect the cultural integration and experience of an individual or a learner.

Transformative learning is not just an individual experience. It can occur in a virtual and community context as well. It does not have to involve a formal or nonformal learning activity. It can be part of a lifelong learning experience. In addition, transformative learning is not exclusively the result of critical reflection. Spirituality and emotion also play a role. In fact, journaling (King, 2004) and the use of romantic fiction (Jarvis, 1999) have been suggested as contributors to transformative learning. Lyon (2000) and Zieghan (2000) have conducted studies on intercultural experience that stressed the role of emotion in transformative learning. It is difficult to argue that such spiritual reliance results exclusively from prior spiritual involvement because it was observed in both religious and nonreligious participants. Finally, the role of social networking and technology has emerged as a contributing factor to the transformational experience, thus corroborating previous research suggesting that the virtual interactions of individuals or learners, the degree of life experiences of the virtual participants, and the significance of their emotional connection can be transformational (Zieghan, 2001). The findings of several studies indicated that direct, personally engaged, and stimulating learning experiences foster transformative learning (Mallory, 2003; Feinstein, 2004; King, 2004). As King (2005) cautioned, practitioners addressing facets of transformative learning in relationship with context and culture may need to look beyond the realm of traditional Western-based critical thinking processes to better understand adult experience in coping with change, especially after a traumatic event such as an earthquake. These implications are related to the following recommendations for practitioners addressing facets of transformative learning in relationship to culture and context.

Design and Implement Cross-Cultural Responsive Teaching and Learning Activities

Cross-cultural responsive teaching and learning activities that offer a safe environment for both rational and emotional discourses can contribute to self-efficacy, provided the learner is invited to compare and contrast uniqueness and differences. The use of cross-cultural responsive teaching and learning must not be at the mercy of the process. Practitioners should set aside specific times for formal expression (critical discourse) and reflection (critical reflection) on cross-cultural beliefs, assumptions, and values. This should be the moment to introduce the (a) "What if beliefs, assumptions of _____ about _____ (issue, topic) are not completely accurate or misleading?" questions; (b) "How would you deal with your beliefs, assumptions about _____ (issue, topic) if their fundamentals are misleading or no longer relevant?" questions; (c) "Did you consider _____ (alternative ideas)?" questions; and (d) "What do you think about _____ (fact, evidence, information)?" questions.

Contextualize the Historically Based Assumptions

Practitioners need to understand that historically based assumptions, including conspiracy theories, emerge in a context that is ripe for facilitating such emergence. In other words, these assumptions remain in the meaning schemes of individuals or learners based on a context that fosters their persistence. Therefore, the holder of assumptions always has a rational or irrational justification. The context of the justification must be acknowledged first before any critical reflection can take place. Sometimes opportunities for transformation may exist inside the emotional discourse of assumptions. Making value judgments without an understanding and acknowledgment of the context may not only hinder transformative learning taking place, but also may negatively influence credible interactions between educator and learner.

Use Spirituality, Reliance, and Emotion as Assets

Although rational discourse is an important catalyst for transformation, it may be insufficient in relation with culture and context. Learning is not just a matter of rationality. Learning requires an emotional and spiritual connection in some instances. The emotional connection plays a role in either intrinsic or extrinsic motivation of both the educator and the learner and in the interactions between educator and learner. The spiritual connection is not intended necessarily in a religious way. It can be the departure point to help the learner navigate between the known "experience" and the unknown (new knowledge). Besides using spirituality and emotion as assets when necessary, practitioners can use other spirituality/emotion reliance–based strategies such as inviting qualified guest speakers into a learning environment, organizing site visits, highlighting video documentaries, or organizing study-abroad programs.

Design Virtual and Community-Based Learning Activities

Participation in community discourse (virtual or face-to-face) can alter one's frame of reference about some aspects of the world and contribute to transformative learning (Cranton, 2006). Practitioners can customize virtual and community–based learning activities that have potential for self-reflection, discussions on assumptions, beliefs, and values in a respectful and nonthreatening forum.

Practice a Humanizing Pedagogy

Humanizing pedagogy is the adoption of dispositions to consider the learner dealing with a disorienting dilemma, not just as a learner but also as a partner with which the practitioner engages in a teaching and learning journey for change. Although transmission and acquisition of knowledge and skills are important, such a journey requires the development of respectful and compassionate rapport between educator and learner. A humanizing pedagogy can dislocate the practitioner from an academic comfort zone to help the learner deal with setbacks, discouragement, and cynicism vis-à-vis the learning experience.

LIMITATIONS

The findings summarized in this chapter add to existing literature on transformative learning. However, given the convenient sampling procedures used to select the participants and the small scope of this research, the recommendations are limited to the extent that practitioners want to test them when addressing facets of transformative learning in relationship with context and culture.

REFERENCES

Bell, C. C. (1997). *Revolution, romanticism, and the Afro-Creole protest tradition in Louisiana, 1718–1868*. Baton Rouge: Louisiana State University Press.

Brasseaux, C. A., & Glenn, R. C. (Eds.). (1992). *The road to Louisiana: The Saint-Domingue refugees, 1792–1809*. (D. Cheramie, Trans.). Lafayette: Center for Louisiana Studies, University of Southwestern Louisiana.

Christian, M. (1965). *The battle of New Orleans: Negro soldiers in the battle of New Orleans*. New Orleans: Battle of New Orleans, 150th Anniversary Committee of Louisiana.

Clark, M. C., & Wilson, A. (1991). Context and rationality in Mezirow's theory of transformational learning. *Adult Education Quarterly, 41,* 75–91.
Cranton, P. (1994). *Understanding and promoting transformative learning: A guide for educators of adults.* San Francisco, CA: Jossey-Bass.
Cranton, P. (2006). *Understanding and promoting transformative learning: A guide for educators of adults* (2nd ed.). San Francisco, CA: Jossey-Bass.
Dirkx, J. M. (1998). Knowing the self through fantasy: Toward a mytho-poetic view of transformative learning. In J. C. Kimmel (Ed.), *Proceedings of the 39th Annual Adult Education Research Conference* (pp. 137–142). San Antonio: University of Incarnate Word and Texas A&M University.
Dolby, N. (2004). Encountering an American self: Study abroad and national identity. *Comparative Education Review, 48,* 150–174.
Feinstein, B. C. (2004). Learning and transformation in the context of Hawaiian traditional ecological knowledge. *Adult Education Quarterly, 54,* 105–120.
Freire, P. (2000). *Pedagogy of the oppressed* (20th anniv. ed.). New York, NY: Continuum.
Hall, G. M. (1992). *Africans in colonial Louisiana the development of Afro-Creole culture in the eighteenth century.* Baton Rouge: Louisiana State University Press.
Jarvis, C. (1999). Love changes everything: The transformative potential of popular romantic fiction. *Studies in the Education of Adults, 31*(2), 109–123.
Kein, S. (Ed.). (2000). *Creole: The history and legacy of Louisiana free people of color.* Baton Rouge: Louisiana State University Press.
King, K. P. (2004). Both sides now: Examining transformative learning and professional development of educators. *Innovative Higher Education, 29,* 155–174.
King, K. P. (2005). *Bringing transformative learning to life.* Malabar, FL: Krieger.
LeCompte, M. D., & Schensul, J. J. (1999). *Analyzing and interpreting ethnographic data: Ethnographer's toolkit* (Vol. 5). Walnut Creek, CA: AltaMira.
Lyon, C. (2002). Trigger event meets culture shock: Linking the literature of transformative learning theory and cross-cultural adaptation. In J. Pettit et al. (Eds.), *Proceedings of the 43rd Annual Adult Education Research Conference* (pp. 237–242). Raleigh: North Carolina State University.
Mallory, J. L. (2003). The impact of a palliative care educational component on attitudes toward care of the dying in undergraduate nursing. *Journal of Professional Nursing, 19,* 305–312.
Merriam, S., Caffarella, R., & Baumgartner, L. M. (2007). *Learning in adulthood: A comprehensive guide* (3rd ed). San Francisco, CA: Jossey-Bass.
Mezirow, J. (1991). *Transformative dimensions of adult learning.* San Francisco, CA: Jossey-Bass.
Mezirow, J. (2000). Learning to think like an adult: Core concepts of transformation theory. In J. Mezirow & Associates (Eds.), *Learning as transformation: Critical perspectives on a theory in progress* (pp. 3–34). San Francisco, CA: Jossey-Bass.
Miller, S. B. (2004, March 3). Haiti chaos reverberates for expatriates in American cities. *Csmonitor.com.* Retrieved from http://www.csmonitor.com/2004/0303/p03s02-ussc.html
Savicki, V. (Ed.). (2008). *Developing intercultural competence and transformation: Theory, research and application in international education.* Sterling, VA: Stylus.

Strauss, A., & Corbin, J. (1998). *Basics of qualitative research: Techniques and procedures for developing grounded theory.* London, England: Sage.

Taylor, E. W. (2000). Fostering transformative learning in the adult education classroom. *The Canadian Journal of the Study of Adult Education, 14,* 1–28.

van Manen, M. (2001). *Researching lived experience.* London, Ontario, Canada: Althouse.

Wolcott, H. F. (2001). *Writing up qualitative research.* Thousand Oaks, CA: Sage.

Ziegahn, L. (2000). Adult education, communication, and the global context. In A. L. Wilson & E. R. Hayes (Eds.), *Handbook of adult and continuing education* (pp. 312–326). San Francisco, CA: Jossey-Bass.

Ziegahn, L. (2001) "Talk" about culture online: The potential for transformation. *Distance Education, 22,* 114–150.

PART II

LEARNING IN RELATIONSHIP WITH CULTURE,
CONTEXT, AND TECHNOLOGY

CHAPTER 16

RHYTHM, RHYME, REEL, RESISTANCE

Transformative Learning Using African American Popular Culture

I. Malik Saafir

> *"Slaves, be obedient to your masters, for this is right in the Lord." My grandmother made up her mind then and there that if she ever learned to read or if freedom ever came she would never read that part of the Bible.*
> —Howard Thurman (as cited in Goodwin, 1973/n.d.)

History has shown that African American music and biographical narratives have been and continue to be a powerful force to inspire social change. This chapter proposes ways adult educators can use African American music and biographical narratives to teach adult learners how to transcend the cultural norms that endorse racism, sexism, classism, heterosexism, and xenophobia. Educators can select African American songs based on their historical context and signification of cultural resistance and use a postcolonial biblical andragogy to examine the lives of African American women and men who have transcended cultural norms through film and literature.

This inclusion of multiple voices may inspire students to transcend norms in their daily lives.

The usage of the biblical text to promote chattel slavery led African slaves to critique the text based on its perpetuation of systemic oppression, thereby causing them to approach the biblical text with a hermeneutics of suspicion. Africans' folk theology was an amalgamation of Western Christian (e.g., biblical narratives) and African (e.g., African traditional religions such as Voodoo and Hoodoo) sources. African slaves' praxis of "hermeneutical freedom" within the parameters of Western Christianity produced a folk religion that concealed the counterhegemonic practices inscribed in their preaching, songs, and worship (Wimbush, 1995, p. 100). African American folk religion allowed African slaves to question the meaning of God and God's relevance to their daily experiences of chattel slavery.

African slaves used particular biblical narratives that communicate liberation and denounce other narratives that supported chattel slavery. Out of this practice of hermeneutical freedom by African slaves emerged the "invisible institution" that became the precursor for the African American Church (Wimbush, 1995, p. 100). The inauguration of the African American denominations—for example, Baptist, Methodist, Episcopal, Pentecostal, Presbyterian, and such—in mainstream America eventually led Blacks to approach the biblical text as "inerrant," that is, the unquestioned assumption that the biblical text is without error and reproof. Accordingly, the basis of the concept of biblical inerrancy is the subjugation of human experience to the unquestioned authority of the Bible. As a result, the rise of the biblical inerrancy in the African American Church has compromised its legacy as an institution that cites particular biblical narratives that communicate liberation and denounce other narratives that support oppression. This chapter explores how postcolonial biblical criticism reconnects the African American Church to its legacy of hermeneutical freedom. Critical race theory, spirituality, and transformative learning (hereafter referred to collectively as CST) can be used in postcolonial biblical criticism.

Critical Race Theory

Critical race theory is not a panacea, but instead a means by which to identify the function of racism as an institutional and systemic phenomenon.
—Stovall (2005, p. 106)

Critical race theory (CRT) emerged in response to the social construction of race and its legitimization of the social, political, and economic inequalities experienced by persons of color. CRT allows persons of color to use the concept of race to combat the restraints of categorical racism until liberated from anti-Black racism. Thus, race matters for CRT because it has tremendous social, political, economic, and cultural currency because of its various uses in the United States. This theory gives educators, scholars, activists, and persons of color the aptitude to

1. name and discuss the pervasive, daily reality of racism in U.S. society which serves to disadvantage people of color;
2. to expose and deconstruct seemingly "color-blind" or "race-neutral" policies and practices which entrench the disparate treatment of non-White persons;
3. legitimize and promote the voices and narrative of people of color as sources of critique of the dominant social order which purposefully devalues them;
4. revisit civil rights law and liberalism to address their inability to dismantle and expunge discriminatory socio-political relationships;
5. change and improve challenges to race-neutral and multicultural movements in education which have made White... behavior the norm. (Stovall, 2005, p. 96)

CRT is an interdisciplinary approach that "recognizes the most crucial link between the disciplines to lie in the recognition of racism as endemic to daily life and the inclusion of 'real life experience' to claim space for scholarship often 'silenced' in the academy" (Stovall, 2005, p. 97; Tate, 1995). This theory also foregrounds the lived experiences of persons of color based on their creative resistance to categorical racism. African Americans historically responded to the mental, emotional, and physical brokenness created by anti-Black racism using African American folk religion.

Spirituality

The ability to create, imagine, and come to further insight through symbol, metaphor, and art is part of the experience of being human that is so often ignored in education.
—Tisdell (2009, p. 457)

One can trace the origins of African American folk religion back to chattel slavery. African slaves used the cultural mediums of art, literature, music, dance, and theater to articulate their lived experiences and creatively resist anti-Black racism. African American folk religion employed the symbols, rituals, and sacred narratives of Western Christianity to create a religious discourse for enslaved and free Africans to describe their lived experiences. Africans' exigencies of political liberation adjudicated their understanding of Western Christianity, thereby problematizing their slave masters' racist theology, apologetics, and polemics that justified chattel slavery. One may construe Africans' critical awareness of the incommensurability of their slave master's religion with their lived experiences of chattel slavery as subversion.

Consequently, Africans' conscientization of the mental, emotional, and physical brokenness (caused by the dehumanizing effects of chattel slavery) allowed African slaves to invert and subvert the colonial and imperial logic of their slave masters through colonial mimicry. It is easy to find the colonial mimicry in African American folk religion in Africans' subversive appropriations of the religious languages and symbols of Western Christianity (Ghandi, 1988). Otherwise stated, African slaves deployed the religious languages and symbols of Western Christianity, under the guise of being faithful practitioners of the slave master's religion, to organize insurrections and participate in emancipatory movements such as the Underground Railroad. This subversive practice gave enslaved and free Africans the ability to create a shared religious discourse based on giving the symbols, rituals, and sacred narratives of the slave master's double meaning. For instance, the slave masters heard conformity through conversion while the African slaves heard liberation through subversion in the lyrics of the Sorrow Songs. These songs communicated when and where to meet to board the Underground Railroad.

This religious discourse is a spiritual discourse because it is based on describing enslaved and free Africans' emancipatory journey from brokenness (dehumanizing effects of anti-Black racism) toward wholeness (liberation from anti-Black racism) (Tisdell, 2008, p. 28). The spiritual experiences of Africans cannot be divorced from the ongoing struggle of African Americans against anti-Black racism. Today, African American folk religion and popular culture allows African Americans to remember the legacy of chattel slavery, Jim Crow segregation, and the Civil Rights Movement through "spiral learning" (Tisdell, 2008, p. 32). Spiral learning allows adult learners to remember past experiences to reclaim their voices and redefine their relationship to those experiences. Tisdell (2002) observed in her discussion with women adult educators who shared the "importance of using spirituality as a grounding place to continue to do social action ... [by] balancing inner reflection with outward social action" (p. 136). The Dr. William H. Robinson School of Practical Theology (SPT) invites adult learners to remember their experiences of racism, sexism, heterosexism, and xenophobia by articulating their journey from brokenness to wholeness through transformative learning.

Transformative Learning

> *We cannot critically reflect on an assumption until we are aware it. We cannot engage in discourse on something we have not identified. We cannot change a habit of mind without thinking about it in some way.*
> —Patricia Cranton (2002)

African American folk religion and popular culture emerged as a spiritual discourse to communicate "emancipatory knowledge" (Cranton, 2002, p. 64). This knowledge is transformative insofar as it allows African Americans to question critically the pervasiveness of internalized and externalized oppression found in the lyrics of songs, performance of rituals, reading of sacred narratives, and characterizations of anti-Black racism in theater and film. At the SPT, we invite each adult learner to participate in small group discussions and exercises, which facilitate the transmission of emancipatory knowledge. "If the individual critically examines, opens herself to alternatives, and consequently changes the way she sees things, she has transformed some part of how she makes meaning out of the world" (Cranton, 2002, p. 64). The SPT facilitates transformative learning, which is also spiral learning insofar as it challenges the assumptions of adult learners by asking them to reflect critically on the origins of these assumptions through African American folk religion and popular culture.

In Cranton's abridged version of Mezirow's (1975) popularized stages of transformative learning, the following are not stages but facets of transformative learning advocated by Cranton:

- Activating Event: an activating event that typically exposes a discrepancy between what a person has always assumed to be true and what has just been experienced, heard, or read;
- Articulating Assumptions: articulating assumptions, that is, recognizing underlying assumptions that have been uncritically assimilated and are largely unconscious;
- Openness to Alternatives: critical self-reflection, that is, questioning and examining assumptions in terms of where they came from, the consequences of holding them, and why they are important [and] being open to alternative viewpoints;
- Discourse: engaging in discourse, where evidence is weighed, arguments assessed, alternative perspectives explored, and knowledge constructed by consensus;
- Revision of Assumptions and Perspectives: revising assumptions and perspectives to make them more and better justified;

- Acting on Revisions: acting on revisions, behaving, talking, and thinking in a way that is congruent with transformed assumptions or perspectives (Cranton, 2002, p. 60).

These facets of transformative learning provide a rubric for adult learners to name when and where they find themselves in the small group discussions and exercises. The SPT course offerings use the interdisciplinary approach of CRT, the cultural mediums of African American spiritual discourse, and the aforementioned facets of transformative learning to promote self and social transformation.

Critical Race Theory, Spirituality, and Transformative Learning (CST)

The employment and integration of the CST into the curriculum and instruction at the SPT allows adult learners to remember, reinterpret, and revise their critical and uncritical responses to cultural norms. The basis of this integrative teaching strategy is the confluence of "instrumental, communicative, and emancipatory knowledge" (Cranton, 2002, p. 64). At the SPT, we use instrumental knowledge to examine the diverse fields of science and social sciences that illegitimate racial taxonomy, communicative knowledge to explore African Americans' responses to cultural norms, and emancipatory knowledge to teach adult learners how to transcend these cultural norms.

In short, the SPT serves as the foreground and entry point to bring CRT into the conversation on how the social construction of race co-determined African Americans' response to anti-Black racism. These conversations give way to remembering the spiritual discourse produced by African American folk religion and popular culture to reflect critically on African Americans' lived experiences of racism, sexism, heterosexism, and xenophobia. African Americans participate in the aforementioned facets of transformative learning by passing through the perspectives and experiences of each other. The SPT allows adult learners to spiral back to the past and forward to the present using the five approaches proffered in postcolonial biblical andragogy that coincide with the six aforementioned facets of transformative learning:

- Readying the Ground (Activating Event) and Remembering (Articulating Assumptions)
- Remembering (Openness to Alternatives)
- Reflecting (Discourse)
- Reinterpreting (Revision of Assumptions and Perspectives)
- Re-searching (Acting on Revisions) (Lee, 2007, p. 51).

These were the five approaches used in a 2-year adult education program that introduced participants to postcolonial biblical criticism using African American popular culture. At the SPT, we designed this program to facilitate spiral learning through group discussions and exercises for each participant recovering from brokenness caused by domestic violence, substance abuse, unemployment, underemployment, and marginalization. The remainder of this chapter will use Table 16.1 to illustrate how adult educators, program planners, and others may use CST to promote transformative learning.

Practical Application at the SPT

African American Spirituals

I designed the first course offered at the SPT to introduce the origins of African American folk religion during chattel slavery. This course used the lyrics in African American spirituals to illustrate how Africans approached the biblical text with a hermeneutics of freedom. Howard Thurman's grandmother corroborated this point by teaching her grandson to select only parts of the Bible that did not endorsed slavery (Oliver, 2007). For instance, participants examined the lyrics of the Sorrow Song entitled, "Mary Don't You Weep." This song highlights how Africans interweaved narratives in the Hebrew Bible and New Testament to articulate their faith in a God who consoles the brokenhearted and liberates the captives. Participants raised questions concerning the song's reference to Mary and Martha found in the New Testament and the Pharaoh's Army found in the Hebrew Bible in the following verses: "Oh, Mary don't you weep, Tell Martha not to mourn, Pharaoh's Army, They got drowned in the sea."

This course challenged the unquestioned assumptions each participant held about the biblical text and demonstrated Africans' praxis of hermeneutical freedom. Participants in turn reflected on how certain parts of the biblical text effectively or ineffectively spoke to the brokenness in their lives and community. They also shared their interpretations of select biblical passages that were silent on the topics of racism, sexism, heterosexism, and xenophobia. The spiritual discourse that emerged highlighted the multiple and divergent interpretations each participant held about the biblical text. These group discussions and exercises sought to re-search how participants can reclaim the integrity of their voices by connecting with the lyrics of Sorrow Songs.

African American Blues

The second course I offered explored the continuation of lyrical subversion in African American blues during Jim Crow segregation. This course

268 ■ I. M. SAAFIR

TABLE 16.1 Courses Taught at the SPT

Postcolonial Biblical Criticism	Spirituals	Blues	Rhythm and Blues	Film
What are examples of readying the ground?	Lecture given on African American Sorrow Songs.	Lecture on the response of blues to Jim Crow America.	Lecture on the inception and response of soul music to liberation movements.	Lecture on African American women and liberation movements.
What are examples of remembering?	Participants evaluated the song, "Mary Don't You Weep."	Participants evaluated the song, "Strange Fruit."	Participants evaluated the song, "Mercy, Mercy, Me (The Ecology)."	Participants were shown documentaries on African American women and the Civil Rights Movement.
What are examples of reflecting?	Participants are asked to compare the brokenness in the song to the brokenness in lives of enslaved and free Africans.	Participants are asked to explain the metaphors used in the blues song to describe the lynching of African Americans.	Participants are asked to explore the lyrics and explain the images in the music video to describe the turmoil in America in the 1960s and 1970s.	Participants are asked to examine the role of women today in mainstream America.
What are examples of reinterpreting?	Participants were asked to identify and explain a biblical passage that spoke against their understanding of justice.	Participants were asked to compare the metaphors in selected passages in the Book of Psalms with selected lyrics from blues songs.	Participants were asked to compare the environmental destruction referenced in the song with the environmental destruction referenced in a documentary on climate change.	Participants were asked to compare the role of women in the home and at work today with women in the Liberation Movement.
What are examples of re-searching?	Participants were asked to re-search the brokenness in their life and how the Bible speaks to their condition or remains silent.	Participants were asked to re-search their life and share metaphors of social, economic, and political lynching in society.	Participants were asked to re-search their conservation of energy by examining urban, rural, work, and recreational areas.	Participants were asked to re-search the ways they can fight for gender justice in their lives and communities. Participants were also asked to compare the role of men in fighting for gender justice in their lives and communities.

included selected lyrics from popular blues songs to illustrate how African Americans responded to the horrors of the lynching campaign of anti-Black racists. In order to explain the link between the song and the biblical text, I divided participants into groups and asked them to do a comparison between a selected Psalm in the Hebrew Bible and the lyrics of the blues song entitled, "Strange Fruit." Then I provided photographs of lynched African Americans and asked students to compare the photos with the image of a Roman crucifixion in the first century. Afterwards, participants compared the lynching of African Americans to the lynching of Jesus of Nazareth in the New Testament (Cone, 2007).

Through comparing the lynching tree and the Roman cross, participants linked the brutalities inflicted on African American bodies to the brutalities inflicted on the body of Jesus of Nazareth in the New Testament (Cone, 2007). This comparison also helped participants understand how African slaves cited particular biblical narratives that communicate liberation based on their experience of chattel slavery in the Hebrew Bible and New Testament. This course also allowed participants to pass through the lived experiences of African Americans and biblical characters who experienced the blues. The spiritual discourse found in blues songs about brokenness encouraged participants to challenge the fears and hatred that produce violence in their lives and community. These conversations led to critical reflections on how love, hope, and faith can lead to wholeness. Participants returned to the root causes of their blues to re-search ways to heal from their past. This spiraling back to Jim Crow America and forward to the Civil Rights Movement led participants to examine the social, economic, and political conditions that supported the domination of one group over another group.

African American Rhythm and Blues

The third course I offered sought to continue the conversation on how African American blues spoke to their brokenness and introduce African American rhythm and blues as a means to wholeness. This course introduced the apex of the Civil Rights Movement, the inception of the Black Power Movement, and the response of rhythm and blues artists to both movements. I chose the songs of Curtis Mayfield, Stevie Wonder, and Marvin Gaye because of their lyrical content, which spoke to the brokenness in America caused by bigotry, greed, war, poverty, and environmental destruction. These songs provided vivid images of the turmoil produced by fear and the hope for peace produced by love.

For example, I invited the participants to watch and listen to Marvin Gaye's "Mercy, Mercy, Me (The Ecology)" on YouTube (erkd1, 2008). Participants reflected on the images in the video that showed pollution and environmental disasters throughout the world. Afterwards, I asked them to create four groups based on the following categories: urban, rural, corporate, and recreational environment. Each group drew an eco-friendly environment based on their understanding of energy efficiency, renewable energy, and waste management. As I observed each group, the participants drew examples of light bulb replacements, recycling containers, efficient public transportation, bike trails, eco-friendly parks, and urban gardening. These groups also responded to the social, economic, and political conditions that support or undermine environmental justice.

African American Film

The final course I offered compared African American women in the Civil Rights Movement and Black Power Movement to women in the Hebrew Bible and New Testament. Critical questions arose regarding how best to introduce the concept of patriarchy and promote gender justice in the African American Church. Participants in this course studied the victimization of African American women during colonialism and neocolonialism while they were fighting for liberation for the entire community. The course also discussed ways the African American Church and community has historically disempowered women based on the religious and moral prejudices that women are inferior, irrational, and divinely mandated to embody servitude.

The exposure and critical examination of the experiences of African American women showed how African American men were culpable in perpetuating and condoning patriarchy in small group discussions and exercises. I divided men and women evenly into small groups and gave them critical questions to remember and reclaim the voices of African American women in the African American Church. These discussions decentered the male-dominated voices in the Hebrew Bible and New Testament by focusing solely on the representation of women in the biblical text.

I also encouraged men and women to examine whether they relate to one another based on prescriptive gender-constructed roles, and I challenged them to think about how these roles may be oppressive or liberating. Participants took seriously the power and privilege given to men and women based on gender roles. For example, after viewing the documentaries on the lives of Ida B. Wells, Fannie Lou Hamer, and Shirley Chisholm, I asked students to create three groups. Men and women in each group passed through the challenges and brokenness of each woman in the documentaries with "compassionate spirituality" (Kyung, 1990, p. 89).

The grounding of compassionate spirituality is the realization that "the self and community are one" (Kyung, p. 89). This type of spirituality allows participants to see the impact of patriarchy on the whole community and not just on individuals. A critical awareness of the social constructions of cultural norms requires that one empathetically listen with others and share in one another's journey from brokenness to wholeness. This awareness evoked African American men to participate in the emancipatory struggle of African American women, thereby transcending the patriarchal and sexual norms that constitute the African American Church and community.

Personal Reflections: Spirituality and Liberation

Postcolonial biblical criticism demands that the adult educator and learner journey together in the process of self-recovery through healing and transformation. A deep influence on me is the work and life of Mercy Matthew, an Indian Catholic laywoman and activist at a refugee camp, whose spirituality is paradigmatic to what I propose as a postcolonial biblical andragogy (Kyung, 1990). Matthew's spiritual growth "came in three phases which she names immersion, activity, and multiplication of oneself" (Kyung, 1990, p. 90). I use these three phases to invite participants to respond ethically to the categories of race, sex, class, and heterosexuality.

The first phase, *immersion* means creating a process of self-declassification while transcending the hegemonic practices of racism, sexism, classism, and heterosexism. CST can assist adult learners in the process of self-declassification. Participants discover how the dominant culture constructed each category during colonialism. They also learn about how one particular group obtained positions of authority and affluence over another group based on the aforementioned cultural norms. Participants explored how the dominated group fought for liberation during neocolonialism by examining liberationist movements. They challenged one another to respond ethically to ideologies that cause one group to misconstrue another group as morally and intellectually inferior based on their classification. This process allowed participants to declassify themselves by no longer responding to each other with cognitive and emotive distance, but compassionate spirituality.

The second phase, *activity*, involves not only the process of self-declassification but becoming active in the grassroots organizations, workshops, seminars, bible studies, conferences, and missions that reclaim the voices of marginalized groups in the African American Church and community. The third phase, the *multiplication of oneself*, requires the dominant group to recede to the background once those whom they are actively leading have been empowered. In other words, those of the dominant group who have privilege and power in the African American Church and community should actively stand as vanguards for justice and remove the structural barriers that colonization created. This will eventually lead to the perpetual multiplication of oneself in the lives of others as each group seeks to transcend the hegemonic norms that created both. We can best understand the multiplication of oneself at the moment when both groups imagine a world not classified by race, sex, class, and heterosexuality, but a world that is truly postcolonial.

CONCLUSION: SPIRITUALITY AND LIBERATION

Transformative learning as a means of decolonization is an indispensable tool for adult educators in the African American Church. Historically, African Americans did not have to unveil anti-Black racism, because it was unconcealed during chattel slavery, the Abolitionist Movement, the Civil War, Reconstruction, Post-Reconstruction, Jim Crow segregation, and the Civil Rights Movement because of the agentive powers operating "above ground." Today, outside of the displaced ruptures of overt forms of oppression, the hegemonic practice of racism, sexism, classism, and heterosexism are "underground" within the institutional practices of the African American Church and community.

The SPT allows African Americans to discover when, where, how, and why hegemony is operative in the African American Church and community. This school also serves as a locale for persons of color to practice hermeneutical freedom by reconnecting them to African American folk religion and popular culture. This type of connection will allow adult educators and adult learners to begin the process of self-recovery, self-declassification, and "self-actualization" (hooks, 1994). Compassionate spirituality takes seriously participants' struggle for authenticity as they pass through each other's experience of privilege, power, affluence, oppression, and marginalization based on the categories of race, sex, class, and heterosexuality. In short, there is a direct connection between self-actualization—as the power to remove cultural and institutional barriers that deny full access to dignity, self-respect, and self-determination—and CST. Hence, the 2-year program sponsored by the SPT allows participants to find peace through the broken pieces of their lives.

Further Research

Much work remains for using CST as a learning strategy. This chapter proffers only one of the many ways adult educators can use postcolonial biblical criticism to promote transformative learning. I look forward to gaining more insight from adult educators in the fields of critical race theory, spirituality, and transformative learning. These fields provide a critical lens to explore, examine, and articulate the lived experiences of persons of color. The effective use of CST creates a pedagogical relationship between adult educators and adult learners that transforms the classroom into a democratic space. This space can provide a plethora of empirical evidence for theorists and practitioners to verify the personal and social effects of CST in adult education.

REFERENCES

Cone, J. (2007, November 23). Strange fruit: The cross and the lynching tree. *Bill Moyers Journal.* Retrieved from http://www.pbs.org/moyers/journal/11232007/watch.html

Cranton, P. (2002). Teaching for transformation. In J. M. Ross-Gordon (Ed.), Contemporary viewpoints for teaching adults effectively. *New Directions for Adult and Continuing Education, 93,* 63–71. San Francisco, CA: Jossey-Bass.

erkd1. (2007, July 8). *Mercy mercy me (the ecology) Marvin Gaye* [video]. Retrieved from http://www.youtube.com/watch?v=IkYx—x9wa0&feature=related

Ghandi, L. (1988) *Postcolonial theory: A critical introduction.* New York, NY: Columbia University Press.

Goodwin, M. E. (1973/n.d.). Racial roots and religion: An interview with Howard Thurman. *Chicken Bones: A Journal.* Retrieved from http://www.nathaniel-turner.com/racialrootsandreligion.htm

hooks, b. (1994). *Teaching to transgress: Education as the practice of freedom.* New York, NY: Routledge.

Kyung, C. (1990). *Struggle to be the sun again: Introducing Asian women's theology.* New York, NY: Orbis Books.

Lee, B. (2007). When the text is the problem: A postcolonial approach to biblical pedagogy. *Religious Education, 102*(1), 44–61.

Mezirow, J. (1975). *Education for perspective transformation: Women's reentry programs in community colleges.* New York, NY: Center for Adult Education, Teachers College, Columbia University.

Oliver, B. J. (2007). The mind, ministry, and mysticism of Howard Thurman. *Baptist History and Heritage.* Retrieved from http://www.findarticles.com/p/articles/mi_m0NXG/is_3_42/ai_n24927506/

Stovall, D. (2005). A challenge to traditional theory: Critical race theory, African American community organizers, and education. *Discourse: Studies in Politics of Education, 26*(1), 95–108.

Tate, W. (1995). Critical race theory and education: History, theory and implications. *Review of Research in Education, 22,* 195–247.

Tisdell, E. J. (2002). Spiritual development and cultural context in the lives of women adult educators for social change. *Journal of Adult Development, 9*(2), 127–140.

Tisdell, E. J. (2008). Spirituality and adult learning. In S. Merriam (Ed.), Special issue: Third update on adult learning theory. *New Directions for Adult and Continuing Education, 119,* 27–36. doi: 10.1002/ace.303

Tisdell, E. J. (2009). Spirituality and adult learning. In R. Lawrence (Ed.), *Proceedings of the Adult Education Research Conference*, Vol. 50 (pp. 414–415). Chicago, IL: National-Louis University.

Wimbush, V. L. (1995). In reading texts as reading ourselves: A chapter in the history of African-American biblical interpretation. In F. Segovia & M. A. Tolbert (Eds.), *Reading from this place, volume 1: Social location and biblical interpretation in the United States* (pp. 95–108). Minneapolis, MN: Fortress.

CHAPTER 17

TRANSFORMATIVE LEARNING EXPERIENCES OF BLACK AFRICAN INTERNATIONAL STUDENTS

Alex Kumi Yeboah and William H. Young III

This chapter provides information for teachers and researchers to understand transformative learning experiences of Black African international students, pre-arrival transformative learning experiences, and factors that promote transformative learning experiences of Black African students. Through discussion of transformative learning concepts for adult learners, this chapter addresses questions including, What are the transformative learning experiences of Black African international students? What are the pre-arrival transformative learning experiences of Black African international students? What are the factors that promote transformative learning experiences of Black African international students? What are the possible future trends and recommendations for the study?

According to the Institute of International Education (IIE, 2009) *Open Door Report*, the United States is the leading destination for higher education among international students in the world. The number of interna-

Pathways to Transformation, pages 275–289
Copyright © 2012 by Information Age Publishing
All rights of reproduction in any form reserved.

tional students increased 7% to a record high of 623,805 in the 2007–2008 academic years. In 2008–2009, the population of international students in the United States increased 7.7 % over the previous year to a high of 671,616 students. The majority of international students comes from Asia, Europe, Latin America, and Canada, but recently there has been a steady increase of students from sub-Saharan Africa. For instance, the population of African students in the United States increased by 3.6% in 2008–2009 to 36,937 students, and the number of students from sub-Saharan Africa in the United States increased by 2.2% in 2008–2009 to 32,491 students (IIE, 2009). Moreover, international students contributed $13.49 billion in 2005–2006 and nearly $20 billion in the 2009–2010 academic years to the United States economy for tuition and fees, living expenses, and related costs (IIE, 2010). The data in Table 17.1 show the origin of international students from sub-Saharan Africa in the United States (IIE, 2009).

According to Dei (1994), the continent of Africa has numerous challenges such as lack of educational resources, political instability, infrastructural facilities, high rate of illiteracy, and health problems. According Picker (2006), with the increasing population of adult learners, it is difficult for students in sub-Saharan Africa to gain admission to the few institutions available because of inadequate infrastructural facilities and the lack of competent and qualified university faculty. There is also the desire among international students to study in the United States with the goal of having access to the available educational resources such as technological resources, financial assistance, and scholarships (Kung, 2007). Additionally, a U.S. degree is highly valued across the continent of Africa (Picker, 2006). The image of wealth and economic prosperity in the United States makes most international students believe that the United States is the best place to pursue higher education (Erichsen, 2009; Kung, 2007).

TABLE 17.1   International Student Mobility by Region

Place of Origin	2008–2009 Total
Angola	544
Benin	328
Botswana	298
Burkina Faso	568
Burundi	85
Cameroon	1,826
Cape Verde	100
Central African Republic	42
Chad	138
Comoros	23
Congo	208

TABLE 17.1 International Student Mobility by Region

Place of Origin	2008–2009 Total
Democratic Republic of Congo	247
Cote d' Ivoire/Ivory Coast	806
Djibouti	13
Equatorial Guinea	94
Eritrea	168
Ethiopia	1,583
Gabon	262
Gambia	328
Ghana	2,988
Guinea	190
Guinea-Bissau	17
Kenya	5,877
Leosotho	61
Liberia	261
Madagascar	123
Malawi	315
Mali	479
Mauritania	59
Mauritius	221
Mozambique	89
Namibia	60
Niger	249
Nigeria	6,256
Reunion	8
Rwanda	366
Sao Tome & Principe	2
Senegal	642
Seychelles	9
Sierra Leone	173
Somali	40
South Africa	1,703
St Helena	40
Swaziland	156
Tanzania	1,217
Togo	381
Uganda	836
Zambia	743
Zimbabwe	1,269
Sub-Saharan Africa	32,491

Source: Open Doors 2009 Report on International Educational Exchange; Institute of International Education–International Student Mobility by Region–Africa 2008–2009

TRANSFORMATIVE LEARNING DEFINED

Background

Transformative learning is the process by which adult learners critically examine their beliefs, assumptions, and values in light of acquiring new knowledge and begin a process of personal and social change called "reframing" in perspective (Mezirow, 1990). According to the IIE (2009) *Open Door Report*, the rapid global changes in the social, economic, technological, political, and academic environments have resulted in increasing the population of international students in the United States, including those from sub-Saharan Africa. This situation has motivated experts to look into the trends of transformative learning experiences among international students. Taylor (2008) argued that in the present diverse and globalized world, there is an interdependency with the environment wherein people face constant life changes. According to Ritz (2010), transformative learning experiences among international students varies due to factors such as differing cultures, languages, educational background, and personality traits. Adults are better prepared than are children to evaluate the soundness of their beliefs and understandings and the dependability of their way of making meaning of new experiences.

The chief proponent of transformative learning, Jack Mezirow, first identified transformative learning among women reentering higher education. Mezirow (1978) investigated the experiences of these women as "Rather than merely adapting to changing circumstances by more diligently applying old ways of learning, and discover a need to acquire new perspectives in order to gain a more complete understanding of changing events" (p. 3). Mezirow (1991) described perspective transformation as the process of how adult learners could revise their meaning structures. The act of culturally defined frames of reference is inclusive of meaning schemes and meaning perspectives. Meaning perspectives are a general frame of reference, worldview, or personal paradigm involving "a collection of meaning schemes" made up of higher-order schemata and theories (Mezirow, 1991). Meaning perspectives operate as perceptual filters that organize the meaning of experiences. As one assimilates the new experience into these structures, it either reinforces the perspective or gradually stretches its boundaries depending on the degree of congruency. The transformed meaning perspective is the development of a new meaning structure with the consequences of questioning values and beliefs (Mezirow, 1991).

The concept of "frame of reference" consists of two dimensions, namely, habit of mind and point of view. Habit of mind is a broad, abstract, orienting, and habitual way of thinking, feeling, and acting that, influenced by assumptions, constitutes a set of cultural, political, social, educational, and economic codes (Mezirow, 1997). It also includes dimensions of sociolinguistic, moral-ethical, epistemic, philosophical, psychological, and aesthetic perspectives, which include sets of immediate specific expectations, beliefs, feelings, attitudes, and judgments (Mezirow, 2000). The habit of mind, expressed in a particular point of view, includes the constellation of beliefs, value judgments, attitudes, and feelings that shape a particular interpretation. The habit of mind is more durable, and it is subject to change through the process by which adult learners solve problems and identify the need to modify assumptions (Mezirow, 1997).

Brookfield (1986) stated that personal learning is the act by which adult learners come to reflect on their self-image, change their self-concepts, question their previously uncritically internalized norms, and reinterpret their current and past behavior from their perspective (p. 213). Merriam and Caffarella (1999) acknowledged that learning from experience involves one's readiness to acknowledge an experience (concrete experience), viewing the experience from a different perspective (reflecting observation), ability to analyze so that ideas and concepts can be developed (abstract conceptualization), and ability to put into practice concepts learned (active experimentation) from Kolb's learning theory (1984).

Mezirow's original research explained ten phases of perspective transformation as (a) A disorientating dilemma; (b) Self-examination with feelings of guilt or shame; (c) Recognition that one's discontent and the process of transformation are shared and that others have negotiated a similar change; (d) Exploration of options for new roles, relationships, and actions; (e) A critical assessment of assumptions; (f) Provisional trying of new roles; (g) Planning of a course of action; (h) Acquisition of knowledge and skills for implementing one's plans; (i) Building of competence and self-confidence in new roles and relationships; and (j) A reintegration into one's life on the basis of conditions dictated by one's new perspectives (Mezirow, 1978, 1991; Taylor, 1998). According to Cranton (1994), King (1997), and Tisdell (2000), there are other factors such as culture, immigration, and social and financial challenges that contribute to transformative learning experiences of adult learners. Tisdell (2003) criticized Mezirow for lack of attention to the unconscious and spirituality. According to O'Sullivan (2002), spirituality in the context of transformative learning is aspiring toward social justice and interconnectedness and having a relationship to a higher power.

King (2003) conducted a study of feminist research and pedagogy in the shadow of tragedy about how international adult learners construct a response in lifelong learning. Participants in the study were from Belize, Ghana, Sri Lanka, and the Dominican Republic. All the participants agreed that others are different from themselves when they learned to accommodate the strengths in building shared communities. King (2003) concluded that many of the adult learners experienced transformative learning as a result of shifts in emotions and perceptions from shock, fear, and intense grief that emanated from the tragedy of September 11, 2001. According to Mezirow (2000), two elements of transformative learning are critical reflection or critical self-reflection. The adult learner gets the chance to validate the best judgment. With critical reflection, the adult learner rationalizes new points of view without dealing with the deep feelings that accompanied the original meaning perspective. King (1997) concluded in a mixed-method study that adult learners' experience facilitated transformative learning, as did occurrence of other life changes such as immigration, emotional issues, changing jobs, and/or residence. Cultural values can also shape the choice of the adult learners' assumptions to examine the new perspectives of subsequent behaviors (King, 1997). According to Mezirow (1997), human communication grounds transformative learning, which is the process of using a prior interpretation to construe a new or revised interpretation of the meaning of one's experience in order to guide future action.

In the context of the Black African international student, perspective transformation will provide new ways to examine the experiences of acculturation, intercultural awareness, and language acquisition. It affords Black African international students the opportunity to critically analyze issues as they try to fit new knowledge into their unexamined and unspoken beliefs. Avoseh (2001) asserted that the values of Africans lean more toward the collective rather than that of the individualistic concept of responsibility. According to Avoseh, the African traditional system comprises the spiritual, communal, and political dimensions and values. The spiritual dimension includes influences from the metaphysical world wherein the individual is responsible to the community and has spiritual obligations. The communal learning dimension emphasizes one's commitment to the interest of the "corporate existence of the community," and the political dimension is the responsibility to serve the interest of the nation before oneself through the effort of the community's family and spiritual duties.

The most common themes of Mezirow's transformative learning theory (1978, 1991, 1997, 2000) are the centrality of experience, centrality of reflection, and rational discourse. Experience is socially constructed, thus, it is possible to deconstruct based upon individual adult learners' process of the knowledge and act. According to Avoseh (2001), in sub-Saharan African society, there is no individual without the collective support. The collective support includes human beings, the world of nature, and the world of spirits. The tools of culture (family, gender, language, spirits, and status) will shape one's experience to promote transformative learning experience. The different languages (about 800 recognized ethnic languages), cultures, values, and beliefs in sub-Saharan African society enhance the collective nature of learning. Dei (1994) contends that adult learners from sub-Saharan Africa are influenced by both native and Western cultures of historical antecedents resulting from colonialism and the spread of Western cultures in Africa. Growing up to understand other cultures makes the learner in sub-Saharan Africa develop the potential to offer new coping skills for taking information from the outside world. The meaning-making process that differs from those of their cultures allows them to continuously change and do self-examination that transpires into transformative learning (Merriam & Ntseane, 2008). Cranton (2000) supports the idea by stating that individuals develop a sense of self and find their voices. Cultural values like collectivity appear to be the most common cultural entity of the people. The group to which one belongs, not individual characteristics, determines one's identity. The people of the sub-Saharan African region embrace connectedness, spirituality, and the concept of family (Avoseh, 2001). There are the ideas that respect for the human life, self, and mutual help are important. Likewise, the people place great value on cooperation, love of generosity, harmony, and the preservation of the sacred (Avoseh, 2001).

Preece (2004) stated that transformational learning is a complex process contextualized in the individual's interpretation and meaning making of the environment and culture. According to Preece, transformational learning occurs when Black African international students are able to develop the self through inner awareness from previous knowledge and question assumptions or reality of an issue that applies to them. According to Merriam and Ntseane (2008), transformative learning experience among Black African international students is often about recognizing an inner voice, intuitive guide, or self-examination. Considering the above assertions, Taylor (2008) suggested that it is practical for faculty and university policymakers to know more about transformative learning experiences of international adult learners, including Black African international students.

PRE-ARRIVAL TRANSFORMATIVE LEARNING EXPERIENCES OF BLACK AFRICAN INTERNATIONAL STUDENTS

Upon their arrival in the United States, Black African students do have pre-arrival transformative learning experiences in their host countries by virtue of the different cultural and educational experiences they are accustomed to because of colonialism (Dei, 1994). The educational system in sub-Saharan Africa, based on either the British or the French (European) systems, places little emphasis on student participation in the classroom, independent project-based learning, and research projects. The teacher becomes the center of attention (teacher-centered learning), and students depend on them for knowledge and do not question authority (Picker, 2006). Acquisition of knowledge is more of rote memorization and sequentialization in the processing of information. The ability to develop critical thinking or consciousness in order to become conscientized to intervene in the world as transformed students is minimal (Freire, 1970). Black African international students fall within the conceptual framework of Freire's concept of dependency and lack of free thought (conscientization). The ability to develop critical consciousness among African students will provide them the power to transform and apply what they have learned in the classroom. The type of education they receive at home (sub-Saharan Africa) lacks innovation and creativity to develop skills to solve problems in the community (Picker, 2006). However, it depends on the country the student is coming from, as not all of the countries in sub-Saharan Africa are experiencing a poor educational state. A few Black African international students have privileged family backgrounds and enjoy Western culture at home, making them no different than their peers in the United States. The majority of Black African international students come from poor or underprivileged families that receive foreign education, but the students have limited opportunities to self-examine their lives and make changes.

Adult learners in Sub-Saharan Africa undergo many transformative phases in their academic life because of the colonial legacy left behind and the different cultures created (Merriam & Ntseane, 2008). For example, formal schooling is of the Western education standards and disconnected from the life of the community of students. One receives education by way of disassociating the learner from his/her oral code of the cultural community. According to Dei (1994), the adult grows to not accept or be proud of the community's history and heritage. It is, however, noticeable that the majority of the students want to learn the local knowledge and indigenous experiences, but they also want to come out of their formal schooling with degrees that are "transferrable" in globalized contexts. According to Palmer (1999), adult learners in Africa learn the value of spirituality in the community. They understand that there are connections to humility, healing, the value of wholeness, self and collective empowerment, liberation, and reclaiming the vitality of life. Adult learners from sub-Saharan Africa enter the United States with different cultural values and beliefs. They might speak French, Arabic, or English with a different accent. The majority of Black African international students in the United States are multilingual, as they can speak English and French, or Arabic and French, or English and Arabic, in addition to their native languages such as Hausa, Zulu, Youroba, Akan, Mende, Swahili, Somali, and others. It is interesting to note that international students from sub-Saharan Africa bring with them comprehensive and depth of knowledge in global affairs to the United States. This comes from their educational background and the content of their curriculum (Dei, 1994).

FACTORS THAT PROMOTE TRANSFORMATIVE LEARNING OF BLACK AFRICAN INTERNATIONAL STUDENTS IN AN AMERICAN UNIVERSITY

King (2005) enumerated that there are practical strategies for promoting transformative learning when presented with an emphasis on being critically reflective. These include case studies, collaborative learning, collaborative writing, critical incidents, discussions, interviews, student presentations, journals, and research papers. Cranton (2002) lists "seven facets of transformative learning" that would enhance a particular learning environment to promote transformation to include (a) an activating event that typically exposes a discrepancy between what a person has always assumed to be true and what has just been experienced, heard, or read; (b) critical self-reflection, that is, questioning and examining assumptions in terms of from where they came, the consequences of holding them, and why they are important; (c) articulating assumptions, that is, recognizing underlying assumptions that have been uncritically assimilated and are largely unconscious; (d) being open to alternative viewpoints; (e) engaging in discourse, where evidence is weighed, arguments assessed, alternative perspectives explored, and knowledge constructed by consensus; (f) revising assumptions and perspectives to make them more open and better justified; and (g) acting on revisions, behaving, talking, and thinking in a way that is congruent with transformed assumptions or perspectives (pp. 65–66).

There are many factors that tend to promote transformative learning experiences of international students including Black African students from sub-Saharan Africa (Taylor, 1998). These include critical thinking skills, classroom discussions, discovering the voice of Black African international students, and learner support. Black African international students will one way or the other experience transformative learning associated with education and noneducation with the aid of the above factors indicated by Cranton (2002) and King (2005).

Critical Thinking Skills

Transformative learning is a highly individualized experience and calls for the individual to develop critical reflection to question assumptions and examine self from the previous experience or knowledge (Cranton, 2002). Critical thinking is the process of examining assumptions that include beliefs, values, and ways of understanding (Brookfield, 1987). Black African international students are used to listening to the teacher, and they hardly understand the teaching and learning styles in the United States upon their arrival to the various universities or higher institutions of learning in which they may find themselves. The disorientation the students' experience is an attribute of cultural differences and lack of English language proficiency. The students are also used to the lecture method and learning by memorization with little or no student participation in the classroom considering the common use of discussions, participatory research, case studies, project-based learning, problem solving, and self-evaluation in the classroom (Dei, 1994). It is beneficial for students to do classroom activities that will include assignments to research or critique scholarly journals in their respective academic fields to help promote critical thinking skills. This will enable them to have opportunities to do reflective thinking such as cognitive, critical, and narrative elements of examining issues (King, 1997). King (2005) explained that international students transform from inveterate silent members to class leaders through such learning opportunities. Students will use their knowledge base to make an informed decision and reflect on their experiences. Both Brookfield (1995) and Cranton (1994) described at length various ways to empower the adult learner with the ability to critically assess their personal beliefs, values, and assumptions. Critical learning occurs when the learner compares new ideas to existing knowledge, and there is continuous interplay of questions and answers.

According to Cranton (1994), educators can use critical thinking to empower learners by relinquishing some of their position power in the classroom. The educator should encourage critical self-reflection and include the learner in decision making by including questions, experiential learning, critical reflections, journaling, and constructing conscious-raising experiences in the classroom. These will serve as an impetus to make students challenge previously unexamined values, beliefs, and assumptions.

Discovering the Voice of Black African International Students

Black African international students do experience some adjustment problems such as financial difficulties, loneliness, homesickness, depression, confusion, lack of English proficiency, academic difficulties, discrimination, and lack of close family support upon arrival in the United States. Ritz (2010) described adjustment as the process of adaptation that over time follows a U-shaped curve. At first, the change seems easy for students. Then follows a "crisis" in which students feel less well-adjusted, somewhat lonely and unhappy, and finally students begin to feel better adjusted again, becoming more integrated into the foreign community. The orientation programs in most colleges are not comprehensive enough for students to receive information before and after arrival to be able to adjust to the campus environment (IIE, 2009). Black African international students are not used to the individualistic nature of life in the United States. In this situation, it becomes difficult for them to establish friendly relations with American students because they are used to the group or collective culture that used to shape their learning process, and they conform to the rules of the group and ideals of communal cultures. Financial problems are also not an exception to Black African international students upon arrival, during, and after their education in the United States. The majority of African students find it hard to pay for tuition, accommodations, transportation, and other expenses (IIE, 2008). These challenges make them experience disorientating dilemmas and states of disequilibrium as the first stage in Mezirow's 10 stages of perspective transformation (Mezirow, 1990). The above situations may in turn affect Black African international students' academic performance and in some cases, force them to drop from their program of study. These lead students to what Cranton (2002) calls radical changes in the life or rocky turbulence of their current situation and perspectives across the life span (King, 2005). It also throws off balance the need to create perspectives and views for learning (King, 2009).

The next stage for these students is when they begin to engage in self-examination as to why they have lost status and are experiencing changing perspectives in their lives. These experiences allow the Black African international students to do self-assessment in order to discover their voice. This voice becomes an expression of self-understanding, identity, and acceptance (King, 2009). To discover one's voice serves as a tool for individuals to empower themselves, and is an indication that they are now in the position to reexamine themselves and express their own beliefs and values in their new environment (Cranton, 1994). This supports King's (2009) assertion that after some time, learners in transformation had these observations: "I see things differently now," "I am much more open-minded to views other than mine," "I have had such a radical change in my view of issues," and "I have more self-confidence than I ever dreamed possible." The ability of Black African international students to express their voice concerning challenges they experience may lead to an integration of self-evaluation and empowerment as a vital tool for transformative learning (King, 1997).

Classroom Discussions

Black African international students are generally passive, submissive, and hardly contribute or participate in classroom discussions (Merriam & Ntseane, 2008). They must acknowledge that they are in the process of cultural shock upon arrival in the United States. It would be significant for educators to create a good physical environment, such as spacious conducive areas of learning, technology-friendly classrooms, learner support resources, and an all-inclusive classroom that can break the walls of hesitancy that many international students bring to the educational experiences (Brookfield, 1986). The classroom learning environment should be supportive to help one's values and assumptions. This will enable the adult learner to use her critical thinking skills to question assumptions and past experiences. Educators should engage Black African international students in discussions and critical analysis of tasks so that the students can reflect on the meaning of the content of study. Engaging in discussions will allow students to have opportunities to express their problems and find solutions. These discussions can be achieved through collaborative group work, problem-based learning, online courses, and project-based learning.

Learner Support

With difficulties in English language proficiency, different learning styles, and unfamiliar cultural systems, Black African international students experience problems adjusting to the teaching and learning patterns in the United States. According to Picker (2006), some, not all, are unaccustomed to taking classes online or are not familiar with media resources in the classroom. These students seem to struggle to keep pace with the academic work at the initial stages (Picker, 2006). Black African international students in their new destination may be looking for support and assistance in the new academic environment (IIE, 2007, 2008). There are many learner support systems to help the Black African international students in the United States in their transformative learning processes. According to Bloom (1995) and Daloz (1987), learner support is the means of providing physiological, emotional, and technical assistance to the learner when needed. It is important to provide support to the learners in their movement to a new perspective or understanding, which helps the learners to accept the new threshold of knowledge. To make learner support more effective, educators will have to create group interactions, mentoring opportunities, and support learner actions. Educators will also have to create a nonjudgmental class attitude and a culturally friendly classroom environment. Support could be in the form of providing close personal attention, clear expectations, specific assignments, and technological support. Faculty support is an important step in helping students in their perspective transformations. This is a powerful instrument on the journey to transformation.

Daloz (1987) acknowledged that mentoring makes room for the learner or mentee to create new ways of asking questions about the learning process and the environment. Mentoring also assists students in dealing with human relations, which are instrumental in their learning transformations. According to Daloz, it is also practical for mentors to express positive expectations as a means of effective advising since international students often view mentors as powerful allies. Mentors intercede on the students' behalf, translate aspects of an unknown environment, and protect students. Good mentors provide a mirror in order to help students extend their capacity for self-awareness (Daloz, 1999, pp. 209–229).

FUTURE STUDIES AND RECOMMENDATIONS

This chapter contributes to transformative learning theory with specific reference to how Black African international students deal with their academic, social, and psychological transformations in the United States. This chapter demonstrates that adult learners from sub-Saharan Africa are subject to African, European, and Middle-Eastern cultural influences as referenced by Merriam and Ntseane (2008). The multitude of rich learning experiences allows them to have a wider frame of reference and meaning making of knowledge.

The educational implication of this chapter is that it has created awareness of the challenges adult learners from sub-Saharan Africa face as part of their journey to transformative learning experience. The chapter highlights the role culture plays in the transformative learning experience of individual adult learners or groups of adult learners from sub-Saharan Africa. For example, the chapter discusses how adult learners from sub-Saharan Africa become acclimated to the new classroom environment and the strategies that need to be developed by educators and policymakers in higher education to help the students create changes to adapt to the social cultures in the United States. The chapter provides information for faculty on the best strategies to promote transformative learning experiences for adult learners from sub-Saharan Africa in the United States. It further allows faculty who work across cultures to develop methods and cross-cultural expertise. Faculty need to be aware of the cultures of Black African international students and how best to integrate the students into the American educational and cultural systems.

We recommend a future investigation of the relationship between the transformative learning experiences of Black African international students by demographic origin and college program. We also suggest a comparative study of transformative learning experiences of American students who take overseas courses in sub-Saharan Africa and Black African international students who study in the United States. Furthermore, future research should investigate factors that promote the transformative learning experiences of adult learners from sub-Saharan Africa. There can be more research in areas of the relationship between learning styles and transformative learning experiences of Black African international students.

REFERENCES

Avoseh, M. B. M. (2001). Learning to be active citizens: Lessons of traditional Africa for lifelong learning. *International Journal of Lifelong Education, 20*(6), 479–486.

Bloom, M. (1995). Multiple roles of the mentor supporting women's adult development. In K. Taylor & C. Marienau (Eds.), *Learning environment for women's adult development: Bridges towards change. New Directions for Adult & Continuing Education, 65*, 63–72.

Brookfield, S. D. (1986). *Understanding and facilitating adult learning.* San Francisco. CA: Jossey-Bass.

Brookfield, S. D. (1987). *Developing critical thinkers.* San Francisco, CA: Jossey-Bass.

Cranton, P. (1994). *Understanding and promoting transformative learning: A guide for educators of adults.* San Francisco, CA: Jossey-Bass.

Cranton, P. (2000). Individual differences and transformative learning. In J. Mezirow & Associates (Ed.), *Learning as transformation.* San Francisco, CA: Jossey-Bass.

Cranton, P. (2002). Teaching for transformation. In J. M. Ross-Gordon (Ed.), *Contemporary viewpoints on teaching adults effectively: New directions for adult and continuing education, 93*. San Francisco, CA: Jossey-Bass.

Daloz, L. A. (1987). *Effective teaching and mentoring: Realizing the transformational power of adult learning experiences.* San Francisco, CA: Jossey-Bass.

Daloz, L. A. (1999). *Mentor: Guiding the journey of adult learners.* San Francisco, CA: Jossey-Bass.

Dei, G. J. S. (1994). Afrocentricity: A cornerstone of pedagogy. *Anthropology & Education Quarterly, 25*, 3–28.

Erichsen, E. (2009). *Reinventing selves: International students' conceptions of self and learning for transformation.* Digital dissertation. (UMI No. AAT 338757)

Freire, P. (1970). *Pedagogy of the oppressed.* New York, NY: Herder & Herder.

Institute of International Education (IIE). (2007). *Open Doors 2007 report on international education exchange.* New York, NY: Institute for International Education.

Institute of International Education (IIE). (2008). *Open Doors 2008 report on international education exchange.* New York, NY: Institute for International Education.

Institute of International Education (IIE). (2009). *Open Doors 2009 report on international education exchange.* New York, NY: Institute for International Education.

Institute of International Education (IIE). (2010). *Open Doors 2010 report on international education exchange.* New York, NY: Institute for International Education.

King, P. K. (1997). Examining activities that promote perspective transformation among adult learners in adult education. *International Journal of University Adult Education, 36*(3), 23–37.

King, P. K. (2003). Exploring feminist research and pedagogy in the shadow of tragedy: International perspectives construct a response in lifelong learning. *Radical Pedagogy, 5*(2). Retrieved August 2011, from http://radicalpedagogy.icaap.org/content/issue5_2/02_king.html

King, P. K. (2005). *Bringing transformative learning to life.* Malabar, FL: Krieger.

King, P. K. (2009). Evolving research of transformative learning based on the learning activities survey. *SERIES: Adult education special topics: Theory, research and practice in lifelong learning* (pp. 3–94). Charlotte, NC: Information Age.

Kolb, D. A. (1984). *Experiential learning: Experience as a source of learning and development.* Englewood Cliffs, NJ: Prentice Hall.

Kung, H. (2007). *Dancing on the edge: International students' transformative journeys in the United States of America.* Digital dissertation. (UMI No. AAT 3271223)

Merriam, S. B., & Caffarella, R. S. (1999). *Learning in adulthood: A comprehensive guide.* San Francisco, CA: Jossey-Bass.

Merriam, S. B., & Ntseane, G. (2008). Transformational learning in Botswana: How culture shapes the process. *Adult Education Quarterly, 58*(3), 183–197.

Mezirow, J. (1978). *Education for perspective transformation: Women's re-entry programs in community colleges.* New York, NY: Teachers College, Columbia University.

Mezirow, J. (1990). *Fostering critical reflection in adulthood: A guide to transformative and emancipatory learning.* San Francisco, CA: Jossey-Bass.

Mezirow, J. (1991). *Transformative dimensions of adult learning.* San Francisco, CA: Jossey-Bass.

Mezirow, J. (1997). Transformative learning: Theory to practice. In P. Cranton (Ed.), *Transformative learning in action: New directions in adult and continuing education.* (pp. 5–12). San Francisco, CA: Jossey-Bass.

Mezirow, J., & Associates (2000). *Learning as transformation: Critical perspectives on a theory in progress.* San Francisco, CA: Jossey-Bass.

O'Sullivan, E. (2002). The project and vision of transformative education: Integral transformative learning. In E. O'Sullivan (Ed.), *Expanding the boundaries of transformative learning: Essays on theory and praxis* (pp. 1–12). New York, NY: Palgrave.

Palmer, P. (1999). *The grace of great things: Recovering the sacred in knowing, teaching, and learning.* Retrieved May 2010, from http://www.couragerenewal.org/?q=resources/writings/grace

Picker, M. (2006). Out of Africa. *Diverse: Issues Higher in Education, 23,* 14.

Preece, J. (2004). *Education for transformational leadership in Southern Africa.* Paper presented at the Regional Conference on Leadership Development Program: LeaRN, Gaborone, Botswana.

Ritz, A. A. (2010). International students and transformative learning in a multicultural formal educational context. *Educational Forum, 74,* 158–166.

Taylor, E. W. (1998). *The theory and practice of transformative learning: A critical review.* (ERIC monograph Information Series No. 374). Columbus, OH: ERIC Clearinghouse on Adult, Career, and Vocational Education.

Taylor, E. W. (2008). Transformative learning theory. *New Directions for Adult & Continuing Education, 119,* 5–15.

Tisdell, E. J. (2000). Spirituality and emancipatory adult education in women adult educators for social change. *Adult Education Quarterly, 59,* 308–335.

Tisdell, E. J. (2003). *Exploring spirituality and culture in adult and higher education.* San Francisco, CA: Jossey-Bass.

CHAPTER 18

FACILITATING TRANSFORMATIVE LEARNING OPPORTUNITIES IN HIGHER EDUCATION CONTEXTS FOR ADULT LEARNERS IN ONLINE AND VIRTUAL SPACES

Kathleen P. King and Shelley Stewart

This chapter develops an idea that may meet with resistance from some people acquainted with transformative learning. It reveals that extensive dialogue, discourse, and negotiation may be elements of online and virtual spaces in higher education that instructors can plan, design, and implement to create opportunities for transformation. Virtual and online communities in higher education provide fertile opportunities to facilitate transformative learning in many ways. The co-authors have experienced it and taught others how to facilitate it. The understanding and framework shared herein assists faculty, program planners, administrators, and faculty developers in making informed decisions about whether or not to have transformative learning as a planned learning opportunity for their online courses and curricula.

TRANSFORMATIVE LEARNING UNLEASHED

Web 2.0 technologies such as blogs, podcasts, wikis, and social media have generated new forms of information acquisition and sharing, both in society and in higher education in particular (Rudestam & Schoenholtz-Read, 2010). In a survey conducted by Kim, Bonk, and Zeng (2005), they found that among the most highly predicted pedagogical techniques for the online future of higher education were group problem solving, collaborative tasks, and problem-based learning. They also found that peer-to-peer collaborative tools were at the forefront of emerging technologies. Google Docs is an example of one such peer-to-peer collaborative tool, allowing multiple online users to simultaneously edit the same file in real time. Through applications and processes such as these, learners and scholars worldwide can collaboratively construct knowledge more easily than ever before.

These trends and research findings illustrate a pattern that can teach higher education faculty and instructional designers a great deal. However, for this to happen, a shift needs to occur so that the attention shifts away from the sole focus of "how to," which is often embedded within classes. Instead, instructors need to build a foundation to explore and discover the best means to use technology to cultivate relationships and substantial learning. It appears that even in a significantly decentralized learning environment inundated with 21st-century information technology, the potential for sculpting new knowledge is dependent on the building of human relationships and communities as well as mobilizing the learning potential of groups (Rudestam & Schoenholtz-Read, 2010).

MISSED OPPORTUNITIES

When one discusses online and virtual learning, there is the risk that readers will identify with their experience of online instruction, whether it is good or bad. In comparison to the vast opportunities dynamic online communities offer, some online courses, which some faculty and universities are still promulgating today, are poorly constructed (King & Griggs, 2007; Moore & Kearsley, 1996, 2005). Interaction is an essential aspect of the educational experience (Dewey & Bentley, 1949/1989; Laghos, 2009). When there are distance learning courses that make little effort to involve students in interaction, Moore and Kearsely (1996) apply the concept of transactional distance. Transactional learning theory (Dewey & Bentley, 1949/1989) supports the view that geographical distance does not have to be a negative consequence in the learning process. Instead, significant learning occurs when learner involvement, dialogue, and analysis of the content is integral to the course, regardless of the geographical distance of participants.

Indeed, a valid criticism of some digital learning environments is the dominance of presentational content that students passively receive (Moore & Kearsley, 2005). Such experiences do not create environments that engage learners in understanding the details, limits, and extensions of knowledge. Dewey defined, promoted, and facilitated experiential learning because it enabled the learner to come to inquiries of knowledge and build schemas to comprehend new information and examine its truth, connections to other domains of knowledge, and applications. In later years, educators have learned that blending intellectual exploration with dialogue, discussion, and action affords integration of the brain's hemispheres and thus provides a more robust foundation for understanding, storage, recall, application, and innovation (Begley, 2007; Johnson & Taylor, 2006; Sundberg, Sunal, & Mays, 2006; Zull, 2002). Based on the research of online and virtual learning, it is clear that instructors can create such learning experiences in these environments. However, just as with face-to-face classrooms, they will not happen by themselves.

In most cases, instructors need to plan and facilitate such significant learning. Conrad and Donaldson (2004), as well as Palloff and Pratt (2001, 2005), describe many successful strategies to engage online learners in dialogue, discussion, and exploration of content in ways that excel at mastering understanding at higher levels as defined by Bloom (1956) (analysis, synthesis, evaluation). Moreover, another exciting outcome emerges from this online and virtual environment: participants also build capacity for constructing knowledge (Vygotsky, 1978) in virtual collaborative environments. These virtual collaborative environments are the very climates in which they will carry out their professional and academic pursuits today and in years to come (Altbach, Berdahl, & Gumport, 2005; Christensen, Johnson, & Horn, 2008; Prensky, 2001, 2008; Tapscott, & Williams, 2006).

REVIEW OF RELATED LITERATURE

Situated Learning in Virtual and Online Learning Communities

While most might be familiar with using Facebook and Skype for updates and sharing with friends and family, the literature describes virtual communities more broadly. Consider that in 2000, Rheingold was already discussing the power of online relationships to have the potential to parallel traditional interactions: "Virtual communities are social aggregations that emerge from the NET when enough people carry on...discussions long enough, with sufficient human feeling, to form webs of personal relationships in cyberspace" (para. 27).

When instructors leverage learning with opportunities for sustained interaction spanning time and space, it stretches the concept of what a learning community (Senge, 1994) can be. Porter helps capture these possibilities in this description of an online learning community as "a group of people who communicate with each other across the Internet to share information, learn more about a topic, or work on a project of mutual interest" (2004, p. 193). Much like a collaborative group in face-to-face contexts, online communities have the same goals, but they offer new dimensions of connectivity, access, and support. Indeed, research illustrates that online learning communities can result in greater learning outcomes, higher retention rates, and increased support between peers; these findings reflect the importance of online learning communities (Zaphiris & Ang, 2009).

Researchers have extensively discussed online and virtual learning communities in the literature since 2000. Among significant voices in the development of this research and related facilitation models are Palloff and Pratt (2001, 2005). As distance learning has developed over the last several decades, educators and researchers have realized that dialogue and community are of core importance for learning to achieve many of its critical outcomes. The 21st-century workforce and the academy (Partnership for 21st Century Skills, 2004) both require an extensive amount of skill in communication and collaboration, in addition to a host of content area skills. Learning communities are a powerful platform to hone these skills in a moderated, private space bound by the goal of learning.

A deconstruction of the theoretical basis of the extensive body of work regarding online and virtual learning communities reveals that Lave and Wenger (1991) situated that learning and learning communities are the foundation. Moreover, the familiar concepts of Senge's (1994) learning communities have the same roots (Lattuca & Stark, 2009). Online communities and online learning, which leverage relationships for education, access the same dynamic process and power of situated learning.

Situated learning occurs when students discover new understanding through interaction with their environment; usually incredible content absorption dominates the moment of exploration, testing, and critical thinking (Lave & Wenger, 1991). One can see that situated learning is a powerful "teachable moment," an opportune climate for new ideas, discoveries, and innovation. By realizing that online learning communities can foster online situated learning, the same characteristics of situated learning, learning communities, and accountable learning relationships apply: respect, safety, and accountability, to name a few. This vantage point of online learning and virtual learning communities opens the door to an even more significant connection.

Transformative Learning

In 1978, Mezirow began publishing research regarding women who reentered college later in life and experienced significant change: transformative learning. He proposed a 10-stage model that outlined the essential cognitive stages and actions that occurred during the process. Not until the late 1990s was research greatly expanded, and it includes several examples of transformative learning of adults as they are engaged in learning technology and online learning (King, 1999, 2002, 2003, 2005, 2010; Kitchenham, 2005, 2006; Lari, 2008; Wasnick, 2007). Across these studies, evidence emerges that technology-mediated relationships can serve effectively in supporting learners through transformative learning experiences.

Furthermore, the literature is replete with studies and books that describe ways to craft and design transformative learning experiences to support significant student learning (Cranton, 1996, 2001; Mezirow & Associates, 1990, 2000; Mezirow, Taylor, & Associates, 2010). However, on a scarce discussion focused on the connection to virtual learning communities as a facilitative tool for transformative learning, there have been few models proposed to guide transformative learning in practice. King (2005) provides a Transformative Learning Opportunities Model (TLOM), which addresses this need in a dynamic manner. In King's TLOM, there are two major strands of action: What the Teacher Does and What the Student Does. These parallel strands are similar to those portrayed in other curriculum and instructional planning models (Lattuca & Stark, 2009); however, in this more learner-centered approach, King describes a dynamic flow of needs, goals, and aspirations from students to teacher. In this manner, even a traditional classroom can begin to incorporate more student participation in curriculum choice and portions to engage students and build greater, relevant outcomes. Due to its dynamic and responsive feedback pattern, the TLOM provides a robust framework for guiding the initiation and development of learning communities in higher education environments.

The core of the TLOM, however, is the transformative learning opportunity (King, 2005). These learning experiences are crafted in a way to provide freedom for learners to engage in critical reflection, self-assessment, and transformation. A critical characteristic of the TLOM is that transformative learning opportunities are offered with no strings attached to learners. They also need to be designed and delivered in a climate that is respectful and safe for self-assessment, dialogue, and development. When facilitated through an online platform, it is critical that the TLOM is effectively using online and virtual learning in higher education with these same hallmarks and characteristics. Learners are free to question themselves and convention; they are supported in their views, and they learn to resolve differences of opinion and conflict.

Transformative Learning in Relationship

What are the dynamics needed for individuals to scaffold the stages of transformative learning? As just a brief sampling, transformative learners often need to be able to

- overcome the questioning and resistance to new ideas;
- stand up to accusations of defying tradition;
- withstand pressure from society, family or friends;
- critically analyze the pros and cons of their decisions;
- evaluate the repercussions, consequences, and issues which could arise from their decisions; and
- test or try different ways of thinking or acting (King, 2005; Mezirow & Associates, 1990).

Likewise, in the literature of counseling and therapy, experts know that many adults facing such challenges benefit from discussing their conflict with other people (Carnevale & Pruitt, 1993). It is not that they seek someone to tell them what to do; rather, they are looking for a chance to dialogue about the situation and co-create solutions. This is the power of socially constructive knowledge Vygotsky (1978) identifies in education, and which in formal educational settings is usually accessed through collaborative and cooperative groups. In these instances, instructors may pose artificial situations in the format of cases, simulations, or role-plays, and the learners engage in working through them together. The dynamic is one of learning relationships at work to solve a dilemma.

At the root of successful learning relationships, instructors and researchers have identified several essential elements:

- Safe environments;
- Accountability;
- Confidentiality, privacy, and protection of reputation—no gossip;
- Openness and acceptance—no one is attacked or degraded for their beliefs or views;
- Ground rules of equal participation and voice; and
- Sharing of responsibilities (Caffarella, 2002; King, 1997, 1998, 1999; Stewart, 2008).

Transformative Learning in Relationship in Action

Two examples of where one can see transformative learning in relationship in action in higher educational virtual and online environments include opportunities for collaboration and coaching/mentoring support. Dialogue, discourse, and negotiation (internal) are foundational elements of transformative learning (Mezirow & Associates, 1990) and are core components in each of the activities listed above.

Consider the opportunities for virtual peer collaboration, which may be included in traditional or online classrooms. Having group projects in which students choose various roles to work through in a simulated situation is powerful learning. An example of such could be experiencing curriculum development as faculty members or participating in a business start-up as entrepreneurs. Such activities can break through the barriers of time and space via simple, inexpensive online platforms such as private discussion boards (group designations inside Blackboard) or private wiki groups (Pbwiki, Wikispaces, etc.) set up specifically for the assignment. In these spaces, the participants can even use substitute names representing their roles, explore the complexities of the situations, and have to negotiate the construction of a solution as they solve problems along the way. The power of such learning experiences can even exceed the stimulation and learning of familiar educational role-playing games such as Where in the World is Carmen San Diego? Sim Civilization, Civilization V (http://www.civilization5.com/), or Karma Tycoon (www.karmatycoon.com/), because they are built on the complex dynamics of relationships in an accountable formal educational setting.

Most higher education faculty have a terminal degree in their field and have experienced academic mentoring through the educational process. However, the benefits of their mentoring experiences were mostly dependent on the individual they had as a mentor and their relationship with that individual (Ragins, Cotton, & Miller, 2000). A powerful experience occurs when academic mentors invest in the dissertation process and the professional development of their learners. In these instances, the mentoring process aligns more with the now-prominent professional coaching literature (Hawkins & Smith, 2007; Homan & Miller, 2008; Hunt & Weintraub, 2007) than customary academic mentoring. In the professional coaching approach, one guides individuals into discovering tools and strategies to identify their strengths and weaknesses, to develop learning and professional goals, to discover resources, to seek opportunities, and to cultivate an attitude of lifelong, continuing professional development (Hawkins & Smith, 2007). The central vehicle for such learning is dialogue and the coach-participant relationship; this is a relationship of peer learning that challenges assumptions and encourages seeking the participants' chosen discovery and direction.

Online and virtual technologies are widely used in the professional coaching field today, as people are working with coaches across their nation and the world. No longer bound by mere geography, professionals can work with a coach from across the globe via free phone service (Voice over Internet Protocol [VoIP]), SKYPE video, remote computer desktop displays, private blogs, wikis, and e-mail. Structuring and facilitating these learning opportunities uses many of the same guidelines as face-to-face engagement. However, because one does not have visual clues to understand a person's feelings or attitudes, the voice, text, and spoken word have to be more specific and extensive. This need helps cultivate stronger written and verbal communication skills for everyone involved. The example of virtual professional coaching provides a powerful model of academic coaching at a distance. No longer does one have to be restricted to a professional or dissertation mentor who is in close proximity. Whether one enrolls in an online PhD program or seeks support through the tenure process, one can reach out to experts across the world to build coaching relationships that will be transformative for personal and professional development.

EXAMPLES OF TRANSFORMATIVE LEARNING EXPERIENCES IN VIRTUAL AND ONLINE SPACES

In this section, we describe a model that helps instructors plan transformative learning opportunities. In addition, three cases demonstrate specific examples of transformative learning opportunities using virtual and online spaces. The first case uses the platform of Second Life, the next uses several tools integrated together for collaborative groups (a wiki or Google Docs), and the final one uses Elluminate Live! Some readers may have experience with one or more of these technologies, which they can build upon. The emphasis is not only on introducing the technologies briefly within the context of higher education but also effecting means to plan, implement, and facilitate their use as transformative learning opportunities. Therefore, for each example, please consider:

1. How such methods could be used in various content areas and teaching contexts,
2. How one might incorporate dynamic feedback from learners to faculty in the midst of the learning process,
3. How one might design the lesson with opportunities to incorporate the student feedback, and
4. The benefits to one's field of study to cultivate reflective practice (Schon, 1987) through academic training.

In these ways, faculty will be applying critical aspects of King's TLOM (2005), described earlier, to the learning, mentoring, and coaching relationships. Incorporating virtual and online learning communities fuels such opportunities further. While these examples may provide greater clarity of what is possible with a few examples, please do not allow these examples to stifle creativity or innovation. The intent is that these scenarios will be the seeds of similar or entirely different development implementations as is appropriate and fruitful with specific populations of learners.

Shadowing an Expert in Real Time

Consider the risk involved in a rookie being on the police force for the first week. The daily news headlines have examples of police deaths in the line of duty. Much like the flight simulator made practicing the skills of flying a plane solo a reality for pilots in training, instructors may use virtual simulations with powerful results for other fields, such as the preparation of law enforcement specialists.

Second Life is a vibrant virtual environment to discover ready-made communities that can be used "as is," rented, purchased, and/or modified based on the specific instructional needs (Hudson & Degast-Kennedy, 2009). Consider an approximate reproduction of your community's Main Street and 12 miles square of surrounding side streets. A virtual replica of this environment can be the training ground for new police and firefighters. As other people carry on the routines of their lives in this simulated environment, they select their occupation and profile, or assume that of someone they *would* have known.

Learning opportunities abound; as new situations arise, the community members follow assigned scripts as arsonists, breaking and entering into residences and commercial buildings. The rookie police learners practice the protocols they learned to recite; but will they be able to react appropriately under pressure? Will they know how to think critically to handle the next time when variables and complications change the situation?

Faculty might consider a parallel scenario for their own discipline, but in this example, the first round may include rookies exploring the virtual community solo through a virtual representation of themselves (an avatar). When designed with progressive complexity, such experiences effectively teach the vital role of logical extension, analysis, and synthesis. In a future round of training, the rookie might put her skills to the test as she shadows an expert security trainer who serves as a model and coach in life-like situations.

While learners are using the virtual simulation, they can also pass along information to the faculty member to provide suggestions about new cases they would find beneficial to train for; they can comment on the complexity of the cases (too simple or too complex) and provide direction regarding how to introduce new learners to the format most effectively. Learner feedback will be invaluable in formatively improving and customizing the learning environment for each round and as a standard.

In this manner, while using real-life settings, novice law enforcement officers could gain valuable awareness, experience, and practice in many essential skills, but within the safety and convenience of virtual learning. Instructors could couple this approach with small group and large group discussion to debrief rounds of interaction and reflect on issues, lessons, and strategies. A virtual environment affords the students the power of relationship complemented by real-life dialogue. Essential shifts of perspective to being alert in dangerous situations and rapid critical decision making are another type of transformative learning. These virtual rookies have accomplished these goals within a safe, supportive, and collaborative environment. Now when advancing into real-life situations, they have a more complex perspective to navigate the many variables that surround their daily work.

One Strategy for Facilitating Effective Virtual Groups

Instructors can encourage students to engage in social construction of knowledge (Vygotsky, 1978) via several Web 2.0 technologies including Google Docs, wikis, and synchronous, Web-based courseware (virtual classrooms). Instructors from all levels and disciplines frequently ask that their students work in groups online (and face-to-face) but abandon the strategy when conflict ensues. Inevitable as it is, conflict is not inherently good or bad; it is the framework and strategies by which we handle it (or ignore it) that determines ultimate success or failure (Lewicki, Saunders, & Minton, 1999). This example outlines one such framework for the implementation of successful group work online using Web 2.0 technologies. In addition, ongoing strategies for preventing (some instances of) and dealing with inevitable conflict are presented.

By participating in groups, students gather feedback, exchange innovative ideas, and develop a sense of multicultural understanding from their peers (future colleagues). This type of knowledge construction among peers sets the stage for professional development, growth, and leadership. A course wiki enables students to use a digital-age tool to collaborate. Students build the infrastructure of their learning community by using a wiki to select topics, assign roles, and communicate. By using Google Docs, learners virtually collaborate to design, develop, and revise their ideas.

Certainly, the establishment and subsequent success of a group project lies in the philosophy that group work is a process, not a one-time event.

Therefore, each step of the process will be delineated alongside suggested Web 2.0 tools that aid in facilitating the method.

- The first step in this process is to identify the objective(s) and outcome(s) in order to link them.
- Secondly, build a wiki, editable by all stakeholders in the group process. The wiki serves as a tool that instructors and students can access and edit for sign-up and role-assignment purposes. A suggested framework for the Group Project Wiki can be found at https://sites.google.com/a/mail.usf.edu/group-projects-online/ (Stewart, 2010).
- The third step is to provide students with an outline and/or grading rubric for the group project. This provides guidance for students to develop their own group project.
- The next step is to prepare and exhibit examples of exemplary group projects.
- Next, provide an explanation of the group project parameters. This explanation could be produced with presentation tools and posted in a learning management system (LMS) or Web site. It allows students to understand the expectations.
- Students then sign-up on the group project wiki, self-selecting topic and role. A marginal amount of points or credit could be awarded for completing this task on time. This step allows students to take an active role in selecting their preferred topic and role.
- Next, create "Groups" in Blackboard (or other LMS). This provides for multimodal communication channels among group members.
- The next step involves the group members (students). The Communication Coordinator contacts the rest of the group members. Group members agree on the frequency and mode of communication, that is, Communication Plan & Task Assignments, then the leader submits Communication Plan & Task Assignments to instructor. A key to this step is that the instructor now communicates only with the group leaders. This reduces the number of people with which the instructor needs to interact while providing an effective conduit of feedback. In the case of when communication comes from another member of the group directly to the faculty member, it is good to refer them back to the group leader to reinforce this pattern of communication.
- In the next step, students view the Google Docs Tutorial (available at http://services.google.com/apps/resources/overviews/welcome/topicDocs/index.html). Through the use of Google Docs, as group members coordinate work among each other, they can collaborate anytime, anyplace. The group leader reports any potential "issues" to the instructor. The Communication Coordinator re-

ports any gaps in communication to the group leader, who in turn, reports them to the instructor in a timely manner. The instructor works with the group leader to address concerns and feedback and resolve any issues that might arise.
- The next step is optional but saves time for the instructor in the long run: the compiler may submit a draft of the group project to the instructor via the Google Docs link. The instructor provides formative feedback. Group members can then improve and refine their project prior to final submission. Finally, the compiler submits the final project to the instructor for grading.

Synchronous Sessions Facilitate Virtual Learning Communities

Students express much enthusiasm at the fact that their work can be shared and edited via Internet cloud technology platforms, anytime, anyplace. Synchronous online sessions are able to facilitate virtual learning communities by allowing learners the convenience of meeting virtually in a fully functional classroom. Elluminate Live! is one such synchronous, Web-based courseware system. (Free resources with a similar virtual platform and capabilities include Dimdim.com and Yugma.com for example.) Elluminate Live! emulates the face-to-face classroom online by including such features as hand-raising, discussion rooms, and whiteboard functionalities. Using the whiteboard, text, chat, and VoIP, students can interact in similar fashion as they would in a traditional classroom.

Instructors can design this real-time, virtual platform and use it to facilitate the incorporation of learner needs and goals. For instance, one can use the onboard polling system to identify how many participants are familiar with the system and what tools they are comfortable using. The instructor can also easily see and track who is participating and thereby make sure all have a chance to voice opinions, provide responses and examples, and participate fully. In addition, these virtual presentation designs include branching formats coupled with brief whole-group quizzes or polls. In this manner, the instructor might present a few slides of material and ask a few in-depth questions to see if participants can analyze and apply the information accurately. If so, the session continues as planned; if not, additional slides are presented to supplement the learning experience, or more time is spent to discuss and flesh out details, and consider questions and alternatives until participants and instructor are satisfied. In this manner, the experience becomes more interactive, customized to student needs, and collaboratively constructed by a specific virtual learning community.

Facilitating Transformative Learning Opportunities in Higher Education Contexts ▪ **303**

These shared learning experiences (Flecha, 2000) enhance meeting possibilities for face-to-face students outside of scheduled classroom time while facilitating the gathering of online students who otherwise might never meet one another beyond the learning management system. Social construction of knowledge (Vygotsky, 1978) occurs, enabled by the use of technological tools, as students assemble together to explore their individual curiosities while at the same time considering the thoughts, actions, and reactions of their peers.

Recommended strategies/best practices for promoting interaction in the online synchronous classroom include (a) respecting diverse talents and perspectives, (b) facilitating discussion, (c) assigning group work, (d) emphasizing time on task, (e) providing feedback, and (f) building social presence (Chickering & Gamson, 1987; Stewart, 2008).

LOOKING AHEAD

Future Opportunities for Innovation in Practice

It is critical for instructors and students alike to realize that online learning and community building is a process, not a one-time event. Online groups may not proceed in a completely linear fashion but move back and forth between growth stages and steps (McGrath & Hollingshead, 1994). Future opportunities for creating transformative learning experience in online and virtual spaces mean that faculty and students alike can take advantage of using Web 2.0 technologies to not only develop, grow, and sustain collaborations, but also to evaluate the process of collaboration. This opportunity for evaluation is very important because members may contribute to the group effort in a variety of ways, some of which may be more helpful than others. One powerful strategy is to develop the best ways to integrate collaborative online tasks with assessment (MacDonald, 2006) on both the individual and group levels. Benefits to this approach include

- ensuring active participation by all students,
- determining the most equitable means for students to be heard in virtual and online conversations,
- discover barriers that might inhibit their willingness or ability to participate, and
- identify effective means to support and cultivate participation for different populations and contexts.

Of critical consideration for virtual learning communities, faculty should expect conflict, at least occasionally (Palloff, & Pratt, 2001). The wise instructor anticipates conflict and deals with it effectively using the following recommended techniques. First, inform students that the faculty member's role is that of facilitation of group processes. The group is in charge of assigning and completing the tasks successfully. Convey to students up front that conflict is expected among group members and can be challenging, but it is manageable. Explain that this is why there are specific group member roles. Second, resist the temptation to resolve conflict among group members individually. Communicate only with the group leader. This not only reduces the number of students the instructor has to communicate with, but requires the students experiencing the conflict to express it to their group leader. As the conflicted students articulate their irritation with the group or member, they have time to "cool off" emotionally (the intensity of a situation wanes with time) and consider possible solutions. Require the group leader to present several resolutions, and leave it to the group to gain consensus on which solution they will pursue. In other words, facilitate mediation; however, do not dictate actions or outcomes.

It is known that the facilitation of successful virtual communities depends on several variables: (a) the provision of expectations, articulated at the formation of the community and built upon group consensus; (b) anticipation and management of conflict; (c) students' self-selection of roles; and (d) delineated milestones throughout the learning and community building process, not exclusively at the end (Palloff & Pratt, 2005, 2007; Stewart, 2008). Future studies can advance this understanding and practice further.

Future Research

Scanning the literature and current practice of virtual learning communities, future research may focus in this area related to the dynamics of learning, faculty development, and innovative extensions in specific contexts. As indicated, future research in this area may fruitfully examine the dynamics of virtual communities, specifically how they form, evolve, and flourish. The need for the pursuit of these efforts is great. Online and virtual learning is advancing more rapidly in higher education than expected (Allen & Seaman, 2009). In addition, instructors increasingly use virtual learning communities for a greater number of critical activities, so the related skills will be essential for success.

Examining effective means to train and support faculty in developing and facilitating such online communities for varied higher education content and contexts is important because one size does not fit all (King & Lawler, 2003). In addition, providing models for faculty to continue to develop and refine their efforts will increase the body of scholarship of teaching and learning (Boyer, 1990), supporting the advancement of research and practice.

One might expect that, given specific contexts and content areas, innovations may not fit in the general scope of practice. The breadth of potential applications within higher education ranges from liberal arts simulations to virtual experiences of science experimentation and individualized nanotechnology, which are only a few examples of possible content-specific innovations that could transform the ways in which we think of, plan, and deliver teaching and learning. Learning communities, which explore concepts and join their experiences to build greater insights and perspectives, promise to create new challenges and research agendas for the psychology and sociology of learning, the neuroscience study of learning, and instructional design.

CONCLUSION

In this chapter, we have presented several case examples of the development and facilitation of transformative learning through virtual and online learning communities. From both a theoretical and empirical perspective, there is little question as to the necessity and effectiveness of interaction and collaboration to achieve deep and meaningful learning outcomes (Garrison & Vaughan, 2008). While higher education institutions can and must address the changing expectations of the millennial generation and the wave of technological innovations through the deliberate and consistent use of Web 2.0 technologies, instructors can maximize this opportunity as a means to develop transformative learning opportunities rather than traditional formats of learning.

Change is not easy. However, transforming teaching in new dimensions such as those proposed is a challenge from which faculty and students alike have much to gain. Collaboration, reflective practice, critical thinking, co-learning, and lifelong learning are vital to the virtual learning communities of today and tomorrow. Who will lead our colleges into the discovering our future within and beyond these technologies?

REFERENCES

Allen, I. E., & Seaman, J. (2009). *Learning on demand: Online education in the United States*. Babson, MA: Babson Survey Research Group and The Sloan Consortium.

Altbach, P. G., Berdahl, R. O., & Gumport, P. J. (Eds.) (2005). *American higher education in the twenty-first century*. Baltimore, MD: John Hopkins University Press.

Begley, S. (2007). *Train your mind, change your brain*. New York, NY: Ballantine.

Bloom, B. S. (1956). *Taxonomy of educational objectives*. New York, NY: Longman.

Boyer, E. (1990). *Scholarship reconsidered: Priorities of the professoriate.* San Francisco, CA: Jossey-Bass.

Caffarella, R. S. (2002). *Program planning for adult learning* (2nd ed.). San Francisco, CA: Jossey-Bass.

Carnevale, P. J., & Pruitt, D. (1993). *Negotiation in social conflict.* Pacific Grove, CA: Brooks/Cole.

Chickering, A. W., & Gamson, Z. F. (1987). Seven principles of good practice in undergraduate education. *AAHE Bulletin.* Retrieved February 24, 2008, from http://www.uis.edu/liberalstudies/students/documents/sevenprinciples.pdf

Christensen, C. M., Johnson, C. S., & Horn, M. B. (2008). *Disrupting class: How disruptive innovation will change the way we learn.* New York, NY: McGraw-Hill.

Conrad, R., & Donaldson, J. (2004). *Engaging the online learner.* San Francisco, CA: Jossey-Bass.

Cranton, P. (1996). *Transformative learning in professional development.* San Francisco, CA: Jossey-Bass.

Cranton, P. (2001). *Becoming an authentic teacher in higher education.* Malabar, FL: Kreiger.

Dewey, J., & Bentley, A. F. (1949/1989). Knowing and the known. In J. A. Boydston (Ed.). *John Dewey: The later works Volume 16* (pp. 1–279). Carbondale: Southern Illinois Press.

Flecha, R. (2000). *Sharing words: Theory and practice of dialogic learning.* Lanham, MD: Rowman & Littlefield.

Garrison, R., & Vaughan, N. (2008). *Blended learning in higher education: Frameworks, principles and guidelines.* San Francisco, CA: Jossey-Bass.

Hawkins, P., & Smith, N. (2007). *Coaching, mentoring and organizational consultancy: Supervision and development.* New York, NY: Open University Press.

Homan, M., & Miller, L. J. (2008). *Coaching in organizations.* Hoboken, NJ: Wiley.

Hudson, K., & Degast-Kennedy, K. (2009, April). Canadian border simulation at Loyalist College. *Journal of Virtual Worlds Research, 2*(1), 3–11.

Hunt, J. M., & Weintraub, J. R. (2007). *The coaching organization: A strategy for developing leaders.* Thousand Oaks, CA: Sage.

Johnson, S., & Taylor, K. (2006). The neuroscience of adult learning. *New Directions in Adult and Continuing Education, 110.* Hoboken, NJ: Jossey-Bass/Wiley.

Kim, K. J., Bonk, C. J., & Zeng, T. (2005). *Surveying the future of workplace e-learning: The rise of blending, interactivity, and authentic learning.* Retrieved June 14, 2010, from http://www.publicationshare.com

King, K. P. (1997). Examining learning activities and transformational learning. *International Journal of University Adult Education, 36* (3), 23–37.

King, K. P. (1998). *A guide to perspective transformation and learning activities: The Learning Activities survey.* Philadelphia, PA: Research for Better Schools.

King, K. P. (1999, Fall). Unleashing technology in the classroom: What adult basic education teachers and organizations need to know. *Adult Basic Education: An Interdisciplinary Journal for Adult Literacy Educators, 9* (3), 162–175.

King, K. P. (2002). *Keeping pace with technology: Educational technology that transforms. Vol. 1.* Cresskill, NJ: Hampton.

King, K. P. (2003). *Keeping pace with technology: Educational technology that transforms. Vol. 2: Faculty development in higher education.* Cresskill, NJ: Hampton.

King, K. P. (2005). *Bringing transformative learning to life*. Malabar, FL: Krieger.
King, K. P. (2010). *The handbook of the evolving research of transformative learning* (10th anniv. ed.). Charlotte, NC: Information Age.
King, K. P., & Griggs, J. K. (Eds.). (2007). *Harnessing innovative technologies in higher education: Access, equity, policy and instruction*. Madison, WI: Atwood.
King, K. P., & Lawler, P. A. (Eds.). (2003, June). New perspectives on designing and implementing professional development for teachers of adults. *New Directions in Adult and Continuing Education, 98*. San Francisco, CA: Jossey-Bass.
Kitchenham, A. (2005). Adult-learning principles, technology and elementary teachers and their students: The perfect blend? *Education, Communication & Information 5*(3), 285–302.
Kitchenham, A. (2006). Teachers and technology: A transformative journey. *Journal of Transformative Education, 4*(3), 202–225.
Laghos, A. (2009). E-learning communities. In P. Zaphiris (Ed.), *Social computing and virtual communities*. Hoboken, NJ: CRC.
Lari, P. (2008). *Understanding teaching experiences: Faculty transitions from traditional to online classrooms*. Doctoral dissertation, North Carolina State University, Raleigh.
Lattuca, L. R., & Stark, J. S. (2009). *Shaping the college curriculum*. San Francisco, CA: Jossey-Bass.
Lave, J., & Wenger, E. (1991). *Situated learning*. Cambridge, England: Cambridge University Press.
Lewicki, J., Saunders, D. M., & Minton, J. W. (1999). *Negotiation: Readings, cases and exercises*. New York, NY: McGraw-Hill.
MacDonald, J. (2006). *Blended learning and online tutoring: A good practice guide*. Aldershot, England: Gower.
McGrath, J., & Hollingshead, A. (1994). *Groups interacting with technology*. Thousand Oaks, CA: Sage.
Mezirow, J. (1978). *Education for perspective transformation: Women's re-entry programs in community colleges*. New York, NY: Teachers College, Columbia University.
Mezirow, J., & Associates (1990). *Fostering critical reflection in adulthood*. San Francisco, CA: Jossey-Bass.
Mezirow, J., & Associates (2000). *Learning as transformation: Critical perspectives on a theory in progress*. San Francisco, CA: Jossey-Bass.
Mezirow, J., Taylor, E., & Associates. (2010). *Transformative learning in practice*. San Francisco, CA: Jossey-Bass.
Moore, M., & Kearsley, G. (1996). *Distance education: A systems view*. Belmont, CA: Wadsworth.
Moore, M., & Kearsley, G. (2005). *Distance education: A systems view* (2nd ed.). Belmont, CA: Wadsworth.
Palloff, R., & Pratt, K. (2001). *Lessons from the cyberspace classroom: The realities of online teaching*. San Francisco, CA: Jossey-Bass.
Palloff, R., & Pratt, K. (2005). *Collaborating online: Learning together in community*. San Francisco, CA: Jossey Bass.
Palloff, R., & Pratt, K. (2007). *Building online learning communities: Effective strategies for the virtual classroom*. San Francisco, CA: Jossey-Bass.

Partnership for 21st Century Skills. (2004). *Framework for 21st century learning.* Tucson, AZ: Retrieved August 12, 2009, from http://www.21stcenturyskills.org/documents/frameworkflyer_072307.pdf

Porter, L. R. (2004). *Developing an online curriculum: Technologies and techniques.* Hershey, PA: Information Science.

Prensky, M. (2001). Digital natives, digital immigrants. *On The Horizon, 9*(5), 1–6. Retrieved September 8, 2008, from http://www.emeraldinsight.com/journals.htm?articleid=1532742

Prensky, M. (2008, June). Young minds, fast times: The 21st century digital learner. *Edutopia.* Retrieved September 25, 2008, from http://www.edutopia.org/ikid-digital-learner-technology-2008

Ragins, B. R., Cotton, J. L., & Miller, J. S. (2000). Marginal mentoring. *Academy of Management Journal, 43*(6), 1177–1194.

Rheingold, H. (2000). *The virtual community: Homesteading on the electronic frontier.* Retrieved September 18, 2010, from http://www.rheingold.com/vc/book/intro.html

Rudestam, K. & Schoenholtz-Read, J. (Eds.). (2010). *Handbook of online learning* (2nd ed.). Thousand Oaks, CA: Sage.

Schon, D. A. (1987). *Educating the reflective practitioner.* San Francisco, CA: Jossey-Bass.

Senge, P. (1994). *The fifth discipline: The art and practice of the learning organization.* New York, NY: Doubleday.

Stewart, S. (2008). *A study of instructional strategies that promote synchronous dialogue online.* (Doctoral dissertation). Available from ProQuest Dissertation database. (UMI No. 3347372)

Stewart, S. (2010). A model for facilitating group projects online using Web 2.0 technologies. *Group Projects Online.* Retrieved from https://sites.google.com/a/mail.usf.edu/group-projects-online/

Sundberg, C., Sunal, D., & Mays, A. (2006). Problem solving and coping strategies used in online environments. In V. Wright, C. Sunal, & E. Wilson (Eds.), *Research on enhancing the interactivity of online learning* (pp. 175–196). Charlotte, NC: Information Age.

Tapscott, D., & Williams, A. D. (2006). *Wikinomics: How mass collaboration changes everything.* New York, NY: Portfolio.

Vygotsky, L. (1978). *Mind and society.* Retrieved from http://www.marxists.org/archive/vygotsky/works/mind/index.htm

Wasnick, J. (2007). *Transformative learning in online learning.* (Doctoral dissertation). Available from ProQuest Dissertation database. (UMI No. 3259579)

Zaphiris, P., & Ang, C. S. (Eds.) (2009). *Social computing and virtual communities.* Boca Raton, FL: CRC Press.

Zull, J. (2002). *The art of changing the brain.* Sterling, VA: Stylus.

CHAPTER 19

VIDEO TECHNOLOGY

Transforming Reflective Practice

Sejal Parikh and Christopher Janson

The concept of transformative learning has been a valuable lens through which educators have viewed their work in the development of adult learning since it was first proposed and described by Mezirow in the 1970s (Brock, 2010; Mezirow, 1991; Trotter, 2006). Since that time, the theory and tenets of transformative learning have provided the framework for, and been applied to, numerous methods and practices of adult education (Grossman, 2009; Ritz, 2010; Vescio, Bondy, & Poekert, 2009; White, 1999). In this chapter, the authors continue this tradition of applying elements of transformative learning theory in order to frame the development and use of video technology as a method to develop adult learners' reflective capacity and practices. Thus, building from Mezirow's (1997) own definition of transformative learning, we define transformative learning in relationship to video technology as the process of effecting change in adult student learners' frame of reference through the use and analysis of video journals.

REFLECTIVE PRACTICES AND TRANSFORMATIVE LEARNING

Mezirow (1997) defined transformative learning as "the process of effecting change in a frame of reference" (p. 5). Essentially, transformative learning theory is predicated on the notion that adult learners have accumulated significant experiences that involve all the perceptual, relational, affective, and cognitive elements that both compose and inform those experiences. The central endeavor for educators working with adult learners, then, is to facilitate a process through which those adult learners can begin to reflect upon and critically examine and question those frames of reference. Ultimately, the desired outcome of transformative learning is for adult learners to integrate and employ ways of knowing and practicing that are built not from the ideas, values, and approaches of others swallowed whole, but instead are synthesized through active integration with one's own ideas, values, perceptions, and meanings (Mezirow, 2000).

Mezirow (1997) described frames of reference as being composed of two dimensions that he referred to as "habits of mind" and "point of view" (p. 5). Mezirow described habits of mind as far-reaching and abstract ways of relating and behaving that are heavily influenced by the cultural, political, social, and psychological assumptions that permeate every individual's life in society. When human services practitioners encounter an experience in practice, their far-reaching and abstract ways of relating and behaving coalesce to a point of view that then guides their interpretations of those experiences. Mezirow noted that habits of mind are generally challenging for practitioners to critique and reflect on, whereas points of view are more easily accessible to practitioners and thus are more commonly examined and reflected upon from the standpoints of both the dilemmas their experiences present. Additionally, the process through which they address those dilemmas as well as the outcome of their interventions or practices can also be examined.

Rationale and Importance of Reflective Practice for Transformative Learning

Transformative learning occurs when adult learners change their frames of reference by reflecting critically on the assumptions that underlie their habits of mind and points of view (Mezirow, 1997). Educators in the field of adult learning need to encourage, prepare, and invite students to become aware of their own assumptions and to reflect on them, as well as on the assumptions of others that inform their own. Only by structuring learning experiences to purposefully promote reflection can instructors nurture the development of adult students' transformative learning.

Reflective learning opportunities should focus on the experiences of students in the context of their burgeoning professional practices (Mezirow, 2000). It is when adult learners reflect on their experiences and practices that they can then begin to reflect on the assumptions that informed those experiences and practices. In many ways, when adult learners begin to develop their capacity to reflect, they also begin to take control of their learning and move toward autonomy and self-directedness. The increased self-agency that is nurtured through the reflective processes facilitates transformative learning and can then lead to transformed practice. In this way, "transformation represents a new way of thinking as well as a new way of acting" (Vescio et al., 2009, p. 1).

Process of Reflection

The process of reflection has been described within contexts other than transformative learning. However, across these various descriptions, there are common elements, the foremost being the idea that reflection involves taking the unprocessed, raw material of experience and engaging with it in order to make meaning (Boud, 2001). As such, reflection is necessary if practitioners are to increase their effectiveness by reframing their experiences in the field (Schön, 1983). Neufeldt, Karno, and Nelson (1996) also contextualized this element of reflection by describing how it often begins with a persisting issue or problem of practice and proceeds with a search for deeper and different understandings of that issue or problem as well as potential solutions to it.

Reflection has also been described as the process adult learners engage in to not only make deeper meaning from experiences but also as the process in which they examine their assumptions and attitudes that inform those experiences. Although adapted to the context of adult learners by Mezirow (1997), this description has its origins in the work of Dewey (1933), who proposed that beliefs regarding practice must be a focus of reflection.

Finally, those preparing, training, and supervising adult learners in education and human services programs face the persisting challenge of nurturing students' abilities to integrate their disciplines' theories and conceptual models to actual practice. This developmental process is challenging, but many have maintained that it can be enabled through reflection (Brandt, 2008; Kolb, 1984; Wilson, 2009). Kolb (1984) used the term *praxis* to describe how reflection mediates the learner's struggle to reconcile theory and practice. Kolb emphasized that intentional reflective practice serves to not only close the gap between theory and practice, but that reflection can and should transform both by enriching understanding of theory while simultaneously developing the ability to practice more effectively through foundational theoretical approaches. In contrast to Kolb's definition, Freire (1973) described praxis as "reflection and action upon the world in order to transform it" (p. 47). In doing so, Freire also positioned reflection as not simply a mechanism to integrate theory and practice but as a foundation of transformative action.

DISCUSSION OF LEARNING IN RELATIONSHIP TO TECHNOLOGY

Technology and Reflective Practice

Given the continued explosion of technological advancement, it should come as no surprise that emergent technology has increasingly been identified and used as a vehicle for reflection. The use of technology has been promoted as a favorable platform for either individual or group reflection (White, 1999). This is particularly the case for the use of constructing reflective practices for adult learners within a supervised context. The use of computers to support the reflection required for transformative learning has created an alternative to traditional direct observation and face-to-face interaction for adult learners in education and human services programs (Yang, 2009). By creating an alternative to direct observation or face-to-face interactions, the use of video addresses the time constraints that many supervisors of adult learners in experiential courses experience. This is particularly the case with the use of video reflective journaling in that it acknowledges the simple reality that adult learning is not limited to times interacting directly with supervisors.

Use of Video Journaling to Engage Transformative Learning

Most examples of the use of video to prepare adult learners has centered on the delayed examination of their direct work with clients or students (Wang & Hartley, 2003; Welsch & Devlin, 2006). Some of these descriptions and examinations of the use of video to review work with students and clients even directly discuss the transformative possibilities of its use (Rosaen, Luneberg, Cooper, Fritzen, & Terpstra, 2008; Sewall, 2009). However, very little has been written about the use of video journals as a method to enable and develop reflective capacity and practices (Parikh, Janson, & Singleton, 2010), a central element to transformative learning.

Mezirow (1997) noted that the central idea of transformative learning is to provide opportunities for adult learners to "actively engage the concepts presented in the context of their own lives and collectively critically assess the justification of new knowledge" (p. 10). The use of video journaling with students is intended to do just that. Either in response to a prompt focusing on problems in the field or through self-directed exploration of the integration of theoretical knowledge and practice, adult learners record video reflections that are designed to activate reflexivity. Along with others (Greiman & Covington, 2007), the co-authors have found that adult learners prefer that their mode of reflection be verbal rather than writing (Parikh et al., 2010). Unencumbered by perceived constraints of the writing process, adult learners can record video reflections that meet central criteria for transformative learning as identified by Mezirow (1997). That is, the use of video journaling can be transformative because it supports "critical reflective thought, imaginative problem posing, and discourse that is learner centered, participatory, and interactive, and it involves group deliberation and group problem solving" (p. 10). When adult learners engage in reflective video journaling, they are provided with the opportunity to not only examine their frames of reference during the act of recording the reflections but are also able to review and reflect upon the video journal artifact in order to reflect on the reflective process they engaged in to create the artifact in the first place. This type of reflection can yield learning characterized as "double-loop" by Argyris and Schön (1978). Resonant with the core aim of transformative adult learning, Argyris and Schön propose that when engaged in single-loop learning, learners modify their actions based upon the difference between their expected and obtained outcomes or perceptions. However, when engaged in double-loop learning, learners question the underlying perceptions, assumptions, values, and processes that initially led to the outcomes and perceptions. Once individuals are able to perceive and change those perceptions, assumptions, values, and processes, then double-loop learning has occurred. By first recording and then examining video reflective journals, adult learners begin to develop reflexivity toward the exploration of their frames of reference that may limit their effectiveness.

Video Journals as a Medium for Meaningful Reflection

Video journaling can be used as an effective means of self-reflection. In particular, Wang and Hartley (2003) noted that the use of video technologies may have the ability to document complex events that occur in teaching and learning experiences. This method of documentation can provide for a richer mechanism to capture thoughts that occur in the classroom and experiential settings. Wang and Hartley also posited that reflecting can allow students the opportunity to share their experiences, observations, and discussions. Particularly, reflections can allow adult learners to capture their thoughts within a certain context. For example, in the context of experiential learning, learners can process their work that occurs in the field, their thoughts about their skill development, and other professional or ethical considerations that may arise.

Further, Osterman and Kottkamp (2004) suggested that through reflection, learners can resolve issues that occur in practice and can foster critical self-examination. The authors also noted that reflection allows individuals to learn about the assumptions they hold and to explore what is often left unspoken (Osterman & Kottkamp, 2004). With the use of video reflections, adult learners may reveal thoughts, feelings, and emotions that otherwise may be unspoken and, in turn, can reflect upon those reflections at a later time, thus allowing for deeper self-reflection and self-analysis. This assumption is supported by Moon (2004), who stated, "use of journals involves the acknowledgement of the expression of emotion which is considered to be more a complete form of learning... This is not learning that takes place 'only from the neck-up.' It is a gut-level type of learning" (p. 27). Given that reflective video journals support authentic reflection (Parikh et al., 2010), learners can begin to process their experiences and make meaning of their work (Moon, 2004).

Video Journals as Evidence of Self-Growth and Self-Development

Reflection is a process that has the capacity to influence self-growth and development. For example, through the use of reflective journaling, adult learners may examine their own assumptions, theories, beliefs, and thoughts (Pasch, 1995). Moon (1999) also noted that reflection is an underpinning of self-development. Moreover, reflection can facilitate personal learning that can lead toward empowerment and self-development. Given that video technology allows for repeated viewing (Wang & Hartley, 2003), reflective video journals offer learners the opportunity to reexamine their video reflections, thus allowing for deeper self-reflection.

Initial research has illustrated positive outcomes for the use of reflective video journaling. For example, the co-authors conducted a phenomenological study with seven participants who created reflective video journals during their internship course. The study revealed that video reflections supported student self-development and self-growth (Parikh et al., 2010). These findings support Griffith and Frieden (2000), who noted that the reflective process can promote counselor development. Additional research findings indicated that reflecting on video mirrored the counseling process as it allowed participants to understand the importance of clear communication, understand the importance of nonverbal communication, and fostered authenticity (Parikh et al., 2010).

BEST PRACTICES THAT SUPPORT TRANSFORMATIVE LEARNING

Expectations and Ethical Considerations

Although video journaling can be an effective means of reflection, it is important to note that there are expectations, parameters, and ethical considerations that should be considered prior to implementation. First, as indicated in previous research, the mere thought of creating a video journal had the potential to cause feelings of discomfort and apprehension (Parikh et al., 2010). Griffith and Frieden (2000) pointed out that since self-reflection is a mechanism that encourages reflection on a deeper level, individuals may uncover hidden or past trauma. Accordingly, individuals who have this type of reaction ought to be referred to counseling services. Prior to implementation, educators should also set clear guidelines regarding what is expected from the reflective journal. Some considerations include (a) setting up clear standards to protect confidentiality, (b) offering students the choice as to whether or not the video will be shown outside of supervision or to their classmates in a supervisory group setting, (c) considering the use of prompts to which students can respond, (d) limiting the type of content that students choose to share on video, and (e) setting clear standards as to how the reflection will be assessed. The American Counseling Association's (ACA, 2005) code of ethics prescribes best practices regarding self-growth experiences. The ethical guidelines are clear that evaluations of these types of experiences should be based on academic standards rather than how much an individual chooses to self-disclose.

Use in Experiential Learning

Transformative learning can be supported through experiential practice. Osterman and Kottkamp (2004) referred to learning theorists such as Dewey, Lewin, and Piaget, who suggested that effective learning and behavioral change occurs when it first begins with experience. Posner (2005) took this idea further and insisted that, "If you merely 'do' your field experience without thinking deeply about it, if you merely allow your experiences to wash over you without savoring and examining them for their significance, then your growth will be greatly limited" (p. 21).

Given the multitude of settings in which adult learners may practice, it is also important to consider that solutions cannot always be directly translated across settings. In turn, reflective video journals can foster reflection and process learning that is relative to the settings in which learners practice their work (Osterman & Kottkamp, 2004). Moon (2004) stated that when journals complement field experiences, learners can connect their own unique experiences to establish theory and meaning. Additionally, by moving beyond one's preconceived ideas, reflecting can provide the opportunity to reframe experiences (Hubbs & Brand, 2005). These statements clearly illustrate the importance of learners engaging in reflection while practicing in the field. In this context, by reviewing previously recorded video journals, adult learners have the opportunity to make meaning of their experiences even after the initial reflection. In turn, this may translate into a deeper personal and philosophical understanding of their work.

Use in Supervision

The opportunities to reflect on one's video reflection may occur within the individual and group supervisory settings. Bernard and Goodyear (2004) discussed the notion that supervision is a distinct intervention. Specifically, supervision can foster professional development while ensuring client welfare (Bernard & Goodyear, 2004). Given that reflective video journals can support self-growth and development (Parikh et al., 2010), supervisors should assist their supervisees with their development in the cognitive, affective, and behavioral domains (Granello & Hazler, 1998). Further, Roberts (2001) noted that time with supervisors for reflection and processing may enhance supervisees' skill development and decision making. Through interaction in the supervisory setting, reflection can also be modeled in order to help supervisees develop their own reflective style (Skovholt & Ronnestad, 1992). Vaccaro and Lambie (2007) referenced the various uses of technology in supervision. In this case, using video technology allows supervisors to manage what segments can be used as a teaching tool. Having the ability to start and stop a video reflection allows time for processing, questioning, and further reflection. The video also allows the supervisor to focus on affective elements and nonverbal cues of the reflection in addition to what is reflected verbally.

The group supervision setting may also be a beneficial environment to process reflective video journals. Borders and Brown (2005) argued that through feedback, brainstorming, and exposure to diverse clients and settings, group supervision allows supervisees to learn from one another. The authors also stated that group supervision offers supervisees the opportunities to see each other's frustrations and anxiety. Similarly, video journals give supervisees a mechanism by which they can both see and hear what their peers are experiencing. The use of video technology allows groups to process what supervisees experienced in the moment.

Evaluation Methods

Reflective journals are considered to be useful in processing practices in the field and making meaning of experiences (Moon, 2004; Wang & Hartley, 2003). Therefore, if reflective video journals are going to be used in field experience courses and assessed by a supervisor, there are some considerations for evaluation methods. First, supervisors should consider a standard of care when assigning the reflective video journals for part of a course grade. According to the ACA (2005), evaluations for self-growth experiences should be based upon academic standards rather than self-disclosure. Supervisors should consider creating a rubric that outlines expectations for reflective video journals. Such expectations could outline specific prompts that should be responded to, length of time of the reflection, and how frequently the reflection should occur. Grades can then be assigned according to whether or not the points in the rubric were addressed. Supervisors may also consider evaluating reflective video journals based on whether students addressed their own skill development, thoughts, and feelings rather than talking about ancillary concepts that have little bearing on self-growth and professional training.

DISCUSSION

Use in Multicultural Education

Reflective video journals can also be used as a platform to process multicultural training and development. Sue et al. (1998) discussed how examining one's attitudes, cultural competence, knowledge, and ability to work with culturally diverse groups as a necessary function of working with diverse populations. Accordingly, video journals provide the opportunity for adult learners to engage in authentic self-reflection, process their diverse experiences (Parikh et al., 2010), explore their prejudices, and examine preconceived ideas (Osterman & Kottkamp, 2004). Further, Sue and Sue (2003), asserted that there can be emotional consequences when individuals engage in self-analysis of the attitudes, beliefs, and feelings related to cultural differences. Video journals, therefore, give learners the opportunity to process their feelings as they watch their own videos. Under supervision, adult learners can answer questions about what they are feeling and thinking as they are reflecting on multicultural issues.

Use in Immersion Experiences

Pederson (2000) stated that cultural immersion experiences allow individuals to view situations through their own lens while being able to see another's perspective. Cultural immersion allows students to learn by working with and alongside diverse groups. While these experiences have the ability to increase cultural awareness, they also have the potential to increase emotional stress (Pederson, 2000). As such, reflective video journals provide adult learners with the ability to share their emotions in a safe and supportive environment. Additionally, learners have the ability to go back and view their reflections to gauge their progress, identify areas of continued concern, and be able to point out their own areas of self-development. Transformative learning can be documented on video as students can see their actual development over time and can process what skills and knowledge they have acquired that contributed to their growth.

Future Areas of Research

The co-authors' initial research study supported the use of video journals as a tool that promotes authentic reflection and self-development (Parikh et al., 2010). Future research could examine the use of this approach in individual and group supervision settings. Research could also be conducted to examine the effectiveness of video journals to support multicultural education courses and immersion experiences. Researchers might also investigate how video journaling and other technological methods support transformative practice.

CONCLUSION

Reflective journaling is a multilayered mechanism by which adult learners can make meaning of their experiences, engage in self-growth, and process their learning (Dewey, 1933; Schön, 1983). Video journaling adds another layer that promotes authentic reflection and allows learners to take part in processing their own self-development. Video reflections can be useful in experiential learning, which in turn can transform the learner into an intentional practitioner. Furthermore, the use of this type of technology allows students to go back and review their reflections, thus allowing for one to see their growth and transformation over time. Multicultural training and development can also be influenced by the practice of video journals as it cultivates that environment for authentic self-reflection. While the supervisory process can support learners individually, group supervision can also provide for strong dialogue, connections among learners, and an environment that supports collaborative learning. Overall, reflective video journals have the potential to foster self-development and support adult learners as they engage in practices that are transformational in nature.

REFERENCES

American Counseling Association. (2005). *ACA code of ethics.* Alexandria, VA: Author.

Argyris, C., & Schön, D. (1978). *Organizational learning: A theory of action perspective.* Reading, MA: Addison-Wesley.

Bernard, J. M., & Goodyear, R. K. (2004). *Fundamentals of clinical supervision.* Boston, MA: Pearson.

Brandt, C. (2008). Integrating feedback and reflection in teacher preparation. *ELT Journal, 62*(1), 37–46.

Borders, L. D., & Brown, L. L. (2005). *The new handbook of counseling supervision.* Mahwah, NJ: Lawrence Erlbaum.

Boud, D. (2001). Using journal writing to enhance reflective practice. In L. English & M. Gillen (Eds.), *New directions for adult and continuing education* (pp. 9–17). New York, NY: John Wiley.

Brock, S. A. (2010). Measuring the importance of precursor steps to transformative learning. *Adult Education Quarterly, 60*(2), 122–142.

Dewey, J. (1933). *How we think: A restatement of the relation of reflective thinking to the educative process.* Boston, MA: D.C. Heath.

Freire, P. (1973). *Education for critical consciousness.* New York, NY: Continuum.

Granello, D. H., & Hazler, R. J. (1998). A development rationale for curriculum order and teaching styles in counselor education programs. *Counselor Education and Supervision, 38,* 89–105.

Greiman, B. C., & Covington, H. K. (2007). Reflective thinking and journal writing: Examining student teachers' perceptions of preferred reflective modality, journal writing outcomes, and journal structure. *Career and Technical Education Research, 32,* 115–139.

Griffith, B. A., & Frieden, G. (2000). Counselor preparation: Facilitating reflective thinking in counselor education. *Counselor Education and Supervision, 40,* 82–93.

Grossman, R. (2009). Structures for facilitating student reflection. *College Teaching, 57*(1), 15–22. doi:10.3200/CTCH.57.1.15-22

Hubbs, D. L., & Brand, C. F. (2005). The paper mirror: Understanding reflective journals. *Journal of Experiential Education, 28*(1), 60–71.

Kolb, D. A. (1984). *Experiential learning: Experience as the source of learning and development.* Englewood Cliffs, NJ: Prentice Hall.

Mezirow, J. (1991). *Transformative dimensions of adult learning.* San Francisco, CA: Jossey-Bass.

Mezirow, J. (1997). Transformative learning: Theory to practice. *New Directions for Adult and Continuing Education, 74,* 5–12.

Mezirow, J. (2000). Learning to think like an adult: Core concepts of Transformation Theory. In J. Mezirow & Associates (Eds.), *Learning as transformation* (pp. 3–34). San Francisco, CA: Jossey-Bass.

Moon, J. (1999). *Reflection in learning & professional development.* Sterling, VA: Stylus.

Moon, J. A. (2004). *A handbook of reflective and experiential learning: Theory and practice.* New York, NY: RoutledgeFalmer.

Neufeldt, S., Karno, M., & Nelson, M. (1996). A qualitative study of experts' conceptualization of supervisee reflectivity. *Journal of Counseling Psychology, 43,* 3–9. doi:10.1037/0022-0167.43.1.3

Osterman, K. F., & Kottkamp, R. B. (2004). *Reflective practice for educators: Professional development to improve student learning* (2nd ed.). Thousand Oaks, CA: Corwin.

Parikh, S., Janson, C., & Singleton, T. (2010). *A qualitative investigation of video journaling as a method of reflective practice.* Manuscript submitted for publication.

Pasch, S. H. (1995). Assisting and assessing the development of preservice teachers in academic and clinical settings. In S. W. Soled (Ed.), *Assessment, testing, and evaluation in teacher education* (pp. 159–188). Norwood, NJ: Ablex.

Pederson, P. B. (2000). *A handbook for developing multicultural awareness.* Alexandria, VA: American Association for Counseling and Development.

Posner, G. J. (2005). *Field experience: A guide to reflective teaching* (5th ed.). Boston, MA: Pearson Education.

Ritz, A. A. (2010). International students and transformative learning in a multicultural formal educational context. *The Educational Forum, 74,* 158–166.

Roberts, W. (2001). Site supervisors of professional school counseling interns: Suggested guidelines. *Professional School Counseling, 4*(3), 208–216.

Rosaen, C. L., Luneberg, M., Cooper, M., Fritzen, A., & Terpstra, M. (2008). How does investigation of video records change how teachers reflect on their experiences? *Journal of Teacher Education, 59*(4), 347–360.

Schön, D. (1983). *The reflective practitioner: How professionals think in action.* New York, NY: Basic.

Sewall, M. (2009). Transforming supervision: Using video elicitation to support preservice teacher-directed reflective conversations. *Issues in Teacher Education, 18*(2), 11–30.

Skovholt, T., & Ronnestad, M. H. (1992). Themes in therapist and counselor development. *Journal of Counseling and Development, 70,* 505–515.

Sue, D. W., Carter, R. T., Casas, J. M., Fouad, N. A., Ivey, A. E., Jensen, M., . . . Vasquez-Nuttall, E. (1998). *Multicultural counseling competencies: Individual and organizational development.* Thousand Oaks, CA: Sage.

Sue, D. W., & Sue, D. (2003). *Counseling the culturally diverse. Theory and practice* (4th ed.). New York, NY: John Wiley and Sons.

Trotter, Y. D. (2006). Adult learning theories: Impacting professional development programs. *Delta Kappa Gamma Bulletin, 72*(2), 8–13.

Vaccaro, N., & Lambie, G. (2007). Computer-based counselor-in-training supervision: Ethical and practical implications for counselor educators and supervisors. *Counselor Education and Supervision, 47,* 46–57.

Vescio, V., Bondy, E., & Poekert, P. E. (2009). Preparing multicultural teacher educators: Toward a pedagogy of transformation. *Teacher Education Quarterly, 36*(2), 5–24.

Wang, J., & Hartley, K. (2003). Video technology as a support for teacher education reform. *Journal of Technology and Teacher Education, 11*(1), 105–138.

Welsch, R. G., & Devlin, P. A. (2006). Developing preservice teachers' reflection: Examining the use of video. *Action in Teacher Education, 28*(4), 53–61.

White, C. (1999). It's not just another new thing: Technology as a transformative innovation for social studies teacher education. *Journal of Technology and Teacher Education, 7*(1), 3–12.

Wilson, A. L. (2009). Reflecting on reflecting on practice. *New Directions in Adult and Continuing Education, 123,* 75–85.

Yang, S-H. (2009). Using blogs to enhance critical reflection and community of practice. *Educational Technology & Society, 12*(2), 11–21.

RELATIONSHIP WITH ADULT EDUCATION AND THE HUMAN SERVICES FIELDS

CHAPTER 20

ADVANCING TRANSFORMATIVE THEORY

Multifold and Cyclical Transformation

Fujuan Tan and Lee Nabb

As defined in the field of adult education, transformation occurs when one has difficulty incorporating a new experience into the mental matrix of perceptions largely built on prior experiences (Merriam, Caffarella, & Baumgartner, 2007; Mezirow, 1990, 2000). Although recent discourse writing from a research perspective has identified different levels at which transformation can occur, and different areas in which it can occur, researchers have focused very little on transformation from a learner perspective concerning the multiple layers of transformation that can occur simultaneously. Moreover, most of the literature depicts transformation as a linear, sequential process in accord with the dominant model (Brock, 2010; Erickson, 2007; Moon, 2011; Taylor, 1997, 2007, 2008). Some attention has been given to perspective dilemmas in terms of reverse culture shock (Christofi & Thompson, 2007), and some research has emerged to challenge the singular, linear concept of the transformative process (Brock, 2010; Taylor, 1997, 2005, 2007, 2008). Notwithstanding, the literature seems vacuous concerning the deeper concept of transformation and its occurrence when one traverses contexts from the familiar to the unfamiliar, let alone back to the familiar and so on. Not only do international experiences prompt myriad types of transformation, as the number of international students enrolling in U.S. programs continues to increase (IIE, 2011a, 2011b), sensitivity to their transformative experiences becomes ever more pertinent in providing effective education (Hoff, 2008; Hunter, 2008; Savicki, 2008). For these reasons, after a review of literature concerning current perspectives on adult education transformational theory, we will explain new notions of multifold and cyclical transformation and explore using two separate case studies of international students enrolled in U.S. graduate programs.

BACKGROUND

First developed by Jack Mezirow in 1978, transformative learning theory reflects an idea quite different from merely adding to an already existing knowledge base (Clark, 1993), or expanding "already established cognitive capacities" (Kegan, 2000, p. 48). Transformation concerns how one interprets life experience and makes meaning from it. Thus, experience, critical reflection, and some kind of resulting development are foundational concepts in transformation (Merriam et al., 2007). More specifically, according to Mezirow's theory, transformative learning denotes a process resulting in a change that occurs after one experiences something one cannot readily incorporate into one's existing worldview. Such an experience brings on a disorienting dilemma, which triggers self-reflection and a critical assessment of assumptions. After such critical reflection, recognizing that others have gone thorough similar processes, one explores options for forming new roles, relationships, and actions. One then invents a new plan of action and reintegrates into the environment with a new, transformed perspective (Mezirow, 1991). In short, "transformative theory is about change—dramatic, fundamental change in the way we see ourselves and the world in which we live" (Merriam & Caffarella, 1999, p. 319).

Mezirow's 10-step, or -phase process has been described as "linear" (Taylor, 1997, p. 43) or "sequential" (Moon, 2011, p. 24) in nature. Although Mezirow (1995) himself has admitted that the process need not always follow the exact sequence he depicts, he still asserts that it follows some kind of variation of the process (Erickson, 2007; Mezirow, 2000), and has continued to include all 10 steps or phases in his writing (Brock, 2010; Mezirow, 1985, 1994, 2000). Perhaps because in its development, Mezirow intended his process to be comprehensive and universal (Erickson, 2007; Mezirow, 1994), it arguably became, and remains, "the most extensive theoretical conceptualization of transformative learning" (Clark, 1993, p. 49).

Mezirow's paradigm has informed and stimulated practice in transformative learning for decades and continues to do so (Brock, 2010; Erickson, 2007; Taylor, 2007). Unfortunately, its dominance may also have caused some limitations. "The ubiquitous acceptance of Mezirow's... transformative learning theory has often led to an uncontested assumption that there is a singular conception of transformative learning, overshadowing a growing presence of other theoretical conceptions" (Taylor, 2008, p. 7). Moreover, the 10-phase model he identified in his research has presented a "Catch-22" for researchers, who "can be accused of attempting to fit the data to the phases or to find the phases in the data" upon replicating the theory in research (Erickson, 2007, p. 68).

Although overshadowed by, and perhaps underappreciated because of, the dominance of Mezirow's model (Taylor, 2005), research into transformative learning has provided different conceptualizations on how one may view the process and in what contexts it can take place. The process has been conceptualized and observed as "more recursive, evolving, and spiraling in nature" (Taylor, 1997, p. 44). Recent conceptions and delineations identify different psychological and sociological lenses through which to examine different kinds of transformation (Taylor, 2005) as well as different factors to consider, such as "the role of spirituality, positionality, emancipatory learning and neurobiology" (Taylor, 2008, p. 7); and recent trends have been enumerated that identify areas in which transformation can occur and merit further research (Merriam et al., 2007). Such alternate views suggest that transformation can occur at multiple levels, simultaneously, and repeatedly (Brock, 2010; Taylor, 1997, 2005, 2007, 2008). Put another way,

> Transformational learning is a complex learning experience that incorporates influences, considerations, and meaning for many areas of adult learners' lives.... In exploring transformational learning, it has become increasingly apparent that our understanding may need to be extended and developed further to begin to account for these many dimensions and inter-relationships. (King & Wright, 2003, p. 103)

Participants and researchers have identified study-abroad experiences as having great potential for transformative learning. Such transitions can provide disorienting dilemmas that hold promise for changing worldviews (Hunter, 2008) and "nurturing more transformation in learners than if they were to stay on campus in a home country" (p. 101). Moreover, the number of international students pursuing study-abroad experiences, thus placing themselves in positions for such potential transformation, is increasing (Hoff, 2008), including the number of students from diverse countries and cultures who come to study in the United States (Hoff, 2008; Pandit, 2009).

The literature reflects considerable research on the transformation of international students (Hoff, 2008; Hunter, 2008; Savicki, 2008), but this research also tends to reflect linear thought. Although relatively new, the notion of "reverse culture shock," or the culture shock international students experience when they return to their home countries after immersion in other cultures for substantial periods of time, has received some attention, most of which is quantitative in nature and lacking depth of experiential descriptions. Such research assumes, rather than examines, some sort of transformation. The relatively little qualitative research in this area tends to focus on the culture shock and reverse culture shock itself and how one copes with it (Christofi & Thompson, 2007) rather than on what has caused it. Although this concept transcends one-directional thinking, it has not extended to a cyclical concept.

The increasing number of international students studying abroad and the realization of their potential to undergo transformation have generated attention to the outcomes of international study experiences and in finding ways to assist in the transformative learning process (Hoff, 2008; Savicki, 2008). Such assistance is a skill that can be learned (Savicki, 2008). Some admonish this assistance as a responsibility of adult educators (Mezirow, 1991). This zeal is understandable under the realization that educators of international students can either broaden worldviews and enrich life experience or reinforce "old patterns of thought, behavior, and sentiment" (Hunter, 2008, p. 105), and "validate culturally insensitive and close-minded perceptions of difference" (p. 106). Notwithstanding, and with good reason, other scholars caution of the ethical issues raised in influencing, or even examining, the transformative process (Merriam et al., 2007).

The following sections introduce the concepts of multifold and cyclical transformation using two case studies involving international students who have studied in the United States. With an understanding that methodology is a plan, or design "lying behind the choice and use of particular [research] methods" which are "techniques...used to gather and analyze data" (Crotty, 1998, p. 3), the first case study used an autoethnographic methodology to research the international learning experience of chapter co-author Fujuan Tan during her first years of study in the United States. The second case study used an ethnographical methodology to research the experiences of a fellow international student also studying in the United States, coming from, and returning to, China. The method of case study facilitates an adequate understanding of these particular cases and thus the concepts they convey rather than to facilitate an understanding of, or generalization to, other cases (Stake, 1995). The intent is to foster new ways of contemplating and examining transformation as well as to underscore the importance of international transformation. The hope is to initiate a dialogue ultimately resulting in ethical facilitation of international transformation for positive outcomes.

MULTIFOLD TRANSFORMATION

Transformation can take place in a variety of ways. The myriad contexts and levels at which it can occur have generated several classifications and schemes of delineation. *Multifold transformation* expresses the idea that several different instances of transformation can arise from the same overall experience. Moreover, instances of transformation and the processes that lead to them can occur simultaneously, and parts of them overlap. These instances of simultaneous, shared, and overlapping transformation are layers or folds. Therefore, more precisely, multifold transformation is the idea that multiple layers of transformation can occur from one overall experience. Evolving discourse accommodates the suggestion or idea that one experience can produce discomfort that leads to several kinds of disorienting dilemmas. One disorienting dilemma can generate several layers of critical reflection leading to numerous changes in perspective or perceptions with which one reintegrates (see theoretical and research discussions in Brock, 2010; King & Wright, 2003; Merriam et al., 2007; Mezirow, 1997; Taylor, 2007, 2008; Taylor, Marienau, & Fiddler, 2000).

Although multifold transformation can be very complex and diverse, for the sake of conveying the idea and processes clearly and succinctly, the use of a model or framework is appropriate. Mezirow's (1978) 10-step process of transformative learning is among the most noted models (Brock, 2010). However, later research disputes that all such stages exist and presents evidence that other stages unidentified by Mezirow might occur (Taylor, 1997). Mezirow himself states that not all steps are required for perspective transformation to occur (1994) and that the stages do not necessarily follow the expressed sequence (1995). Notwithstanding, from Mezirow's model, four main components of the transformative learning process have been identified: (a) experience, which can come in myriad dimensions from direct to vicarious; (b) critical reflection, the critical self-examination and revision of assumptions that structure experience interpretation; (c) reflective discourse, which seeks other opinions to test, understand, and possibly refine new perceptions; and (d) action, which can be immediate, delayed, or continued and range from a simple decision to political protest (Merriam et al., 2007). Note that these are components, not stages; they convey no particular sequence, prerequisites, or relational limitations. Therefore, the following case study uses these components to describe three layers of transformation that occurred as a result of one overall experience. The experience was an initial online learning course taken by co-author Fujuan Tan shortly after she arrived in the United States to engage in a graduate program in adult education. She describes her transformation with respect to the areas, or folds, of technology, language, and culture.

CASE STUDY ONE

Several years ago, I came to pursue graduate studies at a university in the Western United States. I was a top-ranked student in my home country of China. Holding a master's degree in English, I was confident in my ability to speak and understand this second language and had studied Western culture. Upon arriving, I thought I was more than ready to begin graduate studies in this new environment. So bold was I when I first arrived, I contemplated taking four courses the first semester. Since I had a full graduate assistantship, I cautiously decided to take only three. I was glad I did. I experienced culture shock despite my preparation; but the most discomfort came upon taking my first online course in my program of study.

Technology

Experience. I was very uneasy, and thus disoriented, with technology. I had never taken an online course before. Upon registering for the course, I received some basic instructions on how to access the electronic delivery system. Initially logging into the course was very stressful as I entered a world for which I was completely unprepared. I did not know where or how to begin. Exploring the venue helped little. I was unsure about every aspect. I found reading online discussions, a large part of the course, difficult. I thought I could read them more effectively, and more comfortably, if I printed them out; so I tried to print out entire discussions. This method proved cumbersome and ineffective as new entries to these discussions occurred continuously, making complete printouts impossible. I also remained very concerned about submitting assignments. I was not sure I was doing it right and perceived I was sending them to "nowhere." I would e-mail the instructor upon every submission to make sure he received it. For important project submissions, I asked another, more experienced, graduate assistant to sit and watch as I submitted assignments to confirm I was using the correct procedure. The first couple of weeks, I felt quite stressed and frustrated and even lost interest and confidence in the course.

Critical Reflection. At about the 2-week point, I began to question my abilities. I wondered what business I had taking an online course. I also wondered whether my past education had all been for naught. Being on campus, I knew I needed and could obtain help. I shudder to think of what would have happened had I actually taken the course from a distance. In a reflective process lasting about 3 weeks, with the help of conversations and actions described in the components below, I reevaluated my perspectives on technology and the trust (or lack thereof) I placed in it. As my perceptions changed from this self-reflection, I became more and more comfortable with online learning and technology in general.

Reflective Discourse. Early in the dilemma, the instructor of the course explained to me what a threaded discussion was and showed me how to participate in one. He also showed me where and how to find course materials and submit assignments. Over the first several weeks of the course, I e-mailed the instructor to ensure he received my posted assignments. I also solicited the input of another more experienced graduate assistant, who took time to converse with me about the technology, confirm that it was reliable when used correctly, and verify that I was indeed using it correctly.

Action. I decided to take action by scheduling meetings with the instructor and the graduate assistant; I obtained a more informed (changed) perspective and concomitant comfort. Later on, I decided to place more trust in technology. As a result, I not only came to enjoy online courses, but I actually taught educational technology courses my last 2 years in the program.

Language

Experience. Disorientation also occurred in the online course as a result of language. I observed native speakers describing personal experiences in threaded discussions. I wondered why they shared so much information about such things as their travels and families. I was unaccustomed to this kind of discussion in classrooms and did not see how it related to academic learning, which made me uncomfortable. I found the assumption that everyone understood the subtle variances of the kind of language used in such discussions disconcerting. Native speakers used various kinds of slang without explaining the meaning. Because my culture discouraged me from asking for such explanations (for fear of "losing face"), these parts of the discussions were lost to me. Abbreviations were another cause of miscommunication. For instance, one person used the abbreviation NCLB for the "No Child Left Behind" Act. I had no idea what this meant until much later when I finally asked another student in the course what it meant. By that time, the discussion was well in the past, and I had missed more meaning and understanding. Miscommunication due to language took other forms as well. For instance, in one discussion, a student capitalized the word bad for emphasis. Mistaking BAD for an acronym, I mustered the courage to ask its meaning, only to discover that BAD meant bad and nothing more. I was embarrassed for asking what I was sure others would see as a stupid question.

Critical Reflection. As stated earlier, I initially questioned my abilities, and whether what I had learned, particularly about the English language in this respect, was worthwhile knowledge. Through discussions described below, and self-examination of my current situation, past experience in the course and further back in my educational life, I began to realize that I was not the only person in this situation. I also realized that my perceptions of inadequacy of self and education were not useful or accurate, and that I did not have to view the situation and challenges so negatively. I then began to analyze my abilities, and I asked questions concerning how best and most advantageously to change my perspective regarding my situation and relationship to the English language. I realized that, to me, the charms of language are in its flexibility, variable descriptiveness, and subtle nuances. I needed to learn the electronic lingo of American English and get over my reluctance to ask questions and participate if I were to survive the program.

Reflective Discourse. I expressed my situation and frustration to three international friends (two Chinese and one Filipino), who confessed similar feelings about language challenges in online courses. I then spoke with a very close American friend in the program who offered perspective-challenging and -changing questions like, "How many people do you suppose can speak English as a second language as well as you?" "How many people do you suppose could go to another country and undergo a doctoral program in a second language on their own merits?" and then, "Why are you not confident in your already-proven abilities?" These conversations were very influential in further critical reflection and the actions described below.

Action. First I decided that I was worthy and did indeed deserve to be in the program, and that I could use this experience to further develop and hone my English skills. I decided to view my situation as a unique, rare, and perhaps once-in-a-lifetime opportunity to experience English in a native-speaking country where I could learn all the various vernacular and colloquial usages. I went to the library to check out books on slang and read daily newspapers. I made a point to participate as actively as possible in online discussions using acronyms and idioms when possible and appropriate. I soon realized I did not need to worry about embarrassment due to lack of language skills. The more I participated, the more comfortable I became, making valuable contributions to class. I regained my confidence and established a sense of well-being. I decided not to let future challenges I would undoubtedly face hinder my attitude or progress.

Culture

Experience. As one might guess, other disorientation occurred from the challenges of cultural difference. Aside from the discomfort of discussing personal experiences in class, something not done where I come from, opportunities to share cultural information, and thus foster a sense of community, were few in the electronic, asynchronous format. I did not see evidence of encouragement for such sharing. There were no explicit instructions to share personal information, and I avoided providing cultural perspectives in assignments for fear of losing points. As a result, I felt alienated and found making acquaintances, professional contacts, and friends difficult. I also had difficulty with time management. My culture teaches students to strive for perfection and thus, only to provide the best quality information or answers to questions possible. Operating under these values caused me to spend an inordinate amount of time reading everything as thoroughly as I could, including all postings, in order to see how others were commenting and ensure I would not embarrass myself by posting something off topic, inappropriate, or misinformed. I would then wait until late in the week to post, which was often inconvenient and did not allow for flexibility in my schedule.

Critical Reflection. This form of disorientation caused me to examine critically the utility of certain cultural values in my new environment—to reassess culturally conditioned assumptions. I considered whether saving face, or placing so much emphasis on what others think about me, was important or necessary in this new culture and learning environment. I also contemplated the place of my home culture's values on perfection, reservation, and courtesy. I pondered whether I could say what I really thought and do what I really wanted in class discussions, and whether I should share course-related cultural experiences without invitation. As this reassessment continued, I worked to explore options, establishing a new plan of action.

Reflective Discourse. In this instance, online course discussions operated as reflective discourse. I observed that the natives did not hold my values toward education, and thus did not act as I did regarding the course. They seemed not to prepare as much as I had been trying to before posting to discussions, and they seemed quite comfortable interjecting personal information and topics, not only in discussions, but also in other shared assignments.

Action. Upon critical reflection and reflective discourse, I decided that the learning process and the sharing of information, experience, and knowledge was more important and valuable to me than following a protocol of reservation and perfection, especially when such protocol were adversely affecting my learning. I decided to adopt some of the native behaviors. I balanced timeliness, creativity, and quality, posting earlier and using less time to do so to capitalize on commentary and response. I also offered more information about my culture in assignments as well as discussions, making the course more meaningful to me, and hopefully, expanding the knowledge and understanding of my classmates and creating broader worldviews necessary for global interaction. Thus, my contributions enhanced the overall learning experience and outcomes of the course for everyone involved.

Implications

Hopefully, the case study above demonstrates the idea that transformative learning need not adhere to a singular, linear conception. Along with more recent, but less prevalent research, this example shows that transformation can occur on numerous levels (King & Wright, 2003; Taylor, 2008). To reiterate and forward the idea that multiple levels of transformation can occur from one experience, we offer this autoethnographic exhibition, with its multiple levels of dilemmas, critical reflection, reflective discourse, and action, spawning from one overall experience, through the conception we call *multifold transformation*.

CYCLICAL TRANSFORMATION

As suggested earlier, transformation is not always a linear or one-directional process. The concept of *cyclical transformation* conveys the idea that the transformative process can be recurrent, perhaps even rhythmic in nature (Taylor, 1997). Such cycles can occur and recur as one transitions from a familiar environment to an unfamiliar environment, and then after substantial exposure to this new environment, back to what used to be the familiar environment. Transformation occurs as a result of both transitional periods and may occur again in both instances if the cycle repeats itself, perhaps less intensely in subsequent iterations until one achieves adequate familiarity with both environments and reaches saturation, stability, or equilibrium. International students traveling to and from other countries are distinctively subject to this kind of transformation. The next case study illustrates this kind of cyclical transformation by describing the international student experiences of a colleague we will call Feng, a Chinese graduate student studying in the United States several years ago. As in the previous case study, this one uses the four major components of transformation of form and structure to present the cycling through of the experience of traveling from China to the United States, the United States back to China, and from China back to the United States.

CASE STUDY TWO

Being a highly ranked student in China and speaking her second language of English relatively proficiently, Feng was eager to come to the United States under scholarship and begin her doctoral program in communications. She was excited and proud on her first day in this new country, as she had accomplished something she barely dared to think about before. Although jet-lagged and fatigued from the new environment, she cheerfully toured her new surroundings and took copious amounts of pictures, which she dutifully sent electronically to friends and family back home. She was quick to make new friends in those first days of exposure, getting to know other students, especially a couple of other graduate assistants in the same program who happened to be American.

China to the United States

Experience. Excitement changed to discomfort as Feng began to experience cultural differences leading to disorienting dilemmas. One such instance of discomfort came when she asked one of her new friends for her cell phone number, a matter of course in China. The new friend declined, informing Feng that she did not use her cell phone much and giving her an e-mail address and office phone number instead. Another point of discomfort arose when Feng was invited to lunch by one of these new friends. At the end of the meal, Feng was surprised to learn that everyone would pay his or her own bill. In China, when friends went to lunch, the initiator always paid; others would initiate and pay another time. More academically, Feng became disillusioned initially by the demeanor of American professors and the atmosphere of the classes. Unlike their Chinese counterparts, American instructors seemed informal, relaxed, and often admitted they did not have all the answers. Moreover, students in this new culture were seemingly very "loose" in the classroom, conducting themselves very casually, daring to put themselves on a more equal level with instructors and routinely sharing personal experiences.

Critical Reflection. These and other uncomfortable experiences left Feng questioning her decision to take on this international educational endeavor and wondering whether she should go back to China. As she underwent self-reflection and critical evaluation of cultural values, Feng realized that the new customs were not really bad, just different. Through reflective discourse and actions described below, she discovered that most of the behaviors actually had some advantages. She valued the more private nature of American culture and found it liberating to decline food and drink offerings, giving information, or social invitations with no embarrassment or complications. She especially liked the simplicity of each person paying for his or her own meal during lunch or dinner outings, thus making some of her fellow Chinese students uncomfortable when she practiced the custom with them. She began to feel more comfortable in the academic environment as well, enjoying the more casual and equal nature of classes and their participants. Feng enjoyed the ability to talk to professors as colleagues, share personal experiences and knowledge of her culture with instructors and peers, bring food or drink into the classroom, or leave to get a drink or go to the bathroom at such callings. Perhaps most valuable to her was the ability to create and develop her own research ideas and projects in class.

Reflective Discourse. Reflective discourse was spread over a substantial period (perhaps months) as Feng continued to have all manner of social experiences and conversations both inside and outside of class with Americans and Chinese friends.

Action. She began to assimilate some of the behavior to operate more efficiently. She followed what seemed to be the standard American protocol of social occasions, allowing herself and others the option of being more private, less obligated to share certain contact information and details about personal life, as well as assuming responsibility only for oneself at various outings involving food and drink. Following the example of her American classmates, she gave up her customary formal behavior and acted more casual in classes, engaging in more conversation and activities, even allowing herself to enjoy the occasional snack, drink, or personal break.

The United States Back to China

Experience. After a substantial period in the United States, Feng went back to China for a summer. Upon arrival, she was surprised at the feeling of detachment. The city and streets seemed unfamiliar. Discomfort intensified as she felt the cultural pressure of obligation to attend banquets and dinners in her honor. Not only did she balk at so much food, she resented feeling forced to drink alcohol as friends and family made toast after toast to her and others. Family and friends met Feng's attempts to refuse dinners or drinks with social disapproval. Social custom extended to obligatory visits with former superiors, the seriousness and formality of which made her uncomfortable. Her mother insisted she visit all her extended family members. She spent the initial weeks as isolated as possible, feeling alienated, and not knowing what to do.

Critical Reflection. Early on, Feng missed the freedom of the United States, where people "minded their own business" and one could eat and drink or not, and visit people or not, at one's own discretion with relatively no repercussions. She also missed the leisure and freedom of the American classrooms she came to enjoy. She wanted to behave according to the perspective she had developed in the United States but knew such conduct was unacceptable in China. As time went on, Feng began to see the good in both cultures and understand the reasons behind social customs. She was then able to reach a compromise in her values and strike a balance in her actions.

Reflective Discourse. The conversations that took place during, or regarding the abovementioned occasions and visits, constituted much of the reflective discourse in which Feng engaged. She also confided in some of her closer friends in China about her feelings and consulted select friends and mentors with whom she maintained contact in the United States. These latter people, understanding more of her feelings and situation, provided Feng with nonconfrontational communion more conducive to deliberation.

Action. Feng initially resisted Chinese convention, not liking being obligated to attend social events and meetings, which she now saw as unnecessarily formal. Nor did she want to visit family and have to answer their questions. She argued with her mother in favor of staying home regardless of the social sanctions she faced. Gradually, Feng began to relent, softening her resistance into compromise. Realizing her initial attitude was fruitless and unhealthy, she decided to see the good in both cultures and incorporate desirable aspects whenever possible. By the end of summer, Feng had attended enough social events, meetings, and visits to maintain peace and reputation, eating and drinking just enough to show respect without overindulging (not an easy task). Life became easier as Feng developed her new perspective and adjusted her behavior accordingly.

China Back to the United States

Experience. When the summer ended and Feng returned to the United States, she found herself feeling uncomfortable again. The environment seemed unfamiliar.

Critical Reflection. As she analyzed the reasons for this feeling, she discovered that she caused the disorientation by her reluctance to immerse herself in a culture she knew she would eventually have to leave and would not be able to live by where she inevitably had to go.

Reflective Discourse. She consulted with counselors and confided in friends. These people helped her to realize the most effective approach to the situation was to enjoy the aspects of the culture in which she lived and the values and behavior she admired and had developed with the understanding that she would be able to adapt once again to the culture of her homeland when she returned.

Action. Feng did as her counselors and friends suggested and enjoyed being part of the American culture as long as she was there. Knowing that situations and perceptions constantly change, she decided to deal with her return to China when it actually occurred.

Implications

Emerging research and ideas about transformative learning indicate that, instead of being one-directional, the transformative process might be "more recursive, evolving, and spiraling in nature" (Taylor, 1997, p. 44). To support this notion, we offer the above ethnographic case study presented from a cyclical angle, as well as the concept of *cyclical transformation*.

CONCLUSION

Case Study One suggests that transformation can occur at multiple levels simultaneously. Moreover, it supports the idea that multiple levels of transformation can occur from one overall experience. This might suggest that one can interpret one experience in manifold ways, according to one's immersion in multiple contexts. Case Study Two supports developing research that the transformative process can occur in other than a linear fashion. It can be, in at least some instances, viewed as something akin to cyclical in nature. We chose to convey our studies using the four components purported to be standard in transformative learning in order to reinforce these ideas. Also, the way in which we have presented information hopefully conveys the idea that transformation can be chronic or acute (Brock, 2010), or perhaps both; that it does not necessarily have to follow an ordered sequence, and that the occurrence of several of its components can overlap or intertwine.

Whether or not an educator views aiding transformation as ethical and a learned skill, he or she should be able to provide education that is more effective by understanding more about the occurrence of transformative learning. In the case of international students who are a rich, concentrated, and a growing source for transformative learning, educators knowing that transformation is ripe to occur can take steps to mitigate the triggering experience. Moreover, these educators can take steps to make the outcome positive for all involved, including the international students, his or her classmates, the course instructor, and others who will experience repercussions in the future. This could be a challenge for online instructors, as the number of national and international students who enroll in online courses increases. Perhaps technology will someday make the issue obsolete; but right now, such learning experiences lack the immediate and personal interaction in which students can observe verbal inflections and visual cues so important to community building and learning. Moreover, online courses seldom provide the ability for students to meet outside of class where they share cultural information, give support, and develop personal relationships. Online educators should understand that online students and instructors only improve the learning experience for all by fostering an understanding of, and sensitive response to, cultural differences and their affects in the classroom.

Transformation is an important concept in education for producing personal growth and empowerment (Cranton, 1994). As the world and education become more accessible, and ever more people become exposed to the potential for transformative experiences, understanding transformation as comprehensively as possible becomes more of a priority for those who facilitate learning. As such understanding improves, one can discuss ethical issue concerning levels of involvement with the process and resolve conflicts at societal and personal levels. Moreover, educators of those who undergo transformation can learn how to practice in such a way as to at least not obstruct, if not facilitate the process, and take measure to promote desirable outcomes. In hopes of advancing such developments in transformative learning theory and practicality, we have offered and explained the concepts of multifold and cyclical transformation, or the ideas that transformation can occur in multiple layers and iterations. Examination can now focus on how these kinds of transformations occur, how students who experience them can be more comfortable with and empowered by them, and what educators can, and should, do to foster these conditions.

REFERENCES

Brock, S. (2010). Measuring the importance of precursor steps to transformative learning. *Adult Education Quarterly, 60*(2), 122–142.

Christofi, V., & Thompson, C. L. (2007). You cannot go home again: A phenomenological investigation of returning to the sojourn country after studying abroad [Electronic version]. *Journal of Counseling & Development, 85,* 53–63.

Clark, M. C. (1993, Spring). Transformational learning. *New Directions for Adult and Continuing Education, 57,* 47–57. doi:10.1002/ace.36719935707

Cranton, P. (1994). *Understanding and promoting transformative learning: A guide for educators of adults.* San Francisco, CA: Jossey-Boss.

Crotty, M. (1998). *The foundations of social research: Meaning and perspective in the research process.* Thousand Oaks, CA: Sage.

Erickson, D. (2007). A developmental re-forming of the phases of meaning in transformational learning. *Adult Education Quarterly, 58*(1), 61–80.

Hoff, J. (2008). Growth and transformation outcomes in international education. In V. Savicki (Ed.), *Developing intercultural competence and transformation: Theory, research, and application in international education* (pp. 92–107). Sterling, VA: Stylus.

Institute of International Education (IIE). (2011a). *Open Doors data: International student trends.* Retrieved from http://www.iie.org/Research-and-Publications/Open-Doors/Data/International-Students/Enrollment-Trends/1948-2010

Institute of International Education (IIE). (2011b). *Open Doors fast facts*. Retrieved from http://www.iie.org/Research-and-Publications/Open-Doors/Data/~/media/Files/Corporate/Open-Doors/Fast-Facts/Fast%20Facts%202010.ashx

Kegan, R. (2000). What "form" transforms? A constructive-developmental perspective on transformational learning. In J. Mezirow & Associates (Eds.), *Learning as transformation: Critical perspectives on a theory in progress* (pp. 35–70). San Francisco, CA: Jossey-Bass.

King, K., & Wright, L. (2003). New perspectives on gains in the ABE classroom: Transformational learning results considered. *Adult Basic Education, 13*(2), 100–123.

Merriam, S. B., & Caffarella, R. S. (1999). *Learning in adulthood: A comprehensive guide*. San Francisco, CA: Jossey-Bass.

Merriam, S. B., Caffarella, R. S., & Baumgartner, L. M. (2007). *Learning in adulthood: A comprehensive guide* (3rd ed.). San Francisco, CA: Jossey-Bass.

Mezirow, J. (1978). *Education for perspective transformation: Women's re-entry programs in community college*. New York, NY: Teachers College.

Mezirow, J. (1985). A critical theory of self-directed learning. In S. Brookfield (Ed.), *Self-directed learning: From theory to practice* (pp. 7–30). San Francisco, CA: Jossey-Bass.

Mezirow, J. (1990) How critical reflection triggers transformative learning. In J. Mezirow & Associates (Eds.), *Fostering critical reflection in adulthood: A guide to transformative land emancipator learning* (pp. 1–20). San Francisco, CA: Jossey-Bass.

Mezirow, J. (1991). *Transformative dimensions of adult learning*. San Francisco, CA: Jossey-Bass.

Mezirow, J. (1994). Understanding transformation theory. *Adult Education Quarterly, 44*(4), 222–232.

Mezirow, J. (1995). Transformation theory of adult learning. In M. R. Welton (Ed.), *In defense of the lifeworld* (pp. 39–70). Albany: State University of New York Press.

Mezirow, J. (1997). Transformative learning: Theory to practice. *New Directions for Adult and Continuing Education, 74*, 5–11.

Mezirow, J. (2000). Learning to think like an adult: Core concepts of transformation theory. In J. Mezirow & Associates (Eds.), *Learning as transformation* (pp. 3–33). San Francisco, CA: Jossey-Bass.

Moon, P. (2011). Bereaved elders: Transformative learning in late life. *Adult Education Quarterly, 61*(1), 22–39.

Pandit, K. (2009). Leading internationalization. *Annals of the Association of American Geographers, 99*(4), 645–656.

Savicki, V. (2008). Experiential and affective education for international educators. In V. Savicki (Ed.), *Developing intercultural competence and transformation: Theory, research, and application in international education* (pp. 92–107). Sterling, VA: Stylus.

Stake, R. (1995). *The art of case study research*. Thousand Oaks, CA: Sage.

Taylor, E. W. (1997). Building upon the theoretical debate: A critical review of the empirical studies of Mezirow's transformative learning theory. *Adult Education Quarterly, 48*(1), 34–59.

Taylor, E. W. (2005). Making meaning of the varied and contested perspectives of transformative learning theory. In D. Vlosak, G. Kielbaso, & J. Radford (Eds.), *Proceedings of the 6th International Conference on Transformative learning* (pp. 459–464). East Lansing: Michigan State University.

Taylor, E. W. (2007). An update of transformative learning theory: A critical review of the empirical research (1995–2005). *International Journal of Lifelong Education, 26*(2), 173–191.

Taylor, E. W. (2008). Transformative learning theory. *New Directions for Adult and Continuing Education, 119,* 5–15.

Taylor, E., Marienau, C., & Fiddler, M. (2000). *Developing adult learners: Strategies for teachers and trainers.* San Francisco, CA: Jossey-Bass.

CHAPTER 21

THE SELF IN TRANSFORMATION

What Gets Transformed in Transformative Learning?

Ted Fleming

Mezirow's Theory of Transformative Learning has become a well-established paradigm in which adult learning is understood. Its development and critique has taken place in journals such as *Adult Education Quarterly*, *Journal of Transformative Education*, and in a number of other publications (Mezirow, Taylor, & Associates, 2009). However, it is surprising that there is little of significance published on how frames of reference are developed in the first instance. An elaboration of the genesis of frames of reference might be suggestive as to how they could be transformed. One possible reason for this absence may be that in attempting to trace the origin and development of frames of reference one is inevitably drawn to areas of psychology such as psychoanalysis, individual life history, and the social and cultural contexts in which our meaning schemes or habits of mind are developed or indeed, to research and theory about child development.

This chapter will illustrate how Bowlby's Attachment Theory is of profound and neglected importance for understanding transformative learning. It will outline Bowlby's main ideas and current research findings on adult attachment. It will conclude with suggestive connections that will add not only to the understanding of Transformation Theory but highlight the implications for facilitating transformative learning.

JOHN BOWLBY AND ATTACHMENT THEORY

John Bowlby's (1907–1991) work as a child psychiatrist with children from poor backgrounds led him to explore the causes of delinquency (1944)—a term widely used then—the nature of the child's ties to mother (1958), the meaning of separation anxiety (1960a), and the significance of grief and mourning for young children (1960b). He outlined a theory in three volumes of *Attachment & Loss* (1969, 1973, 1980). Ainsworth made significant contributions to the theory and studied the stress resulting from separation of child and mother, called the strange situation (Ainsworth, Blehar, Waters, & Wall, 1978).

Bowlby (1973) saw both separation from the mother and social deprivation as detrimental to a child's psychological development, but the emphasis on the role of the mother should not be interpreted as in any way blaming mothers for the insecurity of children. Feminists object that Bowlby is using biology to justify what is essentially a cultural product of our own "patriarchal but father-absent" society (Holmes, 1993, p. 47). Bowlby took a dim view of anything that kept a mother from her infant, but was clear, even in early work, that "the role of a child's principal attachment-figure can be filled by others than the natural mother" (1969, pp. 303–304). The view that only the natural mother could provide care was dismissed by saying, "no such views have been expressed by me" (pp. 303–304). It could be the father who provides a secure base for the child. If the mother is blamed for the insecurity of the child, this allows society to abdicate responsibility for its role in shaping the child and also allows fathers to be absent. The primary carer, man or woman, parent or not, can perform the role of providing a secure base for the child.

Attachment is an enduring tie with a person who provides security. Bowlby observed that the child's attachment figure provides a secure base from which the infant can safely explore her environment and to which she can return if she experiences danger. Attachment is the process whereby infants and young children "develop deep confidence in their parents' protection" and this enduring tie provides security (Goldberg, 2000, p. 8). The child's experience of attachment strongly influences subsequent reactions to stress, relationships, self-esteem, sense of security, and identity. If a parent is not available through neglect, illness, or inattention, this may result in insecure attachments. Bowlby (1969) observed that the child's attachment figure appeared to provide a secure base (a developmental platform) from which infants could safely explore their environment and to which they could return if stressed or in perceived danger or need (p. 304). In their fourth year, the child can begin to tolerate separation and keep alive a sense that the caregiver, though absent, is still available. For Bowlby (1979), parenting involves providing appropriate responses to the child's need for security, but as many as one in three children grow up without this experience (p. 136).

Secure and Insecure Attachments

Children introject their experience of being cared for and as a result have a model of themselves as valued, a greater sense of "felt security," and more optimistic views of social relationships. Such children are securely attached (Bowlby, 1969, p. 339). This security is a result of the carer being sensitive (maternal sensitivity) and responsive to the needs of the child for security. Such a carer may be characterized as psychologically available to the child, emotionally expressive, and flexible in dealing with babies.

Insecure attachments have been categorized as anxious, avoidant, and disorganized. These attachments are defensive strategies that are the child's attempt to maintain contact with inconsistent or rejecting carers. The anxious attached child is preoccupied with the carer and reluctant to explore even in their presence. The carer of an anxious attached child (Bowlby, 1969, p. 338; 1973, p. 245) is more likely to be inconsistent in their responses, insensitive to signals from the child, inept at engaging in physical contact, and show little spontaneous affection (Gomez, 1997, p. 161).

The avoidant attached child is usually unconcerned with either the presence or absence of the carer and does not express attachment needs in order to avoid rejection. The primary carer in this case may exhibit low levels of response to the distress of the child, who is encouraged to get on with life and not make too many demands on the carer, who may be uncomfortable with close contact; even if the carer has positive feelings toward the child, these may be overshadowed by feelings of resentment or anger.

Finally, the disorganized attached child (Main & Solomon, 1986) is associated with consistently inadequate care, a parent who is seriously depressed, or who even subjects the child to maltreatment. In this case, the child may experience the carer as frightening and as a result, may be unable to maintain a consistent strategy for engaging in attachment behaviors.

Strange Situation

According to Ainsworth et al. (1978), when the carer leaves a young child alone in a room or when a stranger approaches, the child may experience separation anxiety. Ainsworth used this *strange situation* as an analytical tool to assess attachment style. A secure child is likely to be upset when the carer leaves but will seek comfort from her when she returns. Insecure avoidant children, on the other hand, hardly notice the presence of their carer, show few overt signs of distress when the carer leaves, and mostly ignore the carer when they do return. The anxious child is often inconsolable when the carer leaves and is not easily pacified on their return.

Internal Working Models

Attachment operates by each child developing an internal representation of their experience of relationships, an Internal Working Model (IWM) of social relating. Like an architect's model, it represents the individual's perception of the world of relationships and guides social interactions (Bowlby, 1969, p. 80; 1973, p. 237). A securely attached child has internal working models that see the world as a safe place and themselves as responsive, caring, and reliable. An insecurely attached child is more likely to be cautious toward others and see themselves as less worthy of attention and love (Holmes, 1993, p. 79). Although IWMs can be revised in the light of experience, they are not always, or indeed easily, accessible to conscious examination and change because they are laid down unconsciously in early life (Bowlby, 1973, p. 367). Parents' relationships with their children are influenced by their own IWMs, and in this way, IWMs are transmitted across generations (Bowlby, 1969, p. 348).

Mind-Mindedness

Recent research has developed the important concept of "mind-mindedness" to describe the ability of a parent to understand and respond not only to the infant's feelings but also to their thinking (Meins et al., 2002). Carers' "proclivity to comment appropriately on their infants' mental states and processes" is related in research to secure attachments (Meins et al., 2001, p. 637). Mind-mindedness is an indicator of a relationship that is more likely to produce secure attachments. Mind-mindedness reframes Bowlby's concept of maternal sensitivity and involves the carer being "willing to change her focus of attention in response to cues from the infant" (Meins et al., 2001, p. 638). An examination of these selected ideas from

Attachment Theory will be linked to Transformation Theory later in the chapter. First, one more body of research findings on adult attachment will assist in making the proposed connection with the Theory of Transformative Learning more secure.

ADULT ATTACHMENT

Attachment style and behaviors persist through life (Bowlby, 1988, p. 126) and undergo developmental transformation. Bowlby saw that

> Whatever representational models of attachment figures and of self an individual builds up during childhood and adolescence, tend to persist relatively unchanged into and throughout life. As a result he tends to assimilate any new person with whom he may form a bond, such as a spouse or child, or employer or therapist, to an existing model... and may continue to do so despite repeated evidence that the model is inappropriate. (Bowlby 1979, p. 142)

Goleman's popular work on *Social Intelligence* acknowledges the importance of a secure base for human relationships; and in researching the connection between attachment and adult relationships, he found that the secure adult is confident of a partner's love and regularly turns to the partner for support, especially when upset (2006, pp. 162–172, 194). Secure adults have internalized "rules" and strategies that allow them to be aware of when they are distressed and when to actively seek comfort from others. They are also able to engage with emotions, neither fearing them nor avoiding them and, moreover, not preoccupied with them (Goleman, 2006, p. 194). Adults with secure attachments will be better able to cope with and embrace new experiences, new ideas, and will even (of importance for adult learners) accept the supports offered. A secure attachment style is a positive indicator of success at reaching one's goals (including learning goals). Insecure adults who are anxious tend to be preoccupied with the anxiety brought on by new experiences. They are more likely to be overwhelmed with feelings of loss and are more likely to be disoriented and unable to avail themselves of support from colleagues or teachers. Anxious attached adults (including students) are likely to worry and tend to be unable to turn off the worry (Goleman, 2006, p. 196). The role of the teacher of adults then is one of building secure and safe spaces in which the anxiety is addressed and a secure base created.

Avoidant adults distance themselves cognitively and in their behavior from the source of stress (Belsky, 2002, p. 167). Those with an avoidant style overly rely on cognitive factors; may ignore or deny emotional reactions, such as anxiety or fear; and may not be able to turn on the worrying brain signals (Feeney & Noller, 1996, p. 105). Avoidant adults are less likely to seek support, are less satisfied with the support available, and mistrust those who offer support. This is in contrast to those with anxious attachments who focus on the emotional dimensions of experience rather than the cognitive aspect. Whether students are secure or insecure, this will impact on their feelings, attitudes, and behavior and how they react in a learning situation.

A secure attachment facilitates optimal motivation for achieving one's goals because it enables individuals to view achievement in positive terms and to fully focus on effective ways of reaching their goals (Eliot & Reis, 2003, p. 328). In contrast, anxious attachments undermine motivation and achievement because they lead to viewing tasks less positively. Research in this area by Eliot and Reis (2003) supports the general view that secure attachments in adulthood assist in achieving one's goals, and insecure attachments interfere with exploration and in achieving one's goals by evoking avoidance or anxiety. This adds a new dimension to our understanding of adult motivation to learn.

The internal working models (or meaning schemes) of adults affect cognitive, emotional, and behavioral responses to others in family, work, and in all communications. They affect how data is evaluated and experienced, accepted, rejected, or ignored; how communications are interpreted and responded to; and how others are evaluated. Cognitive responses may lead to giving selective attention to others and biases in memory, and they may impact inferences and explanations. Emotional response patterns and behavior are also influenced by our IWMs. In any activity that involves thinking, the question arises as to how one's IWMs influence that thinking? The thoughts we have, what we remember, what we consider important, how we interpret and make sense of events, is influenced by these models. Those with anxious attachments will focus on the emotional rather than the cognitive aspects, and those with avoidant style will overly rely on the cognitive factors and ignore or deny emotional reactions such as anxiety or fear (Feeney & Noller, 1996, p. 105). Attachment theory and the concept of IWMs help us elaborate what Mezirow (2007, p. 11) calls meaning schemes.

The strange situation is not only a reality that brings to the fore one's attachment style, it is also a precondition for learning. A teacher of adults has traditionally been described as one who initiates wonder (Aristotle, 1998, p. 7), creates perplexity (Dewey, 1933, p. 11) or, in the words of Maxine Greene (1995), makes the familiar strange. Adult education provides strange situations for learners when an adult joins a course or program for the first time or when they explore new ideas. Such experiences bring to the fore one's attachment style. This is understandable as much of the discourse in adult education centers around the anxiety of "going back to school" and the low self-confidence a learner often feels on joining a new group for the first time. In addition, these ideas of Bowlby (1969, 1973) also prompt us to see that new ideas, new points of view, and new learning can have a similar impact, even if the student has successfully navigated their way into the classroom. The ability of a learner to cope with new knowledge is hugely influenced by their strategies for coping with the strange situations brought about by new learning that triggers attachment behaviors. Students make meaning of the strange situations in ways that are consistent with their internal working models. Whether they are secure or insecure will impact on their feelings and attitudes and how they make meaning and act in these situations. The logic of the strange situation is possibly what Greene means when she talks about the teacher as stranger (Greene, 1995, p. 92).

This understanding is consistent with Bowlby's own views. For instance, Bowlby envisages the role of the therapist as providing the conditions in which a patient can explore their representational models of themselves and their attachment figures with a view to reappraising and restructuring them in the light of the new understandings acquired and the new experiences one has in the therapeutic relationship (Bowlby 1988, p. 138). He goes on to describe the role of the therapist as providing the patient with a secure base from which the past may be explored. Therapy involves assisting the patient to explore the ways he/she now engages in relations with significant others and what unconscious biases there may be in one's close or intimate relationships. The therapist encourages the patient to explore how the current situation is an expression of how one's own experiences in childhood may continue to impact on current relationships and helps in recognizing that the models the patient has of oneself and one's relationships may or may not be appropriate to the present or future, or indeed may not have been justified at all (Bowlby, 1988, p. 138). In this way, "one may cease to be a slave to old and unconscious stereotypes and to feel, think and to act in new ways" (Bowlby, 1988, p. 139). This is the site in which an understanding of how transformative learning can be understood, reframed, and facilitated.

Paying attention to the student as having a mind and feelings is not new to adult education. It is in fact a precondition for all interactions. It is a precondition for the Communicative Action of Habermas, which is so influential in the articulation of the Theory of Transformative Learning (as cited in Honneth, 1996, pp. 71–75). However, insights from attachment theory give a solid and additional grounding for attending to the student in this way, as one with a mind and feelings. Mind-mindedness is developmental. As Greene says, while emphasizing the role of the teacher in supporting learning, I see teachers "becoming a friend of someone else's mind" (1995, p. 38). Mind-mindedness is a useful way of supporting adults in the process of learning and supporting the move toward secure attachments.

MEZIROW'S THEORY OF TRANSFORMATIVE LEARNING

According to Mezirow's theory, the most significant adult learning involves becoming aware of the ways in which unquestioned assumptions that act as taken-for-granted beliefs, attitudes, and values, constrain and distort how one makes sense of the world. Frequently, these assumptions originate in childhood experiences. These unquestioned assumptions as frames of reference have two dimensions. One involves habits of expectation (meaning perspectives) that serve as filters or codes that shape, constrain, or distort our meaning making. The other involves points of view (meaning scheme) or individual beliefs, judgments, attitudes, and such (Mezirow, 2007, p. 11). Attachment styles and internal working models are good examples of psychological filters or codes that continue to influence ways of feeling and acting in adulthood. These internal working models are frames of reference as described by Mezirow (2007, p. 11).

In transformative learning theory, a key role is given to meaning as the organization of experience. Individuals order experiences, relate them to previous experiences, and use them to make decisions about how to act in the future. This organization of experience allows the individual to order and classify events and recognize feelings associated with events. By perceiving experience as having a pattern that is recognizable, one can learn (Marris, 1991, p. 78). The process of growing up is at least partly the process of developing these organizations of meaning. The activity of adult learning involves the process of changing these organizations of meaning. Transformative learning theory adds a critical dimension by emphasizing how these organizations of meaning are transformed by critical reflection on taken-for-granted assumptions.

One's attachment style and internal working models are psychological dimensions of meaning schemes. In transformation theory, it is these meaning schemes or frames of reference that get transformed (Mezirow, 2007). The internal working models are exactly what Mezirow means by psychological filters or codes "that shape and delimit and often distort our experience" (Mezirow, 2007, p. 11). One can associate the process of transformation with the development of new internal working models. It is also consistent with attachment theory and transformative learning theory to see the creation of perplexity as a prompt for transformative learning. In addition, a changed IWM may be an improvement on a previous one, and it is better if it meets Mezirow's criteria. A transformed frame of reference is "more inclusive, differentiating, more open to alternative perspectives and more integrative of experience" (Mezirow, 2007, p. 11). This may also be a good set of criteria for judging a "better" internal working model. It is at least a real possibility that development and growth are best supported by more secure attachment styles.

What gets transformed in transformation theory? Attachment styles and internal working models get transformed, and the understanding of transformation theory can thus be expanded and enhanced in a number of ways. According to Mezirow, the process of transforming a frame of reference commences with a disorienting dilemma and concludes with a reintegration into community with a new set of assumptions. This is suggestive of a process of altering or transforming one's attachment style and internal working models. Mezirow's disorienting dilemma is reminiscent of the strange situation. Each has in common an experience that what was taken for granted or assumed does not hold anymore. In the case of the child, it is the departing attachment figure or the arrival of a perceived danger, possibly another person. In the case of the adult engaged in transformative learning, it might be the apprehension felt by the arrival at new learning situations or exploration of new ideas. The strange situation has the added importance for transformation theory in that it allows us to identify the experience of disorientation as a sense that things do not fit anymore; previously taken-for-granted meanings do not hold. The profound sense of loss implied in that experience may precipitate or bring to the fore our own attachment style. If learners are secure, they are more likely to react with less anxiety and a decreased possibility of avoiding issues and situations.

As one's attachment style informs one's way of relating to others, it is suggested here that a significant kind of adult learning involves the developmental task of moving toward more secure attachments. One dimension of transformative learning involves the process of developing new internal working models. It is also consistent with attachment theory to see the creation of perplexity as a way of prompting transformative learning. Human development is being redefined here as the transformation of attachment styles and internal working models. Bowlby (1973, p. 368; 1988, p. 126) did envisage attachment as a lifelong learning project. Finally, it is the usefulness of mind-mindedness, though not carrying the full weight of critical reflection so important for transformation, that leads to seeing the importance of paying attention to one's mind that underpins the importance of a process of facilitating adult transformation.

This study of Bowlby's attachment theory allows a more thorough understanding of how society and culture construct child-rearing practices and have a profound impact not only on the child but on the entire learning life of that individual. Attachment theory provides a lifelong learning project that brings together deep psychological patterns as well as the reproduction of society. These ideas take on board, in a way reminiscent of Erich Fromm's work, how the individual and society are inextricably connected. Marris (1991, pp. 79–80) posits,

The experience of attachment is the first crucial link between sociological and psychological understanding: the experience of attachment, which so profoundly influences the growth of personality, is itself the product of a culture, and a determinant of how that culture will be reproduced in the next generation—not only the culture of attachment itself but all our ideas of order, authority, and control.

At the core of a critical adult learning theory is the necessity to imagine and theorize about how the cultures and societies in which we live and interact with influence the ways in which people relate to each other. This is helpful in understanding more thoroughly how adult learning may be enhanced or distorted by secure or insecure attachment styles and internal working models. Finally, the move toward more secure ways of relating and exploring the world is a lifelong learning project of the most significant personal and political importance.

Mind-mindedness for adults is what is being proposed. When adults develop secure attachments, as a consequence, the next generation of children learns secure attachment as well. This begins a positive cycle or attachment and facilitates continuous growth. Meaning schemes, as articulated by Mezirow (2007, p. 11), can now be understood as having a genesis in childhood experiences and in society. The process involved in the development and transformation is a lifelong learning project.

REFERENCES

Ainsworth, M. D. S., Blehar, M. C., Waters, E., & Wall, S. (1978). *Patterns of attachment*. Hillsdale, NJ: Lawrence Erlbaum.
Aristotle (1998). *The metaphysics*. New York, NY: Penguin.
Belsky, J. (2002). Developmental origins of attachment styles. *Attachment and Human Development, 4*(2), 166–170.
Bowlby, J. (1944). Forty-four juvenile thieves: Their characters and home lives. *International Journal of Psychoanalysis, 25*, 19–52.
Bowlby, J. (1958). The nature of the child's tie to his mother. *International Journal of Psychoanalysis, 39*, 350–373.
Bowlby, J. (1960a). Separation anxiety. *International Journal of Psychoanalysis, 41*, 89–113.
Bowlby, J. (1960b). Grief and mourning in infancy and early childhood. *The Psychoanalytic Study of the Child, 15*, 9–52.
Bowlby, J. (1969). *Attachment and loss Vol 1: Attachment*. New York, NY: Basic.
Bowlby, J. (1973). *Attachment and loss Vol 2: Separation, anxiety and anger*. New York, NY: Basic.
Bowlby, J. (1979). *The making and breaking of affectional bonds*. London, England: Tavistock.

Bowlby, J. (1980). *Attachment and loss Vol 3: Loss, sadness and depression.* New York, NY: Basic.

Bowlby, J. (1988). *A secure base: Clinical applications of attachment theory.* London, England: Routledge.

Dewey, J. (1933). *How we think. A restatement of the relation of reflective thinking to the educative process.* Boston, MA: DC Heath.

Eliot, A. J., & Reis, H. T. (2003). Attachment and exploration in adulthood. *Journal of Personality and Social Psychology, 85*(2), 317–331.

Feeney, J. & Noller, P. (1996). *Adult attachment.* London, England: Sage.

Goldberg, S. (2000). *Attachment and development.* London, England: Arnold.

Goleman, D. (2006). *Emotional intelligence: The new science of human relationships.* New York, NY: Random House.

Gomez, L. (1997). *An introduction to object relations.* London, England: Free Association.

Greene, M. (1995). *Releasing the imagination: Essays on education, the arts and social change.* San Francisco, CA: Jossey-Bass.

Holmes, J. (1993). *John Bowlby and attachment theory.* London, England: Routledge.

Honneth, A. (1996). *The struggle for recognition: The moral grammar of social conflicts.* Boston, MA: MIT Press.

Marris, P. (1991). The social construction of uncertainty. In C. M. Parkes, J. Stevenson-Hinde, & P. Marris (Ed.) *Attachment across the lifecycle.* London, England: Routledge.

Main, M., & Solomon, J. (1986). Discovery of a new, insecure-disorganized/disoriented attachment pattern. In T. B. Brazelton & M. Youngman (Eds.), *Affective development in infancy.* Norwood, NJ: Ablex.

Meins, E., Ferynhough, C., Wainwright, R., Gupta, M. D., Fradley, E., & Tuckey, M. (2001). Rethinking maternal sensitivity: Mothers' comments on infants' mental processes predict security of attachment at 12 months. *Journal of Child Psychology and Psychiatry, 42*(5), 637–648.

Meins, E., Ferynhough, C., Wainwright, R., Gupta, M. D., Fradley, E., & Tuckey, M. (2002). Mind-mindedness and attachment security as predictors of theory of mind understanding. *Child Development, 73*(6), 1715–1726.

Mezirow, J. (2007). Adult education and empowerment for individual and community development. In B. Connolly, T. Fleming, A. Ryan, & D. McCormack (Eds.), *Radical learning for liberation 2*, (pp. 10–17). Maynooth, Ireland: MACE.

Mezirow, J., Taylor, E., & Associates (2009). *Transformative learning in practice: Insight from community, workplace and higher education.* San Francisco, CA: Jossey-Bass.

CHAPTER 22

EXPLORING POSITIVE LIFE CHANGES IN RESPONSE TO CANCER

Perspective Transformation and Posttraumatic Growth

Allen C. Sherman, Avinash Thombre, and Stephanie Simonton

Life-threatening illnesses such as cancer confront patients with daunting burdens. Difficult challenges often include taxing treatments, altered lifestyles, and uncertainty about the future. In recent years, however, there has been growing recognition that some individuals perceive positive life changes in addition to harrowing ones. Some patients discover unexpected shifts in the way they see themselves, their relationships, or the world around them. These positive sequelae do not obscure the tumultuous changes that illness brings. However, they suggest that a greater level of complexity than sometimes assumed characterizes other diseases. Health researchers have used concepts such as "posttraumatic growth" (Tedeschi & Calhoun, 2004), "benefit-finding" (Tennen & Affleck, 2002), and "adversarial growth" (Linley & Joseph, 2004) to describe these changes. Among the most widely used and better elaborated conceptual models is posttraumatic growth.

A burgeoning literature has sought to explore perceived growth among patients with cancer. Interestingly, these efforts by health researchers have proceeded largely independently from the extensive work on transformational learning developed by adult education and communication specialists (e.g., Courtenay, Merriam, & Reeves, 1998; Mezirow, 1991, 2000; Mohammed & Thombre, 2005). For the most part, scholars from these divergent disciplines have moved in separate orbits. There may be value in cultivating greater contact and exchange.

In this chapter, we briefly explore some of the parallels between these conceptual formulations—posttraumatic growth and perspective transformation. A review of recent empirical findings among cancer patients and a consideration of some of the factors that might contribute to perceived growth in response to illness follows. Finally, we touch on some of the debates and uncertainties that have characterized work in this area and offer comments about the road ahead.

CONTRASTING POSTTRAUMATIC GROWTH AND PERSPECTIVE TRANSFORMATION

The possibility of positive changes following disorienting experiences has captured the attention of scholars across diverse disciplines. Those familiar with Mezirow's model of perspective transformation (1991, 2000), which has had a broad impact on educators and human service providers, may find much that is familiar in Tedeschi and Calhoun's model of posttraumatic growth (2004; Calhoun & Tedeschi, 2006), which has kindled considerable interest among behavioral scientists and health investigators. Posttraumatic growth involves positive changes experienced as a result of struggling with highly challenging life circumstances. A crisis (e.g., life-threatening illness) ruptures fundamental, tacit assumptions about the self and the world (e.g., Janoff-Bulman, 1992; Parkes, 1971). Preexisting beliefs and goals are unable to assimilate one's experience; instead, the individual is impelled toward the painful process of revising and rebuilding these structures in a way that can better accommodate his/her new reality. The process of schema repair sets the stage for personal growth. Cognitive processing plays a prominent role. Initial responses to traumatic experiences tend to be automatic and unbidden, marked by oscillations between intrusive ideation on the one hand and emotional numbing on the other (Horowitz, 1976; Janoff-Bulman, 1992). Over time, processing is thought to become more deliberative and reflective (Calhoun & Tedeschi, 2006). Individuals who are actively engaged in efforts to reevaluate basic assumptions and create new meanings (i.e., to reconfigure the "assumptive world") are considered most likely to demonstrate personal growth (Taku, Cann, Tedeschi, & Calhoun, 2009). In addition, the likelihood of growth is thought to be influenced by a range of other factors, including aspects of the situation (e.g., sufficiently "seismic" to shatter the assumptive world), the individual's capacity to manage ensuing emotional distress (e.g., coping), the individual's personal resources (e.g., openness to experience), and the social context (e.g., supportive responses, cultural models of growth).

There are some compelling parallels between posttraumatic growth and Mezirow's theory of perspective transformation (1991, 2000). Both frameworks construe these changes as fundamental life transitions. In both, the transition is set in motion by a disconcerting triggering situation, which Mezirow refers to as a "disorienting dilemma." According to both models, growth stems not from the dilemma itself but from struggling with the experience and creating new meaning. Both frameworks emphasize that the old working models or tacit assumptions through which experience is filtered and organized, which Mezirow labels as "meaning perspectives," are found to be limiting and inadequate. In both models, the process of revising basic assumptions is a difficult and effortful undertaking. Deliberative cognitive processing (which Mezirow refers to as "premise reflection") plays a critical role in both formulations. Finally, the immediate social environment and broader culture context are a strong influence in both frameworks.

Of course, these models are not without their salient differences. For example, Tedeschi and Calhoun (2004; Calhoun & Tedeschi, 2006) have devoted more attention to formulating specific domains or areas of life in which growth may emerge (i.e., altered relationships, an enhanced sense of personal strength, a heightened appreciation for life, deepened spirituality, and new possibilities/goals). Another difference concerns the circumstances thought to precipitate growth. For Mezirow (1991), in keeping with his roots in higher education, the "disorienting dilemma" may include commonplace occurrences such as poems or pictures as well as more "epochal" events. For Tedeschi and Calhoun (2004), who ground their model in trauma work, the triggering circumstances are severely disruptive. Both models consider factors that might contribute to growth; however, Tedeschi and Calhoun's framework more fully articulates the potential impact of the type of triggering event, the personal resources that an individual brings to it, and the supportive responses the person receives from others. Moreover, the role of intrusive or automatic cognitive processing (commonly observed among trauma patients) has greater weight in Tedeschi and Calhoun's model as an initial response to the crisis. Both models highlight the importance of effortful, deliberative processing in revising core assumptions and creating new meaning. However, Mezirow's formulation depicts a more distinctly rational, logical analysis ("critical reflection"), though nonlinguistic intuitive processing ("presentational construal") tempers the model. The role of personal intent ("line of action"), of authenticating new understanding (i.e., "rational discourse"), and of taking concrete action once assumptions have been restructured, also receive somewhat greater weight in Mezirow's model. Finally, Mezirow identifies a series of 10 phases involved in the process of transformation, each of which contributes to clarified meaning (Brock, 2010).

Positive Changes Among Cancer Patients

A rapidly expanding body of research has examined positive perceived changes in response to the crisis of cancer. For the most part, researchers construed these changes as posttraumatic growth or benefit finding; few oncology studies explicitly addressed perspective transformation (e.g., Thombre & Sherman, 2009; Thombre, Sherman, & Simonton, 2010), though as noted, there is considerable overlap among these constructs. In studies across a range of different malignancies, a large proportion of patients have pointed to favorable outcomes (for reviews, see Sawyer, Ayers, & Field, 2010; Stanton, Bower, & Low, 2006). Positive sequelae have emerged whether these experiences were explored using open-ended inquiries or standardized instruments. Prevalence estimates are variable (e.g., the number of participants reporting at least one positive change has ranged from 53% to 91%; Fromm, Andrykowski, & Hunt, 1996; Sears, Stanton, & Danoff-Burg, 2003; Tallman, Shaw, Schultz, & Altmaier, 2010; Taylor, Lichtman, & Wood, 1984). Clearly, however, many patients believe that their confrontation with illness has brought beneficial as well as seriously adverse alterations in their lives. Moreover, several studies indicated higher reports of growth among cancer patients relative to healthy controls (e.g., Andrykowski et al., 2005; Cordova, Cunningham, Carlson, & Andrykowski, 2001; Tomich, Helgeson, & Vache, 2005; see Frazier & Kaler, 2006 for conflicting results).

Factors Contributing to Positive Changes

What factors contribute to positive perceived changes among cancer patients? Table 22.1 summarizes some of the interesting results.

Findings regarding *demographic background* have been highly variable. Younger patients, women, and those from ethnic minority groups have reported higher levels of growth in some studies (for reviews, see Helgeson, Reynolds, & Tomich, 2006; Stanton et al., 2006). However, other investigations have reported null findings (e.g., Bellizzi, Miller, Arora, & Rowland,

TABLE 22.1 Correlates of Perceived Growth Among Cancer Patients

Variable	Promising Findings	Inconsistent Findings
Demographic background (e.g., age, gender, education)		✔
Illness characteristics (e.g., stage, time since diagnosis, treatment modalities)		✔
Subjective appraisals of disease threat	✔	
Intrusive ideation		✔
Efforts to reevaluate worldviews/ deliberative cognitive processing	✔	
Coping via positive reframing, religious coping, or active coping	✔	
Social support received	✔	
Optimism		✔

2007; Harrington, McGurk, & Llewellyn, 2008; Schulz & Mohamed, 2004). Similarly, basic *medical characteristics* (e.g., tumor stage, time since diagnosis, type of treatment) have demonstrated inconsistent and often negligible relationships with perceived growth (e.g., Cordova et al., 2007; Kinsinger et al., 2006; Lelorain, Bonnaud-Antignac, & Florin, 2010; Schroevers, Helgeson, Sanderman, & Rachor, 2010; Urcuyo, Boyers, Carver, & Antoni, 2005). On the other hand, patients' *subjective appraisals* of threat have been somewhat more reliably tied to perceived growth (e.g., Cordova et al., 2001; Cordova et al., 2007; Sears et al., 2003; Widows, Jacobsen, Booth-Jones, & Fields, 2005; for exceptions see Thombre et al., 2010; Weiss, 2004). This finding is in keeping with Tedeschi and Calhoun's (2004) model, which posits that the crisis must be sufficiently jarring to rupture core assumptions.

Emotionally laden, *intrusive ideation* is often an initial response to disruptive events. The posttraumatic growth model (Calhoun & Tedeschi, 2006) posits that automatic, unbidden ideation reflects preliminary efforts to integrate the experience—an early step in a process that, for some, ultimately leads to growth (Taku et al., 2009). Within the oncology setting, however, empirical findings have been inconsistent; some investigations noted associations between intrusive ideation and perceived growth (Jaarsma, Pool, Sanderman, & Ranchor, 2006; Mystakidou, Tsilika, Parpa, Galanos, & Vlahos, 2008; Sears et al., 2003) while others did not (e.g., Carboon, Anderson, Pollard, Szer, & Seymour, 2005; Cordova et al., 2001; Manne et al., 2004). Thus, this remains an area for further study.

Beyond the effects of intrusive ideation, the models of Tedeschi and Calhoun (2004) and Mezirow (1991) both highlight the importance of more purposeful, *deliberative cognitive processing* in contributing to growth. In particular, they underscore the process of reevaluating core assumptions (i.e., the "assumptive world," or "meaning perspectives") that new circumstances challenged. This has been a point of considerable debate in both the adult education (e.g., Courtenay et al., 1998; Merriam, 2004; Taylor, 1997) and behavioral science (McMillen, 2004; Wortman, 2004) literatures. Some writers have questioned the centrality of schema reconstruction and the portrayal of it in a deliberative, reflective manner.

To what extent is growth propelled by efforts to reconstruct basic schemas or worldviews? Preliminary investigations offered little evidence to support this hypothesis (Carboon et al., 2005; Park, 2004; Park & Fenster, 2004). However, these studies assessed the *content* of basic beliefs (e.g., expectations of fairness or benevolence) rather than perceived disruptions and reevaluation of these beliefs (Thombre et al., 2010). Recent investigations have focused more specifically on participants' efforts to reappraise core assumptions in response to life crises (i.e., process rather than outcome) (Cann et al., 2010; Park, Edmondson, Fenster, & Blank, 2008; Thombre et al., 2010). Research with leukemia patients, for example, suggested that those who devoted greater efforts to reconsidering core beliefs or worldviews in the wake of their illness in turn reported greater personal growth (Cann et al., 2010). We found similar results in a qualitative study (Thombre & Sherman, 2010) and in a subsequent quantitative investigation (Thombre et al., 2010) among cancer patients in India. More broadly, outside of the cancer literature, other studies have underscored the effects of deliberative cognitive processing after various types of crises (e.g., Nolen-Hoeksema & Davis, 2004; Taku, Calhoun, Cann, & Tedeschi, 2008; Taku et al., 2009). Together, these investigations imply that "cognitive work" or active reflection may play a significant role in promoting growth.

Other studies have explored the influence of *coping*. One might expect more effective coping strategies to enhance one's possibilities for adaptation and transformation. Perhaps not surprisingly, positive reframing (i.e., efforts to recognize benefits in the illness) has been associated with increased reported growth in cross-sectional and longitudinal studies (Harrington et al., 2008; Porter et al., 2006; Schroevers & Teo, 2008; Sears et al., 2003; Widows et al., 2005). Additionally, religious coping (Lelorain et al., 2010; Schroevers & Teo, 2008; Urcuyo et al., 2005) and active coping (e.g., Kinsinger et al., 2006; Lelorain et al., 2010; Luszczynska, Mohamed, & Schwarzer, 2005; Schroevers & Teo, 2008) were tied to increased perceived growth. Similar findings have emerged in other populations (Prati & Pietrantoni, 2009).

Investigators also have examined different dimensions of *social support* (e.g., received vs. available; positive vs. negative reactions). A more receptive social environment provides emotional encouragement, alternate perspectives, and perhaps role models for growth. Consistent with these expectations, in the broader literature, higher levels of support related to greater perceived growth (Helgeson et al., 2006; Prati & Pietrantoni, 2009). Among cancer patients, findings have varied somewhat according to the particular type of support examined. The strongest results have emerged for the role of support *received* by the individual (as opposed to simply being available). In several studies, increased received support was related concurrently (Schwarzer, Luszczynska, Boehmer, Taubert, & Knoll, 2006) and prospectively (Schwarzer et al., 2006, Schroevers et al., 2010; Schulz & Mohamed, 2004) to increased perceived growth. Findings have been mixed regarding other domains, such as available support (e.g., Bellizzi et al., 2007; Bozo, Gundogdu, & Buyukasik-Colak, 2009; Pinqart, Frohlich, & Silbereisen, 2007; Porter et al., 2006; Schroevers et al., 2010), or negative, undermining reactions (i.e., Cordova et al., 2001; Cordova et al., 2007). Additional dimensions of support that merit further exploration include having role models for growth (Weiss, 2004), and discussing these changes with others (Cordova et al., 2001).

Another area of study has focused on *personality characteristics*. One might expect patients who come to the illness with greater personal resources to experience the greatest growth. Alternately, however, individuals with ample, adaptive resources, whose preexisting assumptions remain essentially unchallenged, might have little opportunity for growth. Much of the research on personality variables has focused on optimism. Investigations among cancer patients have yielded mixed results (e.g., Bellizzi et al., 2007; Bozo et al., 2009; Harrington et al., 2008; Pinqart et al., 2007; Tallman et al., 2010; Urcuyo et al., 2005), perhaps due in part to the particular version of the optimism measure that was used. Other personal factors that might shape the experience have yet to receive much attention among cancer patients, including, for example, emotional expression (Mann et al., 2004), openness to experience (Jaarsma et al., 2006), tolerance for ambivalence, and cognitive complexity.

In sum, increased perceived growth in response to cancer has been associated with a number of personal and contextual factors, including appraisals of the illness as more threatening or stressful, greater efforts to reevaluate core assumptions, increased reliance on adaptive coping strategies, and increased received support from others. Further research using longitudinal designs and medically homogenous samples would help confirm these relationships and clarify how they change across different phases of illness. In view of its theoretical importance, there is a need for more work to examine deliberative cognitive processing, including patients' efforts to reevaluate violated beliefs and goals ("premise reflection"). Thus far, much of this research has relied on cross-sectional designs (see Park et al., 2008 for an exception). Moreover, few investigations have focused explicitly on how patients restructure personal goals rather than only beliefs (for examples, see Emmons, Colby, & Kaiser, 1998; Lykins, Segerstrom, Averill, Evans, & Kemeny, 2007; Neter, Litvak, & Miller, 2009)—this would be a fruitful direction for future research. More broadly, there is a need to distinguish among different kinds of helpful and less adaptive cognitive processing in response to health crises (e.g., social comparisons, causal attributions, benefit-seeking, etc.). Some progress has been made in developing assessment tools to facilitate this work (e.g., Pakenham, 2007; Williams, Davis, & Millsap, 2002), but further refinement would be an important next step.

Questions, Controversies, and Future Directions

How well do conceptual models of posttraumatic growth and perspective transformation fit with empirical findings? Clearly, a large number of patients report positive as well as negative personal changes in response to illness. Favorable changes seem evident regardless of the particular approach used to assess these experiences (e.g., narratives, standardized measures).

What these changes represent is somewhat less clear. First, there is ambiguity as to whether all the positive changes reported among cancer patients necessarily rise to the level of "growth" or "transformation." No doubt some changes reflect modest, circumscribed outcomes (i.e., recognition of "benefits") as opposed to fundamental shifts in underlying meaning structures and ways of relating to the world (i.e., "growth/transformation"). There is considerable overlap among different measures of positive change (e.g., Perceived Benefit Scale, Posttraumatic Growth Inventory, Thriving Scale; Joseph et al., 2005). Nonetheless, preliminary evidence suggests that "posttraumatic growth" is distinct from "benefit-finding" (e.g., Sears et al., 2003); much more work needs to be done in this area.

Most approaches to evaluating growth have focused on which domains of life have been altered (e.g., changes in self, relationships, philosophy of life) or which underlying schemas have been reevaluated (e.g., religious beliefs, fairness, control). However, another approach is to consider the structure rather than only the content of altered beliefs and goals. For Mezirow (1991), transformed perspectives are those that have become "more inclusive, discriminating, integrative, and permeable (open)" (p. 193). Surprisingly few empirical studies have sought to examine these features. Interesting methods developed to assess structural characteristics of cognitive processing (e.g., Segerstrom, Stanton, Alden, & Shortridge, 2003) and goal strivings (Emmons et al., 1998; Pöhlmann, Gruss, & Joraschky, 2006) might be helpful in discriminating modest changes from transformative ones.

Aside from ambiguity regarding which positive outcomes reflect fundamental transformation as opposed to more peripheral changes, there is also uncertainty as to whether these accounts are real or illusory. Most of the research reviewed in this chapter relied on participants' retrospective judgments. On the one hand, there is no one better positioned than these individuals themselves to observe the complex alternations in their lives. On the other hand, however, self-reports of change may be markedly influenced by recall biases and self-enhancement processes (e.g., McFarland & Alvaro, 2000; Tennen & Affleck, 2009; Widows et al., 2005). For example, research on temporal comparison processes has shown that individuals tend to enhance self-worth by derogating their past selves, inaccurately recalling their previous attributes as less favorable than their current qualities (Widows et al., 2005; Wilson & Ross, 2001). As a result of these and other biases, perceived change may have little relationship to actual change (Frazier et al., 2009). Thus, there has been longstanding debate as to whether accounts of growth represent substantive changes or adaptive illusions (Taylor & Armor, 1996).

Other investigators have supported retrospective assessments of growth, noting that individuals often relate painful changes as well as positive ones—a pattern that seems more credible than blanket endorsements of improvements. Moreover, social desirability bias (e.g., Park, Cohen & Murch, 1996; Weinrib, Rothrock, Johnsen, & Lutgendorf, 2006) is not a strong influence on commonly used instruments. In several investigations (Park et al., 1996; Shakespeare-Finch & Enders, 2008; Thombre et al, 2010), self-reports of growth have been modestly but significantly corroborated by family or friends. Finally, more recent versions of these instruments have been modified to include negative as well as positive changes, with the expectation that this may diminish response bias (e.g., Baker, Kelly, Calhoun, Cann, & Tedeschi, 2008; Joseph et al., 2005). Some conceptual frameworks (Zoellner & Maerker, 2006) suggest that growth involves *both* components: illusory coping efforts, which are prominent at first and preserve core assumptions; and a subsequent self-transcendent experience, which transforms core assumptions. Among patients undergoing radiotherapy, retrospective judgments of growth seemed to encompass both veridical and illusory processes. Self-reported growth related both to *actual* changes over time in personal goals, and to *perceived* (but not actual) changes in personal characteristics (Ransom, Sheldon, & Jacobsen, 2008).

On the whole, the meaning of personal accounts of growth or transformation remains uncertain. Studies that use prospective designs to examine positive outcomes on repeated occasions over time will be more revealing than those that rely solely on retrospective judgments (Tennen & Affleck, 2009). Efforts to discover how perceived growth has resulted in actual changes in day-to-day behavior (e.g., new volunteer work or religious practices), or in alterations that are evident to loved ones, will be helpful as well. Although these approaches have their own limitations (i.e., internalized shifts in meaning structures may not always be evident in overt behavior), a number of writers have emphasized that taking action is an essential element of genuine growth (Hobfoll, Canettii-Nisim, Galea, Johnson, & Palmieri, 2007; Mezirow, 1991).

Questions also remain regarding the *process* of growth or transformation in response to illness. Under what circumstances is growth experienced as deliberative and purposeful versus more reflexive and automatic (McMillan, 2004; Tedeschi & Calhoun, 2004)? Moreover, when does one experience gradual and incremental versus a more abrupt, discontinuous change? Both conceptual models emphasize the conscious, effortful nature of reconstituting core assumptions—reworking valued goals and beliefs that no longer seem viable (Calhoun & Tedeschi, 1998; Mezirow, 1991). According to Tedeschi & Calhoun (2004), one typically experiences the process as an arduous struggle to keep one's head above water, not a sunny search for enlightenment. A sense of growth often seems to emerge spontaneously—a surprising discovery (Calhoun & Tedeschi, 1998; Mezirow, 1991). Overall, however, we know little about the factors that might contribute to the experience of growth as gradual versus sudden, or purposeful versus unintended. These writers have speculated about divergent pathways to growth (e.g., the influence of prelinguistic, intuitive "presentational" processing [Mezirow, 1991] or "chaotic" cognitive styles [Calhoun & Tedeschi, 1998]), but systematic research remains quite limited.

Somewhat more information is available about the timing of posttraumatic growth relative to the triggering experience. Although sometimes growth or transformation requires a considerable period of time, research with cancer patients suggests that this is not necessarily the case. Studies conducted at different points in the trajectory of disease, from diagnosis through treatment and long-term survivorship, have demonstrated perceived growth early in the course of care (e.g., Manne et al., 2004; Thombre et al., 2010); very long intervals may not be required. Some writers are skeptical about the veracity of growth reported in the early aftermath of stressful events, suggesting that these accounts are apt to reflect positive illusions rather than substantive change (Sumalla, Ochoa, Blanco, 2009; Zoellner & Maerker, 2006). Thus far, there is little evidence to go on, and this remains an open question.

Other investigators have begun to explore how growth may continue to change and evolve over the course of illness and recovery. Some longitudinal studies have noted increased reports of positive change over time (Pinquart et al., 2007; Schwarzer et al., 2006; Tomich & Helgeson, 2004). Of course, these group averages mask more diverse patterns among individual participants, with increases among some in tandem with decrements among others. Tracking these individual trajectories of growth or transformation may be especially illuminating.

Finally, another intriguing area that has begun to receive greater attention involves the cultural context in which growth or transformation unfolds. Some writers initially questioned whether posttraumatic growth would have much relevance outside of the United States, given the importance Americans ascribe to triumphing over adversity and embracing happy endings (McMillan, 2004; Pals & McAdams, 2004). However, a number of investigations have evaluated perceived growth among cancer patients in very different cultural settings, including Turkey (Bozo et al., 2009), Hong Kong (Ho, Chan, & Ho, 2004), Malaysia (Schroevers & Teo, 2008), and India (Thombre & Sherman, 2009; Thombre et al., 2010); similarly, other studies have documented perceived growth following other types of traumatic experiences in diverse regions of the world (e.g., Taku et al., 2008; Taku et al., 2009). These studies have been noteworthy in verifying the prevalence of perceived growth or transformation in non-Western settings. However, few studies have focused specifically on how distinctive features of the cultural landscape might color growth. In previous work, we explored the experience of patients with recently diagnosed cancer in Western India. Among the salient themes that seemed tied to transformation were culturally embedded beliefs about the cycle of life and death, karma (the consequences of one's actions), and dharma (one's duty at each phase of the life cycle) (Thombre & Sherman, 2009; Thombre et al., 2010). There needs to be further research to help clarify how socially constructed roles, beliefs, goals, and epistemologies may facilitate growth, or constrain it. Table 22.2 lists a summary of some of the intriguing questions that merit future study.

TABLE 22.2 Areas for Further Study Regarding Perceived Growth Among Cancer Patients

Target Area

Exploring changes in perceived growth over the course of illness

Distinguishing actual growth from adaptive illusions, at different phases of illness

Discriminating peripheral/minor positive changes from more central/transformative ones

Examining the structural characteristics of new beliefs or goals (e.g., level of differentiation, complexity, permeability, or conflict among them)

Exploring process characteristics of perceived growth (i.e., gradual vs. discontinuous; effortful vs. unintended changes)

Investigating types of deliberative cognitive processing that might contribute to growth, such as sense-making (e.g., causal attributions, information-seeking, religious frameworks) or benefit-seeking (e.g., search for personal, relational, or existential changes)

Charting cultural influences on perceived growth

Exploring eudemonic or positive outcomes that may be associated with perceived growth (e.g., wisdom, forgiveness, gratitude, altruism, empathy, acceptance of mortality)

Examining behavioral or physiological correlates of perceived growth that might influence health outcomes (e.g., lifestyle changes, treatment adherence, decision making about treatment options, symptom reporting, changes in neuro-endocrine function or proinflammatory cytokines)

CONCLUSIONS

Perceptions of personal growth in response to cancer are not uncommon. Clearly, it would be a tragic disservice to romanticize the burdens that patients experience; cancer is not a self-improvement exercise. Nonetheless, some individuals report *both* buffeting and enrichment of their lives as a result of their struggle with illness. The meaning of these positive changes, and the forces that propel them, have become the subject of intensive inquiry. For the most part, efforts to understand life transitions within the framework of posttraumatic growth have proceeded separately from similar efforts undertaken by scholars studying perspective transformation. We look forward to a more active dialogue among these investigators as they continue to explore the complex and creative ways in which individuals adapt to "epochal," life-altering events.

REFERENCES

Andrykowski, M. A., Bishop, M. M., Hahn, E. A., Cella, D. F., Beaumount, J. L., Brady, M. J., ... Wingard, J. R. (2005). Long-term health-related quality of life, growth, and spiritual well-being after hematopoietic stem-cell transplantation. *Journal of Clinical Oncology, 23*, 599–608.

Baker, J. M., Kelly, C., Calhoun, L. G., Cann, A., & Tedeschi, R. G. (2008). An examination of posttraumatic growth and posttraumatic depreciation: Two exploratory studies. *Journal of Loss and Trauma, 13*, 450–465.

Bellizzi, K. M., Miller, M. F., Arora, N. K., & Rowland, J. H. (2007). Positive and negative life changes experienced by survivors of non-Hodgkin's lymphoma. *Annals of Behavioral Medicine, 34*, 188–199.

Bozo, O., Gundogdu, E., & Buyukasik-Colak, C. (2009). The moderating role of different sources of perceived social support on the dispositional optimism-posttraumatic growth relationship in postoperative breast cancer patients. *Journal of Health Psychology, 14*, 1009–1020.

Brock, S. E. (2010). Measuring the importance of precursor steps to transformative learning. *Adult Education Quarterly, 60*, 122–142.

Calhoun, L. G., & Tedeschi, R. G. (1998). Posttraumatic growth: Future directions. In R. G. Tedeschi, C. L. Park, & L. G. Calhoun (Eds.), *Posttraumatic growth: Positive changes in the aftermath of crisis* (pp. 211–238). Mahwah, NJ: Lawrence Erlbaum.

Calhoun, L. G., & Tedeschi, R. G. (2006). The foundations of posttraumatic growth: An expanded framework. In L. G. Calhoun, & R. G. Tedeschi (Eds.), *Handbook of posttraumatic growth: Research and practice* (pp. 3–23). Mahwah, NJ: Lawrence Erlbaum.

Cann, A., Calhoun, L. G., Tedeschi, R. G., Kilmer, R. P., Gil-Rivas, V., Vishnevsky, T., & Danhauer, S. C. (2010). The Core Beliefs Inventory: A brief measure of disruption in the assumptive world. *Anxiety, Stress, & Coping, 23*, 19–34.

Carboon, I., Anderson, V. A., Pollard, A., Szer, J., & Seymour, J. F. (2005). Posttraumatic growth following a cancer diagnosis: Do world assumptions contribute? *Traumatology, 11,* 269–283.

Cordova, M. J., Cunningham, L. L. C., Carlson, C. R., & Andrykowski, M. A. (2001). Posttraumatic growth following breast cancer: A controlled comparison study. *Health Psychology, 20,* 176–185.

Cordova, M. J., Giese-Davis, J., Golant, M., Kronenwetter, C., Change, V., & Spiegel, D. (2007). Breast cancer as trauma: Posttraumatic stress and posttraumatic growth. *Journal of Clinical Psychology in Medical Settings, 14,* 308–319.

Courtenay, B. C., Merriam, S. B., & Reeves, P. M. (1998). The centrality of meaning-making in transformational learning: How HIV-positive adults make sense of their lives. *Adult Education Quarterly, 48*(2), 65–84.

Emmons, R. A., Colby, P. M., & Kaiser, H. A. (1998). When losses lead to gains: Personal goals and the recovery of meaning. In P. T. P. Wong, & P. S. Fry (Eds.), *The human quest for meaning: A handbook of psychological research and clinical applications* (pp. 163–178). Mahwah, NJ: Lawrence Erlbaum.

Frazier, P. A., & Kaler, M. E. (2006). Assessing the validity of self-reported stress-related growth. *Journal of Consulting and Clinical Psychology, 74,* 859–869.

Frazier, P., Tennen, H., Gavian, M., Park, C., Tomich, P., & Tashiro, T. (2009). Does self-reported posttraumatic growth reflect genuine positive change? *Psychological Science, 20,* 912–919.

Fromm, K., Andrykowski, M. A., & Hunt, J. (1996). Positive and negative sequelae of bone marrow transplantation: Implications for quality of life assessment. *Journal of Behavioral Medicine, 19,* 221–240.

Harrington, S., McGurk, M., & Llewellyn, C. D. (2008). Positive consequences of head and neck cancer: Key correlates of finding benefit. *Journal of Psychosocial Oncology, 26,* 43–62.

Helgeson, V. S., Reynolds, K. A., & Tomich, P. L. (2006). A meta-analytic review of benefit finding and growth. *Journal of Consulting and Clinical Psychology, 74,* 797–816.

Ho, S. M. Y., Chan, C. L. W., & Ho, R. T. H. (2004). Posttraumatic growth in Chinese cancer survivors. *Psycho-Oncology, 13,* 377–389.

Hobfoll, S. E., Canetti-Nisim, D., Galea, S., Johnson, R. J., & Palmieri, P. A. (2007). Refining our understanding of posttraumatic growth in the face of terrorism: Moving from meaning cognitions to doing what is meaningful. *Applied Psychology, 56,* 345–366.

Horowitz, M. J. (1976). *Stress response syndromes.* New York, NY: Aronson.

Jaarsma, T. A., Pool, G., Sanderman, R., & Ranchor, A. V. (2006). Psychometric properties of the Dutch version of the Posttraumatic Growth Inventory among cancer patients. *Psycho-Oncology, 15,* 911–920.

Janoff-Bulman, R. (1992). *Shattered assumptions: Toward a new psychology of trauma.* New York, NY: Free Press.

Joseph, S., Linley, P. A., Andrews, L., Harris, G., Howle, B., Woodward, C., & Shevlin, M. (2005). Assessing positive and negative changes in the aftermath of adversity: Psychometric evaluation of the Changes in Outlook questionnaire. *Psychological Assessment, 17,* 70–80.

Kinsinger, D. P., Penedo, F. J., Antoni, M. H., Dahn, J. R., Lechner, S., & Schneiderman, N. (2006). Psychosocial and sociodemographic correlates of benefit-finding in men treated for localized prostate cancer. *Psycho-Oncology, 15,* 954–961.

Lelorain, S., Bonnaud-Antignac, A., & Florin, A. (2010). Long term posttraumatic growth after breast cancer: Prevalence, predictors, and relationships with psychological health. *Journal of Clinical Psychology in Medical Settings, 17,* 14–22.

Linley, P. A., & Joseph, S. (2004). Positive change following trauma and adversity: A review. *Journal of Traumatic Stress, 17,* 11–21.

Luszczynska, A., Mohamed, N. E., & Schwarzer, R. (2005). Self-efficacy and social support predict benefit finding 12 months after cancer surgery: The mediating role of coping strategies. *Psychology, Health, & Medicine, 10,* 365–375.

Lykins, E. L. B., Segerstrom, S. C., Averill, A. J., Evans, D. R., & Kemeny, M. E. (2007). Goal shifts following reminders of mortality: Reconciling posttraumatic growth and terror management theory. *Personality and Social Psychology Bulletin, 33,* 1088–1099.

Manne, S., Ostroff, J., Winkel, G., Goldstein, L., Fox, K., & Grana, G. (2004). Posttraumatic growth after breast cancer: Patient, partner, and couple perspectives. *Psychosomatic Medicine, 66,* 442–454.

McFarland, C., & Alvaro, C. (2000). The impact of motivation on temporal comparisons: Coping with traumatic events by perceiving personal growth. *Journal of Personality and Social Psychology, 79,* 327–343.

McMillen, J. C. (2004). Posttraumatic growth: What's it all about? *Psychological Inquiry, 15,* 48–52.

Merriam, S. B. (2004). The role of cognitive development in Mezirow's transformational learning theory. *Adult Education Quarterly, 55,* 60–68

Mezirow, J. (1991). *Transformative dimensions of adult learning.* San Francisco, CA: Jossey-Bass.

Mezirow, J. (2000). Learning to think like an adult. In J. Meziow & Associates (Eds.), *Learning as transformation: Critical perspectives on a theory in progress* (pp. 3–33). San Francisco, CA: Jossey-Bass.

Mohammed, S. N., & Thombre, A. (2005). HIV/AIDS stories on the World Wide Web and transformative perspective. *Journal of Health Communication, 10*(4), 347–360.

Mystakidou, K., Tsilika, E., Parpa, E., Galanos, A., & Vlahos, L. (2008). Posttraumatic growth in advanced cancer patients receiving palliative care. *British Journal of Health Psychology, 13,* 633–646.

Neter, E., Litvak, A., & Miller, A. (2009). Goal disengagement and goal re-engagement among multiple sclerosis patients: Relationship to well-being and illness representation. *Psychology and Health, 24,* 175–186.

Nolen-Hoeksema, S., & Davis, C. G. (2004). Theoretical and methodological issues in the assessment and interpretation of posttraumatic growth. *Psychological Inquiry, 15,* 60–64.

Pakenham, K. I. (2007). Making sense of multiple sclerosis. *Rehabilitation Psychology, 136,* 257–301.

Pals, J. L., & McAdams, D. P. (2004). The transformed self: A narrative understanding of posttraumatic growth. *Psychological Inquiry, 15,* 65–68.

Park, C. L. (2004). The notion of growth following stressful life experiences: Problems and prospects. *Psychological Inquiry, 15,* 69–76.

Park, C. L., Cohen, L., & Murch, R. (1996). Assessment and prediction of stress-related growth. *Journal of Personality, 64,* 71–105.

Park, C. L., Edmondson, D., Fenster, J. R., & Blank, T. O. (2008). Meaning making and psychological adjustment following cancer: The mediating roles of growth, life meaning, and restored just-world beliefs. *Journal of Consulting and Clinical Psychology, 76,* 863–875.

Park, C. L., & Fenster, J. R. (2004). Stress-related growth: Predictors of occurrence and correlates with psychological adjustment. *Journal of Social and Clinical Psychology, 23,* 195–215.

Parkes, C. M. (1971). Psycho-social transitions: A field for study. *Social Science and Medicine, 5,* 101–115.

Pinguart, M., Frohlich, C., & Silbereisen, R. K. (2007). Cancer patients' perceptions of positive and negative illness-related changes. *Journal of Health Psychology, 12,* 907–921.

Pöhlmann, K., Gruss, B., & Joraschky, P. (2006). Structural properties of personal meaning systems: A new approach to measuring meaning in life. *Journal of Positive Psychology, 1,* 109–117.

Porter, L. S., Clayton, M. F., Belyea, M., Mishel, M., Gil, K. M., & Germino, B. B. (2006). Predicting negative mood state and personal growth in African American and White long-term breast cancer survivors. *Annals of Behavioral Medicine, 31,* 195–204.

Prati, G., & Pietrantoni, L. (2009). Optimism, social support, and coping strategies as factors contributing to posttraumatic growth: A meta-analysis. *Journal of Loss and Trauma, 14,* 364–388.

Ransom, S., Sheldon, K. M., & Jacobsen, P. B. (2008). Actual change and inaccurate recall contribute to posttraumatic growth following radiotherapy. *Journal of Consulting and Clinical Psychology, 76,* 811–819.

Sawyer, A., Ayers, S., & Field, A. P. (2010). Posttraumatic growth and adjustment among individuals with cancer or HIV/AIDS: A meta-analysis. *Clinical Psychology Review, 30,* 436–447.

Schroevers, M. J., Helgeson, V. S., Sanderman, R., & Rachor, A. V. (2010). Type of social support matters for prediction of posttraumatic growth among cancer survivors. *Psycho-Oncology, 19,* 46–53.

Schroevers, M. J., & Teo, I. (2008). The report of posttraumatic growth in Malaysian cancer patients: Relationships with psychological distress and coping strategies. *Psycho-Oncology, 17,* 1239–1246.

Schulz, U., & Mohamed, N. E. (2004). Turning the tide: Benefit finding after cancer surgery. *Social Science and Medicine, 59,* 653–662.

Schwarzer, R., Luszczynska, A., Boehmer, S., Taubert, S., & Knoll, N. (2006). Changes in finding benefit after cancer surgery and the prediction of well-being one year later. *Social Science and Medicine, 63,* 1614–1624.

Sears, S. R., Stanton, A. L., & Danoff-Burg, S. (2003). The Yellow Brick Road and the Emerald City: Benefit finding, positive reappraisal coping, and posttraumatic growth in women with early-stage breast cancer. *Health Psychology, 22,* 487–497.

Segerstrom, S. C., Stanton, A. L., Alden, L. E., & Shortridge, B. E. (2003). A multidimensional structure for repetitive thought: What's on your mind, and how, and how much? *Journal of Personality and Social Psychology, 85,* 909–921.

Shakespeare-Finch, J., & Enders, T. (2008). Corroborating evidence of posttraumatic growth. *Journal of Traumatic Stress, 21,* 421–424.

Stanton, A. L., Bower, J. E., & Low, C. A. (2006). Posttraumatic growth after cancer. In L. G. Calhoun & R. G. Tedeschi (Eds.), *Handbook of posttraumatic growth: Research and practice* (pp. 138–175). Mahwah, NJ: Erlbaum.

Sumalla, E. C., Ochoa, C., & Blanco, I. (2009). Posttraumatic growth in cancer: Reality or illusion? *Clinical Psychology Review, 29,* 24–33.

Taku, K., Calhoun, L. G., Cann, A., & Tedeschi, R. G. (2008). The role of rumination in the coexistence of distress and posttraumatic growth among bereaved Japanese university students. *Death Studies, 32,* 428–444.

Taku, K., Cann, A., Tedeschi, R. G., & Calhoun, L. G. (2009). Intrusive versus deliberative rumination in posttraumatic growth across US and Japanese samples. *Anxiety, Stress & Coping, 22,* 129–136.

Tallman, B., Shaw, K., Schultz, J., & Altmaier, E. (2010). Well-being and posttraumatic growth in unrelated donor marrow transplant survivors: A nine-year longitudinal study. *Rehabilitation Psychology, 55,* 204–210.

Taylor, E. W. (1997). Building upon the theoretical debate: A critical review of the empirical studies of Mezirow's transformative learning theory. *Adult Education Quarterly, 48,* 34–59.

Taylor, S. E., & Armor, D. A. (1996). Positive illusions and coping with adversity. *Journal of Personality, 64,* 873–898.

Taylor, S. E., Lichtman, R. R., & Wood, J. V. A. (1984). Attributions, beliefs about control, and adjustment to breast cancer. *Journal of Personality and Social Psychology, 46,* 489–502.

Tedeschi, R. G., & Calhoun, L. G. (2004). Posttraumatic growth: Conceptual foundations and empirical evidence. *Psychological Inquiry, 15,* 1–18.

Tennen, H., & Affleck, G. (2002). Benefit-finding and benefit-reminding. In C. R. Snyder & S. Lopez (Eds.), *Handbook of positive psychology* (pp. 584–597). New York, NY: Oxford University Press.

Tennen, H., & Affleck, G. (2009). Assessing positive life change: In search of meticulous methods. In C. L. Park, S. C. Lechner, M. H. Antoni, & A. L. Stanton (Eds.), *Medical illness and positive life change* (pp. 31–49). Washington, DC: American Psychological Association.

Thombre, A., & Sherman, A. C. (2009). Understanding perspective transformation among recently diagnosed cancer patients in western India, *in review.*

Thombre, A., Sherman, A. C., & Simonton, S. (2010). Posttraumatic growth among cancer patients in India. *Journal of Behavioral Medicine, 33,* 15–23.

Tomich, P. L., & Helgeson, V. S. (2004) Is finding something good in the bad always good? Benefit finding among women with breast cancer. *Health Psychology, 23,* 16–23.

Tomich, P. L., Helgeson, V. S., & Vache, E. J. N. (2005). Perceived growth and decline following breast cancer: A comparison to age-matched controls 5-years later. *Psycho-Oncology, 14,* 1018–1029.

Urcuyo, K. A., Boyers, A. E., Carver, C. S., & Antoni, M. H. (2005). Finding benefit in breast cancer: Relations with personality, coping, and concurrent well-being. *Psychology and Health, 20,* 175–192.

Weinrib, A. Z., Rothrock, N. E., Johnsen, E. L., & Lutgendorf, S. K. (2006). The assessment and validity of stress-related growth in a community-based sample. *Journal of Consulting and Clinical Psychology, 74,* 851–858

Weiss, T. (2004). Correlates of posttraumatic growth in married breast cancer patients. *Journal of Social and Clinical Psychology, 23,* 733–746.

Widows, M. R., Jacobsen, P. B., Booth-Jones, M., & Fields, K. K. (2005). Predictors of posttraumatic growth following bone marrow transplantation for cancer. *Health Psychology, 24,* 266–273.

Williams, R. M., Davis, M. C., & Millsap, R. E. (2002). Development of the Cognitive Processing of Trauma scale. *Clinical Psychology and Psychotherapy, 9,* 349–360.

Wilson, A. E., & Ross, M. (2001). From chump to champ: People's appraisals of their earlier and present selves. *Journal of Personality and Social Psychology, 80,* 572–584.

Wortman, C. B. (2004). Posttraumatic growth: Progress and problems. *Psychological Inquiry, 15,* 81–90.

Zoellner, T., & Maercker, A. (2006). Posttraumatic growth in clinical psychology: A critical review and introduction of a two component model. *Clinical Psychology Review, 26,* 626–653.

ABOUT THE EDITORS

Carrie J. Boden McGill, PhD, served University of Arkansas at Little Rock (UALR) faculty 2007-2012 and served as Associate Professor of Adult Education and Program Coordinator for the Master's Degree in Adult Education. At UALR she taught a variety of classes, including all core and several seminar courses. Dr. Boden McGill joined Texas State University in 2012 and serves as Associate Professor and Chair of the Occupational Education Program.

Dr. Boden McGill holds a PhD in curriculum and instruction with an emphasis in adult education from Kansas State University, MFA in creative writing from Wichita State University, and BA in English language and literature from Bethel College. Her memberships include the Arkansas Association for Continuing and Adult Education, American Association of Adult and Continuing Education, and Women Expanding Literacy Education Action Resource Network. Dr. Boden McGill serves as a member-at-large for the Commission of Professors of Adult Education and as a director on the Board of the Adult Higher Education Alliance.

Dr. Boden McGill's research is primarily in the areas of self-directed learning, personal epistemology, transformative learning, and teaching and learning strategies. Recent publications and presentations focus on the mentoring experiences of graduate students, the effects of mindfulness practices on personal epistemological beliefs, and various methodologies that can be implemented in distance education and classroom settings.

Dr. Boden McGill has an interest in international education, and she recently participated in a faculty exchange program with Karl-Franzens Universität in Graz, Austria. She has also been on the planning committees for several international conferences and serves as an associate editor for *The International Journal of Learning*. She has coordinated a Sister Cities International Exchange with La Salle University in Cancun, Mexico, traveled to South America as a Fulbright Scholar with Project ECHO, and participated in the NGO Forum on Women in Beijing, China.

Sola M. Kippers, PhD, is core faculty in the Harold Abel School of Social and Behavioral Sciences, Department of Counseling at Capella University. She facilitates instruction in online courses in the Mental Health Counseling master's degree program. Dr. Kippers also serves on several department committees.

Dr. Kippers holds a PhD in Counselor Education and supervision from the University of New Orleans. Additionally, she is a Licensed Professional Counselor-supervisor and Licensed Marriage and Family Therapist in Louisiana. She holds national certification as a Certified Rehabilitation Counselor. Dr. Kippers' clinical experience is in chemical dependency and vocational counseling with adult clients. She is a member of the American Counseling Association, National Rehabilitation Association, Louisiana Counseling Association, and Louisiana Association of Counselor Educators and Supervisors.

Dr. Kippers' research interests are related to best practice in counseling supervision and transformative experiences in counselor supervision. She has presented extensively at state, regional, and national counseling conferences. In 2000, she co-authored (with Drs. Veach, Remley, and Sorg) the article, "Retention Predictors Related to Intensive Outpatient Programs for Substance Abuse Disorders," published in the American Journal of Drug and Alcohol Abuse.

ABOUT THE CONTRIBUTORS

Shelly Albritton, PhD, serves as associate professor at the University of Central Arkansas in the Department of Leadership Studies. She served as a teacher and school leader in public schools for many years and teaches graduate students who aspire to be school leaders. She earned her Doctor of Philosophy degree in the Department of Educational Leadership and Research of the College of Psychology and Education from the University of Southern Mississippi, Hattiesburg. Dr. Albritton serves as a co-leader of one of Arkansas' Scholastic Audit teams and is a trainer for Arkansas' teacher evaluation system. As a result of her experiences in public school with at-risk students, with Scholastic Audit, and as a certified trainer of Arkansas' teacher evaluation system, she has dedicated herself to coaching and engaging in meaningful conversations with existing and emerging school leaders in their acquisition of the knowledge and skills required of 21st-century instructional leaders.

Candice Dowd Barnes, EdD, is assistant professor in the Department of Early Childhood and Special Education at the University of Central Arkansas. Dr. Barnes teaches undergraduate courses in learning theories and integrated curriculum planning. Her background in early childhood education and leadership has led to her work as a classroom teacher, administrator of community-based early care and education programs, and coordinator of an early childhood administration degree program. Dr. Barnes currently serves as chair of the Dispositions Committee for her department. She is also chairperson of the Board of Directors for Mothers for Education and has spent several years as a professional development consultant for school districts (PK–8) and community-based early childhood programs.

Elizabeth Bondy, PhD, is professor and director of the School of Teaching and Learning in the College of Education at the University of Florida. A member of the Curriculum, Teaching, and Teacher Education faculty, she is passionate about her doctoral seminar in Critical Pedagogy, out of which this chapter developed. Dr. Bondy studies teaching, learning, and learning to teach in high poverty elementary schools. She, Lauren, and Alvarez thank the Critical Pedagogy Crew—Aliya, Chris, Desi, Elyse, Jess, and Katrina—without whom there would be no chapter.

Freddie A. Bowles, PhD, is assistant professor of Curriculum and Instruction at the University of Arkansas, Fayetteville. She teaches in the Master of Arts in Teaching program, specializing in foreign language education. Her research interests include language preservation, language acquisition, and cultural competence. Freddie is active in the American Council on the Teaching of Foreign Languages (ACTFL), Teaching English to Speakers of Other Languages (TESOL), and the Association of Teacher Educators (ATE). She holds office in several professional organizations including the Arkansas Foreign Language Teachers Association and the Iota Chapter of Delta Kappa Gamma. Freddie is faculty advisor for the Kappa Delta Pi chapter and the Native American Student Association. She was nominated to be a faculty mentor for the Bridge Scholar Program for underrepresented populations. She has numerous publications concerning the state of foreign language education, American Indian language preservation, and instructional strategies for pedagogy classes.

D. Alvarez Caron is a doctoral student in Curriculum and Instruction at the University of Florida with a focus on Teaching and Teacher Education. Her research interests are Whiteness in teacher education, educational policy, and K–12 education. Her teaching experience includes teaching African American and Latino students in the K–12 setting, White preservice teachers, and White and African American inservice teachers.

Teresa (Terry) J. Carter, EdD, is assistant professor in the School of Education at Virginia Commonwealth University in Richmond, Virginia, and coordinator of the MEd program in Adult Learning. She holds a master's degree in education and human development and a doctorate in executive leadership in human resource development from The George Washington University. Her doctoral dissertation explored transformative learning through developmental relationships among midcareer women. Before teaching in higher education, Terry worked in the corporate sector as a training and development professional. Her research interests include transformative learning and reflective practice, learning through relationships, and teaching and learning with technology. Terry has presented at numerous national and international conferences on transformative learning, including the American Association for Adult and Continuing Education and the International Conference on Transformative Learning.

Javier Cavazos Jr. is a doctoral student in counselor education at Texas A&M University-Corpus Christi. Javier has published a number of articles that have appeared in the *Journal of School Counseling, Professional School Counseling, American Secondary Education, Journal of Creativity in Mental Health, Journal of Latinos and Education,* and the *Arizona Counseling Journal.* His research focuses on factors that help Hispanic students pursue and succeed in higher education. In addition, he would like to dedicate this book chapter to his mother and grandparents. They have been instrumental in providing emotional, financial, and spiritual support. Javier also would like to acknowledge his number one mentor (Dr. Michael Johnson) who helped him become involved in research and who believed in his academic potential. Javier would not be in a doctoral program without his mentoring relationship with Dr. Johnson. When Javier is not writing or studying, he enjoys reading for pleasure, playing golf, and running.

Katrina Cook, PhD, is assistant professor in the School of Education and Kinesiology at Texas A&M University, San Antonio, where she teaches graduate level courses for counselors in training. She has 18 years of experience working as a school counselor. She is also a licensed professional counselor and licensed marriage and family therapist and has provided counseling services in substance abuse treatment centers, MHMR group homes, private practice, and community agencies. In 2008, she earned a doctoral degree in Counselor Education and Supervision, and began a new chapter in her life as an assistant professor.

Mark J. Cooper, PhD, LPC, is professor in the department of early childhood and special education at the University of Central Arkansas, a licensed professional counselor, and Director of the Mashburn Center for Learning. He has been a contributing author to the *Autism Asperger's Digest*, a national magazine devoted to children, adolescents, and adults with autism spectrum disorders, and has also written for numerous other journals including *Focus on Autism and Other Developmental Disorders, Rural Special Education Quarterly, Phi Delta Pi Record, Children and Families,* the *Journal of Early Education and Family Review,* and the *National Forum for Educational Administration and Supervision.* Dr. Cooper has written *Bound and Determined to Help Children with Learning Disabilities Succeed,* published by Learning Disabilities Worldwide. Dr. Cooper uses the venues of teaching, counseling, consulting, writing and speaking to help teachers and parents guide, manage, and teach children and adolescents more successfully.

Stacy England, LPC, is a PhD candidate in the counselor education and Supervision program at Oregon State University. She currently works with Project Respond in Portland, Oregon, providing mobile mental health crisis services to underserved populations. In addition, she teaches in the counseling program at Portland State University. Passionate about education, she strives to create classroom and supervision learning environments that honor and acknowledge the whole self. In addition to transformational, somatic, and embodied learning, her research interests include working alliance and advocacy.

Elizabeth Anne Erichsen, PhD, is assistant professor in the Education Doctoral Programs at North Dakota State University. Her research interests include transformative learning, adult learner identity development, international and comparative education, qualitative research methods, and the integration of instructional technology into diverse learning environments. She is interested in writing as methodology, particularly in the ways in which writing in all its forms—therapeutic, academic, poetic, private, published, experimental, conventional and creative—is a method of narrative research.

Laura Fazio-Griffith, PhD, NCC, LPC-S, LMFT, received her PhD from the University of New Orleans in May of 2002 in Counselor Education. She is a licensed professional counselor supervisor, a licensed marriage and family therapist, a registered play therapist supervisor, and a National Certified Counselor. Dr. Fazio-Griffith was the clinical director for the Counseling and Training Center of Families Helping Families of Greater New Orleans for approximately 5 years. She provided individual, group, and family counseling as well as supervision for master's level counseling interns. She has been an adjunct assistant professor at the University of New Orleans, Southeastern Louisiana University, and Louisiana State University. She was the president of LACES from 2004 to 2006. She serves as treasurer on the Louisiana Association for Play Therapy Executive Board. Her research interests include group work, personality disorders, supervision, and play therapy. She is currently assistant professor of counselor education at Southeastern Louisiana University.

Janet Filer, PhD, associate professor in the Department of Early Childhood and Special Education at the University of Central Arkansas. Dr. Filer teaches graduate classes in assessment, working with families, transdisciplinary practices, and methods with children from birth to age 5. In addition, Dr. Filer is Discipline Coordinator for Special Education at the University of

Arkansas Medical Sciences (UAMS) LEND program. Lastly, she has worked extensively with the State of Arkansas' Part C (Age 0–3) and Part B (Age 3–5) programs.

Brandé Flamez, PhD, is professor at Walden University. She received her doctoral degree in counselor education in supervision at Texas A&M University-Corpus Christi. She has presented at numerous conferences nationally and internationally. Her articles have appeared in the *Journal of Technology in Counseling*, *Journal of Counseling Research & Practice*, *The Family Journal: Counseling and Therapy for Couples & Families*, *Journal of Professional Counseling: Practice, Theory, & Research*, and the *Arizona Counseling Journal*. Richard De Vos once said, "Few things in the world are more powerful than a positive push. A smile. A word of optimism and hope. A 'you can do it' when things are tough." Brandé would like to dedicate this chapter to all the mentors who took extra time to support, encourage, and believe in their mentees.

Ted Fleming, EdD, is Director of the Centre for Research in Adult Learning and Education at the National University of Ireland, Maynooth. His MA and EdD in adult education are from Teachers College, Columbia University. His research interests include mature students in higher education, transformative learning and the work of Jürgen Habermas. His most recent publications include a co-edited book on *Habermas, Critical Theory and Education* (Routledge). Other co-authored works include *Even Her Nudes Were Lovely* (Irish Museum of Modern Art); *Where Next? A Study of Work and Life Experiences of Mature Disadvantaged Students in Three Higher Education Institutions* (Irish Combat Poverty Agency). Most recent research includes an EU-funded longitudinal and narrative study of access, retention and noncompletion of nontraditional students in higher education across eight EU countries. He has also published articles and papers on Bowlby and Honneth, whose work has implications for understanding adult learning.

Emmanuel Jean Francois, PhD, is assistant professor of human services and educational leadership at the University of Wisconsin Oshkosh. He is the author of *Global Education on Trial by U.S. College Professors* (2010).

Nancy P. Gallavan, PhD, is professor of teacher education at the University of Central Arkansas (UCA). She specializes in the analysis and practice of teaching, cultural competence, multicultural education, performance-based assessments, and social studies education in the Master of Arts in Teaching (MAT) Program at UCA. Nancy is active in the American Educational Research Association (AERA), the Association of Teacher Educators (ATE), the National Association of Multicultural Education (NAME), and the National Council for the Social Studies (NCSS). She has more than 100 published peer-reviewed articles, chapters, and books. Nancy's books with Corwin Press include *Secrets to Success for Beginning Elementary School Teachers* and *Secrets to Success for Social Studies Teachers*, co-written with Ellen Kottler. Nancy also authored *Developing Performance-Based Assessments in Grades K–5*, *Developing Performance-Based Assessments in Grades 6–12*, *Navigating Cultural Competence in Grades K–5*, and *Navigating Cultural Competence in Grades 6–12*.

Pi-Chi Han, EdD, grew up in a very traditional Chinese family in Taiwan. She received her EdD from the University of Arkansas, in Fayetteville, Arkansas. She has been impacted by both Chinese and American cultures. She has had strong interest in the issue of exploring intercultural effectiveness (ICE) competencies since her doctoral study. Besides her active scholarly presentations in the United States, Dr. Pi-Chi Han has presented papers internationally in Finland, Japan, France, China, Taiwan, and Australia. Recently she was invited as a visiting international faculty fellow by the Chinese Academy of Social Science (CASS), Beijing. Dr. Pi-Chi Han is also an educator of global workforce development and a consultant in developing global talent and intercultural competence. She joined the University of Missouri-St. Louis in the fall of 2007. Her research interests have been focused on the issues of investigating ICE competencies for various demographic groups and developing global talents and global leadership.

Christopher Janson, PhD, is assistant professor in the Department of Leadership, Counseling, and Instructional Technology at the University of North Florida. Janson was a junior high school teacher and high school counselor before his work in academia. His research interests include school counselor skill and dispositional development regarding interprofessional relationships in schools; educational leadership; career, academic, and motivational development of urban school students; and transformative pedagogy. Janson is also a program developer for a university-community school grant partnership focused on increasing career and college readiness for urban students living in high-poverty communities. Janson has published in journals such as *Professional School Counselor*, *Journal of School Leadership*, and *Journal of Special Education Leadership*. He received his undergraduate and MA from Central Michigan University, his teaching certification from Michigan State University, and his PhD from Kent State University.

Leann M. R. Kaiser, PhD, is assistant professor in the School of Education at Colorado State University and an affiliate faculty in the School of Education and Counseling at Regis University. Her academic interests include adult teaching and learning theory, community building in the classroom, learner development in distance education, and adult outdoor education. She is also interested in nontraditional roles for female faculty members through her research and experience as a distance educator and mother working from home.

Kathleen P. King, EdD, is professor of higher education the University of South Florida in Tampa and president of Transformation Education LLC. She formerly served as a professor and research center director at Fordham University. King's areas of research include faculty development, distance learning, transformative learning, and diversity issues. An award-winning author (20 books), she is a popular keynote speaker, faculty mentor, and consultant. Recent publications include *The Professor's Guide to Taming Technology* (with Cox), *Handbook of Evolving Research in Transformative Learning* (10th anniv. ed., 2009); and *Empowering Women through Literacy* (2009; with Miller). Examples of recent awards she received for her educational research and contributions include being inducted into the International Continuing and Adult Education Hall of Fame (2011), and awards from AERA, ACHE, POD Network, and NYACCE. Through distance technologies, Dr. King and her collaborators have reached over 6.5 million learners. Kathy earned her doctorate in higher education from Widener University in 1997. For more information visit www.kpking.com and www.TransformationEd.com

Patty Kohler-Evans, EdD, completed her Doctor of Education degree in special education from the University of Memphis. She served as the director of the Division for Exceptional Children in the Little Rock School District, Little Rock, Arkansas, for over a decade. While there, under her leadership, the district hosted the state's first conference on inclusive practice. Dr. Kohler serves as a consultant in co-teaching, and has written and presented on this practice. She is a Strategic Instruction Model Professional Developer and works with teachers across the state of Arkansas providing professional development in this research-validated methodology. She also serves as an executive coach with public school principals.

Ellen L. Marmon, PhD, associate professor of Christian Discipleship and Mentored Ministry at Asbury Theological Seminary in Wilmore, Kentucky, earned her PhD in educational psychology from the University of Kentucky; an MA in Christian education from Asbury Theological Seminary in 1995; an MA in English from the University of Kentucky, and a BS in education from Miami University (Oxford, Ohio). Her interests include transformative learning, teaching the full narrative of the Bible, cross-cultural training for missions (local and global), and contextualizing discipleship for oral cultures. Travels have taken Ellen to Israel; Bihar, India; and to Kenya many times for teaching and serving with Worldwide Hearts and Hands. Ellen's parents live where she was raised in Anderson, Indiana. She enjoys serving in her local church and vacationing with her sister's family. When she is not outdoors or with friends, she just might be cheering on her favorite driver at a NASCAR race.

Julien C. Mirivel, PhD, is a graduate of the University of Colorado at Boulder and serves as associate professor in the Department of Speech Communication at the University of Arkansas at Little Rock. His teaching and research interests focus on improving communication praxis. He has published in various academic journals and edited volumes. He also earned several awards for excellence in teaching. In 2011, he won the Faculty Excellence Award in Teaching for the College of Professional Studies at the University of Arkansas at Little Rock.

Lee Nabb, PhD, acquired a BA from Southern Illinois University with a major in religious studies and a minor in classical civilization. He went on to study religion for one more year in Temple University's doctoral program before returning to Illinois and acquiring an MSEd in adult and continuing education from Northern Illinois University. From there he went to law school at Syracuse University and worked as a consultant in environmental legal issues for 3 years. He then attended the University of Wyoming, where he received his PhD in adult and postsecondary education and worked as an assistant lecturer for a year. He is currently licensed to practice law in New York and Illinois, and assistant professor of adult and higher education at Morehead State University.

Sejal Parikh, PhD, is assistant professor of counselor education the University of North Florida in the Department of Leadership, Counseling, and Instructional Technology. Sejal is certified in K–12 guidance and counseling in the state of Florida. She has experience as a professional school counselor working in elementary, high school, urban, and suburban school settings. She received her PhD in counseling from the University of North Carolina at Charlotte where she was the recipient of the Dean's Distinguished Dissertation Award for Social Sciences. In 2010, Sejal was selected as one of the first cohort members of Community Scholars at the University of North Florida. Her primary research focus includes social justice and advocacy in school counseling, multicultural counseling, and school counselor training and development.

Julie Prindle, PhD candidate, is a licensed clinical social worker living in Portland, Oregon. In her private practice, North Portland Narrative Therapy, she serves adolescents, families, and couples. She works with a goal of helping people transform the problem story and move in the direction of their preferred self, family, relationship, and future. Her 18 years of experience include wilderness adventures with adolescents, service coordination with runaway and homeless youth, Director of Counseling in an alternative high school, and providing supervision to graduate students and counselors seeking licensure. She teaches school social work as an adjunct in the Graduate School of Social Work at Portland State University. She is currently completing her doctoral degree at Oregon State University with an emphasis in counselor education.

I. Malik Saafir, MDiv, is lead consultant for the Janus Institute for Justice and resident theologian for the Dr. William H. Robinson Jr. School of Practical Theology. He holds a BA in philosophy and history from the University of Arkansas at Little Rock where he was a Ronald E. McNair Scholar. He holds a Master of Divinity from Vanderbilt Divinity School where he was a Kelly Miller Smith Scholar. He has devoted his career to the examination of the intersections between religion, ethics, and culture, seeking to bridge the gap between the academy, church, and community. His research interests include liberation and practical theology, African American and postcolonial Biblical criticism, Africana philosophy, culture studies, and ethics.

Varunee Faii Sangganjanavanich, PhD, is assistant professor of counselor education in the Department of Counseling at The University of Akron in Akron, Ohio. Her work focuses on multicultural competencies in clinical counseling and supervision, career counseling and development, and counselor education. She received her doctoral degree in counselor education and supervision from the University of Northern Colorado. She has authored and co-authored a number of professional publications and presentations in the field of counseling and counselor education.

Allen C. Sherman, PhD, is associate professor and director of the Behavioral Medicine Division at the Winthrop P. Rockefeller Cancer Institute, University of Arkansas for Medical Sciences. Much of his research has focused on understanding quality-of-life outcomes, personal meaning, and spiritual involvement among patients with cancer or other serious illnesses.

Michelle Kelley Shuler, PhD, is assistant professor in the Department of Psychology and Counseling at Northeastern State University, Tahlequah, Oklahoma, where she teaches graduate level courses for counselors in training. She has over 10 years of experience working with diverse populations as a licensed professional counselor and licensed alcohol and drug counselor. In 2009, she received a doctoral degree in counselor education and supervision, from the University of Texas as San Antonio. During her work as a doctoral student, she engaged in writing her spiritual autobiography and has appreciated the insights gained from the completion of the reflective exercise.

Stephanie Simonton, PhD, is associate professor and Director of Program Development in the Behavioral Medicine Division at the Winthrop P. Rockefeller Cancer Institute, University of Arkansas for Medical Sciences. Her research has focused on end-of-life care, family adjustment, and psychosocial interventions among individuals with cancer or other illnesses.

Shelley K. Stewart, PhD, is the elearning facilitator at the University of South Florida College of Education. She coordinates the development of quality online courses in partnership with the Media Innovation Team at the USF eCampus. Shelley's research interests include instructional strategies that promote dialogue in online courses, course conversions, online course redesign, and the role of emotions in online learning. She earned her PhD in instructional technology from the University of South Florida in 2008.

Gabriele Strohschen, EdD, has worked for more than 20 years in adult education and training, nationally and internationally, in NGOs and in higher education. She received her doctoral degree from Northern Illinois University. Dr. Strohschen joined DePaul University as director for the graduate program of the School for New Learning (SNL) in 2003. She designed and implemented the SNL's graduate program for our international campus in Bangkok, Thailand. During her directorship at SNL, she also designed and implemented the MA in educating adults and formulated the design of the Center for the Education of Adults. Dr. Strohschen maintains her connection to the not-for-profit world and continues to work with organizations locally, nationally, and internationally. She works primarily with organizations in Chicago's disenfranchised, urban communities. Internationally, she works in Afghanistan, China, Germany, Kenya, Mexico, and Thailand on action research projects in the areas of program and staff development, program evaluation, and teacher training.

Daniel Stroud, PhD, is a counselor educator and Clinical Mental Health Program coordinator at Oregon State University-Cascades. The 2010 recipient of the Teaching Excellence Award at OSU-Cascades, he has taught psychopathology and diagnostics, counseling theories, group and advanced group counseling, research methods, adult learning, introduction to counselor education, multicultural counseling, practicum and internship. His research interests focus on enhancing graduate learning environments, group work, and problematic behavior.

Fujuan Tan, PhD, holds a BA in English education from Ludong University in Yantai, China, an MA in foreign languages and applied linguistics from Chinal Ocean University in Qingdao, China, and a PhD in adult and postsecondary education from the University of Wyoming. With over 7 years experience working and teaching in adult English as a second language (ESL) education and as a coordinator of international exchange programs, she is currently a faculty member in the College of Foreign Languages at Ludong University. Her research interests include adult ESL, culturally responsive and experience-based education as well as transformative learning.

Avinash Thombre, PhD, is associate professor in the Department of Speech Communication at the University of Arkansas at Little Rock. His research has explored perspective transformation among individuals with a range of medical conditions, including cancer, HIV, and burn injuries across different cultural contexts.

Lauren Tripp is a doctoral student in curriculum and instruction at the University of Florida with a focus in adolescent literacy. Her research interests include the possibility of seeing literacy as a cultural practice and using multimodal literacy to empower marginalized students, as well as designing embedded professional development to empower teachers to broaden their definition of literacy. She is interested in the power of professional learning communities and their potential for transformation and authentic school reform, and she believes that all teachers are called to be both gentle and brave with their students.

Joshua C. Watson, PhD, is associate professor of counselor education on the Mississippi State University, Meridian campus. An accomplished author, he has authored over 45 publications and has presented at several state, national, and international professional counseling conferences. In recognition of his scholarship, Dr. Watson has received numerous awards, including the Ralph F. Berdie Memorial Research Award, Herb Handley Memorial Research Award, American College Counseling Association's Outstanding Research Award, the Mississippi Counseling Association's Distinguished Research Award, and the Mississippi State University College of Education Faculty Research Award. Prior to beginning his tenure at Mississippi State University, he received his doctorate in counseling and counselor education from The University of North Carolina at Greensboro.

Angela Webster-Smith, PhD, completed her doctor of philosophy degree in educational psychology and research from The University of Memphis. In Memphis she served as founding principal of two independent schools and as a consultant for public charter school design. She has been a faculty member in the United States and abroad. Now as assistant professor of leadership studies at the University of Central Arkansas, she teaches and explores reflectivity in leadership, in teaching and learning, and in individual success. She is also passionate about cultivating hope-based schooling for all learners. Webster-Smith speaks nationally on the topic of self-reflection, serves on the board of trustees of a charter school and as an executive coach with public school principals. She continues to serve as a consultant in curriculum design, public relations, human resources management, and as an inclusion broker. She hosts a radio show, *Reflective Living with Dr. Angela*, and is active in the National Council of Professors of Educational Administration and the Association of Teacher Educators.

Alex Kumi Yeboah is a doctoral candidate in curriculum and instruction with an emphasis in adult education at the University of South Florida, Tampa, Florida and originally from Ghana, West Africa. He is currently a high school social studies and adult education teacher. His research interests are transformative learning of international adult learners, comparative adult education, and distance education in sub-Saharan Africa.

William H. Young III, EdD, has been either an administrator or faculty member in higher education since 1968. He has served as an instructor, assistant professor, associate professor, and professor. Administratively, he has served as a dean, assistant dean, department chair, campus director, graduate program director, administrative coordinator, assistant coordinator, and staff associate. He has been involved in the publication of three books, several book chapters, and many refereed journal articles. Dr. Young is considered a leading authority on continuing education, continuing higher education, and continuing professional education. He is also actively involved in human resource development and community college leadership.